1981

LATIN AMERICA
IN ITS LITERATURE

LATIN AMERICA IN ITS CULTURE
César Fernández Moreno, Series Editor

LATIN AMERICA IN ITS LITERATURE
César Fernández Moreno and Julio Ortega, Editors

LATIN AMERICA IN ITS ARCHITECTURE
Roberto Segre, Editor

LATIN AMERICA IN ITS ART
Damián Bayón, Editor

LATIN AMERICA IN ITS MUSIC
Isabel Aretz, Editor

Latin America in Its Literature

César Fernández Moreno,
General Editor

Julio Ortega,
Assistant Editor

Ivan A. Schulman,
Editor of the English Edition

Translated from the Spanish
by Mary G. Berg

HM
HOLMES & MEIER PUBLISHERS, INC.
New York / London

First published in the United States of America 1980 by
Holmes & Meier Publishers, Inc.
30 Irving Place
New York, N.Y. 10003

Great Britain:
Holmes & Meier Publishers, Ltd.
131 Trafalgar Road
Greenwich, London SE10 9TX

English translation and new material
Copyright © 1980 by Holmes & Meier Publishers, Inc.

Original Spanish edition:
América Latina en su literatura © Unesco 1972
Copublished 1972 by Siglo XXI, Mexico, and Unesco.
This book has been published
with the financial assistance of Unesco.

LIBRARY OF CONGRESS CATALOGING IN PUBLICATION DATA

Fernández Moreno, César.
    Latin America in its literature.

    (Latin American in its culture ; 1)
    Translation of América Latina en su literatura.
    Bibliography: p.
    Includes index.
    1. Latin American literature—History and criticism.
I. Ortega, Julio.   II. Schulman, Iván A.   III. Title.
IV. Series.
PQ7081.F3713   860'.9   79-26626
ISBN 0-8419-0530-4

MANUFACTURED IN THE UNITED STATES OF AMERICA

Contents *860.9 M842*

PART FIVE: THE SOCIAL FUNCTION OF LITERATURE

Introduction to the Series

> ...America is the country of the future. In future times, its historical importance will be shown, perhaps in the struggle between North America and South America.... It is a country of nostalgia for all those who are tired of the historical museum of the Old Europe.... What has happened here so far is only the echo of the Old World and the reflection of that other way of life. But as a country of the future, America does not interest us, since the philosopher does not prophesy.
>
> Hegel[1]

WHAT IS LATIN AMERICA?

Y bien: a century and a half have gone by since Hegel prophesied about America while saying that he refused to do so. What he saw as the future is now America's present; the continent which was nature for him is already history. He spoke of North and South America: one of the strongest nations in the world is now established in North America. And South America, under its extended name of Latin America, represents one of the present world's most polemical ideas: a series of factors have brought it to the forefront of public attention.

Meanwhile, the demographic explosion, if we accept that technological term for the fact of birth: the rhythm of the growth of its population is the greatest of any of the major regions of the world: 2.8 percent annually. Right now there are more than 342 million inhabitants, irregularly distributed over 21 million square kilometers.[2] This explosion, which is occurring within the economic context called underdevelopment, threatens to transform itself, in turn, into a political explosion. And following upon this chain of explosions, or explosion in links, Latin America has been experiencing another: the cultural, which is of specific interest to us here.

Nevertheless, the term Latin America continues to be notoriously imprecise. What is Latin America? In the first place, why *Latin*? All Latinity began in Latium, a small territory adjacent to the city of Rome, and expanded out in concentric circles through historical time: first until it included the whole of Italy, then spreading to that part of Europe colonized by the Roman Empire, later being restricted to the countries and zones which spoke languages derived from Latin, and finally transported to the American continent which those

Europeans had discovered and colonized. In this way, Latin America turned out to be the fourth ring of that gigantic expansion.

Of the nations which accomplished the discovery, conquest, and colonization of the new continent, three were linguistically Latin: Spain, Portugal, and France. The most comprehensive historical concept of the region, however, should include all the territories of the new continent which were populated by these powers, opposed as a block to Anglo-Saxon America, concentrated in the north. "Already by the end of the nineteenth century," says Estuardo Núñez, "distinctions are beginning to be made between that which is *North American* and that which is *Latin American*, based upon the occurrence of the political phenomenon of the independence of the North.... Among French writers in particular (and perhaps among all the Europeans) new terms for the things of non-Saxon America come into use: *états latins d'Amérique* which appears as early as an 1882 book, *peuples latino-américains, démocraties latines de l'Amérique....*"[3]

These new terms correspond to a concept which is simultaneously racial, cultural, and political. But they come, as Núñez himself points out, to replace other terms which were merely geographical designations: *Amérique méridionale, Amérique septentrionale, Amérique du Sud, Amérique australe*. These terms were more limited and therefore clearer; in them, South America gave itself over in its entirety to its geographic identity: split sensually on its Atlantic side by its three great deltas, planetarily sustained on its Pacific side by the irrefutable Andes.

By replacing that geographic *South America* with the already political *Latin America* without clearly indicating the step taken, those French writers create confusion about the supposed Latinity of America: in the old geographic concept, the terms was reserved for the meridional subcontinent, basically Iberoamerican (Spanish and Portuguese); the new term also includes the French established in various areas of the three Americas, especially in Canada. We could imagine, then, that this concept of what is Latin American was created by the French not only as a scientific contribution but also in order to compensate in the area of culture for the diminution or loss of their political power in the Americas, the fading of Louis Napoleon's dream. Canada, in a part of which the strongest present-day subsistence of that French cultural power is rooted, has tended correlatively to maintain its bilingualism, attempting to avoid an excessively sharp differentiation between its two idiomatic and cultural zones. The preservation of French is even more useful in that portion of the country which, being Anglophonic, is less protected from the cultural influence of its powerful Anglo-Saxon neighbor.

Along the southern border of the United States, the cultural tension is of the inverse sort, and Anglo-Saxon America sees itself invaded by a vaporous breath of Latinity which rises up against and over its boundaries like the steam that lifts the lid of a boiling pot. In this case, Latin America is moving in on Anglo-Saxon America from beneath, thanks to a kind of demographic capillarity which ascends from Mexico, Cuba, Puerto Rico. It is a tardy but effective answer which tends to compensate, through human fertility, for the Latin territories which were lost during the formative period of our nations. Immediate consequence: Spanish is today the second language of the United States.

The global situation of the Americas thus returns us to the old opposition between the Spanish and the Anglo-Saxons and, further back, between the Roman (Latin) Empire and its external enemies. The confrontation Hegel foresaw between the Americas of North and South would not be, then, anything other than the reiteration, on American ground, of a fundamentally European situation. If we try, then, to return ourselves to the initial historical situation of American man, the adjective of the term Latin America blurs and we find ourselves submerged in the geographic dimension of the noun, obviously prior to and different from anything European.

This is how the great cultures which existed before the discovery seem to us, especially those of Mesoamerica and the Andes. The conquest of the sixteenth century nearly annihilated these great cultures, but, at the same time, it gave them new dialectic life insofar as it transformed them into the *terminus ante quem* of a process of Westernization. This process also affected the other populations of America which were less evolved at that time: those which were generically called *Indians* by the discoverers, misled by the colossal geographical error which caused them to believe that they had landed in Asia.

But this is not all. There is another factor, radically not Latin but not Anglo-Saxon either, which has come to enrich the situation even more, and also to universalize it: the extensive African contribution to the culture of the Americas. This contribution is rooted, certainly, in prehistoric time. The theory of "drifting continents" explains that America, in a remote geological time, formed a single physical unit with Africa and that only later, when it was pulled apart by the plutonic forces of our planet, did it take on its individuality as a continent. In this fabulous adventure, the flora and fauna of Africa were carried off by the American continent, but not its men.[4]

The Africans themselves came to America much later. In the green and transparent Caribbean, in that sea which docilely lets its intimate depths be seen, on the islands of that sea which are incrusted with a double luxurious border of moss and sand, the merciless phenomenon of the slave trade, the instrumentalization of men of one color by men of another color, took place beginning in the sixteenth century. One hundred million Africans were captured and taken to America; of them all, two thirds perished on the journey. Nevertheless, this process had the surprising result that we can now see: those slaves repaid their masters by transmitting to them all they had been able to conserve of their ancestral cultures, teaching them a whole gamut of activities ranging from singing and dancing to fighting for their liberty.

African America makes itself felt strongly not only in the Caribbean islands but also in the adjoining continental areas, that is, in the north of South America and in the south of North America, since these islands share their cultural physiognomy with the neighboring coastal areas, also marked by plantation economy. In this way, the interposition of the African culture between the Latin and the Anglo-Saxon constitutes an enrichment of the classic scheme from which the very concept of Latin America had emerged: the two divergent Americas converge in a third culture until they form a great region, a single Afro-America, a human bridge which tends to unify culturally the two enormous subcontinents which constitute the Americas. In this new zone, the boundary between the two colonizing cultures—the Latin and the Anglo-Saxon—is not even always precise, since both have coexisted here and still coexist. This is true to such an extent that the Caribbean seems to unite South and North America as much or more than the slender mountainous transition of Central America: the passage from Latin America to Anglo-Saxon America takes place both along the length of that Mesoamerica (of Indian tonality) which extends from Panama to California, and across the intermittent insular isthmus (of African tonality) which extends from Guyana to Florida.

This intermediate zone of Afro-America, which with greater precision we call the Caribbean, turns out to be also an accentuation, an only slightly less than didactic example of that characteristic plurality which gives birth to the cultural identity of all of our America: multiple Indian, European, Asiatic, and above all African contributions intercross in its totality. This is also an example of the exercise of the most accentuated colonialisms which America has suffered and, correlatively, of the most energetic revolutions which, beginning with the Haitian, have been opposed to those colonialisms.

As we can see, the sum total to which we are brought by the idea of Latinity amply overflows its historical origins. And this semantic expansion does not end here, certainly. The new immigratory currents of the second half of the nineteenth century will spill over, finally, into the socioeconomic gaps of Latin America, will be concentrated in its great ports, and will multiply the mixture of races and cultures to the point of making it really world-inclusive.

Some say of a child that he is identical to his father, others say he is just like his mother; they are all right. The same may be said of Latin America: that it is identical to its mother (the land, the cultures before the conquest) and to its father (Spain, Portugal, Africa, and other "fathers" which reached it from outside). But at the same time, and just like that child, America is different from its progenitors and has its own personality. It is "our America," as José Martí showed us; it is our mother who is both one and many, as another of our many contemporary poets says very precisely:

> Madre hay una sola
> América india negra
> mestiza mulata zamba
> inmigrante y española[5]

[There is only one mother America/Indian Black/Mestiza Mulatto Zamba/ immigrant and Spanish]

SOUTH OF A RIVER

Within a cultural complex which is so rich and tense, the possibilities of actions and reactions are almost infinite, even in the intellectual field. Thus the presumed unity of the region becomes more problematical to us as we attempt to delve more deeply into it.[6] The great Argentine essayist Ezequiel Martínez Estrada, for example, tends to compare Latin American problems with African ones, and emphasizes the "aspects of our national life which belong to a kind of history which does not fit into the patterns we had previously taken as models but rather into those of the African countries where slavery and servitude reveal universal and typical similarities to the perceptive observer, forms of life which are common to those peoples who apparently exercise their sovereignty."[7]

The Italian sociologist Gino Germani in his turn points out two concepts which are polar opposites, "diametrically opposed to each other but coinciding in according a real existence to Latin America." The first "insists upon the Latin, or Greco-Roman, Christian, Hispanic or Iberian character of the American subcontinent." In the second, "Latin America is seen as a unit not only in cultural and social terms but also—and above all—in political terms.... the unifying factor originates in an object which is external, antagonistic, and threatening." If in the first of these hypotheses the central factor seems to be cultural and in the second political, it must be observed that both are prefigured by another which is geographic: in the first the "American subcontinent" is referred to, in the second an "external object."[8]

These claims are almost inevitable in any conceptualization of Latin America. Nor would a merely racial criterion serve, one that would oppose Latins to Anglo-Saxons: that concept would be seen to be demolished not only by the presence of the Indians, the Africans, and the various later immigrants, but also by the inseparable mixture of all those races which is seen particularly in the Caribbean. In the inverse sense, we should also compute the Latinity of the United States, not only because of the demographic penetration which we have already indicated, but also because of the Latin origins of more than one of its southern states. For analogous reasons, we should also reject a religious definition which would oppose the Catholicism of Latin America to the Protestantism of the Anglo-Saxon colonies (in view of the large number of Catholics in the United States).

Nor would a purely linguistic concept be acceptable, one which would define Latin America as made up of those countries which speak Spanish or Portuguese. José Luis Martínez reminds us that "of the 254.4 million inhabitants who form the population of Latin America (1968), 164.2 million, or 64.5 percent, speak Spanish; 85.6 million speak Portuguese in Brazil, that is 33.4 percent, and the rest speak French and English."[9] The remaining 2.1 percent, in effect, speak French, English, and even Dutch, especially in the Caribbean, whether in independent countries or in the various remaining colonies. We should also take into account the survival of the pre-Columbian languages (there are bilingual countries, like Paraguay).

Despite this definitional and conceptual difficulty, the contemporary world is rediscovering with new astonishment this complex which insists upon calling itself Latin America, an entity which is still not defined but which obviously has the consistency of something real. In any case, the term Latin America serves as an indication that it is a matter of something which excludes a part of the triple continent called America, that there is insistence that there are at least two Americas, apparently defined by the opposite attraction of the two terrestrial poles. And it is also an exteriorization of its being something more complex than Hispanic or even Iberian America.

It is a question, then, of another unity, no less indefinable than ostensible. I will briefly set down a series of historical coincidences among all these countries which we call Latin American:

1. A certain pre-Columbian culture.
2. The military, political, and economic conquest of these cultures by the West, represented in the majority of the cases by Spain or Portugal.
3. The correlative imposition of a language and a religion.
4. The total or partial deculturation of the pre-Columbian populations.
5. The arrival of the African slaves.
6. An independence movement in the nineteenth century, strongly influenced by British policy.
7. Beginning in the middle of that same century, the arrival of new contingents of immigrants from all over the world.
8. Cultural interaction among all the coexisting human elements.
9. A relative backwardness in the process of industrialization, which permits the localized or generalized maintenance of serious conditions of poverty, contrasting with the wealth of Anglo-Saxon America and thus providing a paradigmatic example of the worldwide North-South economic polarity.
10. At the end of the Second World War, the culmination of a process of transference of political and economic power in the region from Great Britain to the United States. This last note allows a generalization of three of these (2, 6, 10) which indicates a successive dependence of the entire group of nations in relation to an "external object."

All of the political and human formations which make up Latin America are differentiated from each other only by their different quantitative gradations of the ten elements indicated. Gradations which are not sufficient to indicate a qualitative difference within those formations, since they vary within a limited range which reveals the unity within the plurality of cultural identities.

On the other hand, those ten elements all refer to one geographic area. The expression "Latin America" designates—in all the interpretations we have mentioned—a specific geographic area south of the Grande or Bravo River (which marks the boundary of Mexico with the United States). The common usage of this expression (south of the Rio Grande, of the Rio Bravo) may be the proof of its veracity: south of this river there exists a certain homogeneity which is cultural, political, ethnic, linguistic, religious; and this homogeneity extends to Patagonia, more exactly to the tip of Cape Horn, which separates the two gigantic oceans.

THE RECIPROCAL ASTONISHMENT

The three incentives which motivated the Spanish to colonize America have often been pointed out: the warrior impulse, acquired during the reconquest of their own territory from the Arabs; the mysticism of the Catholic mission; and greed (for gold, for slaves, for women). Each historian, each essayist, singles out the one of these incentives that most impresses him, but there is no doubt that the effect of the three factors added together was what shaped this process which would join the two halves of the world into one.

Christopher Columbus was, in a certain sense, a mystic; but that did not prevent him from adopting a whole strategy for seducing the Catholic king and queen of Spain with the gold of the new continent which he had placed on the market...and certainly he succeeded in this (it was already the era of capitalism). Toward this end, he began by writing to the monarchs' notary: "...When I speak only of what has been done on this voyage, which was so fleeting, Your Highnesses will be able to see that I will give you as much gold as you may need in return for the very little assistance which Your Highnesses will give me..." Later he continued to explain the riches discovered on that "so fleeting" first voyage: spices, cotton, resins, lignaloe, slaves, rhubarb, cinnamon, "and a thousand other items of substance."[10] "The gold is most excellent," he wrote before beginning his fourth voyage, "of it treasure may be made, and whoever has it can do whatever he wishes in the world and even manage to send souls to Paradise." From gold to paradise; that could be the title of a biography of Columbus.

We should now mention a fourth factor which is a consequence of the other three: astonishment, the first emotional reaction which flooded the hearts of the discoverers and conquerors when they confronted the object of their discovery and conquest. Columbus's astonishment in regard to America frequently verged on delirium: drawing close to the mouth of the Orinoco, he thought he had discovered one of the rivers that flow out of Paradise; however, a mysterious illness that blinded him temporarily kept him from stepping onto the continent that he was incorporating into Western history. He never could get to Mexico, because he remained entangled in the gigantic spiderweb of the Caribbean islands; but he lucidly foresaw that on the other side of Central America there was another sea. However, he added that a ten-day journey from that sea—the Pacific—"lies the Ganges River." Columbus is, simultaneously, the greatest seer and the greatest madman of history.

Each of the Spaniards who followed Columbus continued to express this astonishment. The Indians who smoked, for example, were described by the conquerors as "men and women who walk along fumigating themselves with a burning firebrand." The city of Tenochtitlán—Mexico—left them stunned with amazement; Díaz del Castillo said that it "looked like the enchanted things that are described in the book of Amadís."[11] And it is as though the atmosphere of a novel of chivalry illuminated the conquest of Mexico. In reality, Cortés himself discovered, farther to the north, the coasts he called California, a name which comes from one of those novels. No one could believe what was happening to him: no one was master of his own destiny. Magellan and Elcan went around the world against their will, driven by the winds. This astonishment sometimes became rejection: the captives whom Moctezuma sent to be sacrificed before Cortés ("who knows if they will wish to drink their blood") occasioned the revulsion and anger of the conquerors. The Captain "got very angry at this...maltreated the one who was giving him blood. He gave him blows with his sword."[12] Spilling his blood, no doubt.

We return with this blood to the point of departure, in order to register the reciprocal astonishment of the Indians before the conquerors. This other side of the same sentiment was documented at first hand by Miguel León-Portilla, who collected the testimonies which reveal the process of the conquest of Mexico from the point of view of the Indians. Confronted with the "undeniable amazement or interest of the ancient world in regard to the things and the men of this continent, we rarely think about the reciprocal admiration or interest which must have been awakened in the Indians by the arrival of those who came from an equally unknown world."

Since time immemorial the stage had been set for this situation. Topiltzin Acxitl Quetzalcóatl, the king of the Toltec kings, had been obliged to emigrate at the end of the tenth century to Yucatán. But the Books of Chilam Balam record the prophecy of his return. And, in effect, he returned to Mexico five centuries later in the person of Hernán Cortés. This is what Moctezuma believed, attributing to Quetzalcóatl the intention of "coming alone, emerging here: he will come to discover the place of his throne and canopy. For this purpose he departed rightly at the time when he left."[13] This is the point of departure for the Indian astonishment: man reencounters his god, who, filled with supposed benevolence, returns to the encounter with his adorer.

And this was, certainly, the first element the Spanish took advantage of in order to consummate their cruel conquest: Hernán Cortés made good use of this advantage. When Moctezuma's messengers, informed that "they walked like two towers or small hills upon the surface of the sea," arrived at those Spanish ships, Don Hernán had them put into leg and neck irons, and ordered the big cannon to be fired. "And in that moment the envoys passed out, fainted. They fell, each one doubled over in his place: they were no longer conscious." One of the "Sad Songs" of the conquest expresses the feeling:

> Ya se ennegrece el fuego, ardiendo revienta el tiro:
> ya la niebla se ha difundido.[14]

[Now the fire blackens, the gunfire flashes and burns/now the smoky haze has spread everywhere.]

From this moment on, the messengers could no longer rest. They insisted, "We are in a hurry, we are going to tell our lord king about this.... We will tell him what we have seen. A thing very worthy of astonishment. Nothing like this has ever been seen! Or, have you ever heard about it before?" They returned amazed to tell everything to their king, who ordered captives to be sacrificed and had the envoys sprinkled with their blood. "The reason for doing such a thing is that they went on a very difficult journey; that they saw the gods; that they fixed their eyes upon his face and upon his head."[15]

There were many other specific astonishments: the most theatrical of them perhaps the reaction of the Aztecs to the Spaniards' skin color: "their bodies are wrapped up all over, only faces emerge. They are white, as if they were of chalk." But soon these white-faced gods began to behave like men. The Spaniards' thirst for gold was seen with disdain by the Aztecs: "Their bodies swell up because of this, it gives them a furious hunger, they crave gold like famished hogs." And another passage describes them before Moctezuma's treasure: "as though they were brutes, they clapped each other on the back: so pleased were they at heart." The Aztecs' attitude was geometrically opposed to that of such distinguished Westerners as Christopher Columbus, Hernán Cortés, the Pizarro brothers. Finally, the Aztecs reduced the Spaniards to the condition of *popolocas*, an Aztec word which means barbarians.

That is to say: the Aztecs did not behave any differently from the Spaniards, the Greeks, or the Romans when faced "with the others."[16] We see ourselves thus led to generalize this idea of reciprocal astonishment, which is part of the clash of any two cultures. It is a matter of a general quality of astonishment in man: astonishment before what is different. But in the case of the discovery of America, the difference was so extreme as to be the equivalent of a Copernican revolution.

FROM ASTONISHMENT TO ART

Astonishment not only disconcerted the Europeans but also provided them with adequate themes and new stimuli for their art which had already been launched during the Renaissance. Lope de Vega offers an example of American themes: in his twilight *Dorotea*, he dreams that Don Bela, his explicitly colonial rival, arrives from the Indies, traveling by sea all the way to Madrid! On his way, he tosses out silver bars and gold coins; his tutor explains to him that "gold is like women, slandered by everyone and desired by everyone." In addition to alchemy, the philosophic miracle-mongering that used metals as a beginning and an end to all things, this golden tidal wave from America to Spain may have been what gave the name of Golden Age to the 180 years of hegemony which Spain enjoyed in all fields during the sixteenth century and part of the seventeenth. As a second aesthetic approximation, the greed for gold, which was as strong in Lope as in Columbus, was replaced by astonishment before the art with which that gold has been worked: no one less that Albrecht Dürer said of the sun disks that "he had never seen such marvelous works, which so filled his own heart with satisfaction."[17]

The inverse geographical relationship seems even more radical: the Indian amazement at European culture, added to the European astonishment at Indian culture, constitute the egg from which will hatch, finally integrated, what we today call Latin American culture. Art is nothing other than the expression of that astonishment, which generates the impulse to share with others what the artist has perceived as extraordinary. This is the impulse which made unexpected writers out of the conquerors themselves, even out of nearly illiterate common soldiers who recounted with effective straightforwardness the surprising truth they saw or imagined they saw. This impulse carries over into contemporary literature, made by the Latin American descendents of those remote populators. In his "Mythical Foundation of Buenos Aires," Jorge Luis Borges continues to express astonishment:

> Y fue por este río de sueñera y de barro,
> que las proas vinieron a fundarme la patria?

> [And was it along this river of dreams and of mud/
> that the prows sailed up to found my country?]

However, this transition from astonishment to art did not occur in Latin America without contradictions. The great pre-Columbian civilizations were rich in architecture, in sculpture, in music (this last has been preserved almost intact until our time). European culture mainly contributed language, religion, and the already very highly developed technology of the West. Very well: upon being defeated militarily, the primitive inhabitants of America—that is, the true Americans—were despoiled of their empires and possessions, receiving in exchange the benefits, very dubious from their own point of view, of the expanding Western culture.

Of course, although they were shoved out toward the frontiers of the empires and transformed into external proletariats, that did not happen so completely that they were obliterated without a trace. They were always present, and they still are today, no longer as an influence but rather as a real component of this new Western world, which thus includes many of the characteristics of their different civilizations, characteristics which are considered today as some of the most outstanding factors in the originality of Latin America. It is thus that, through historical time, the cultural estate of Latin America became polarized and began to offer itself as a sterile option which repeated the situation of the conqueror and the conquered, European and American. That is: (1) on one hand, the cultural remains of the great civilizations which preceded the discovery and conquest, like those which are centered in the contemporary republics of Mexico and Peru; (2) on the other hand, European culture transported by the discoverer and conqueror as one more product of the Western expansion which they represented; that is, as a specifically European activity, although carried out by the colonizers in the new region they had incorporated into their domain.

This dichotomy provoked an opposition which would long falsify the relationship between Latin American and European culture, which would present those remains of the original civilizations which were not affected by the impact of conquest and colonization as the only authentic and original culture of Latin America. Thus, by this definition, European culture is rejected as a colonialist and purely mimetic manifestation.

It was finally possible to overcome the dichotomy by verifying and evaluating the most important event in the field of culture: that from the very fact of the discovery there had been born *ipso facto* a third and totally distinct culture based upon the mental interpenetration demanded by reciprocal comprehension. The Spaniards must have explained Europe to the Americans and America to the Europeans. First the Indians and later the mestizos must have modified their own self-awareness of themselves as Americans. Put in terms of examples: the Indians had to learn about horses and the Europeans about cigars.

The solution of that false option between the American and the European consisted, then, in being both simultaneously, which means not being either one thing or the other, but rather something else altogether: in this case, in being European man modified by American man, and vice versa. This new culture can be called mestizo, due to the rich mixture of races caused by the absence of women on Spanish expeditions, but when cultures are being discussed, abuse of the adjective of racial origin can imply the veiled or unconscious persistence of a racist attitude.

On the other hand, looking at things specifically from the racial point of view, it would be very difficult to single out any culture which is not mestizo. It seems preferable in any case to speak of symbiosis or synthesis, and this is the self-concept which triumphs in Latin American culture. Thus there is recognition not only of the contributions of the autochthonous cultures, but also of those of the discovering European cultures, as well as of the important African contribution which came to America through slavery and, finally, of the rejuvenating currents from the universal sources implicit in the immigration movements of the nineteenth century.

This synthetic concept is perhaps the true (we mean to say the most effective) autocthonous dissidence with European culture, although it may have been historically imposed by the conquerors. However, it is also easy to perceive the impossibility of achieving that synthetic culture anyplace where the most visceral racial blending has not occurred, anyplace where Indians continue to be as marginal to the dominant majority (or minority) as they were during the time of the discovery and conquest.

At the present moment in the historical process, a general overview can discern two principal forms in which Latin American culture manifests itself, two forms which in some more elaborate and complex ways are related to that initial sharp dichotomy between European culture and American culture:

1. A culture which attends preferentially to certain values which it considers essential and which do not relate directly to daily events; values which are not contradictory, meanwhile, with the political and economic line which dominates in each one of the countries of the region. This form of culture is expressed principally through the academies, universities, institutes, libraries, museums, traditional organs of the press... culture carefully in accord with the body of traditional European culture and constantly rejuvenated by the novelties which arrive from a diligent Europe.

2. Another type of culture which we could call existential, directly related to daily life, stemming in complicated ways from the original substratum of the region, but without being reduced to the autocthonous. This attitude not only integrates Latin American culture but even defines it with greater authenticity. As examples, I point out two constants associated with this type of culture: beginning in the first years of the twentieth century, the discontent of young people with certain university structures and, in recent years, the so-called "brain drain" which, while it is particularly noticeable on a scientific and technical level, is also evident in the artistic and literary fields (without doubt as a consequence of the polemical interest in lived reality which is part of this attitude).

In this tense process of the creation of a compound culture, it is perhaps possible to read another chapter of the synthetic destiny which seems consubstantial to America. "The New World," says Paul Rivet, "has been, since the prehistoric era, a center of the convergence of races and peoples.... It is truly curious that the historical period of American evolution should be only a repetition of those ethnic events which conditioned its population. Since it was discovered, America has continued to be a focus of attraction for the most diverse peoples and races, just as it was during its long pre-Columbian formation."[18]

In this way, the possible Asiatic and Oceanic ancestry of all the American peoples, and the possible immemorial geographic intregration of America with Africa, are facts which frame the universality of America in its widest perspective, something like an anticipation of the future world where, beyond races and cultures, all men are one. For man, once his instinctive disorders are overcome, tends to establish a rational order, a world which can be like his own head.

THE UNESCO STUDY

This rationally integrated world is precisely the one which an organization like Unesco seeks to promote. In the particular case of Latin America and the Caribbean, the cultural acceleration which the region has undergone during our century is evident as well as its present impact upon universal culture, and evident, too, is the absence of any clear conceptual characterization of the region and of its cultural products.

Unesco could not do other than register this paradox, and has paid attention to it for some time, trying first to establish a definition of Latin American culture, and then of its worldwide diffusion. The principal project relative to the mutual appreciation of the cultural values of the East and of the West (launched at the General Conference, 1956) is the antecedent of a resolution of the Conference in 1966 which ordered the undertaking of a study of the cultures of Latin America in their literary and artistic expressions, with the purpose of determining the characteristics of those cultures.

This project is part of a much vaster group of activities through which Unesco proposes to encourage the reciprocal knowledge of cultures on a world scale. This group of activities is divided into two stages: a first stage will include the study of the great cultural regions of the present world, and a second (which is intercultural) will focus primarily upon making known to each region that which constitutes the originality of each one of the others. In summary, it is a matter of replacing an atomized vision of the different cultures with another more structured view which is based upon a division of those cultures into great interrelated regions in order that each one of them may be able to utilize the resources of the others for creative purposes.

For Latin America, the initial impulse for these efforts was provided by a meeting which took place in Lima in 1967, attended by a prestigious group of experts from the region.[19] The first task of this meeting was to define the limits and divisions of the region to be studied, which was accomplished with the explanation that it "constitutes a way of introducing a method within the fulfillment of the project but not a division into circumscriptions of an administrative or functional type." Here, then, are the six subregions from north to south as indicated by the Lima meeting, together with a tentative list of the states which compose them:

1. That which—extending the geographic idea of Central America—could be called Mesoamerica, including the following states: Mexico, Guatemala, Honduras, El Salvador, Nicaragua, Costa Rica, and Panama.
2. Cuba, the Dominican Republic, Guyana, Haiti, y las demás Antillas ("and the rest of the West Indies"), as the Lima meeting indicates with a certain haziness. If we understand this subregion to be the Caribbean, we should also include, from a cultural point of view, the following English-speaking states, some of which achieved independence after 1967 (the date of the meeting): Barbados, Dominica, Granada, Jamaica, Santa Lucia, Trinidad, and Tobago (all islands), and also Surinam (Dutch-speaking) although, like Guyana, it is not an island.
3. Colombia and Venezuela, that is, the matrix of the Bolivarian ideal.
4. The three states specially defined by the Andean culture: Peru, Ecuador, and Bolivia.

5. Brazil, which by itself constitutes a subregion, not only because of its enormous size, but also because of its language, Portuguese.
6. The so-called Southern Cone: Argentina, Chile, Paraguay, and Uruguay.

It is possible to reduce these relatively small subregions to two larger ones which include them all: Latin America on one hand, and the Caribbean on the other. This last category would include the more or less Afro-American countries with shores on the Caribbean Sea (either including or not including the continental states, depending on the opinion).

It should be clarified, finally, that this division into subregions only includes the independent states of the region, thus leaving unresolved—as in fact it is—the problem of the cultural Latin Americanness of the still numerous political or cultural enclaves of the three Americas which have not yet achieved their independence, especially in the Caribbean. In respect to these countries, the Lima meeting formulated the following recommendation: "With respect to other territories of the American continent where there can be found a culture of Latin type, but which juridically are not considered by Unesco as being a part of Latin America, the experts recommend that even so they should be studied in the project insofar as it includes them within its cultural concept."

The meeting also had to determine the basic focuses which would guide the study to be undertaken. In this sense, their two most important recommendations were perhaps the following:

1. The Latin American intellectuals, who were the ones called together to collaborate on the study, should consider Latin America as a whole, made up of the present national political formations. In accord with this requirement, the collaborators on the project have felt and expressed their region as a cultural unity, which has encouraged in them the process of self-awareness which the project intends to stimulate.
2. They should also consider the region in contemporary terms, although certainly delving back into the past when it is necessary for the comprehension of the present. This directive has obliged the collaborators to confront the burning questions of the present day, insofar as they take place in the region or have some repercussion within it.

If there are inconvenient aspects of these criteria, they are merely the counterbalances of their advantages. The quality of self-recognition which the study assumes, deprives it of a perhaps more objective vision which could be contributed by critics from outside the region. The consideration of Latin America as a whole requires the leaving aside or at least the paying of less attention to more localized characteristics. The priority of focus on the contemporary may perhaps lead to the postponement of consideration of other values which have been important in the region during the course of its history.

In any case, these and other general principles established in Lima were confirmed and more clearly defined later in a series of special meetings attended by experts in the various fields included in the study. The first of them was that of San José de Costa Rica (1968) on literature, and it was followed by those of Buenos Aires (1969) on architecture and urbanism, that of Quito (1970) on plastic arts, that of Caracas (1971) on music, and that of Bogotá (1976) on festivals and the performing arts.

Each one of these meetings recommended various approaches and methods but in every case it was unanimously decided to compile a series of studies in essay form under the general title of *Latin America in Its Culture*. It is here that we should point out the intentional acuity of that title, the structure of which is repeated in all the volumes of the series. Its originality does not reside, certainly, in the nouns which compose it, but rather in the preposition *in*. This preposition clearly indicates that the object of this study is not the culture in itself, the styles and their evolution, the inventory of the works produced, but rather, specifically, Latin America itself *in* or *through* these cultural manifestations.

On the other hand, Unesco did not neglect the necessity of providing the study with an adequate administrative infrastructure and the opportune intellectual evaluation of the task which was being carried out. In reference to the first of these aspects, the Conference of Ministers of Education and others of Latin America and the Caribbean, meeting in Caraballeda (Venezuela, 1971), recommended that the Center previously established by Unesco in Hanava should take on the functions of Regional Office in the realms of culture and the human sciences, and this was accomplished beginning in July 1972.

In reference to the second aspect, the importance of the meeting in Mexico (1974) should be pointed out, a meeting which covered a broad range of topics and was as significant as an advanced milestone of the project as the Lima meeting (1967) had been as an initial landmark. The meeting, which took place at the Colegio de Mexico, not only outlined the summary of the book about *Latin America in Its Ideas,* but it also established solid bases for the new series entitled *The World in Latin America*, and at the same time accomplished a succinct evaluation of the work done between 1967 and 1974. In regard to this last matter, the meeting in Mexico expressed "its agreement along general lines with the objectives followed by Unesco upon undertaking the integral study of the Latin American cultures... as well as with the criteria taken into account in order to establish the list of topics into which that study has been divided... and with the procedure followed in the selection of editors for the respective volumes."[20]

In summary, the volumes published in Spanish so far in the series *Latin America in Its Culture* are the following: *Latin America in Its Literature* (1972 and subsequent editions), *Latin America in Its Art* (1974 and subsequent editions), *Latin America in Its Architecture* (1975 and subsequent editions), *Latin America in Its Music* (1977). Various related volumes (informative, bibliographic, journalistic) have been published in parallel, and the volumes about Latin America in its ideas and Latin America in its festivals and spectacles are well along in preparation. Meanwhile, the project has begun the transition from its regional cultural phase to its intercultural phase, that is, to the investigation of the relationships between two or more cultures: for this reason, in the new series *The World in Latin America*, begun in 1977 with the publication of *Africa in Latin America*,[21] scholars from outside the region have also been asked to contribute.

In order to accomplish all of these collective projects, Unesco invited the most lucid observers of Latin American and Caribbean reality to contribute, taking into principal account, in their selection, the nominating recommendations of each meeting of experts. The essays submitted by these authors were then coordinated by the Secretariat of the Organization, with the assistance of other specialists charged with watching over and checking each volume of the series.[22] Proceeding thus by successive stages, Unesco is making a great effort to guarantee both the objectivity and the unity of each volume, so that it will not be a mere juxtaposition of individual points of view but rather the product of the reflection of a diversified (and even contradictory) but solidly organized team. Once these two series have been completed, Unesco will perhaps have managed to provide a complete vision of the cultures of Latin America and the Caribbean, in themselves and in their relationship with the different cultures of the world.

Finally, the Intergovernmental Conference on Cultural Policies of Latin America and the Caribbean, which took place in Bogotá in January 1978, furnished the most ample forum for discussion, not only of all the concepts and experiences pertaining to the culture and the cultural patrimony of Latin America and the Caribbean, but also of all of the possibilities for action in regard to this subject, that is, cultural policies.

As it is expressed in the document *Problems and Perspectives*, of the Bogotá conference, "On the whole, the program of cultural studies that Unesco has been carrying out in Latin America and the Caribbean for over ten years can be regarded as one of the major efforts made to date to foster an awareness of regional cultural identity."[23] After approving this document, the conference formulated a series of recommendations of which the most significant in the field of the studies of cultures is that designated as number 58, which indicates the future intercultural trend which is so importantly associated with those studies in Latin America.[24]

CONCLUSION AND BEGINNING

Considering that literature is primarily an intense form of language which, in its turn, is the most direct and profound communicative medium men have at their command to express the spirit of any given community, the Lima meeting had given literature the initial priority in the study of Latin American culture. This decision could not be more correct: the writers of this region express in inevitable form, to phrase it that way, the world of contradictions and lacerations in which they live. This phenomenon is, perhaps, the manifestation of another more general one, described by the Brazilian anthropologist Darcy Ribeiro: it happens today, as has occurred at all times of great historical change (during the Renaissance or during the national independence movements of the nineteenth century), that "a new wave of intellectual creativity and of possible awareness is expressed critically in the world of the disinherited people."[25] In this way, the multiform language of Latin America becomes a literature which is ever more critical, more potent, more universal.

It is for all these reasons, circumstantial and profound, that the series *Latin America in Its Culture* began, in 1972, with the volume dedicated to literature. Today, after several years, Unesco again undertakes, with this same volume, the task of making a non-Spanish-speaking public conscious of the regional effort of self-awareness expressed throughout the entire series, that is, the task of transporting the study from its regional stage to its intercultural stage. *Latin America in Its Literature* has already been published in an abridged edition in French and in an unabridged edition in Polish.[26] The present English-language selection of essays from the Spanish edition is due to the critic and professor Ivan A. Schulman, who is also the author of the introduction to this volume, which amplifies, in the pages which follow, this introduction to the series.

Very well: the knowledge about Latin American literature which may be found in this initial volume should serve us, to begin with, as a basis for reconsidering our original problem: What is Latin America? Perhaps we should know already, since from the beginning the concept has provided the title for this Unesco project, and since the project, while it has still not terminated, has advanced profoundly during the course of the years.

The unity of Latin America seems unquestionable throughout its history and geography, but we have taken care not to presume it to be demonstrated *ab initio*: meanwhile, we cannot forget that during the process of the formation of nationalities which took place during the nineteenth century, that unifying concept was often omitted because of the political and economic circumstances, external to the region, which influenced the process. And from the geographic point of view, it is a commonplace to mention the lack of communication which has plagued the countries of Latin America, especially in regard to the two large linguistic zones into which it is divided (Spanish and Portuguese) not to mention the other languages spoken in the Caribbean.

Despite all these difficulties, Unesco has asked all those who are collaborating on the project to try to compose their essays beginning with this concept of unity. They have been requested to do this in a nondogmatic critical sense, as a working hypothesis which will be proved—or disproved—during the course of the project and at its end. Some two hundred specialists have worked and will have worked on various aspects of the project, chosen from among the most important figures of the Latin American intelligentsia. I think that the very fact that these writers have been asked, as a point of departure, to use the concept of Latin America as a totality, will serve to ensure the arrival, if not at the necessary affirmation of that assumed unity, then at the clearest awareness of the extent to which it exists or can be proved.

We depart from this starting position with the intention of improving upon it: what the project has tried to apprehend is the very concept of Latin America, through its cultural manifestations, reestablished in its unity and contemplated from the vantage point of the present. In a more familiar way we could say that a person is known by his deeds; well then, we attempt to become acquainted with this huge cultural conglomerate through its cultural deeds, through its literary, plastic, architectonic, musical creations; we are trying to find out "who" this region is through the spectacles it produces, through the ideas it emits.

At the present moment, the entire world and not just Latin America is shrinking due to an enslaving technology; at the same time the regions, countries, human groups, are expanding due to the progressive recognition of their cultural identities. In these circumstances, it has become urgent to encourage the definition of the boundaries of each culture. Toward this end, the collaborators on the project are working in the manner of radiologists or psychoanalysts, in the bosom of the most intense manifestations of the Latin American unconscious: its cultural products. Upon this basis they can trace the appropriate rational coordinates: sociological, economic, ideological. It is thus that Unesco hopes to obtain the most precise possible intellectual definition of this idea called Latin America, its relationship to the reality it attempts to designate.

For the time being, we merely have a clear intuition of this region which is imposing its myths, its men, its cultural products upon the world. The objective of this Unesco project is the transformation of this present intuition into that absent concept. This vast collective work will help the Latin American scholars who collaborate on it, as well as the most extensive public it is possible to reach, to become aware of the historical reality, the possible unity, and the originality of the region to which they belong.

Let me be permitted, then, to reiterate in this first volume in English—which will be followed by the others of the same series—what I said in 1972 for the same first volume published in Spanish: that this enterprise, like all those which matter to people, begins with a hopeful ignorance and aims toward a desired knowledge. What is Latin America? The only certain thing we know about it, for the time being, is that it is ours.

CÉSAR FERNÁNDEZ MORENO
August 1979

Notes

1. The author quotes from: *Filosofía de la historia universal*, by Georg Wilhelm Freidrich Hegel, translated by José Gaos, Madrid, Revista de Occidente, 1928, pp. 185-186.
2. See the United Nations' *Demographic Yearbook,* New York, 1978, p. 137.
3. "Lo latinoamericano en otras literaturas" by Estuardo Núñez, Chapter 5 of the first section of the Spanish edition of *Latin America in Its Literature,* Mexico, Unesco-Siglo XXI, 1972, and subsequent editions.
4. It is curious to observe that the separation between North America and South America is also found in the geological order: the two sub-continents were not originally united. The first was part of the continent called Laurentia, together with Greenland and part of the British Isles (islands which much later would provide the origin of the Anglo-Saxon in America): while South America was part of Gondwana, with Africa, Australia, part of Asia and the Antarctic (recovered today by the southern states of Latin America). See Paul Rivet, *Los orígenes del hombre americano,* Mexico, Fondo de Cultura Economicá, 1960; p. 20.
5. From *Pasen a ver,* by Juan Antonio Vasco, Caracas, Monte Avila, 1976.
6. An eloquent sample of the contemporary answers to the question of "What is Latin America?" has been selected by Yolanda Arencibia Huidobro ("La idea contemporánea de América Latina," in the magazine *Culturas,* Paris, Unesco-La Baconnière, No. 3, Vol. 5, 1978).
7. Ezequiel Martínez Estrada, "Prólogo inútil" to his *Antología,* Mexico, Fondo de Cultura Económica, 1964.
8. Gino Germani, "América Latina existe y si no habría que inventarla" in *Mundo Nuevo,* Paris, Vol. VI, No. 36, 1969.
9. "Unity and Diversity," by José Luis Martínez, in this volume.
10. See *Noticias de la Tierra Nueva,* selection by Alberto M. Salas and Andrés R. Vasqúez, Buenos Aires, Eudeba, 1964, p. 34.
11. F.A. Kirkpatrick, *Los conquistadores españoles,* Buenos Aires, Espasa-Calpe, 1940, pp. 22 and 69.
12. See *Visión de los vencidos* [in English as *The Broken Spears*], edited by Miguel León-Portilla, Havana, Case de las Américas, 1972, pp. 46 and 190.
13. *Ibid.,* pp. 30-31.
14. *Ibid.,* pp. 36 and 223.
15. *Ibid.,* pp. 39-40
16. *Ibid.,* pp. 41, 74, 100, 262.
17. *Ibid.,* p. 259.
18. *Los orígenes del hombre americano, op. cit.,* p. 190.
19. Unesco document SHC/CS/85/2, Paris, 1967. José María Arguedas presided over the meeting; Roger Caillois was the representative of the Director General of Unesco.
20. Unesco document SHC-74/CONF. 612/7, Paris, 1975.
21. This book and the others of the series *Latin America in Its Culture* were published in Spanish in Mexico in copublication with Siglo XXI.
22. In the Unesco Secretariat, the responsibility for the project as a whole was entrusted successively to the Division of Studies of Cultures and to the Regional Office of Culture for Latin America and the Caribbean (based in Havana), both dependent on the General Subdirectorship of Culture successively entrusted to Mahdi Elmandjra, Richard Hoggart, and Makaminan Makagiansar. As for the writer of the present introduction, he began his in-

volvement with the project at the Lima meeting (1967) and from then on was in charge of coordinating the different meetings, series, and volumes, initially as the program specialist and then as director of the regional office.

23. Unesco document CC-78/Américacult, 3, Paris, 1977.

24. Unesco document CC/MD/39, Paris, 1978. Issue No. 3, Vol. V of the magazine *Culturas*, referred to here, is especially dedicated to Latin America and the Caribbean, and contains a summary both of the studies sponsored and published by Unesco about the region, and of the Bogotá conference.

25. Darcy Ribeiro, *Las Américas y la civilización*, Vol. I: *La civilización occidental y nosotros. Los pueblos testimonio* (Buenos Aires, Centro Editor de América Latina, 1969).

26. *L'Amérique latine dans sa littérature*, translated and adapted by Claude Fell: Paris, Unesco, 1979; *Ameryka Lacińska w swojej literaturze*, 2 volumes, Cracow, Wydawictwo Literackie Kraków, 1979, under the care of Henryk Wozniakowski.

Introduction to the English Edition:
In Pursuit of a Literature[1]

Musing over the vexing complexities of his native Latin America and how his European companion might gain an understanding of them, one of Alejo Carpentier's characters in *The Rites of Spring* (1978), refers to the "many bad books about Latin America we ourselves [have written, so that we] are lost in a labyrinth of false notions..." But, he adds, with both hope and apprehension, "the word [Latin] *America* subsists. Although I don't think you can understand it very well because..."[2]

The translated essays of this volume constitute a challenge and a counterstatement to the sense of futility Carpentier voices on the question of unraveling the Latin American riddle. And, while the final ellipsis punctuating his character's trailing voice suggests the silence of defeat or the anguish of frustration, it should be noted he previously affirms: the "word [Latin] *America* subsists." It is an affirmation that reflects a cultural pattern of perennial future time, which in turn fosters concepts of faith and optimism in man and his world in the face of historical errors or recurring disasters. It also reflects Carpentier's related obsession, similar to that of so many other Latin American intellectuals, with defining the continent's cultural cosmography, more often than not in terms of a structured cosmogonic reversal, that is, through the search for the "roots," sources, and origins of *America*.

Carpentier's character attempts to describe the confusing multiplicity of his America, and by inference its presence in literature, through a technique of antitheses and enumerations: pampas and mountain ranges, pyramids and galleons, slavers and liberators, baroque cathedrals, marble palaces, and skyscrapers which spring up in the midst of miserable *bidonvilles*[3]—a mosaic of contrasts, some unexpected, some disparate, which Carleton Beals, years earlier, enunciated in a similar fashion to explain the hermetic nature of a literature tied to geo-human elements:

> ...the many subterranean streams, the very soil-wise virtues of Latin American literature have barred it from widespread acceptance outside the continent. Though much of it is imitative of European (particularly French) models, its home-grown roots are too remote from North American experience, its imagery too exotic.

Beals wrote prior to the appearance of the innovative contemporary narrative with its universal appeal. Nevertheless, his paraphrased critical remarks on "classical" or traditional (*criollista*) literature are pertinent to the persistent regional and national themes of Latin American literature, and they serve to explain the limited public it has had in the past:

How—writes Beals—can the reader abroad enjoy or understand our writing if he has not breathed the perfume of our forests, where trees and forests are so different? Can anyone read it properly who has not at least suspected the depths of sorrow in the Indian or loved the subtleties of his plastic decorative art? Who can know it who has not forgotten time and space in dancing the sensual rumba, the languid danzón, the spiraling tango, the virile zamacueca, the beat and rebeat of the marinera? How read it without comprehending our political struggles, our Byzantine polemics, or the tropical grandiloquence of so many human parrots.[4]

Carpentier, through polarities centering on what is ancient and modern, rural or urban; Carleton Beals, through an evocation of Latin America's exotic cultural geography—each describes a world of disparate levels of cultural, social, and economic existence, the totality of which its writers and intellectuals are at loss to encompass fully in order to overcome the elliptic despair expressed by Carpentier's character. As Beals observes, Latin American literature is a unique expression, a literature engendered by "soil-wise" qualities, which have made it appear arcane or exotic. For many years this difference was extolled and defended as a necessary distinction in sensibility between European and Latin American literature. In 1931, for example, Rufino Blanco Fombona referred to this difference with pride: "We are psychologically different from the Europeans: we cannot be the same as they in literature. We have been formed by them and we owe them a debt of gratitude." But in spite of this debt and the mark of European models on Latin American writers, a diversity existed: "Many overly civilized Europeans may be shocked by art forms which are concerned with national problems...Latin Americans are not."[5]

Today the pendulum has swung toward *"mainstream"* literary forms of expression, ones which embrace national or continental realities with greater cognizance of the more universal concepts of writing. Such new emphasis underscores the constancy of Carpentier's protagonist's observation: in an unstable, developing society only the word *America* has fixity. Its literary expression, as a reflection of social norms, whether or not it is innovative and beyond mimesis, as today, is in a constant state of flux.

Comparisons with Europe or with the United States, such as Blanco-Fombona's, by virtue of their persistence in time, indicate a long-standing, unsettling inequality which justificatory affirmations ("we are psychologically different") cannot disguise. For Octavio Paz this special characteristic of Latin American literature is the result of its peculiar relationship to its historical reality: "Our reality is the response of the real reality of Americans to the utopian reality of America. Before having our own historical existence, we began by being a European idea."[6] The issue is socioeconomic and cultural dependency; liberation from it is today's aspiration—liberation from the neocolonial, externally directed ideological, political, economic, and cultural constraints that constitute part of the reality of Third World existence. These constraints are complicted by an internal struggle with historical, unresolved cultural and social problems. In the light of the complexity of these questions and the stumbling blocks in the way of their resolution, Martí's visionary statement that Latin American literature will not exist until Latin America exists—that is, until it acquires political and economic independence and cultural and historical authenticity—strikes an ominous note and may even constitute a deterrent to a critical study of the unifying concept which constitutes the *a priori* assumption of the essays of this volume.

The problems of instability, self-perception, role models, or the self-reflexive desire for "otherness"[7] lie at the base of the insistent querying on the part of Latin American writers and intellectuals about the nature of their cultural identity; its proper reflection in their literary production; the artist's social role or revolutionary commitment; the relation of the nature of their native world to their art, especially in contrast with and in opposition to the pull of European currents and modes of thought. The tension-attraction of local/regional versus universal/European, or of rural versus urban culture is a perennial source of personal anguish; the lot of many writers who take the leap into the cultural mainstream of Modernity, i.e., into the Western stream of culture from a civilization with its primitive roots of underdevelopment still exposed, is, as Carlos Fuentes has noted, one of internal conflict and alienation.[8] That the writers experience a falling away is consistent with the norms of the asystemic, disruptive, self-critical literature of Modernity. But that they are affected by concomitant social dysfunction and adopt an antiestablishment political stance is symptomatic of a Latin American social malaise.

Yet in spite of these problems Latin American literature has come into its own, or mainstreamed, as some put it, during the last ten years. The previous blatant ignorance or begrudging nod, the sporadic English and French translations of the thirties have given way to major widespread critical attention and enthusiasm.

The "boom" of the contemporary novel in the sixties and seventies catapulted Latin American writers into the limelight and gave some—Borges, García Márquez, Cortázar, Fuentes—a sense of belonging to a creative community whose identity went beyond national or regional boundaries. Coming of age has seemed a slow process to Latin Americans. And yet, if one thinks in terms of historical time, it was achieved in a relatively brief span of time. In the post-discovery New World, time consists of some one hundred fifty years of national (or independent) life, preceded by approximately three centuries of colonial rule.

Colonial life (1520–1820) left an impact whose measure of significance in terms of independence of will or of values goes much beyond the terminal point of European domination, that is, the wars of independence. Three hundred years of ingrained patterns of cultural, racial, and social violence, repression, and authoritarianism resulted in the loss of a clearly delineated cultural consciousness and gave rise to notions of ambivalence, servileness, and inferiority. All of these elements left their mark on a literature which began under cultural colonialism by following peninsular modes to which was added a mixture of local descriptions, laden at times with obsessive enumerative detail.

The native, original cultures were either decimated or repressed: those which survived lived a truncated life in the shadow of semiannihilation, marginality, or nonintegration. The violently grafted colonial Hispanic culture ultimately flourished, but at the expense of fostering among Indians, blacks, Chinese, and mestizos complex feelings of social and cultural inferiority, the quandary of origins, and the denial of a participatory role in society.

Independence did not provide quick or easy solutions to these questions. Yet, in spite of the organizational problems of the early national period, especially the generally prevailing political and economic chaos, writers were convinced there was and would continue to be a steady progression toward an ever more perfect society—a conviction that reflected the deeply rooted ideas of the Enlightenment. Steeped in the encyclopedic thought which guided the *criollista* ideological movements of rebellion and independence in the late eighteenth and early nineteenth centuries, and swayed by the reasoned social progress and idealism of positivism, the writers of the post-independence period, while searching for roots, demonstrated their optimism in the future of the newly liberated societies. But, as António Cândido points out in his contribution to this volume, essays as late as Bomfim's *A América Latina* (1901), or as early as Sarmiento's *Facundo* (1847), or Alberdi's *Bases...* (1852), while recognizing the colonial residues in national life, look forward to reform with excessive, even misplaced confidence in sociopolitical reorganization, education, or demographic additions or their geographic redistribution.

The advent of the process of modernization, whose initial manifestations became evident toward the 1850s, produced major shifts in society and literature; the writer and intellectual who earlier—from 1830 on—had in many instances participated in social planning and development, found himself displaced in the transitional precapitalist societies which from premodern agricultural status entered the first stages of industrialization.

These slowly evolving social and economic transformations affected the major centers of wealth and culture first. With the growth there of foreign capital and markets, the *criollo* oligarchs consolidated their national power. Their alliances with foreign capital and the expansion of mercantilism not only relegated the artist to a marginal social role, but created in him a tragic sense of isolation. His vision of reality was altered so that, in effect, it became part of the "modernizing process." His heightened interest in European culture and literatures, his fascination with *objets d'art*, *bibelots*, and Orientalism were the raw materials of a countercultural literature created by the very forces of the culture with which the writer felt at odds. The themes and objects of early Spanish American Modernist literature (1880–1895) may appear to some escapist; but, in fact, in addition to containing a critical social commentary, they are reflections of a new but *internal* vision of distance; contact with foreign markets heightened the writers' interest in foreign cultures; and their new proximity in national culture in turn intensified their influence on the writer. Distance, however, is not merely cultural; it can also denote the physical sense of discovery Paz refers to in relation to the rootlessness of early Latin American literature. For him, the distance factor, especially physical displacement, shapes literary production in the Modernist period; it was "rootlessness [which] permitted us to recover our portion of reality. Distance had to precede discovery... it is not harmful to feed on illusions if we transform them into reality."[9]

The realities of this early period of Modernity were such, however, that art became a commodity, and the artist, in an environment shaped by developing capitalism, found his critical attitudes moving him more and more from the center of an integrated position in the socioeconomic patterns of development to that of the anguished existential "outsider." This rupturing of previously established roles is reflected in a disintegration of literary genres, styles, and language. It is a phenomenon which occurred much earlier in some European centers of wealth, especially those which experienced early industrialization, and it is reasonable to identify its existence with the development of a socially conditioned romantic literature. From a broader point of view, this breakdown of structures and roles, and the rise of asystemic, asymmetrical, discontinuous elements in literature is one of the measures of Latin America's maturation, its partaking of the Western process of the secularization of life and culture: the redirection of man's pivotal role (*homo faber*) at the center of a universe whose structure is linked not only to the rise of romantic ideologies (subjectivity, individualization), but to the more historically distant stages of the Renaissance rejection of medieval traditions, a break which signaled a turning toward the modern world whose perpetual transformations are the signpost of twentieth-century society and its culture.

All of these changes are reflected in Latin American prose and poetry as early as 1870, when a search for the new, often insurrectional forms of expression became associated with what has been traditionally termed Modernism in Spanish America. It can be seen in the highly individualized forms of expression[10]—a first measure in the linguistic transformations which lead to deconstructions, first in "Modernist" literature, then in the "vanguard" prose and poetry of the twentieth century (in the twenties and thirties), and later in our contemporary period, in experimental novels such as Cortázar's *Hopscotch* (1963) where in *Gliglish* he writes: "As soon as he began to amalate the noeme, the clemise began to smother her and they fell into hydromures, into savage ambonies, into exasperating sustales."[11]

Ludic, parodic, and ironic forms of expression acquired tenacity in the Age of Modernity. Even in their incipient nineteenth-century embodiments they belonged to the period we have identified with the modernization of the Latin American economies and its effect, during a lengthy period of development and transformation, on the writers' image of themselves and of the universe. Self-reflexive and critical, they produced a literature of instability, meta-morphosis, and violation. Its quality is frequently bleak, despondent, alienated. But that is because this literature appears at the point at which the tide of the radical and innovating arts, the experimental, technical, aesthetic ideal "that had been growing forward from Romanticism, reaches formal crisis—in which myth, structure, and organization in a traditional sense collapse.... The crisis is a crisis of culture; it often involves an unhappy view of history...."[12]

This sense of crisis became evident in Latin America later than in Europe.[13] It was delayed in part by the chaos and energy of the immediate post-independence period (1820–1870), but largely by the absence of the socio-economic conditions that were the indispensable concomitant factors in catapulting Latin American culture and literature toward Modernity in the post-romantic period. All of which implies that the liberating forces of romanticism, traditionally equated with the seeds of Modernity in Europe, were lacking in Latin America. Its romanticism is, with few exceptions, a pale imitation of European models; as such they lack authenticity, substance, and conviction. By contrast, the literature which initiated the Age of Modernity has all the freeing functions of European romantic literature. This post-romantic Latin American literature is the product of an age of crisis, like its earlier European counterpart, but its characteristics are not necessarily those of the parallel European expression.

To some the modern, experimental works may seem frivolous, escapist, or exotic. Their style may appear arcane, perhaps out of step with socioeconomic underdevelopment. But this is so only to those who see no deeper than the surface textures and are thus unaware of a recurring, underlying anguished quest for order in a chaotic universe, for harmony in a disjointed world, for spiritual solace in a materialistically oriented society. Behind the ornamentation and the private imagistic systems reminiscent of the baroque, is the frequent expression of the affirmation of the individual, the writer's self-enthronement, the yearning for an inventive style capable of encompassing an often inchoate universe whose image the artist seeks to reflect in myriad, untried aesthetic, metaphysic, and ideologic expressions.

In viewing the development of this literature one of the major stumbling blocks in the path of its clear perception—especially in the context proposed by the guiding philosophy of this volume of essays, that is, the concept of a unified Latin American culture—is the prevailing tendency among historiographers of Latin American literature to view its literary evolution as separate from the continent's cultural, historic, and economic development. Sometimes, literary and socioeconomic developments are treated as parallel phenomena. But they are seldom juxtaposed to form a single, coherent composite. To bedevil matters, the continent's literature is too often seen as a product of European culture. And while derivative elements are undeniably present in its works, even today, it is a patent distortion to equate Latin American literature with European schools, trends, or movements. Equally unproductive is the stolid, traditional sequencing of literary movements, action/reaction fashion—beginning with their rapid succession late in the nineteenth century, a classification concept which yields a neat, but often faulty rhythm of changes whose terminology is: for verse, Modernism, post-Modernism, vanguard expressions, post-vanguard expressions, contemporary; for the novel, Modernism, realism, naturalism, *criollismo* (which includes the novel of the jungle, the Indianist novel, the novel of the Mexican Revolution, the gaucho novel, etc.) followed by the novel of the "boom" or the contemporary novel. (The remaining genres, such as essay or short story, are dealt with less rigorously.) A generational scheme, incorporating the same terms, is an alternate approach among the varied attempts at creating order in a composite literature which is, and always has been, chronologically fragmented, that is, characterized by a time lag vis-à-vis trends in its component parts (its national literatures), and further complicated by a constant overlaying (with delayed falling away) of aesthetic and ideologic movements. The persistence of this layering phenomenon can be reduced to speculative theory; but the fact of its existence remains. Its results often appear strange to the uninitiated European-oriented sense of aesthetics. For a cumulative creative process such as we are describing yields literary incongruities, such as a novel which is (all at the same time) Modernist, realistic, and naturalistic, with touches of the romantic.

In an age of individual, often self-negating styles—generational or aesthetic consanguinity notwithstanding—it seems far more fruitful, though polemic, to seek the common ground of Modernity, from whose perspective the development of Modern Latin American literature can be viewed as one in which the "mainstreaming" previously referred to occurs in relation to a multivalent image of Latin America whose presence assumes distinctly different and individual aesthetic and sociohistoric modes, all of which, however, share a desire for uniqueness, not simply in the sense of originality, but by virtue of their attempt at breaking with traditional sacrosanct norms. This search for the new is clearly not exclusively Latin American; Roland Barthes identifies it as the only way left for the contemporary writer to escape the present alienation of society,[14] an alienation which we have already noted harkens back to the inception of modernization and the appearance of Spanish American Modernism and Latin American literary Modernity.

Whether it be in the realm of the linguistic, the aesthetic, or ideologic, underlying all modern literature, prose and poetry, is the need to criticize, to reject reasoned principles, ideas, and structures, all of which have lost their sense in an age characterized by irrationalism. Contradiction, illogic, insurrection, apocalypse have replaced previous notions of reason, order, harmony, and balance. At times, however, writers will formulate a counterstatement to futility and negation by searching for reason, defending idealism, making pleas for human perfectability and historical progress. Such "lapses" are perfectly consistent with the individually contradictory nature of Modernity. Literature from Spanish American Modernism to our day must be seen as an adversary force—with respect to society and itself—a medium through which man expresses his somber role of challenging the social and cultural status quo in a world which has lost its center.

In such a world it is not surprising if writers sometimes question whether there can actually exist a concept of Latin America such as the one defended by César Fernández Moreno in his general introduction to this work. Paz, for example, tells us that time is history, the depository of meaning, and that history provides man with an image of the world. But if, as he posits, post-Modern technology and the excessively sharp edge of criticism have destroyed man's sense of history, and thus his image of the world,[15] one wonders whether it is feasible to conceptualize a coherent, meaningful vision of Latin America. To be sure, Paz's vision of destruction rests on the assumption that Latin America has entered into a post-Modern or post-industrial stage of development, a premise which may be applicable at present to more advanced societies, but for us is a harbinger of the future in the case of Latin America. Still, it is not inconceivable to foresee the advent of Paz's apocalyptic vision, given the socioeconomic interdependency of our contemporary world. We may yet need to resign ourselves to Carpentier's outer limits of faith or belief with respect to origins: "the word [Latin] *America* subsists."

Ivan A. Schulman
September 1979

Notes

1. Some of the ideas expressed in this essay on the subject of Spanish American Modernity are distillations from a forthcoming volume on the subject by Ivan A. Schulman and Evelyn Picon Garfield. See I. A. Schulman's "La dialéctica del centro; notas en torno a la modernidad de Ricardo Güiraldes," *Cuadernos Americanos*, XXXVII (1978), 196–208; "*Non serviam*: Notas en torno a la modernidad de Vicente Huidobro," *Revista Iberoamericana*, nos. 106–107 (1979), 9–17, and a forthcoming essay by I. A. Schulman and E. P. Garfield, "Arqueles Vela: La estética extraVASANTE de la InNegAusencia."

2. The citation is from the Spanish edition *La consagración de la primavera* (Madrid: Siglo XXI, 1978), p. 30. The translation is mine.

3. Ibid., p. 30.

4. "Roots of Latin American Literature," *Saturday Review*, 20 June 1959, 61.

5. Rufino Blanco Fombona, prologue to *Beauty and the Beast* (Madrid, 1931). The translations are mine.

6. "A Literature of Foundations," *TriQuarterly*, Fall/Winter, 1968, 8.

7. See Roberto Fernández Retamar's essay "Our America and the West," *Casa de las Américas*, September–October 1976, 36–57, and my discussion of this question in "From Washington Towards a Sociocultural Latin American Theory," *Escritura*, July–December 1976, 217–221.

8. *The New Spanish American Novel.* (Mexico: Cuadernos de Joaquín Mortiz, (1969), p. 28.

9. "A Literature of Foundations," pp. 10–11.

10. "Invention, Underdevelopment, Modernity" in *Alternating Current*, eighth edition (Mexico: Siglo XXI, 1975), p. 19.

11. Translated by G. Rabassa (New York: Avon Books, 1975), section 68, p. 383.

12. Malcolm Bradbury and James McFarlane, "The Name and Nature of Modernism" in *Modernism* (Middlesex: Penguin Books, 1976), p. 26.

13. See Federico de Onís in his essay "On the Concept of Modernism," *La Torre* 2 (1952), 95–103, where he notes that as far back as 1934 he identified Modernism with the idea of crisis.

14. *The Pleasure of the Text*, translated by R. Miller (New York: Hill and Wang, 1975), pp. 40–41.

15. "The New Analogy: Poetry and Technology" in *The Sign and the Scrawl*, second edition (Mexico: Joaquín Mortiz, 1975), p. 11.

PART ONE

A Literature in the World

1 / Cultural Plurality

GEORGE ROBERT COULTHARD

INDIAN CULTURAL CONTRIBUTIONS

It is essential to establish right from the beginning that there would be no Indian contributions without Spanish as an intermediary, and to a certain extent, this is true of African contributions in regard to French and English, in a purely linguistic sense, since none of the great indigenous cultures posessed an alphabet. The pictographic codices of the Aztecs, Zapotecs, Mayas, and so forth, although extremely beautiful, were incapable of telling stories, "novels," or of recording poems, dramas, or songs; at best they served as *aide-mémoires* and represented historical events, acts of the deities, or dates. If what we have just affirmed is true with respect to Indian "literature," it is even truer in reference to the contribution of Africa, as we will see later on.

Fortunately, in the case of Indian culture, especially that of the Aztec and the Maya-Quiché, the history, mythology, songs, poems, and religious beliefs were written down, in Náhuatl, Quiché, and so forth, thanks largely to the efforts of priests, among whom Father Bernardino de Sahagún stands out. The method consisted of teaching the Latin alphabet to Indian intellectuals and then allowing them to write what they knew of their history and culture in their own languages. Many of these writings have been translated into Spanish and other languages by scholars, and thus we have a considerable body of all kinds of material in collections; for example, the Florentine Codex, the Madrid Codex of the Royal Academy of History, and Songs in the Mexican Language. Many of the originals may be found in European and North American libraries. There are fewer texts from the Andean region, but a number of mestizo writers, whose relatives knew and remembered how things were before the conquest, dedicated themselves to the task of recounting the history as well as describing the beliefs and the customs of Tawantinsuyo, the Inca Empire. Later, ethnologists who were also good writers, like José María Arguedas of Peru and Jesús Lara of Bolivia, collected stories and songs, presenting them in versions of high literary quality.

The first great mestizo interpreter of pre-Columbian reality in Peru is, of course, the Inca Garcilaso de la Vega (1539–1616). Brought up by his Indian mother in Peru, he spent his entire adult life in Spain, where he became an outstanding humanist. He made a permanent name for himself in Spanish letters for his translation of Leon Hebreo's *Dialoghi d'amore*. However, during the last years of his life, in possession of an ample culture and a refined, graceful style, Garcilaso felt impelled to write *Royal Commentaries of the Incas*,* the first part of which appeared in 1609. He probably felt ashamed of the charges of barbarism and savagery which many Spaniards made against his people, and he wished to diminish the scorn which the majority of Spaniards felt for the Indians. When he described the culture of the Incas, he may have idealized it in his eagerness to rescue his people from the stigma of barbarism and inferiority. Marcelino Menéndez y Pelayo, the great Spanish polygraph, writes of the work: "*The Royal Commentaries* are not historical texts, but a utopian novel like that of Thomas More, like Campanella's *City of the Sun*, like Harrington's *Oceana*: a dream of an empire which is patriarchal and ruled with silken reins. To achieve such a lasting effect, a much greater imaginative power than the ordinary is needed, and it is certain that Garcilaso possessed such power, however deficient he may have been in critical discernment."[1] But this condemnation of the historical work recognizes the essentially *literary* nature of it, which has sustained interest in it from the first French translations to Louis Baudin.

The *Commentaries* are, in fact, an imaginative re-creation of the Inca state which takes into account economic and political matters, linguistic, geographical, and climatological conditions, all evoked according to humanistic historiography, a method which permitted the exercise of fancy and fiction as long as the end product was not too distant from reality and verisimilitude. Without a doubt, it reflects the post-Renaissance preoccupation with a Golden Age, since it is not an unadorned and truthful account (although this would have been feasible); yet, the interweaving of fantasy with facts, both in vision and in reality has produced a masterpiece.

In his *Seven Interpretive Essays on Peruvian Reality* (1928), José Carlos Mariátegui wrote an apparent truth when he said: "An Indian literature, if it comes, will come in its own time—when the Indians themselves are ready to produce it." However, one cannot help wondering whether this condition has not been fulfilled already, if not with Garcilaso de la Vega, at least with Felipe Huamán Poma de Ayala in his *New Chronicle and Good Government* (written between 1613 and 1614). They were both mestizos, it is true, but when they speak of their culture and of their past, and, especially in the case of Huamán Poma, of the present, they speak as Indians. Raúl Porras Barrenechea criticizes Huamán Poma for his "semiculture," but he seems to recognize him as an Indian: "There is an authentic note of pain and of complaint, which comes from the unfortunate situation of the Indian in labor transactions, in enforced labor [*mitas*], and in the Indian towns themselves

*Throughout this volume, titles of literary works written in Spanish or Portuguese are given in English whenever English translations have been found to exist. Untranslated works are referred to by their original titles, and are followed by literal English translations (in brackets) on their first appearance. Dates in parentheses refer to publication of the original edition (not of the translation).

which are subject to all the tyrannies."[2] He even recognizes the Indian quality in his style: "It is the method of Inca masonry transposed to the chronicle." However, it is an error to make too much of the semiculture of Huamán Poma. In this "monstrous miscellany," as Porras Barrenechea calls it, there is some of everything: repetitions; lack of clarity at times; a chronology surpassing belief; but at the same time, there are very colorful and even tender evocations of the pre-Incas; biting criticism of the hypocritical behavior of the Spaniards; and even a prefiguration of what Alejo Carpentier would call *marvelous reality* [*lo real maravilloso*], which he discovered in Haiti only to realize later that the whole history of America was soaked in this essence. The mother of the first Inca, Manco Capac, for example, who spoke with devils, and made the rocks, trees, mountains, and lakes talk and answer her questions; the sorcerers who knew how to predict the death of the monarchs of Castille and other worldwide events. His description of the Cori-Cancha during the sacrifices, with the sun gleaming on the gold of the temple and the rainbows formed by the breath of the crowd of Indians in the cold Cuzco dawn, is a masterpiece of Huamán Poma's imagination, since he had not witnessed this spectacle, although very probably some of the old Indians who remembered it had described it to him. Humor is not lacking either, as when he tells how a Spaniard thirsty for gold disguised himself as an Inca and had himself carried on a litter through a town asking for gold and silver, but the Indians, upon seeing a bearded Inca, fled in terror.

Huamán Poma also collected a number of songs in Quechua and Aymará, which have been translated by various authors and constitute a part of the oral literature of the pre-Hispanic era. Many versions exist, but we have chosen two translations by Jesús Lara, which are really re-creations:

> Causa del ser, Viracocha,
> Dios siempre presente,
> Juez que en toda está.
> Dios que gobierna y provee,
> que crea con sólo decir:
> "Sea hombre, sea mujer."
> Que viva libre y en paz
> el que pusiste
> y críaste.
> ¿ Dónde estás? ¿ Afuera
> o dentro, en la nube
> o en la sombra?...[3]

[Cause of being, Viracocha, / Always present God / Judge who is in everything. / God who governs and provides, / who creates by saying only: / "Be a man, be a woman." / May he live free and in peace / he who is placed by you / and cared for by you. / Where are you? Outside / or within, in the cloud / or in the shadow?...]

This poem in particular has a tragic significance, since according to Huamán Poma, the Indians, descendants of Noah, had forgotten everything that referred to God, although with their "slight shadow" of awareness they knew that He existed but, sad people, they went along with a feeling of forlornness and anguish wanting to know who and where God was. Even in one of his drawings he depicts an Indian kneeling asking "Pachacamac, Maypicanqui" ("Creator of the world, where are you?"). According to him it was the Incas who brought in idolatry and the veneration of the Devil. In a love song, a *Jaray arawi*, a song of absence, there is profound grief, very similar in tone and in imagery to the contemporary Quechua songs. Some of them are sung in Spanish, but the style and emotivity are identical:

> La desventura, reina,
> ¿ Nos separa?
> La adversidad, ñusta,
> nos aleja?
>
> Si fueras flor de chinchercoma,
> hermosa mía,
> en mi sien y en el vaso de mi corazón
> te llevaría.
>
> Pero eres un engaño, igual
> que el espejo del agua.
> Igual que el espejo del agua, ante mis ojos
> te desvaneces.
>
> ¿ Te vas, amada, sin que nuestro amor
> haya durado un día?...[4]

[Misfortune, queen, / Does it separate us? / Adversity, princess, / does it distance us? / / If you were a chinchercoma flower, / my beautiful, / on my temple and in the vase of my heart / I would carry you. / / But you are a deception, just like / the mirror of the water. / Like the mirror of the water, before my eyes / you vanish. / / Are you going, my love, before our love / has lasted a day?...]

Aside from historical-literary contributions like those of Garcilaso de la Vega or Huamán Poma de Ayala, dramas of Indian themes written in Quechua exist. Unfortunately, the names of the authors have been lost and various versions exist of some of them. Nevertheless, even though the Inca Empire had no Greek-style theater, or Spanish Golden Age-type theater, it seems indisputable that there were theatrical performances, episodes of the lives of the deities, kings, and so forth, with or without music or dancing. Also, the concept of theater, like that of the novel, is an extremely open one. I will only mention two specific works; it is evident that they were composed and written after the Conquest, but the themes, the sensitivity, the language (even in Spanish translation) testify to a different, non-European, reality.

In *Apu Ollantay*, the theme is purely Indian. It is about the seduction of a daughter of the Inca by an army general, Ollantay. The general wants to marry the princess, who is pregnant, but the Inca rejects his suit with disdain, since, as we know, the Inca's family was a closed caste. Ollantay, although a great captain, does not have royal blood. Full of resentment, he revolts and wars against the Inca for years, thus making himself doubly a criminal according to Inca law. At the end, defeated, he appears before the new Inca Tupaj Yupanki, expecting the death sentence. The Inca, surprisingly, not only pardons him but names him governor of Antisuyo and gives him Kusi Coyllur as his wife. The denouement seems unrealistic given the severity of the Inca laws, inasmuch as he deserves death for having stained the royal blood and for having revolted against the Inca. Jesús Lara, nevertheless, maintains that the denouement is realistic as a dramatic device because, as Garcilaso says, the sun committed his sons to treat the people "with charity, mercy and gentleness," and this denouement shows the public that the Inca could behave like a forgiving father. (In Ricardo Rojas' Argentine version, the Inca orders Ollantay killed, and exiles his daughter, but Rojas had a thesis that he wished to demonstrate by making use of the Inca legend.)

The other theatrical work we will mention is *La tragedia de la muerte de Atawallpa* [The Tragedy of the Death of Atawallpa], which is dominated by a feeling of inevitable catastrophe. It recounts, in dramatized form, the dreams and fears of Atawallpa, the arrival of the Spanish, the death of Atawallpa and the destruction of his empire. One curious aspect is the fact that the Spaniards do not speak, they only move their lips. Felipillo, a mulatto, translates what they indicate, in vulgar, scornful, insulting terms. The reader is astonished by the absolute submission of Atawallpa to his destiny. He seems to surrender to it with absolute impotence; nevertheless, we know that Atawallpa had been a great warrior, a man of action. Is he weighed down by a sense of guilt for having ordered the assassination of the true Inca, Huáscar, and for the slaughter of the whole family of his father, Huaina Capac? (Even Garcilaso, who generally idealizes the Inca regime, says of this event that "more monstrous and more bloodthirsty than that of the Ottomans was the cruelty of Atawallpa.") If such is the case, there is not the slightest allusion to such a feeling of guilt. What is perhaps more probable is that, as in the prophetic books of *Chilam Balam*, written after the disaster of the Conquest, the author projects the fatalism of what has already happened. Jesús Lara used Chayanta's version, which seems to him the most authentic and which, in addition, contains poetic passages of a very Andean character, such as:

> Tarukas de los páramos,
> cóndores de alto vuelo,
> ríos y roquedales,

venid y llorad con nosotros.
Nuestro padre y señor el Inca
nos ha dejado solos,
en honda congoja sumidos.
¿ Qué sombra vamos a buscar
y a quién hemos de recurrir?
¿ En qué martirio viviremos
y en qué lágrimas nos anegaremos?
Atawallpa, Inca mío,
quizá debemos refugiarnos
en las entrañas de la tierra.[5]

[Tarukas of the wilderness, / condors of high flight, / rivers and rocky places, / come and weep with us. / Our father and master the Inca / has left us alone, / submerged in deep anxiety. / What shadow will we seek / and to whom can we appeal? / In what martyrdom will we live / and in what tears will we drown? / Atawallpa, my Inca, / perhaps we should take refuge / in the bowels of the earth.]

We have not included here the so-called Indianist novels, like *Raza de bronce* [Race of Bronze] (1919), by the Bolivian Alcides Arguedas, *The Villagers (Huasipungo)* (1934) or *Huairapamushcas* (1947), by the Ecuadorian Jorge Icaza, *Broad and Alien Is the World* (1940), by the Peruvian Ciro Alegría, because although they deal with the problem of the Indian and describe customs and superstitions, they are basically novels of social protest and reflect very little of the Indian culture in the literal sense. However, it is necessary to make an exception in the case of the Peruvian José María Arguedas. Although he is not pure Indian, he grew up in the Peruvian mountains among Indians and is bilingual in Spanish and Quechua. He did not feel comfortable using Spanish literary language to interpret the feelings of the Indians, who express themselves in Quechua. Thus he undertook the extremely difficult task of finding a way of translating the reality of Indian idiosyncrasy into Spanish. He solved the problem in three ways: by using the words of many Quechua songs, which he translates; by making his Indian characters speak in Spanish, but with phrases and metaphors taken directly from the Quechua; and the Indian characters have a moral code which goes back to the pre-Hispanic era. It would be a serious error on the part of the reader to skip the songs: they are very beautiful, expressive, and Arguedas knows how to arrange them with a skill that reflects his literary mastery. For example, when Ernesto, the principal character of *Deep Rivers* (1958), is saying goodbye to his Indian friends, in order to go to the strange world of the school in Abancay, they sing to him:

No te olvides, mi pequeño
no te olvides.
Cerro blanco

hazlo volver.
Agua de la montaña, manantial de la pampa,
halcón, cárgalo en tus alas
y hazlo volver.
Inmensa nieve, padre de la nieve,
no lo hieras en el camino.
Mal viento, no lo toques.
Lluvia de tormenta,
no lo alcances.
No precipicio, atroz precipicio,
no lo sorprendas.
Hijo mío,
has de volver
has de volver.

[Do not forget, my little one / do not forget. / White ridge / make him return. / Water of the mountain, life-spring of the plains, / falcon, carry him on your wings / and make him return. / Immense snow, father of the snow, / do not injure him on the way. / Bad wind, do not touch him. / Storm rain, / do not reach him. / No precipice, dreadful precipice, / do not surprise him. / My son, / you must return / you must return.]

And in *Todas las sangres* [All Bloods] (1964), the impressive character Rendón Wilka expresses his morality in Quechua terms. For example, to the engineer Cabrejos who tries to bribe him, he answers: "You drunk master! I healthy. I earning money only with work; other money is curse of God; makes ugly worms grow in bone marrow, in the blood too." And to another Indian, who speaks cynically to him, saying "No one is clean," he answers: "No one Carhuamayo? If they throw filth at your head, you are not to blame. If you nourish envy and greed in your soul, you yourself then, then you yourself are dirty." This reminds us of the counsels of the Inca Roca in Garcilaso: "Envy is a termite that gnaws and consumes the entrails of the envious." "He who envies good people reaps only ill for himself, just as the spider does, when it sucks poison." It is a matter, as Alberto Escobar writes very perceptively, of "the invitation to recognize in Quechua the expression of a way of being, of understanding reality and naming it."[6]

In Mexico, as in Peru, preoccupation with the Indian began in the first decades of the twentieth century as part of a movement which was both nationalistic and political. Although a thinker of less breadth than the Peruvian José Carlos Mariátegui, Manuel Gamio, in some of the essays collected under the title of *Forjando patria* [Forging a Fatherland] (1916), emphasized certain fundamental ideas. Among other things, he affirms that the mass of the Mexican people has no feeling for European art imposed by the foreign-influenced bourgeoisie, that "an Indian soul must be forged, even if provisionally" and that in addition to reevaluating the Indian plastic arts it is necessary to "publish the few literary productions of pre-Hispanic origin, almost lost today in museums and dusty libraries, because they are fundamentally important to our literary future."

Two great Mexican scholars dedicated themselves to this enterprise of publication recommended by Gamio: Father Angel María Garibay K. in his *Historia de la literatura náhuatl* [History of Nahuatl Literature] (Mexico, 1953) and Miguel Léon-Portilla in *La filosofía náhuatl, estudiada en sus fuentes* [Nahuatl Philosophy, Studied in Its Sources] (Mexico, 1956). These two writers did not restrict themselves to their two basic works; they also compiled and wrote various books of translations and interpretations which incorporated Aztec *literature* and thought into the general current of Mexican culture. Both affirm the literary value of Aztec literature and thought and compare them to the best literature of other cultures. Garibay, for example, in *La poesía lírica azteca* [Aztec Lyric Poetry] (Mexico, 1937), declares that he had been drawn to the literature of the ancient Mexicans by the same "thirst for beauty" which had impelled him to study Greek and Hebrew literature, and in *La visión de los vencidos* [The Vision of the Vanquished] (Mexico, 1959), a very complete picture of the Conquest from the Indian point of view based on Aztec texts, he states: "It is not an exaggeration to affirm that there are passages in these Indian accounts which are as dramatic as the great classic epics. Because if in the *Iliad* Homer left us the memory of scenes of the most vivid tragic realism, the Indian writers also knew how to evoke dramatic moments of the Conquest."

In *La filosofía náhuatl*, León-Portilla affirms that there existed among the *tlalatinime*, "the Mexican thinkers," a true philosophy, if we accept that a philosophy may be metaphysical, asystematic and literary. This philosophy consists of the recognition of universal transitoriness, but with a way of knowing truth by means of poetry and the cult of beauty (*inxotitl, incuicatl*), the philosophy of songs and flowers: "A valid concept, perhaps, in its essence, for a world as tormented as ours." The essence of this philosophy, a kind of anguished hedonism, may be felt in this poem:

> ¿Es verdad que se vive sobre la tierra?
> No para siempre en la tierra: sólo un poco aquí.
> Aunque sea jade se quiebra,
> aunque sea oro se rompe,
> aunque sea plumaje de quetzal se desgarra,
> no para siempre en la tierra: sólo un poco aquí.[7]

[Is it true that there is life on earth? / Not forever on the earth: only a short while here. / Although jade, it will shatter, / Although gold, it will break, / although quetzal plumage, it will tear, / not forever on the earth: only a short while here.]

and in the beautiful poem included by Father Garibay in *La poesía lírica azteca*:

¿ Qué hará mi corazón?
¿ Acaso sólo en vano vino a la tierra?
¿ Me iré de otra manera
que las flores que fenecieron?
¿ Nada ha de quedar de mi fama
que de algún modo dure?
¿ Nada dejaré en la tierra
cuando me haya ido?
Al menos flores, al menos cantos.
¿ Qué hará mi corazón?
¿ Acaso sólo vino a la tierra en vano?

[What will my heart do? / Could it have come only in vain to the earth? / Will I go in some other way / than the flowers that perished? / Will none of my fame remain / in some way that will endure? / Will I leave nothing on the earth / when I have gone? / At least flowers, at least songs. / What will my heart do? / Could it have come to the earth only in vain?]

The texts can be translated in many ways, since, as Father Garibay suggests, "have we seen the last of the versions of Horace, or of the translations of the Psalms, just to give two examples?" The importance of Father Garibay and León-Portilla consists, of course, in the significance of their basic works of profound erudition, but at the same time, they have managed to establish a wide audience by publishing their translations in books which are suitable for the average reader. There are already many editions of *The Broken Spears: The Aztec Account of the Conquest of Mexico* and *La literatura de los aztecas* [The Literature of the Aztecs] (a selection published in 1964) is a book which is accessible to any reader.

In addition to *The Broken Spears* and *La filosofía náhuatl*, Léon-Portilla has published a marvelous work, *Trece poetas del mundo azteca* [Thirteen Poets from the Aztec World] (1967), which contains long poems by various pre-Hispanic Mexican poets, by Netzahualcóyotl and others, whose names are not known.

The translations from Náhuatl do not in any way exhaust the extremely rich lode of Mesoamerican Indian literature. Real masterpieces have come out of the Maya-Quiché region (Yucatán, Chiapas, Guatemala).

The *Popul Vuh*, known and translated since the beginning of the eighteenth century (the first translation is by the Spanish friar, P. Francisco Ximénez), has become one of America's classics. Although it is a religious book, which recounts the origin of man and the activities of the gods and semigods, it can be read as a novel. In a very broad sense, it is one of the great novels of America, perhaps of the world. With a fantasy free of all limitations of logic (magic plays a primordial role in the book), it recounts the tricks and plots of Hunaphú and Xbalenque in order to destroy the grotesquely proud Vucub-Caquix, the macaw, or to make fun of the lords of Xibalbá, the inferno. If we say that it shares some of the qualities of *A Thousand and One Nights*, of *Alice in Wonderland*, and of the Chinese novel *Mono* by Wu Chêngên, the reader will have some idea of the kind of book it is. The version that is most read today is that of Adrián Recinos, of 1947. It has appeared in many subsequent editions.

El libro de los libros de Chilam Balam [The Book of Books of Chilam Balam] is a less literary book, but despite that it contains lively, strong, and even poetic passages, like the following one from the *Chilam Balam de Chumayel* [The Book of Chilam Balam of Chumayel]:

> There was wisdom in them. There was no sin then. There was holy devotion in them. They lived in health. There was no sickness then; there was no pain in bones; there was no fever among them, there was no smallpox, there was no burning in the chest, there was no stomach ache, there was no consumption. Their bodies were straight and erect then.
>
> It was not thus that the *dzules* behaved when they came here. They taught fear; and they came to wither the flowers. So that their flower would live, they damaged and sucked dry the flower of others.
>
> There was no Higher Knowledge, there was no Sacred Language, there was no Divine Teaching in the gods' substitutes who came here. Castrate the Sun! That is what the foreigners came to do here. And the sons of their sons stayed here amidst the people, who receive their bitterness.[8]

In his translation of the *Libro de los cantares de Dzitbalché* [Book of the Songs of Dzitbalché] (Mexico, 1965), Alfredo Barrera Vásquez presents extremely beautiful poems which do not resemble any European poetry. Thus in the *Kay-Nicté*, "song of flowers" (one must bear in mind that among the Mayas as among the Mexicans, the flower was closely related to sexuality and to fecundity):

> Hemos llegado adentro
> del interior del bosque donde
> nadie
> mirará
> lo que hemos venido a hacer.
>
> Hemos traído la flor de la Plumería
> la flor del chucum, la flor
> del jazmino canino, la flor de...
> Trajimos el copal, la rastrera cañita ziit,
> así como la concha de la tortuga terrestre.
> Asimismo el nuevo polvo de calcita
> dura y el nuevo
> hilo de algodón para hilar; la nueva
> jícara
> y el grande y fino pedernal;
> y nueva pesa;
> la nueva tarea de hilado;

el presente del pavo;
nuevo calzado.
Todo nuevo,
inclusive las bandas que atan
nuestras cabelleras para
tocarnos con el nenúfar;
igualmente el zumbador
caracol y la anciana [maestra]. Ya, ya
estamos en el corazón del bosque,
a orillas de la poza en la roca,
a esperar
que surja la bella
estrella que humea
sobre
el bosque. Quitaos
vuestras ropas, desatad
vuestras cabelleras;
quedaos como
llegasteis aquí
sobre el mundo,
vírgenes, mujeres mozas...

[We have arrived within / the interior of the forest where / no one / will see / what we have come to do. / / We have brought the flower of Plumage / the flower of the chucum, the flower / of the canine jasmine, the flower of... / We brought the copal, the trailing ziit reeds, / and also the shell of the terrestrial tortoise. / Likewise the new powder of hard / calcite and the new / cotton thread to spin; the new / gourd / and the large and fine flint; / and new weight; / the new spinning task; / the present of the turkey; / new footwear. / Everything new, / including the bands that tie / our hair in order to / touch ourselves with the white water lily; / likewise the humming / shell and the ancient [teacher]. Now, now / we are in the heart of the forest, / beside the pool in the rock, / to await / the rising of the beautiful / star which steams over / the forest. Take off / your clothes, unbind / your hair; / be as / you arrived here / upon the world, / virgins, young women...]

It must be added that many writers have made use of the work of authors like Garibay, León-Portilla, and Alfonso Caso for their own creations. We will mention Carlos Fuentes's *Where the Air Is Clear*, Héctor Pérez Martínez's *Cuauhtémoc, vida y muerte de una cultura* [C., Life and Death of a Culture]; and *The Winners*, by the Argentinian Julio Cortázar, one of the most effective passages of which was inspired by various creations of the Maya gods. Nor should we forget two works by Miguel Ángel Asturias, *Las leyendas de Guatemala* [Legends of Guatemala], about Guacamayo and the Sun, the creation of a universally applicable myth, and *Men of Maize*, where marvelous reality or *magic realism* as Seymour Menton calls it, is manifested as a tangible, disconcerting, and enchanting presence.

AFRICAN CULTURAL CONTRIBUTIONS

While Mariátegui said that an Indianist literature would only come when the Indians themselves were in a condition to produce it, he could have made the same observation about the African contribution to the literature of America, with even more justification. The theme of the Negro appears in the first decade of the nineteenth century in the antislavery novels of Cuba. The first, *Francisco*, by Anselmo Suárez Romero, published by the Antislavery Society of London (in English) in 1840 and in Spanish in New York in 1880, was written to stimulate a feeling of revulsion against the horrors of slavery; and José Antonio Portuondo writes that its author "has the indisputable merit of having been the one who perceived most acutely in his time the poetic wealth hidden in the folkloric songs of Negroes and peasants, the latent treasure in Cuban folklore of dances and traditions, of local songs and of rhythms transplanted from Africa."[9] Suárez Romero writes things like the following:

> The drum, for those of the Negro nation and for the creoles who are brought up with them, takes them out of themselves, carries off their souls; hearing it, it seems to them that they are in heaven. But there are songs which do not vary, because they were composed over there in Africa and they came over with the Negro people. The extraordinary thing is that they never forget; they come as small children, years and years go by, they get old and then, when they are only useful as watchmen, they sing them alone in their huts, full of ashes, warming themselves at the fire which burns before them; they remember their homeland, even when they are about to sink into their graves.

Do we find ourselves up against something other than local color, deeply felt perhaps, but local color nevertheless? The great novel by Cirilo Villaverde, *Cecilia Valdés*, part of which appeared in 1839 but was not published in its entirety until 1882 in New York, also deals in depth with the Negro theme, penetrating into the psychology of the Negro, the mulatto, and the slave owner, and containing in seed form, although not as a formula, Césaire's idea "colonisation est chosification." But can we speak of an "African contribution" in regard to these novels? They are novels written by whites who were concerned about the state of the Negro in Cuba. This is true even of Antonio Zambrana's *Francisco* (Santiago, Chile, 1873) in which the author seems to understand the mentality of the Negro with greater subtlety than Suárez Romero, since he does not try to change his characters into Negroes with the psychology of whites, victims of an unjust system. For Zambrana the Negro is a primitive being; let us remember that a few years later the partisans of *négritude* would reclaim primitivism as a positive quality. "Civilized man," he writes, "barely understands a certain order of ideas and emotions, which are in large part artificial and have weakened direct connections with nature. When it is a question of slavery, he compares the idea of civilization with the rough existence of the jungle, and then he decides that the Negro has gained by the change. But the Negro loves what you scorn: his forest, his simple music, his primitive customs. Prove to him that he is happy, be eloquent and rational: his heart tells him something very different." These ideas are, as we have suggested, exactly those which *négritude* will proclaim almost dogmatically when the Franco-West Indians formulate it as a concept some sixty years later.

Can the contents and style of this literature be accepted as African cultural contributions, or would it be more reasonable to reject them completely? It is a matter, as we have said, of the Negro theme, but not written by Negroes or mulattos, and although there are descriptions of dances, ceremonies, Negro attitudes, everything is seen from the outside. Nevertheless, their inclusion in this chapter could, perhaps, be justified, since such a persistent concern could have served to prepare the way for a literature impregnated with genuine African essences. *Africanía*, to use a term by Fernando Ortiz, existed in certain regions of America, especially in the Spanish, French, and English-speaking islands of the West Indies, but on a completely unerudite level. This complex world—superstition, voodoo, customs, songs and dances—had not found a literary expression, it had only been *described*. Thanks, to a large extent, to the works of Fernando Ortiz (*Los negros brujos* [Black Sorcerers], 1906; *Los negros esclavos* [Black Slaves], 1916; *El glosario de afro-cubanismos* [Glossary of Afro-Cuban Expressions], 1924) the existence of this world which is beneath the surface, guessed at and glimpsed, but not known, began to interest many West Indians, mostly Cubans. The possible uses of this popular art began to be examined; and in 1928 "the drums began to respond in the Cuban lyric," as Ortiz himself wrote (*Revista Bimestre Cubana*, 1936, 37:26). It refers to compositions like José Z. Tallet's *La bailadora de rumba* [The Rumba-Dancing Woman] and Alejo Carpentier's *La liturgia ñáñiga* [The Native Liturgy]. But in the three books by Nicolás Guillén—*Motivos de Son* [Themes of Typical Cuban Music] (1930), *Sóngoro cosongo* [untranslatable onomatopoeia] (1931), and especially *West Indies Ltd.* (1934)—we find the authentic Afro-Cuban voice. Rhythms of the Negro music of Cuba, words of Yoruba songs, humor and pathos, all this written about and felt from within, is found in Guillén's poetry of this era. "La balada de los dos abuelos," "Balada del güije," the famous "Sensemayá," are authentically Afro-Cuban in their expression and content; so are poems like "Ebano real" or "Acaná," lines like "Arará cuévano/ arará sabalú" or "Ay, acaná con acaná/ con acaná" and entire poems like:

> Iba yo por un camino
> cuando con la Muerte di.
> —Amigo—me gritó la Muerte
> pero no le respondí,
> pero no le respondí,
> miré no más a la Muerte,
> pero no le respondí.[10]

[I was going along a road / when I met up with Death. / "Friend," Death yelled at me / but I didn't answer him, / but I didn't answer him, / I just looked at Death, / but I didn't answer him.]

The technique is purely African, since the songs of many parts of West Africa are repetitive, with slight variations within the repetitions. So, too, is the Yoruba song in Cuba, in African, or in Spanish. The same phenomenon may be observed throughout the West Indies.

There is not the slightest doubt that the fad of primitivism in Europe and in the United States during the decades 1920–1940 influenced the exploitation of Afro-West Indian culture. But this is the least of it; in addition, all Cuban literature of the nineteenth century had been preparing the ground. Ramón Guirao states very perceptively: "In Cuba, the Negro way, then, does not originate, as it does in Europe, without a tradition or reference to human life."[11] And Marinello suggests that the Negro has come in part to play the role of the aboriginal Indian in Cuba.

Probably the most authentically African novel written in Cuba is Miguel Barnet's *Biografía de un cimarrón* [Biography of a Run-Away Slave] (Havana and Mexico, 1968). It is about the life of a 104-year-old man who recounts how the slaves lived and describes the dances and witchcraft of African origin.

The Afro-West Indian poetry of the Puerto Rican Luis Palés Matos seems clearly a reflection of the antiintellectualism of the era, and is a composite of purely Afro-West Indian ingredients and of neo-Spenglerian theories about the decadence of the West. "The aesthetic sense of the white race has entered into a state of dangerous cerebralization, anulling its cosmic roots," he writes in an article published in *Poliedro* [Polyhedron] (San Juan, 1927). And he calls for an art subordinated "to the pulsing of the blood and of instinct." One may ask to what extent Palés Matos really believed in Afro-West Indian art. Even the first poem of *Tun tun de pasa y grifería* [Rhythm of Popular Music] (San Juan, 1937), "Preludio en Boricua," [Prelude in the Puerto Rican Language] ends with lines of a discouraging tone:

Este libro que va a tus manos
con ingredientes antillanos
compuse un día...
...y en resumen, tiempo perdido
que me acaba en aburrimiento.
Algo entrevisto o presentido,
poco realmente vivido
y mucho de embuste y de cuento.

[This book which goes into your hands / with West Indian ingredients / I composed one day.../...and in summary, time lost / which leaves me in boredom. / Something glimpsed or sensed, / very little really lived / and a lot of bragging and storytelling.]

The West Indian environment is admirably depicted with a rich vocabulary and an exuberant play of images. According to Jaime Benítez in his prologue to the second edition of 1950, this attitude corresponds to the "great spiritual decay of our educated classes." This is probably true, but it is no less true that the Afro-West Indian poetry of Palés Matos is something which has not been lived; it could even be considered as a form of Modernism which only brushes tangentially against the African contribution.

Meanwhile, in Haiti and the West Indies, a Negrist attitude had been forming since the last quarter of the nineteenth century. Anténor Firmin in *De l'égalité des races humaines* (Paris, 1885) and Hanibal Price in *De la réhabilitation de la race noire par le peuple d'Haïti*, had combated the idea of the barbarism of the Negro in Africa and Haiti, of his racial inferiority, and of discrimination. But it was the book by Jean Price Mars, *Ainsi parla l'oncle* (Port au Prince), 1928, which launched an artistic and spiritual movement which is still alive. He not only rejects the idea of inferiority and lack of culture in Africa, but he also studies the customs and beliefs, almost exclusively of African origin, of the Haitian people, calling them "magnificent human material of which the heart, the incalculable awareness, the collective soul of the Haitian people are made." The generation of the thirties and the forties gave itself over to a true orgy of primitivism and Africanism in which a rejection of the cultural values of Europe and a nostalgia for Africa as a lost paradise stand out. Typical examples are: by Carl Brouard: "Drum, when you sound, my soul howls toward Africa"; by Claude Fabry: "I feel that I have the soul of a disheveled African"; by Fabrice Casseus: "Oh tell us your great African rhythm, oh racial drum!" León Laleau laments having to express his heart, which comes from Senegal, in the language of France.

The novelists dedicate themselves to the theme of voodoo, religion of the masses in Haiti. Poetry fills with African flora and fauna, totally different from the Haitian: baobab, siringa, crocodiles, monkeys, jungle, and so forth. These writers, who want to tear off their European clothes and dance naked, who eulogize voodoo, at bottom are executing a dance whose music, despite the African rhythm, is being conducted by a European baton. They even use Creole, incomprehensible outside Haiti and the French West Indies, thinking, not without cause, that it is more linked to Africa than to France. H. Morisseau Leroy translated *Oedipus Rex* into Creole, but it is not only a linguistic translation. The Greek gods are replaced by *loas*, "spirits" of the voodoo pantheon of Haiti.

The outstanding, and almost only, poet of the English West Indies, Claude McKay, deals with themes which are similar to those of the Haitians: nostalgia for Africa, resentment of Europe for having enslaved the Negro and scorned his culture. He also rejoices enthusiastically in the easygoing, unworried life of the Negro (*Home to Harlem*, 1928) and in primitivism.

However, it was the Martiniquean Aimé Césaire who polarized all the Negrism of the West Indies, and in great part, of Africa. Nevertheless, he did not forge his concept of *négritude* based on purely Afro-American elements.

Césaire's *négritude* included consciousness of the black man everywhere in the world. The Haitians had dedicated themselves to overthrowing the supremacy of European culture, but somewhat without rhyme or reason. Césaire, on the other hand, rejected the values of Western civilization, condemned logic, reason, and at the same time proclaimed an exclusively Negro cosmovision:

> Eia pour ceux qui n'ont jamais rien inventé
> pour ceux qui n'ont jamais rien exploré
> pour ceux qui n'ont jamais rien dompté
> mais ils s'abandonnent, saisis, à l'essence de toute chose
> ignorants des surfaces mais saisis par le mouvement de toute chose
> insoucieux de dompter, mais jouant le jeu du monde
> . . .
> étincelle du feu sacré du monde
> chair de la chair du monde palpitant du mouvement même du monde!

[Eia for those who invented nothing / for those who have never explored anything / for those who have never domesticated anything, / but who abandon themselves ecstatically to the essence of all things / ignoring the external surface but possessed by the movement of all things / unconcerned about dominating, / but playing the game of the world / spark of the sacred fire of the world / flesh of the world's flesh throbbing with the movement of the world itself.]

And in the same *Cahier d'un retour au pays natal* (Paris, 1939), he expresses his hatred for logic:

> Parce que nous vous haïssons vous et
> votre raison, nous nous réclamons de la
> démence précoce de la folie flambante
> du cannibalisme tenace

[Because we hate you, you and / your reason, we ask for / the precocious madness,   the flaming madness / of tenacious cannibalism.]

And he proclaims the failure of "white" civilization:

> Ecoutez la monde blanc
> horriblement las de son effort immense
> ses articulations rebelles craquer sous les étoiles dures
> ses raideurs d'acier bleu transperçant la chair mystique

[Hear the white world / horribly tired from its immense effort / creak its rebellious joints beneath the hard stars, / its blue-steel rigidity piercing the mystic flesh.]

A great part of the writing of Césaire and his followers owes its technique to surrealism, although some adherents of *négritude* like the German Jahnheinz Jahn have tried to deny it, by affirming that Negro art always has a clear meaning. In an interview in *Casa de las Américas* (July–August 1958), Césaire himself acknowledges his debt to surrealism. He answers René Depestre: "Surrealism interested me to the extent to which it was a factor of liberation." But he adds: "For me it was the call of Africa," and he describes it as a call to the deep forces, to the unconscious forces, a disintoxication with Cartesianism, with French rhetoric, and he adds significantly: "Submersion in the depths. It was the submersion in Africa for me."

Although the West Indies do not altogether disappear, Césaire seems progressively less and less concerned with Africa, its history, the life of the Negro everywhere, and his writing gradually gives the impression that the African contribution is not so much from the Africanized subsoil of the West Indies as from Africa itself. This is an extremely curious phenomenon.

The African influence exists in the French and British West Indies in the race and color of the inhabitants, most of them black. Little use has been made of the African residues in the folkloric culture and it has not produced anything much in literature, at most some animal fables like *Anansi the Spider*, 1964, by Phillip M. Sherlock of Jamaica. In contrast, the nostalgia for Africa, which was converted into the "return to Africa" political movement by the Jamaican Marcus Garvey, which still endures among the thousands of *rastafaris* of Jamaica, and the inspiration drawn directly from the music, rhythms, and songs of various regions of Africa, seem to have deep roots and are growing. And there is great concern about the black man's place in the contemporary world.

Négritude, the Negro's self-awareness, may have arisen in the West Indies, and it may have emerged from the social and economic conditions of the West Indies, but it is not a narrowly West Indian movement. In his last book, *Masks*, Edward Brathwaite, the poet from Barbados who has spent eight years in Ghana, writes about the culture and customs of the Akan, a nation which speaks Twi. It is not a matter of local color but of the examination of their life style and of his personal reactions as a West Indian who returns. He makes use of rhythms of African songs, and even writes poems almost entirely in Twi: in "The New Ships" he describes his arrival:

> Takoradi was hot.
> Green struggled through red
> as we landed,
>
> Laterite lanes drifted off
> into dust
> into silence.
>
> Mammies crowded with cloths,
> flowered and laughed;

white teeth
smooth voices like pebbles
moved by the sea of their language.

Akwaaba they smiled
meaning welcome

akwaaba they called
aye kooo

well have you walked
have you journeyed

welcome.

You who have come
back a stranger
after three hundred years

welcome.

Here is a stool for
you; sit; do
you remember?

Here is water
dip
wash your hands
are you ready
to eat?

Here is plantain
here palm oil:
red, staining the fingers;
good for the heat,
for the sweat.

Do
you remember?

The poem "Tano" is written almost entirely in Twi, but even in English it
has the rhythm of the tom-tom:

Dam
dam
damirifa
damirifa due
damirifa due

damirifa due
due
due
due

Whom does death overlook?
Whom
whom does death overlook?

I am an orphan
and when I recall the death
of my father

water from eyes
from my eyes
falls upon me

Dam
dam
damirifa
damirifa due
damirifa due
damirifa due
due
due
due[12]

Another interesting fact is that in the Spanish-speaking West Indies and in other regions of America where there are large concentrations of black people (Ecuador, Colombia, Venezuela, Brazil), writers and artists have drawn materials from the quarry of Afro-American folklore. A writer like the Ecuadorian Adalberto Ortiz writes poems like "Contribución" [Contribution] in *El animal herido* [The Wounded Animal] (Quito, 1959), in the manner of Nicolás Guillén. In this poem, lines like this appear:

Invade la sangre cálida de Africa,
de la raza de color,
porque el alma, la de Africa,
que encadenada llegó,
en esta tierra de América
canela y candela dió.

[There is an invasion of the warm blood of Africa, / of the colored race, / because the soul, that of Africa, / which arrived enchained, / in this land of America / yielded cinnamon and light.]

However, Ortiz's interest is in the African *in Ecuador*; he does not wish to return to Africa nor to import literary models by African writers. The same thing happens in Brazil, where the Negro and the mulatto feel very Brazilian despite the fact that Brazil is probably the country where the African heritage in folklore and religion is the strongest. Or perhaps it is for this very reason.

NON-IBERIAN EUROPEAN CONTRIBUTIONS

Immigration

It is perhaps inevitable, especially in certain countries like Argentina, Uruguay, and Brazil, that there should be writing about the immigrants.

Generally, the immigrant appears in two forms. First in opposition to and even in violent clashes with the way of being, the customs and prejudices of the Creoles; this happens in works like *The Foreign Girl* [also in English as *The Immigrant Girl*] (1904), by the Uruguayan Florencio Sánchez, and *The Jewish Gauchos of the Pampas* (1910), by the Argentinian Alberto Gerchunoff; but generally the foreigner ends by being accepted and integrated. Books like these have conclusions which are optimistic and happy. The second form in which the immigrant appears can include elements of the first—contacts, clashes, struggle with nature itself—but at the same time it presents the problem of the Creole, in certain cases inferior to the new arrival. Indications of this tendency may be seen from the "Introduction" to *Life in the Argentine Republic in the Days of the Tyrants; or Civilization and Barbarism*, by D. F. Sarmiento (1845), to Eduardo Mallea's *Historia de una pasión argentina* [History of an Argentine Passion] (1935). However, the masterpiece of this kind of book is undoubtedly *Canaan* (1902), by the Brazilian Graça Aranha. It is not a novel which unfolds easily and ends happily. In the first place there is the conspicuous superiority of the German colonists in their capacity to work and desire to construct, in contrast to the Creole apathy. But despite this, Milkau, a complex and tormented character, recognizes that the greatness of Brazil consists in having conquered a wild and intractable nature. A novel which is rich in ideas, in unforgettable realistic scenes, it unfortunately cannot be summarized briefly. The theme of the immigrant has served to evaluate the effects of immigration upon national life and also to stimulate a close examination of national values.

Literary Influences

Non-Hispanic European influences begin to leave a noticeable imprint on Hispanic American literature beginning with Independence. At the beginning, French influence really predominates; the British or German influences generally come through the French. Certain elements of romanticism are manifested in poetry as well as in the novel and short story. Romanticism is certainly a multifaceted trend: antineoclassical reaction, egocentricity, and historicism are some of its characteristics. But Latin American writers chose what suited them best from the various aspects of romanticism.

First, nationalism in the widest sense of the term: a description of nature according to the models of Chateaubriand, Ossian, Rousseau, Fenimore Cooper; historicism, heavily influenced by Walter Scott, perhaps through the many translations of his works done in Spain. They tended to be repelled by the Middle Ages, perhaps because it reminded them too much of Spanish colonization; thus, they preferred episodes of the time of the Conquest—in which the Indian played the role of the good savage fighting for his freedom against the greedy and traitorous Spaniards—and episodes of the war for independence. The tendency to use linguistic regionalisms may be seen, too, as in Esteban Echeverría's *The Slaughterhouse*, and José Hernández's *The Gaucho Martín Fierro*, which still has many romantic qualities (the character Martín Fierro has a lot in him of the antisocial rebel, of the accursed hero of Byron, Musset, Espronceda, etc.).

In second place, and perhaps related to the first, *costumbrismo*, which may have originated in Spain. Sarmiento, for example, whose *Civilization and Barbarism* is to a large extent *costumbrista*, admired only Larra among the contemporary writers, but of course, Larra was very much influenced by French literature.

In the third place, the attraction of Balzac was enormous and continued until the twentieth century; especially the Balzac of the *Comédie humaine* was very useful as a model for painting the new societies in the process of formation and development. However, to tell the truth, the nineteenth century produced few good novels in Latin America. Two of the better ones: *Cecilia Valdés*, by the Cuban Cirilo Villaverde—very Balzacian despite citing Scott and Manzoni as models—and Jorge Isaac's *María*, where the influence of Chateaubriand is evident.

The second influence, also preponderantly French, appeared with Modernism, and particularly affects poetry. A mixture of Parnassianism and symbolism, it turned its back on America (with exceptions like José Martí and Santos Chocano). The Modernists followed Leconte de Lisle and José María de Heredia, seeking their themes in Japan, China, and in the Orient of *A Thousand and One Nights*. What was worse, they imitated decadentism, the refinement of the senses, the "suggestive magic" of words, imitating the symbolism of the simplest of the symbolists, like Verlaine and the early Mallarmé. They created a literature for a small cultured elite, often pretentious. Their poses as decadentists seemed absurdly out of place in a society where everything needed to be done.

Meanwhile, the mainstream of the novel was flowing through other channels. Authors like Mariano Azuela followed Maupassant, Zola, Daudet, that is, realism-naturalism. Balzac's influence remained strong, as may be seen in Azuela and his attempt to describe the "new bourgeoisie" in his novels, although his style is closer to Maupassant's in its conciseness. In some writers there is a curious mixture of realism, romanticism and modernism, as in Eustasio Rivera's *The Vortex* or the Bolivian Alcides Arguedas's *Raza de bronce* [Race of Bronze].

José Vila Selma recognizes in Rómulo Gallegos influences of Tolstoy, Darwin, D'Annunzio, and Nietzsche, but they are not exactly literary influences; it is doubtful whether characters like Santos Luzardo in *Doña Bárbara* (1929) and Marcos Vargas in *Canaima* (1935) are inspired by the German philosopher's supermen. The fearless he-man already existed in Latin American literature.

We could continue to cite influences or possible influences, but there would be no point in doing so. The fact is that the Latin American writer, whether novelist or poet, with the exception of some of the Modernists, wanted to create a literature in a purely national or Latin American mold.

The same thing has occurred with the contemporary novelists like Carlos Fuentes, Julio Cortázar, Gabriel García Márquez, and Ernesto Sábato. In Fuentes there is possibly the influence of James Joyce (of *Ulysses* in *The Death of Artemio Cruz*, possibly of *Finnegan's Wake* in *A Change of Skin*); "stream-of-consciousness" is seen in many of them, from Miguel Ángel Asturias's *El Señor Presidente* [Mister President], to Ernesto Sábato; it may be that Faulkner has influenced Gabriel García Márquez's *One Hundred Years of Solitude*; but Latin American reality and consciousness penetrate and saturate his novels to such an extent that the question of influences comes to be an almost purely academic matter. As Pablo Neruda has said very sensibly: "The world of the arts is a great workshop in which we all work and help each other, although not everyone may know it or believe it. And, in the first place, we are helped by the work of those who came before us and we already know that there is no Rubén Darío without Góngora, nor Apollinaire without Rimbaud, nor Baudelaire without Lamartine, nor Pablo Neruda without all of them together."[13] As for the novel, Vargas Llosa writes: "I understand that when they had Proust and Joyce, the Europeans took little or no interest in Santos Chocano or Eustasio Rivera. But now that they only have Robbe–Grillet, Nathalie Sarraute, or Giorgio Bassani, why shouldn't they look beyond their own frontiers in search of writers who are more interesting, less lethargic and more lively. Look for yourselves, in European literature of the last few years, for an author comparable to Julio Cortázar, or for a novel of the quality of *Explosion in a Cathedral*, or for a young poet with such a profound and subversive voice as that of the Peruvian Carlos Germán Belli; they are not to be found anywhere. European literature is undergoing a terrible crisis of frivolousness and this has favored the widespread popularity of Latin American writers in Europe."[14]

When they make commentaries like these, it is evident that Neruda and Vargas Llosa are not trying to deny foreign influences, but emphasize rather that such influences, however important they may be, generally do not constitute the essence of Latin American literature; that this literature digests and assimilates them, and utilizing them creates something of its own which is also universal.

However, what serves as a trampoline in spiritual and psychic matters, as well as in the transcription of the American reality itself, is the Latin American living experience. Without falling into an obsession with the "originality" of Latin American literature, it is possible to sustain that from this crucible of influences—aboriginal, African, European and, of course, Spanish—a literature of absolutely distinctive mold has emerged. The proof, as Vargas Llosa proclaims with perhaps excessive arrogance, is that this literature is being translated into almost all the languages of culture, and what is even more important, that the works of Argentinians and Mexicans, Cubans and Chileans, are being read avidly in all of Latin America and in Spain itself.

Notes

1. Marcelino Menéndez y Pelayo, *Historia de la poesía hispanoamericana* (1913), 2:148–149.

2. Raúl Porras Barrenechea, *El cronista indio Guamán Poma de Ayala* (Lima, 1948), p. 67.

3. Jesús Lara, *Poesía quechua* (Mexico, 1947), p. 158.

4. Jesús Lara, *Poesía quechua*, p. 163.

5. Jesús Lara, trans., *La tragedia de la muerte de Atawallpa* (Cochabamba, 1957), p. 181.

6. Alberto Escobar, *Patio de letras* (Lima, 1966), p. 29.

7. León-Portilla, *La filosofía náhuatl*, p. 137.

8. Spanish version: Antonio Mediz Bolio, trans., *Chilam Balam de Chumayel* (San José, Costa Rica, 1930), p. 36.

9. J. A. Portuondo, *Bosquejo de las letras cubanas* (Havana, 1960), p. 24.

10. Nicolás Guillén, *El son entero* (Buenos Aires: Losada, 1947).

11. Ramón Guirao, *Orbita de la poesía afro-cubana, 1928–37* (Havana: Ucar, García, 1939).

12. Edward Brathwaite, *Masks* (London: Oxford University Press, 1968), pp. 37–38, 68–69.

13. Pablo Neruda and Nicanor Parra (Santiago de Chile, 1962), p. 54.

14. "Saludo al margen," *Margen*, no. 1, (Paris, October–November 1966).

2 / Unity and Diversity

JOSÉ LUIS MARTÍNEZ

We are a small human species; we possess a world apart, surrounded by vast seas, new in nearly all the arts and sciences although, in a certain sense, old in the experience of civil society.

SIMÓN BOLÍVAR

COMPLEX LATIN AMERICA

The most unique aspect of Latin America is that it exists as such, that is, as a group of twenty-one countries, with such profound historical, social, and cultural ties that they constitute a single unit in many senses.[1] Other groups of countries may be related by their history and by their race, by their language, and by their religion, or by political or economic pacts. But it is not often that all these connections are found simultaneously, and it is even less frequent that, as in the case of Latin America, the common traits are stronger than the will to individualize and stronger than any dissidence.

Occupying more than half of the American hemisphere, these nations were conquered and colonized in the beginning of the sixteenth century by the Spanish and Portuguese.[2] Since then nineteen of them have retained the Spanish language, and only one, as large as a continent, has retained the Portuguese.[3] They have all experienced parallel histories, cultural formations, and literary developments. But, on the other hand, autochthonous populations and cultures and particular geographical conditions have existed in each zone of America. Common Iberian patterns were imposed upon men, cultures, and nature that encouraged a blending or unifying process, that is, the creation of the community of nations we call *Latin America*, which are very similar in language, cultural formation, religion, ethnic composition, and economic and social structure.

This complex of particular circumstances—that is, recognition of itself as an American extension of European cultures, the acknowledgment of Indian roots of different thicknesses and depths, and the self-awareness of itself as part of a community made up of countries which are identical in many aspects—can explain the insistent questions which Latin American intellectuals tend to ask themselves about their own identity, their originality, and the nature of their culture. Throughout the nineteenth century, American thinkers reflected constantly about the existence, the condition, and the destiny of America; and in our century, a new cycle of more systematic self-questioning began with Pedro Henríquez Ureña's *Seis ensayos en busca de nuestra expresión* [Six Essays in Search of Our Expression] (1928). This mood soon moved on to inquiries into the essential nature of each of the cultural nationalities. The collapse of Europe at the end of the Second World War and the existentialist philosophy which was then in fashion encouraged these inquiries into the existence and the destiny of America and the autonomous qualities of national cultures. Since the vogue has passed, now Latin Americans, instead of theorizing, extend their literature in the world and speak and write about the excellence of their poets and novelists, no longer concerned about whether or not they express America or their respective countries.

THE NINETEENTH CENTURY AND THE APPRENTICESHIP TO LIBERTY

Nineteenth-century Latin American literature pertains to an era of apprenticeship and formation. The first apprenticeship had to be that of liberty and identity. The new countries were formally independent by then and thus felt obliged to extend that independence to matters of spirit, to achieve that which was then called *mental emancipation*, and, consequently, to create an original culture. During the first third of the nineteenth century, literature acquired an intense ideological change which caused it to participate strongly in the complex process of cultural elaboration. No later enterprise in Latin America will possess the force of that initial thrust which proposed to secure our literary emancipation because its struggle was to establish the very existence of America's own literary expression.[4]

In effect, the Latin American generations which appeared during the 1830s, when the new republics began to resolve their internal conflicts—except for Brazil, which was an independent kingdom until 1899 when it changed over to the republican system—undertook the creation of a literature which would express our nature and our customs. In all the countries of the region, poets, novelists, dramatists, and essayists dedicated themselves eagerly to the task of singing the splendors of American nature and of describing and exploring the particular qualities of our character and customs, above all the popular ones which had the greatest flavor and picturesqueness.

From the complex literary panorama of nineteenth-century Latin America, from its ranks of thousands of writers and from the multiplicity of trends and literary currents, three outstanding and representative aspects may be singled out: *costumbrista* narrative, poetry about gauchos and common people, and the prose of thinkers.

Costumbrista Narrative

The *cuadro de costumbres,* or "descriptive sketch," was easily adapted to the literary description of the most evolved Latin American societies in the mid-nineteenth century, in which everyday customs and popular types could be clearly defined. The *costumbristas* described a society in transition: colonial models and customs continued to survive in the upper classes, but the still recent independence had caused many problems to arise and had increased the conspicuousness of the conflicts and social inequalities which the sketches or descriptive articles so humorously satirized.

The extent to which *costumbrismo* became fashionable, especially in Peru, Mexico, Cuba, Colombia, Chile, and Venezuela, was not exclusively due to the desire to imitate Spanish models, such as Mesonero Romanos, Larra, and Estébanez Calderón, but it was also a response to the urgent need for identity which our writers felt and to a search for national and original expression.

The strongest branch of Latin American *costumbrismo* is the novel. However, the simple accumulation of descriptive sketches did not suffice to create a novel of quality, and perhaps because they understood this, only the most highly endowed intellects of the era accepted the challenge and undertook more profound and ample descriptions of the new societies. When they took up the challenge, some of the best novelists, who were stimulated by the weight of the *costumbrista* characters and scenes, shifted, sometimes consciously, from romanticism to realism, thus announcing the maturity of the novel in Latin America.

The relative peace which Brazil enjoyed during the nineteenth century—in contrast with the chronic agitation of Hispanic-America—contributed to the flourishing of the novel in this country during the second half of the century, a novel which in its totality constituted the most important body of fiction in Latin America during this period.

Joaquim María Machado de Assis (1839–1908) is the most eminent figure in Brazilian letters. His life was a pathetic and silent struggle. Born a mulatto, poor, a stutterer, and an epileptic, he defeated his adversities so radically that his works are untouched by any of those shadows of his infancy and are centered only upon man, that is, ordinary men and women of the Brazilian middle class, with the vulgar passions and problems of body and soul. He also turned his back on the jungle, on telluric man, who was anguished by febrile passions, and on stylistic exuberance, in order to present another picture of his country, one of repose and sobriety, of delicate humor which enchants his readers with its acute perceptiveness and sensitivity. As he wrote of Alencar, Machado de Assis's words really explain his own style: "There is a way of seeing and of feeling," he said, "which strikes the intimate note of nationality, independent of the external face of things."[5] In his great novels, *Epitaph of a Small Winner* (1880), *Philosopher or Dog* [*Quincas Borba*] (1891), *Dom Casmurro* (1900), and in his splendid stories, Machado de Assis, intimately Brazilian, is one of the finest universal storytellers.

Colombia also had good novelists of manners and customs during the second half of the nineteenth century, among whom Tomás Carrasquilla (1858–1940) represents one of the peaks of Latin American *costumbrismo*. The case of this nearly forgotten Colombian writer is unique. If one considers the dates of publication of his works (1896–1935), he coincides with the height of Modernism and even with the beginnings of the modern novel. And although he was well acquainted with the writers of his time, he closed himself within his Antioquean region in order to find himself and to try to understand the men of his time. He achieved thus a body of work which formally must be considered within *costumbrista* realism, already out of fashion by then, but which reveals a rare aesthetic quality, a penetrating human vision and a re-creation of the popular language which he found in himself and made part of his literary style. He wrote many stories and four extensive novels, *Frutos de mi tierra* [Fruits of My Land] (1896), about the people of his region; *Grandeza* [Greatness] (1910), about Medellín society; *La marquesa de Yolombó* [The Marchioness of Yolombó] (1926), about an Antioquean city during the eighteenth century; and *Hace tiempos* [In Times Past] (1935–1936), a vast evocation of his own experiences and of places he knew. Carrasquilla is a great extemporaneous novelist whose fame has perhaps begun to be celebrated in the narrative magic of some of his countrymen.

The Mexican *costumbrista* novel has two outstanding narrators, Payno and Inclán. Manuel Payno's (1810–1894) most important novel, *Los bandidos de Río Frío* [The Bandits of Rio Frio], is a charming human comedy about Mexican life during the first half of the nineteenth century. Written as a serialized romance, it is not lacking in gory detail. In addition to these qualities, howver, it includes *costumbrista* details of nearly all the social classes of the epoch, portrayed with great sympathy and narrative efficacy. A unique personality is encountered in Luis G. Inclán (1816–1875), merely a "rancher" whose perceptive words leave us his testimony of love for the land and for the "charrerías" [the doings of the cowboys]. His principal work, *Astucia* [Cunning] (1865–1866), a vast account of the adventures of a band of *charros* [cowboys] who are tobacco smugglers, is a highly colored and cordial panorama of rural Mexican life during the middle of the nineteenth century.

The variety and the contrasts among the classes of Cuban colonial society may be found in realistic descriptions in *Cecilia Valdés* (1839–1879), by Cirilo Villaverde (1812–1894), the first Cuban novelist. The narrator of Chilean life during the second half of the nineteenth century was Alberto Blest Gana (1830–1920). Influenced by Balzac, he described Chilean situations and the lack of communication between the social classes.

Gaucho Poetry

In the mid-nineteenth century, the expanse of Argentinian territory was very thinly populated. "The problem which afflicts the Argentine Republic," wrote Sarmiento in *Facundo* (1845), "is that of extension; the desert surrounds it on every side." On those enormous prairies, on the pampas, while the Indians were being persecuted and annihilated, and the nineteenth century had just begun, there developed a type of nomadic cowboy, Creole or mestizo, who would come to be called a *gaucho*.[6] Those unique inhabitants of the pampas survived, thanks to the abundance of wild horses and cows. Dressed in characteristically distinctive clothing, they wandered ceaselessly from place to place. A picturesque legend was built up around them and their way of life, around the *rastreador* ("tracker"), the *baquiano* ("pathfinder"), the bad gaucho, and the *cantor* or *payador* ("wandering minstrel"), described by Sarmiento in masterful pages.

The wandering life of the gauchos, the distinctive dialect in which they expressed themselves, their adventures, their wisdom, and their decadence were taken up by a series of poets in Argentina and in Uruguay who transformed that mythology into a unique literary creation, gaucho poetry. Like the Mexican *corridos*, these poems are yet another resurgence of the old Spanish ballads, and they are both written, with few exceptions, in octosyllables. The gaucho poems were exceptionally popular, were printed in hundreds of editions, were read around campfires while *mate* was being passed, and many people memorized long sections of them. In 1894 Unamuno celebrated the Hispanic roots of *Martín Fierro*, and a year later, Menéndez y Pelayo affirmed that the gaucho poems were "the most original works of South American literature" and that *Martín Fierro* was "the masterpiece of the genre."

The first poet to write in the gaucho dialect, the Uruguayan Bartolomé Hidalgo (1788–1822) wrote *cielitos* and patriotic dialogues from 1811 on. He anticipated the tone of the great gaucho poems as well as their motifs and characteristic scenes. Like his contemporary, the Mexican Fernández de Lizardi, Hidalgo peddled the *cielitos* he wrote in the streets of Buenos Aires. Hilario Ascasubi (1807–1875), an Argentine Creole, lived multiple experiences. He was a sailor and soldier in the civil wars, traveled through Europe and America, and held various jobs. He played cards with the caudillo Facundo Quiroga and heard him recite entire chapters of the Bible. Among his many gaucho writings, *Santos Vega* (1850–1872) stands out, an enormous poem made up of brief tales and descriptions of pampa customs.

The second generation of gaucho poets is made up of the Argentinians Estanislao del Campo (1834–1880) and José Hernández (1834–1886). Like his friend Ascasubi, whom he admired, del Campo also participated in his country's civil wars. He wrote poems in a conventional language, but he owes his fame to *Fausto* [Faust] (1866), a poem which narrates the conversation of two gauchos, one of whom has attended a performance of Gounod's opera *Faust* and, with wit and humor, tells about it, comments upon it, and analyzes it as though the opera were a series of real events. José Hernández knew and learned about gaucho life thanks to his father's business dealings in the country. He was a public functionary, legislator, and combative journalist. *El gaucho Martín Fierro* [The Gaucho Martín Fierro] (1872), his masterpiece, is the culmination and summary of the genre. This first poem is the story of the rebellion of Martín Fierro, a *payador*, against civilization, which for him is injustice and oppression. Torn away from his happy life, the primitiveness and miseries of military service on the frontiers have been imposed upon him until he deserts and becomes a *gaucho malo*, quarrelsome, drunk, and a killer. The second part, *La vuelta de Martín Fierro* [The Return of Martín Fierro] (1879), recounts the life of the hero with the Indians, among whom he has taken refuge, and his return to the white world. Here Martín Fierro is an old man who remembers and reflects.

One of the merits of *Martín Fierro* is the human truth of its hero. Misfortunes have involved him in evil, but he retains a core of incorruptible honesty, a profound respect for an unwritten code of valor and decency. There is also a very fortunate contrast between the youthful action of the first part and the evocative and sententious tone which dominates the second. Throughout the poem, a superior command of language and its resources is maintained. As employed by José Hernández, gaucho dialect achieves the height of its power.

The Civilizers' Prose

A unique phenomenon may be found in nineteenth-century Latin America. The best prose is not to be found in pure literature but rather in sociological meditations about the ills of our societies, in allegations in favor of civic causes, in historical reflections, in polemical and combative writings and, sometimes, in literary criticism. Perhaps this profound urgency, this burning passion or this anger which give rise to the writings of the Latin American thinkers are what give them their affecting truth and their validity as literary creations.

During the course of the century, nearly all of the countries had men who, beyond ambitions and contingencies, fought generously for liberty and culture. Some of these men were also very fine writers, like the Venezuelan Andrés Bello (1781–1865), the Argentinian Domingo Faustino Sarmiento (1811–1888), the Ecuadorian Juan Montalvo (1833–1889), the Puerto Rican Eugenio María de Hostos (1839–1903), the Peruvian Manuel González Prada (1848–1918), the Mexican Justo Sierra (1848–1912), the Brazilian Ruy Barbosa (1849–1923), and the Cubans Enrique José Varona (1849–1933) and José Martí (1853–1895). And even among the great soldiers, an occasional excellent writer could be found. The Venezuelan Simón Bolívar (1783–1830), author of more than three thousand letters and two hundred speeches and proclamations, wrote with distinctive liveliness and elegance, and was as revolutionary in his style as with arms.

In the case of Bolívar, the pen was only a complement of the sword. In contrast, the Latin American thinkers depended principally upon words. The majority were great polemicists or sustained long ideological campaigns, like Montalvo's against the theocratic dictatorship of García Moreno, and González Prada's against the social injustice and obscurantism of Peruvian society. Nevertheless, side by side with his combative works, the liberalism of which seems naïve to us today, Montalvo wrote the *Capítulos que se le olvidaron a Cervantes* [Chapters That Cervantes Forgot] (1898) and *Geometría moral* [Moral Geometry] (1917), both published posthumously, and remarkable for the elegance and the purity of their prose. And González Prada, in addition to having stimulated the awakening of the social conscience of his country, was a poet who, while he occasionally continued the satiric violence or the political caricatures of his combative prose, did not disdain to re-create ancient forms or to evoke the Indian past of Peru.

In 1842, when they both met in Chile, Bello and Sarmiento carried on a magnificent polemic about the purity of the language or the romantic liberty of expression. Despite all this, Bello's temperament was more suited to the tasks of the scholar and the teacher, although certainly with an eye to reform. He was one of the forerunners of literary emancipation in the two splendid poems called *Silvas americanas* which sing to the landscape and the past of America. Toward the middle of the century, when the Latin American community seemed to have greater coherence, Bello, from Caracas, was invited to Santiago de Chile where he would be the reorganizer of education and of the university, as well as one of the authors of the civil code (1853–1856). His *Filosofía del entendimiento* [Philosophy of Understanding] (1843) was written during those years, as well as his scholarly studies and his treatises on grammar which, together with those of the Colombian Rufino José Cuervo, constitute the most important American contribution in this field.

Sarmiento, on the other hand, was a torrential spirit who possessed equal quantities of combative passion and desire to civilize. His was one of the most intense and productive lives. He fought against tyrannies both with arms and with the pen; he left a masterful treatise, *Facundo* (1845), a lucid diagnosis of Argentine reality and the dilemma of civilization versus barbarism; as president of his country (1868–1874), his accomplishments were substantial. His best works, in addition to *Facundo, Viajes* [Journeys] (1849), *Recuerdos de provincia* [Recollections of Provincial Life] (1850), and so many speeches and journalistic pages, are certainly written hurriedly and tumultuously, as by someone who has a great deal to say and many tasks to tend to, but which, at the same time, expressed his ideas in organic concepts and with perceptiveness. Like Martí, Sarmiento was a natural-born writer and one of the most authentic teachers America has had.

Other American thinkers were also decisive in the moral and cultural formation of their countries. Ruy Barbosa, renowned Brazilian jurist, was the organizer of the republic proclaimed in 1889, an impassioned fighter for the abolition of slavery and a writer of multiple curiosities in his *Cartas de Inglaterra* [Letters from England] (1896). Eugenio María de Hostos, although he was above all an excellent literary critic (*Juicio crítico de Hamlet* [Critical Judgment of Hamlet], 1872), a moralist (*Moral social* [Social Morality], 1888), and a promoter of education in Santo Domingo, had the supreme ambition that his country, Puerto Rico, should achieve independence and form part of a West Indian confederation. Justo Sierra, who was the organizer of Mexican education, founder of the National University—at the inauguration of which (1910) he gave a speech in which he pointed out the necessity of a philosophy and a science "which will defend our country"—and generous guide of national culture, was also a poet, literary critic, and historian in the great *Evolución política del pueblo mexicano* [Political Evolution of the Mexican People] (1900–1901). Although Enrique José Varona, intellectual and skeptic, did not always succeed in his political ambitions, he served Cuban education and was an intellectual stimulus and a writer of polished style in his brief essays and literary criticism (*Desde mi Belvedere* [From My Belvedere], 1907, and *Violetas y ortigas* [Violets and Nettles], 1917).

José Martí was one of those exceptional personalities in whom the passion for a political cause was transformed into a written expression of high literary quality. While still an adolescent, he began to fight with his pen for the independence of Cuba, was condemned to forced labor, and left in exile for Spain (1871). He spent the better part of his life in exile, with the exception of a short stay in Cuba between 1878 and 1879. Nevertheless, he dedicated much of his writing to Cuba and its political problems, although he also wrote a great deal about art, letters, politics, personalities, and events in the Latin American and European countries he visited. He also wrote a long series of chronicles about the United States, where he spent his last fourteen years. When he finally managed to unify his desires and organize the war for independence, he returned to Cuba to die. And although he felt that his hour had come, the patriot and the writer continued to be fused; during his last days he made notes in his diary (*De Cabo Haitiano a Dos Ríos* [From the Haitian Cape to Dos Ríos]), which are full of poetic intent and of observations about nature, side by side with accounts of guerrilla incidents, right up until the night before his death.

Perhaps with the exception of his dramatic and novelistic attempts, in which he let himself be defeated by the rhetoric of the epoch, the rest of Martí's written work, poetry and essays, is of a quality and an authenticity which are very moving. "What will I have written without bleeding?" he asked. And on his pages his spirit bleeds, both in truth and in literary mastery, with a sense for verbal precision as well as an instinct for the felicitous and expressive turn of phrase. Both in his poetry and in his prose, Martí avoids clichés and abstract images or feelings in order to depict concrete entities, familiar, sometimes picturesque and full of personal emotion, and he knows how to transmit them so well that, in the torrent of his prose, they crystallize into palpitating and perfect expressions. This hurried writer, who only wrote to serve his country or to earn his living; this man who gave himself entirely to the cause of liberty for his people and to the cause of America was at the same time a literary innovator and one of the best writers of Latin America.

Modernism

No other literary movement in the cultural history of Latin America, either colonial or independent, provides such evidence of the unity and originality of literature in this part of the world as does Modernism. Over a period of forty years, all the countries of the region participated in Modernism; half of them produced twenty or more important writers—among whom would be found the major poet of Hispanic America—who wrote at least thirty significant books, superior to those which had heretofore been written in their line, and which imposed their influence upon their entire area and, for the first time, upon Spain.

With Modernism, Hispanic America exists as a unit, the internal circulation of which has suddenly become fluid. The first manifestations of the movement appear in Mexico, around 1875, with the simultaneous appearance of twenty-two-year-old José Martí and sixteen-year-old Manuel Gutiérrez Nájera, who begin to manifest new stylistic devices and, above all, a new sensibility. Modernism is already substantially outlined. The clarion call which will give it vitality everywhere and will extend it throughout the continent is heard next in Valparaiso, the opposite geographic corner, where a young Nicaraguan, Rubén Darío (1867–1916), publishes in 1888 a collection of poems and stories with a suggestive title: *Azul...*, which, especially in its prose, introduces an exceptional lyric and an innovative voice. During these years, in Havana and Bogotá, people are reading the poems of Julián del Casal (1863–1893) and José Asunción Silva (1865–1896), sensitive, refined, and tragic.

But the creators of Modernism are still ruled by romantic fate and they die young. By 1896 only Darío remains, if not as the chief, at least the major poet of a constellation which is multiplying itself: in Mexico, with Salvador Díaz Mirón (1853–1928), Luis G. Urbina (1868–1934), Amado Nervo (1870–1919), José Juan Tablada (1871–1945), and Enrique González Martínez (1871–1952); in Colombia, with Guillermo Valencia (1873–1943); in Venezuela, with Manuel Díaz Rodríguez (1868–1927) and Rufino Blanco Fombona (1874–1944); in Peru, with José Santos Chocano (1875–1934); in Bolivia, with Ricardo Jaimes Freyre (1868–1933); in Argentina, with Leopoldo Lugones (1874–1938) and Enrique Larreta (1875–1961); in Uruguay, with José Enrique Rodó (1872–1917) and Horacio Quiroga (1878–1937); and in Chile, with Carlos Pezoa Véliz (1879–1908). After 1896, which represents the peak of Modernism with Darío's *Prosas profanas* [Profane Prose] and *Los raros* [The Strange Ones], the culminating books of the movement are published one after another, until approximately 1915, in Mexico and Buenos Aires, Bogotá and Lima, Caracas and Montevideo.

The collection of studies which Darío called *Los raros* was important because it discussed the principal literary figures of the moment, the French symbolists and Parnassians, in addition to writers of other nationalities like Poe and Ibsen. Such an observant and opportune guide concludes with homage to the Cuban José Martí and a lecture about the Portuguese poet Eugenio de Castro, who introduced free verse poetry in *Horas* [Hours] (1891), which had great influence during those years.

The intense literary activity is manifest also in the magazines which publish, together with local writing, that of the Modernists of other countries as well as

French, Italian, and English translations. The most representative of these publications, the *Revista Azul* [Blue Journal] (Mexico, 1894–1896), presided over by Gutiérrez Nájera until his death, is both American and universal to an exceptional extent. During its three years of publication, it includes contributions by ninety-six Latin American authors from sixteen countries, who are followers of Modernism, without counting the Mexicans. Darío heads the list with fifty-four contributions and is followed by del Casal and Chocano, with nineteen each, and Martí with thirteen. Sixty-nine French writers appeared in translation, among them Baudelaire, Barbey d'Aurevilly, Coppée, Gautier, Heredia, Hugo, Leconte de Lisle, Richepin, Sully Prud-homme, and Verlaine. They appropriately outnumber the Spaniards, who are represented by only thirty-two contributions. And from other nationalities, there are translations of Heine, Wilde, Ibsen, D'Annunzio, of the great Russian novelists, and of Poe, who had already been translated in Mexico in 1869. During years of precarious communications, the extent to which the Modernists managed to become acquainted with each other's work, and to expose their own writings in literary magazines, seems truly remarkable.[7]

Thus for Latin American writers at the turn of the century, Modernism was a taking possession of the world, but it was also a becoming aware of their own time. Seeking beyond the exhausted Spanish romanticism, the creators of the movement perceive, however vaguely, that a vast revolutionary movement of formal renovation and of sensibility has begun in the world, and they decide to form part of it with their own expression. Refusing to accept the vulgarity of the language, they find a first approach in the rigor of French Parnassianism, and new possibilities of refinement, musicality, and imagination in symbolism. Poe, Heine, Whitman, and D'Annunzio will also contribute, but the final result of this synthesis will be entirely original: it will deal with predominantly lyric voices which participate through affinity in a common movement of renovation.

During the initial period and that of the movement's peak, which may be designated as 1905 with the appearance of Darío's *Cantos de vida y esperanza* [Songs of Life and Hope], Modernism creates a distinctive thematic mythology of exotic escapism. A Parnassian and Renanesque Greece is turned to by Gutiérrez Nájera in his *Odas breves* [Brief Odes], del Casal in *Las oceánidas* [The Ocean-Nymphs], and in *Mi museo ideal* [My Ideal Museum], Darío in *Coloquio de los centauros* [Colloquium of the Centaurs] and in the "Responso a Verlaine" [Prayer for Verlaine], and Rodó when he sketches a synthesis of Hellenic civilization in *Ariel* (1900). An Orient more imagined than actually known, and limited to China and Japan, appears in some of Darío's stories, in poems by del Casal, and will serve not only as a thematic but also as a formal inspiration in various books by Tablada which introduce the Japanese haiku into Spanish. On the other hand, Valhalla and the Grail, elves and fairies, Loke and Odín, Wagnerian and Nordic appear in Jaimes Freyre's *Castalia bárbara* [Savage Castilian] (1897). The traditions and personalities of the Old Testament and of the Middle Ages are re-created in stories and poems by Darío ("El arbol del rey David," "Las tres reinas magas," "Los motivos del lobo") and in poems by Valencia ("Palemón el estilista"). An eighteenth-century France, of elegant parties in the manner of Verlaine and of Watteau, appears in poems by Darío, Chocano, and Tablada; and in the general tone of Gutiérrez Nájera and Darío breathes that Francophilia that Juan Valera called "Gallicism of the mind."

Modernism seems to forget American and Hispanic themes. However, Martí and Gutiérrez Nájera used them often, and Darío's stay in Chile moved him to evoke the Herculean strength of Caupolicán in a sonorous sonnet in *Azul.*... After a few years in which autochthonous motifs almost disappear, they reappear in the last phase of Modernism in poets like Valencia, Chocano, and Lugones, together with praise of the Hispanic world and with popular themes. Darío knew Spain and its history very well and also wanted to be the "poet of America." He would succeed in this both through the splendor of his lyricism and because he made himself the spokesman of the Hispanic world ("Salutación del optimista," "A Roosevelt"), of the great Spanish heroes like the Cid and Don Quijote, and because he wrote so many poems ("Triptico de Nicaragua," "Intermezzo tropical," "Oda a la Argentina") in which the presence or the nostalgic memory of his own land and of the American landscape gleam.

Two recurrent symbols also form part of the Modernist mythology, the *azul* or "blue" of Darío's first important book and of Gutiérrez Nájera's *Revista Azul*, perhaps because, as Hugo had said, "l'art c'est l'azur," and the swan, symbol of gratuitous beauty, much employed by Parnassians and symbolists, which will appear in the first Modernists and, in an obsessive manner, in Darío, who, associating it with the myth of Leda, converts it into an emblem of the new poetry. When González Martínez, in 1910, writes the sonnet which begins "Tuércele el cuello al cisne de engañoso plumaje" ["Wring the neck of the swan of deceptive plumage"], and proposes the "wise owl" as a new reflexive symbol, the hour of the swan and of Modernism has reached its end.

These new and old themes and symbols of Modernism, nevertheless, only serve to characterize it. The more profound renovation or revolution of the movement takes place in language and in sensibility; it begins by reacting against careless expression and makes an effort to renovate images and simplify syntax. A distinctive Modernist vocabulary comes into being which seems to limit itself to luxury and to beauty. Poetic language shoud be a unique and surprising creation, and a continual series of discoveries, such as Darío and Lugones achieved, the former in his maturity in the "Epístola a la señora de Lugones" (1907)—a poem which magnificently introduces colloquial language into Spanish-language poetry—and the latter in his *Lunario sentimental* [Sentimental Lunarian] (1909).

The Modernist poets also accomplished a more complex renovation, that of versification. This renovation took place in three ways: first, they sought in the past old forms that were in disuse, like the classic hexameter or ancient meters and forgotten Spanish combinations, like the monorhyme or the hendecasyllable with various accentuation patterns. Second, they gave greater agility and harmony to verse in general and put all the known meters into active use. When Latin American readers shuddered as they read José Asunción Silva's "Nocturno" which begins "Una noche, una noche toda llena de murmullos..." [A night, a night all filled with whispers...], some supposed that a new metric form was being employed; but the poet explained once that the morbid beauty originated formally in a very ordinary fable by Iriarte which says:[8]

> A una mona
> muy taimada
> dijo un día
> cierta urraca

[To a very sly monkey a certain magpie said one day]

However, Silva had put the feet or tetrasyllabic verses together in irregular groups. And third, the Modernists created new meters; they attempted, as did Darío ("Heraldos" in *Prosas profanas*, 1896) and Jaimes Freyre (*Castalia bárbara*, 1897), metric liberty, free verse, and they even theorized about the topic just as Jaimes Freyre did in his *Leyes de versificación castellana* [Rules of Spanish Versification] (1912).

The Modernists frequently sought impressionistic effects based on sensations, like groupings of synesthesias, the visual transpositions of the colors or exercises of monochromatic variations. Vocabulary, themes, symbols, versification, and special effects, all these formal renovations were intended to find adequate expression for a new sensibility. In the moment of Modernism's triumph, Rubén Darío, who said everything and divined everything, thus summarizes the new sensibility in the opening poem of *Cantos de vida y esperanza* (1905):

> Y muy siglo dieciocho y muy antiguo
> y muy moderno; audaz, cosmopolita,
> con Hugo fuerte y con Verlaine ambiguo,
> y una sed de ilusiones infinita.

[And every eighteenth century and very ancient / and very modern; bold, cosmopolitan / strong with Hugo and ambiguous with Verlaine, / and an infinite thirst for illusions.]

But this thirst for illusions and this desire to embrace simultaneously the ancient and the modern will flow easily into doubt, uneasiness, and disenchantment; that is, into a desire to escape and, finally, into a collision against "the black infinite where our voice does not reach." The great poets of the Modernist apogee—Darío, Lugones, Herrera y Reissig, Urbina, and Nervo—show both the triumphal, sensual, and plastic face of life as well as the other, nocturnal and perturbed, which, after the festivities are over, must confront reality and death.

In its totality, Modernism was a unanimous movement in Latin America which fundamentally signified a formal renovation and the full conquest of original expression and modernity. It was a powerful attempt to form part of the world and of the time, to cause all the important voices of the hour to resound in this America and to be heard right along with them. As has been said so many times, with Modernism Latin America takes the initiative and moves ahead of Spain. Now it will be the Spanish writers of the Generation of '98 who will follow the lead of America and recognize the authority of the movement and, above all, of Rubén Darío.

Brazil also experienced a movement of renovation parallel to that of Spanish America, although it was related to it only through coincidences of epoch and of influences. Nor did the Brazilian movement have that unanimous and fervent spirit; it consisted exclusively of the appearance of new trends, among which the Parnassian at first dominated, with Alberto de Oliveira Correa (1857–1937) and Olavo Bilac (1865–1918), excellent poet in *O caçador de esmeraldas* [Hunter of Emeralds] (1904). Later the symbolist group appeared, about 1899, the outstanding poet of which is João de Cruz e Sousa (1863–1898), follower of Verlaine and of Mallarmé in *Broqueis* and *Missais* (1893). Another distinction is that in Brazil the term *Modernism* is not applied to the work of early twentieth-century writers, but rather to those of the vanguard movement, which was begun in 1922 by Mario de Andrade and Manuel Bandeira.

CONTEMPORARY LITERATURE

Considered in its totality, Latin American literature after 1920 reveals two conspicuous trends, vanguardism and social concern, which at certain times have been considered to be antagonistic to each other. The desire to participate in the revolution of artistic expression and meaning, which began at the end of the nineteenth century and was fulfilled during the 1920s, was seen as an exercise in pure literature for those who preferred that literature not serve the cause of its own revolution but rather that of the social and political one which stirs up the world. Although the names of the trends have changed, the two fundamental and still dominant attitudes have remained the same. In more recent years, a new trend has begun to appear, still imprecisely defined, which seems to unite innovation and experimentation with social concern, and which intends to accomplish a more radical revolution of social structures, of sensibility and of conduct, as well as of language and literary forms.

Theater

Following the traditional genre categories, that of drama has been the artistic activity which, in this region, has still not fully reached that transcendence which would provide testimony of its literary importance. During the first decade of the twentieth century, there emerged in Argentina and Uruguay an interesting movement of *costumbrista* theater. It was centered around a family of theatrical impresarios, the Podestás, who were of Italian origin, and their most famous author, the Uruguayan Florencio Sánchez (1875–1910), who did his writing in Buenos Aires. Both Sánchez and his followers wrote social criticism about conflicts between the city and the country, the assimilation of the immigrants, and the moral problems of a still provincial society which was serving its apprenticeship in cosmopolitanism. In Buenos Aires, Montevideo, and Santiago, this theatrical movement acquired authentic vitality. The spectators could recognize their own faces and problems and even their own language in those fictional presentations.

The first steps toward the modernization of the Latin American theater were taken by the following dramatic authors of this period: the Argentinians Conrado Nalé Roxlo (1898) and Samuel Eichelbaum (1894); the Uruguayan Vicente Martínez Cuitiño (1887); the Chilean Armando Moock (1894–1942); and the Mexicans Xavier Villaurrutia (1903–1950), Celestino Gorostiza (1904–1967), and Salvador Novo (1904–). They organized the groups and the theatrical seasons called *Teatro Ulises* [Ulysses Theater] (1928) and *Orientación* [Orientation] (1932).

These eager interests in renovation and in the vanguard were followed by other important movements, like that of the theater of criticism and interpretation of national problems. Contributors included authors like the Brazilian Claudio de Souza (1876–1954), the Mexican Rodolfo Usigli (1905), the Peruvian Bernardo Roca Rey (1918), the Cuban José Antonio Ramos (1885–1946), the Nicaraguan Pablo Antonio Cuadra (1912), and those of the Areyto group, founded in 1935 in Puerto Rico by Emilio Belaval. Theater after 1940 deals with the problematical existence of contemporary man, his solitude, his insecurity, and his confusion, and the conflicts which his sense of responsibility sets for him as he is confronted by violence and injustice.

Poetry

The exhaustion of Modernism during the second decade of the twentieth century does not in the least imply the debilitation of poetry in Latin America. From 1920 until the present day, generations of new poets have appeared who form a great current which is designated initially as vanguard poetry and later, as contemporary poetry. Since the twenties there have been two major trends: one made up of the poets who reacted against certain aspects of Modernism in order to emend excesses or defects in what was called *postmodernism*; and the other composed of more audacious poets who wished to explore the most radical consequences of the tendency of Modernism toward individual creation and the liberty of the artist, denying and destroying the past in a movement which was called *ultramodernism*. The first group's forms of reaction—a search for simplicity and lyric intimacy, reactions against the classic tradition, against romanticism, or against Modernist sensibility and forms by means of irony—in themselves inform us that this group included those who preferred moderate variations on conventional tastes and themes, although that did not preclude the inclusion of such original and interesting poets as the Colombians Porfirio Barba Jacob (1883–1942) and Luis Carlos López (1883–1950); the Argentinians Baldomero Fernández Moreno (1885–1950), Enrique Banchs (1888–1968), and Carlos Mastronardi (1900); the Peruvian José María Eguren (1882–1942); and the Puerto Rican Luis Lloréns Torres (1878–1944).

The *"ultras,"* on the other hand, were the nonconformists and the revolutionaries, the advocates of the "tradition of rupture." Coinciding with the European vanguard movements which appear after the First World War, Latin American poets like the Chilean Vicente Huidobro (1893–1948), the Peruvian César Vallejo (1892–1938), and the Argentinian Jorge Luis Borges (1899) participated actively around 1920, in association with the Spaniards who shared their worries and concerns—Gerardo Diego, Federico García Lorca, Juan Chabás, and Antonio Espina—in movements like that of creationism and other less important ones, which grouped together were called *ultraism*. It was the youthful and iconoclastic era of the *isms*, of the free imagination, which manifested itself above all in such magazines as the Argentinian *Prisma* [Prism] (1921–1922), *Proa* [Prow] (1922–1923), and *Martín Fierro* (1924–1927); the Mexican *Horizonte* [Horizon] (1926–1927), *Ulises* [Ulysses] (1927–1928), and *Contemporáneos* [Contemporaries] (1928–1931); the Cuban *Revista de Avance* [Vanguard Review] (1927–1930); the Peruvian *Amauta* [Inca Sage] (1926–1932); and the Uruguayan *Los Nuevos* [The New Ones] (1920) and *Alfar* [Clay] (1921–1955).

A parallel movement of renovation was taking place in Brazil. It was begun by the poets Mario de Andrade (1893–1945) and Manuel Bandeira (1885–1968) with the celebration of the Week of Modern Art in São Paulo in 1922. The celebration included expositions of paintings and sculpture, concerts and conferences, a clamorous launching of the vanguardism which the Brazilians would call *Modernism*. That same year saw the publication of a book of poems by de Andrade, *Paulicéia desvairada* [Demented Paulicéia], which proposed all of the liberties of a new era for Brazilian poetry: free verse, prosaic and colloquial language, personal and ironic expression, and the search for Indian and popular themes. The writer who was then at the height of his powers, Graça Aranha (1868–1931), would speak out clearly in favor of Brazilian Modernism with his speech-manifesto at the Academy (1924), and he would be joined or followed right to our day by poets such as Jorge de Lima (1893–1953), Rui Ribeiro Couto (1898–1963), Cecilia Meireles (1901–1964), Carlos Drummond de Andrade (1902), Murilo Mendes (1902), and Augusto Federico Schmidt (1906–1965), who as a group constitute one of the most brilliant periods of Brazilian poetry.

Soon the most aggressive and boisterous aspect of those *isms* would subside, but permanent conquests of that vast poetic current would remain: free verse, the elimination of rhyme, the use of typographic compositions, liberty in metamorphic invention, colloquial language, and the enrichment of poetic experience proposed by surrealism. Along beside these characteristics were certain periods of insistent themes like *nativism*, which would involve such poets as the Mexican Ramón López Velarde (1888–1921); the Brazilian Jorge de Lima; the Puerto Rican Luis Palés Matos (1898–1959); the Cuban Nicolás Guillén (1902), and, during certain periods of their work, César Vallejo, Jorge Luis Borges, the Ecuadorian Jorge Carrera Andrade (1902), and the Chilean Pablo Neruda (1904–1973). They gave poetic value to Negro rhythms, to provincial turns of phrase, to the neighborhood epic, and to the secret of the Indian worlds.

These allusions led almost necessarily to the social themes which concerned almost all the nativists and particularly Neruda, perhaps the major poet of Latin America during this period because of his two great poetic corpora, *Residence on Earth* (1931, 1935), and *General Song* (1950).

In addition to these themes and general characteristics of contemporary Latin American poetry, there are many others which only pertain to each of the great poets who have appeared between 1920 and 1940. Thus, the verbal inventiveness and the uneasy spirit of Ramón López Velarde; the acid and original voice, full of human pain and pity, of the Chilean Gabriela Mistral (1889–1957); the classic and popular accents in the vast poetic world of the Mexican Alfonso Reyes (1889–1959), who is also the master of prose and of intellectual curiosity during this period; the lyric refinement of the Cuban Mariano Brull (1891) and of the Argentinian Ricardo E. Molinari (1898). Note also the descriptive sensuality and the verbal imagination of the Argentinian Oliverio Girondo (1891–1967) and of the Mexican Carlos Pellicer (1899); the mixture of vanguardism and classicism in the Nicaraguan Salomón de la Selva (1893–1959); the complex sensibility and the lyric fantasy of the Colombian León de Greiff (1895); the radical and tragic humanity which affects us so in the poetry of César Vallejo; the creation of a universe of intellectual fictions and the rigorous poetic sensibility of Jorge Luis Borges, one of the most influential and original writers; the perceptive poetry of the Mexican José Gorostiza (1901), whose *Muerte sin fin* [Death Without End] (1939) is the most important poem in Latin America during this period. Note also the theological lyricism of the Argentinian Leopoldo Marechal (1900–1970); the formal purity, lyric contention, and humanism of the Mexican Jaime Torres Bodet (1902); the metaphysics of the senses and of the experiences in the Mexican Xavier Villaurrutia (1903–1950) and the Chilean Rosamel del Valle (1900–1963); the tenderness, irony, and colloquial poetry in the Mexican Salvador Novo (1904); and the trace of surrealism in the Guatemalan Luis Cardoza y Aragón (1904).

Since 1940 a new Latin American poetic generation has revealed itself vigorously, with very few traits in common among its members except for their position as witnesses of an unjust and torn-up world. Before such confusion, the following diverse voices are raised: the Argentinians Enrique Molina (1910) and César Fernández Moreno (1919); the Brazilians Vinicius de Moraes (1913) and João Cabral de Melo Neto (1920); the Mexican Octavio Paz (1914); the Chilean Nicanor Parra (1914); the Colombian Alvaro Mutis (1923); the Peruvian Sebastián Salazar Bondy (1924–1965); and the Nicaraguan Ernesto Cardenal (1925). The most outstanding among them is the intense, profound lyric voice of Paz, an extraordinarily lucid spirit in whom the conflicts and cultural experiences of history and of our time intercross.

The Novel

While modern poetry in Latin America presents an organic development, without solutions of continuity, the novel has had a troubled, if not dramatic, development. In Latin America, poetry flows along naturally, and from time to time great poets emerge: Darío, Vallejo, Neruda, Paz. By contrast, the creation of a vigorous and original novel has been one of the greatest literary ambitions of various generations, but judgment has always been withheld as to whether the battle has finally been won. However, there have been two significant peaks: the first occurred between 1924 and 1930, and is somewhat diminished by now; the second, the boom of the Latin American novel, began in the sixties and we still live in its blaze.

Barely past the time of Modernism, the novel attracted extraordinary attention with its great narratives about the Mexican Revolution. The following novels may be of interest to the reader: *The Underdogs* by Mariano Azuela (1873–1952)—which, although it was originally published in 1915, would only be discovered literarily after its sixth edition in 1925; *The Eagle and the Serpent* (1928) and *La sombra del caudillo* [The Leader's Shadow] (1929), by Martín Luis Guzmán (1887); a bitter novel of social denunciation, *Raza de bronce* (1919), by the Bolivian Alcides Arguedas; two excellent novels, the dominant theme of which is the struggle of man with nature: *The Vortex* (1924) by the Colombian José Eustacio Rivera (1889–1928), and *Doña Barbara* (1929), by the Venezuelan Rómulo Gallegos (1884–1968). A delicate counterpoint to this tense dramatism will be provided by two Argentinian narrators: Benito Lynch (1885–1951), who would concentrate on the conflicts of the people of the pampas in a series of novels which begins with *Los caranchos de la Florida* [The Carancho Birds of Florida] (1916) and includes *El inglés de los güesos* [The Englishman of the Bones] (1924) and *El romance de un gaucho* [The Ballad of a Cowboy] (1930); and Ricardo Güiraldes (1886–1927), who would convert man's encounter with nature into poetic imagery in *Don Segundo Sombra* (1926).

However, the works of this generation of founders of the modern novel are regarded with less enthusiasm today than when they first appeared. In effect, the vision that those novelists had of the peasant who fights for his land, of the revolutionary who struggles for justice, and of the conflict of man with nature and with barbarism was still a Romantic vision, sometimes Indianist, and the stylistic devices and methods of composition they had at their disposal were elementary and continued to be linked to realism and naturalism. They were still living in the natural and legendary era, with the historic era only dimly in the future. Nevertheless, those novelists captivated various generations of readers and offered the world a first image of America, thanks to an uncommon quality: authenticity and the vigor of their narrative talent. A page, apparently free of rhetorical artifice, by Azuela, Guzmán, Gallegos, or Lynch is still a masterpiece.

The years which followed this flowering were not very fertile, even when the first important novels appeared during the thirties: *Las lanzas coloradas* [The Red Lances] (1930) by the Venezuelan Arturo Uslar Pietri (1905); *The Villagers (Huasipungo)* (1934), by the Ecuadorean Jorge Icaza (1906); *The Golden Serpent* (1935), by the Peruvian Ciro Alegría (1909–1967); and *Angustia* [Anguish] (1936), by the Brazilian Graciliano Ramos (1892–1953). In general, it is a lackluster decade, characterized by the social novel, which is important in Brazil for the group of novelists headed by Jorge Amado (1903). The germane analysis by the Peruvian critic Luis Alberto Sánchez, *América: novela sin novelistas* [America: Novel Without Novelists] (1933), speaks for this period.

As often happens, facts would soon contradict this pessimistic view, for the decade of the forties saw the appearance of two of the most original narrators of Latin America, the Argentinian Jorge Luis Borges and the Cuban Alejo Carpentier (1904), and of novels and stories which are remarkable for their formal rigor and their novelistic density. Naturalism has been left behind, and a critical attitude in the observation of reality prevails, as in *Yawar fiesta* [Yawar Holiday] (1943), by the Mexican José Revueltas (1914), *The President* (1946), by the Guatemalan Miguel Angel Asturias (1899), *The Edge of the Storm* (1947), by the Mexican Augustín Yáñez (1904), and *Adán Buenosayres* (1948), by Leopoldo Marechal. An imagination ruled by intelligence may also prevail, as in *The Invention of Morel* (1944), by the Argentinian Adolfo Bioy Casares (1914), in *Ficciones* [Fictions] (1944), by Borges, or *The Kingdom of This World* (1949), by Carpentier. For the novelists of this period—as Emir Rodríguez Monegal has observed—their relationship with the vanguard movements is important: "They are, above all, renovators of a vision and of a concept of the language."[9]

During the fifties, writers like Borges and Carpentier reached their moment of greatest productivity, and novelists just beginning to publish important fiction included Juan Carlos Onetti (1909)—*La vida breve* [A Brief Life], 1950—the Chilean Manuel Rojas (1896)—*Hijo de ladrón* [Born Guilty], 1951–and the Venezuelan Miguel Otero Silva (1908)—*Casas muertas* [Dead Homes], 1955. Three Mexican narrators were introduced: Juan Rulfo (1918), with the stories of *The Burning Plain* (1953) and the novel *Pedro Páramo*

(1955); Juan José Arreola (1918), with the extraordinary prose pieces of *Confabulario* [Collection of Schemes] (1952) in which fiction and essay blend; and Carlos Fuentes (1929), who, with *Where the Air is Clear* (1958), opens a new period of the Latin American novel, together with an exceptional Argentinian narrator, Julio Cortázar (1914), who in 1959 published his first memorable book, the stories of *Las armas secretas* [The Secret Weapons].

Thus, through this accumulation of experiences, through this slow conquest of liberty and imagination, through this gradual apprenticeship of techniques and styles, through this struggle with language in which the major expressive concern becomes central, and coinciding with the development of a larger phenomenon of demythification and rejection of social and cultural structures, of sexual revolution, of new norms and life-styles, of dissolving demarcations between the genres and the artistic forms, which together characterize the creation of a sensibility and a style which belong to the present years, the recent apogee of the Latin American novel is produced.

The first period of excellent novels, between 1924 and 1930, was based upon the work of only six major novelists, scattered across Latin America. Now there are almost twice that many, and, whether they write in their own countries, or in other Latin American or European ones, they have established very active communications and alliances among themselves. Their success, the ample and opportune exegesis which their works have received, and the fact that they have achieved an exceptionally widespread readership in their own language and in numerous translations are not unrelated to the parallel appearance of a remarkable generation of critics: the Uruguayans Mario Benedetti (1920), Emir Rodríguez Monegal (1921), and Angel Rama (1926); the Mexicans Emmanuel Carballo (1929) and Carlos Monsiváis (1938); the Chileans Fernando Alegría (1918) and Luis Harss (1936); the Cuban Severo Sarduy (1937); and the Peruvian Julio Ortega (1942).

Here are the names of the novelits who form part of this generation and the titles of their most celebrated works: the Paraguayan Augusto Roa Bastos (1917), with *Son of Man* (1960); Carlos Fuentes, with *The Death of Artemio Cruz* (1962) and *A Change of Skin* (1967); the Brazilian João Guimarães Rosa (1908–1967), with *The Devil to Pay in the Backlands* (1963); the Argentinians Julio Cortázar, with *Hopscotch* (1963) and *La vuelta al día en ochenta mundos* [Around the Day in Eighty Worlds] (1967) and Ernesto Sábato (1912), with *Sobre héroes y tumbas* [On Heroes and Graves] (1962); the Uruguayans Carlos Martínez Moreno (1917), with *El paredón* [The Execution Wall] (1963), and Juan Carlos Onetti, with *The Shipyard (1961), Juntacadáveres* [Corpse-gatherer] (1965), and his *Cuentos completos* [Complete Stories] (1967); the Peruvian Mario Vargas Llosa (1936), with *Time of the Hero* (1963) and *The Green House* (1966); the Cubans José Lezama Lima (1912), with *Paradiso* (1966) and Guillermo Cabrera Infante (1929), with *Three Trapped Tigers* (1967); and the Colombian Gabriel García Márquez (1928) with *One Hundred Years of Solitude* (1967).

This list is neither closed nor definitively established. With the exception of the deceased Guimarães Rosa, they are all at the height of their creativity, and alongside them are novelists of previous generations who continue to write, as well as new writers who are just starting out. Nor can the list of memorable works be considered as comprehensive of all those which form part of this Latin American battering ram which attracts the attention of the world. Some of them will only retain a certain critical esteem and will be forgotten by posterity. All of them reveal a liberty of language and of invention, an undisguised combativeness and a definite participation in the conflicts and currents of contemporary thought which make them significant and alive for the modern reader of our language or any other. Provincialism has been left behind. Of all these novels, one has already achieved, in various languages, a fame which is not only literary but popular, perhaps because it is the masterpiece of this period, García Márquez's *One Hundred Years of Solitude*. It is a book of love and of imagination. It includes everything: history and myth, protest and confession, allegory and reality. Everything is recounted with an ancient art which, when it really appears, defeats all literary formulae. This is a gift as well as a product of the mind and of the spirit, the old secret of storytelling which captivates us once again.

Notes

1.   The present reality of Latin America is somewhat more complex than the simple scheme that was maintained until the middle of the century. The original group of twenty-one countries still exists (Argentina, Bolivia, Brazil, Colombia, Costa Rica, Cuba, Chile, the Dominican Republic, Ecuador, Guatemala, Haiti, Honduras, Mexico, Nicaragua, Panama, Paraguay, Peru, Puerto Rico, El Salvador, Uruguay and Venezuela). However, Puerto Rico is an Associated Free State of the United States and Puerto Ricans have United States citizenship. Since 1960, four new countries have been created: Jamaica, Barbados, Trinidad and Tobago, and Guyana, of predominantly English language, which form part of the "British Commonwealth of Nations."

The name *Latin America* designates, imprecisely and conventionally, the group of twenty-one original. countries, of which nineteen speak the Spanish language, Brazil, the Portuguese, and Haiti, the French. When only the countries of the Spanish language are referred to, they are called *Hispanic America*, and when Brazil is included, they are called *Ibero America*.

The four recently independent countries are usually included in a subregion called the *Caribbean* or the *West Indies*, which sometimes include the other island countries of this zone.

2.   The Spanish and Portuguese were only the initial colonizers and those who occupied the

most extensive zones. Later, the French, Dutch, and English also arrived and occupied various zones. See Silvio Zavala, *El mundo americana en la época colonial,* 2 vols. (Mexico: Purrúa, 1967).

3. Of the 254.4 million inhabitants who form the population of Latin America (1968), 164.2 million or 64.5 percent speak Spanish; 85.6 million speak Portuguese in Brazil, that is 33.4 percent, and the rest speak French and English. Spanish occupies fifth place among the most commonly spoken world languages. The four which are spoken by more people are Mandarin, English, Russian, and Hindi.

4. Cf. José Luis Martínez, *La emancipación literaria de México* (Mexico: Antigua Librería Robredo, 1955).

5. J. M. Machado de Assis, "A estatua de José de Alencar," in *Páginas recolhidas, Obras completas* (Rio de Janiero: Jackson, 1944), pp. 279–280.

6. The word *gaucho* seems to be derived from the Quechua *huacho,* which means "orphan," "abandoned one," "wandering one," or from the Araucanian *gatchu,* "companion."

7. In 1914 the Venezuelan Rufino Blanco Fombona founds the Editorial América in Madrid which publishes, among other things, the "Biblioteca Andrés Bello" in order to make the works of numerous Hispanic-American writers widely available.

8. Baldomero Sanín Cano, "Notas" to the *Poesías* of José Asunción Silva (Paris: Louis Michaud, n.d.), pp. 221–22.

9. Emir Rodríguez Monegal, "Los nuevos novelistas," *Mundo Nuevo,* no. 17 (Paris: November 1967), p. 21.

PART TWO

Ruptures of Tradition

3/Tradition and Renewal

EMIR RODRÍGUEZ MONEGAL

THE TRADITION OF RUPTURE

Rupture as Permanent Process

Three times during this century, Latin American letters have participated in a violent, passionate shattering of the central traditional core which, like a thread of fire, runs through that literature. What happened around 1960, coinciding with the moment of the greatest diffusion of the Cuban Revolution, had occurred previously around 1940, with the cultural crisis motivated by the Spanish civil war and the Second World War and had its most evident antecedent in the other important rupture: that of the vanguard movements of the twenties. Even if the temptations of symmetry are avoided, it is easy to perceive that these three moments of rupture (arbitrarily and deliberately grouped here around round numbers: 20, 40, and 60) correspond to processes which have two simultaneous aspects. If on one hand, each crisis breaks with a tradition and proposes to establish a new system of values, on the other hand, each crisis excavates in the past (immediate or remote) in order to make its revolt legitimate, to create a genealogical tree, and to justify its descent. Occupied with the future they are constructing as well as the past they wish to salvage, the central protagonists of these three crises reflect clearly this double circular movement (forward and backward) which is characteristic of moments of crisis.

But symmetry cannot be carried any farther. Each of the three crises has very specific characteristics and orients its literary material toward very precise objectives which are not the same even when they may be seen to have certain superficial resemblances. For this reason, before examining in its contemporary context this conflict between tradition and renewal which is so evident in Latin American letters today, I think it would be useful to take a quick look at the two confrontations which preceded it while at the same time we attempt to reconsider, parallel to that, their searches and discoveries in order to measure them against those which characterize the current confrontation.

Three Crises and a Common Attitude

If the crisis of the vanguard in Hispanic America in the twenties was simultaneously an updating of the European *isms* and an impassioned

87

liquidation of Modernism (Darío was the victim of his own popularity), it was also, as should not be forgotten, a confused exploration of certain basic values of literary art: technical experimentation carried (in the case of Huidobro) to the extremes of the total destruction of verse and, almost, of the language itself: a most robust affirmation of the fictitious, arbitrary, and playful nature of narrative (as it has been theorized about and until recently practiced by Jorge Luis Borges); the baroque disintegration of the poem and the poet, of the syntax and of the metaphor which some practiced heavily (Neruda, in *Residence on Earth*; some of Vallejo's burning sarcasms). Calling into question a Modernist heritage which had been rendered obsolete by its imitators, the vanguard writers restored strict requirements of form to Hispanic-American poetry and prose, while at the same time questioning that very form. But their exploration of language only went halfway, as did their exploration of the poem or of narrative fiction. Although they produced splendid works, their collective effort seemed to be lost almost immediately. Even the best writers (Huidobro, Borges, Vallejo, and Neruda) seemed to repent quickly of their experimental eagerness and began to seek other goals.

In Brazil, the process was basically the same, but since the nomenclature was very different, it is important to make precise distinctions. Since there is no Modernism, in the Hispanic-American sense of the term, in Brazilian letters at the end of the nineteenth century, the vanguard there which was supported from São Paulo by the organizers of the Week of Modern Art (July 1922) assumes the name of Modernist Movement. Based upon futurism and the French *isms*, this vanguard proposes not only to cut all ties with Portuguese diction and rhetoric, and bring Brazilian literature up to date by intensifying its contact with the European vanguard, but also, and above all, to effect a discovery and interpretation of Brazil. This discovery realized itself through language, myths, and poetic creation. Although it would soon be replaced by another movement with more nationalistic roots (that of northeastern fiction), Brazilian Modernism would leave behind a valuable testimony of its vitality in the works of Oswald de Andrade and, above all, in those of Mario de Andrade. The novel *Macunaíma* (1928), by Mario de Andrade, is the necessary antecedent of more radical and successful experiments like the novel by Guimarães Rosa, *The Devil to Pay in the Backlands* (1956). But if the Modernist vanguard of Brazil also fades away once the fervor of the twenties has passed, its brief and intense production leaves an important mark on Brazilian literature.

The rupture which is centered around the forties often appears to be masked as ambition. These are the years of politically involved literature, of militant art, and of imperialist competition between two cultural giants. The years in which Neruda spurns and abominates his agonized poetry of *Residence on Earth* and writes *España en el corazón* [Spain in My Heart] (1937), the bellicose poems of *Residence on Earth III* (1946), and plans and writes the *General Song* (1950), maintaining in his poetry and in his public declarations that verse is a combat weapon, that the poet is obligated to his countrymen, and that the Latin American creator must concentrate his efforts upon the antiimperialist struggle. During these same years, one of the most popular Brazilian novelists, Jorge Amado, not only writes the biography of the Communist leader Luis Carlos Prestes, but he also embarks on a long narrative cycle about the production of cacao and composes novels, such as *Jubiabá* (1935), which are really tracts advocating social struggle. That both Neruda and Amado would later see themselves forced to change their aesthetics in order to save their literature, is sufficiently symptomatic of the confusion which reigned in certain zones of Latin American letters during those decades.

But these are also the years of the popularization of existentialism (or the existentialisms), and this fact would be sufficient to demonstrate that for the writer the fundamental involvement could not be political or strategic. It is not by coincidence, in the meantime, that while a good part of Latin American literature is oriented toward the sterile polemic of *engagement*, understood almost always to mean stimulus to immediate action, other more important writers of this period (Octavio Paz and Nicanor Parra, Juan Carlos Onetti and José Lezama Lima, Julio Cortázar and João Guimarães Rosa) have little or nothing to do with these basic stances of literary politics.

Despite these profound aesthetic differences, a transcendent preoccupation is revealed in the writings of these authors, a preoccupation which may stem from very different roots—the Catholic religion in Guimarães Rosa and in Lezama Lima, Marxist humanism in Parra, a deep intuition of the divine, but without churches, in Paz, the absurd and alienation in Onetti, metaphysical irony in Cortázar—but which definitely occupies the same inquisitorial space: the destiny of the self, its secret nature, and its insertion into the world. This is their connection with the deepest preoccupations of those years, whether they come from France with Sartre, or may be traced back a little further: to surrealism and Breton, with a hefty dose of Heidegger, in Octavio Paz; to the "black" literature of Céline and Faulkner, in Onetti; to Jarry, Lautréamont and Artaud, in Cortázar; to Thomas Mann, in Guimarães Rosa; to Auden and the English lyric poets of the thirties in Parra; to the Spanish baroque and Don Luis de Góngora, in Lezama Lima. But whatever the source (immediate or remote), of this inquisition, what characterizes each of these writers is his transcendence of the immediate circumstance of *engagement* and his search for an answer which connects his work to the great tradition of universal culture.

In the work of these writers, the only valid *engagement* is with literary creation. The quarry which they seek in their poems or novels is strictly poetic. It is not a coincidence that in the major books they produce (in *Blanco* [Blank] as in *Paradiso*, in *Hopscotch*, as in *The Devil to Pay in the Backlands*) what is questioned is not only the situation of man in his world, the essential and central theme of these works, but also the poetic structure itself, the capacity of language to stimulate and limit creativity, the *form* which is by now inseparable from content because there is no other access to content except through and by means of the form.

In the literature of the sixties, the dilemma is no longer even discussed. There are still commissars, no doubt, who propose a didactic, functional literature of combat. But what characterizes even a literature like that of Cuba since 1959 is the insistence of its best writers on not allowing themselves to be regimented. Today it is an accepted principle there that a writer may be at the service of the revolution and create a work the *engagement* of which is merely aesthetic. Thus it is conceivable that Cortázar should support the Cuban Revolution, yet emphatically refuse to create a literature for the masses, that Borges should be universally denounced by those of the left wing as a writer of official Argentina, yet should be exalted by those same people as an incomparable creator of fiction, that Lezama Lima (in Cuba itself) should publish a book which is esoteric, hermetic, and in ciphers, which not only is not explicitly revolutionary, but which has even violated the mandates against total sexual freedom.

This does not mean that there are not problems and conflicts (within Cuba and outside it) because there are plenty of cultural promoters who still believe in edifying literature, that is, the literature of combat, literature at the immediate service of society and the revolution. But the more profound and independent creators of these years, whatever their beliefs may be or their affiliations as men, have struggled and will continue to struggle for a literature which is primarily involved with literature itself. In this sense, the position of the intellectual and of the writer in Latin America is the position of a critic, of one who does not relinquish his faculty of passionately questioning the reality in which he finds himself.

Thus it follows that what is primarily distinctive about the writing of these years is its attitude of radically questioning writing itself and language. If in poetry, the vanguard (as Paz has said luminously) is in Brazil now, it is because that vanguard is called *concrete poetry*. In the novel, on the other hand, the vanguard is in Cuba and Mexico, in Argentina as well as in Brazil. It is a vanguard which has not broken totally with the most fertile work of the two earlier decades (in more than one sense, it continues and completes that work), but it does propose not to lose time searching for a transcendence other than that which may be found in the work itself. The motto which connects such dissimilar works as *Three Trapped Tigers* and *Betrayed by Rita Hayworth*, Nicanor Parra's *Artefactos* [Artifacts] or the concrete poems of Augusto de Campos, the experimentation of Néstor Sánchez in *Siberia Blues* and that of Severo Sarduy in *From Cuba with a Song*, could be: "a poem or a novel does not *say*: it *is*." Questioning of the work itself, of its structure and its language; questioning of the writing and of the creative role of the writer; questioning of the medium, of the book and of the typography; total questioning.

Each of the crises causes a greater rupture of the creator with a medium which asks of literature that it be anything other than literature. If the vanguard rejected sonnets and confessionalism, if existentialist literature destroyed the prestige of the edifying or protesting narrative and directed its interest toward a highly critical poetry, the literature of the sixties has concentrated fanatically on the analysis of literary process. In each of these ruptures, there is a brusque separation from immediate tradition but at the same time a recognition of ties with some earlier tradition. When concrete poetry experiments with the visual aspect of the object *poem*, it is searching for the same thing Huidobro looked for with his calligrams, which were so controversial. The concrete poets are also following Huidobro when they disintegrate words and fracture them into their bits of sounds, of isolated letters and phonemes. Similarly, many of Néstor Sánchez's experiments would be inconceivable without a previous knowledge of those of Cortázar.

I want to say that rupture exists, but I also want to say that something is continued, changed, and amplified. In the same way, rupture seeks to establish certain genealogies. The vanguard does not always reject everything in the immediate past, and if Neruda can return to Blake, it is also legitimate for Borges to rescue Macedonio Fernández from oblivion and for Huidobro to invoke no one less than Emerson to validate his first original poem, *Adán* [Adam] (1916). The double movement which Paz points out, toward the future and toward the past, allows rupture to be integrated within tradition. Eliot had seen this clearly when he spoke (in one of his essays on "Tradition and Individual Talent") of the double transformation which is effected by every masterpiece: it makes use of a tradition and at the same time alters it profoundly as it adds itself to it. The existence of the *Divine Comedy* profoundly modifies our reading of the sixth canto of the *Aeneid* as well as of the canto in which Ulysses invokes the dead in the *Odyssey*. But the existence of *Ulysses*, that modern odyssey which parodies and corrects the classic one, also modifies our vision not only of Homer, but also of Dante himself: the visit of Leopold Bloom and Stephen Dedalus to the Dublin brothel is also a descent to the world of the dead. Why go on?

Renovation and Revolution

If the quality which best characterizes twentieth-century Latin American letters is the tradition of rupture (as we have seen), it is appropriate to observe that this tradition is not new in Latin American literature. A summary of what has taken place in this literature since Independence allows one to observe that just as the vanguard of the twenties rises up against Modernism, romanticism appears in Latin America as a reaction against neoclassicism and the heritage of Hispano-Portuguese scholasticism. The polemic of 1842 in Chile, in which Sarmiento launches forth against the disciples of Bello and, in passing, against the master himself, is symptomatic of this rupture and contributes to the establishment of its tradition. Modernism, one must remember, also appears in Hispanic-American letters as a rupture with the epigones of romanticism, a rupture which has all the virulence of something new (one must read what

Valera wrote about Darío to understand completely the explosiveness of this novelty) but which at the same time only provides a new instance of that tradition which romanticism itself, in a previous generation, had contributed to establish. For that reason, when the vanguard breaks with the remains of Modernism, the same process is repeated for a third time.

What is behind this almost ritual renovation of a process is something which could be called "questioning of the immediate heritage." When Sarmiento attacks Bello, or Darío attacks the flaccid Hispanic poets, a perfectly natural and inevitable process is occurring: an exhausted tradition is exposed to question, reevaluated, reduced, or canceled out in many of its precepts, and in its place a new assessment, a new tradition, takes over. Such a radical operation, no doubt, can never be achieved without scandal. Borges's injustice toward Darío is equivalent to Sarmiento's injustice in regard to Bello. It is useless for the most precise scholars to insist upon demonstrating (which is easy) that Bello was not an enemy of romanticism and that he was even better acquainted with romanticism than Sarmiento. The image of Bello is altered by the light thrown upon it by the burning polemical words of the Argentine writer. "We the poets are with Sarmiento," Pablo Neruda said to me once, recalling the famous polemic of 1842. What Neruda did not know at that moment was that the poetry he was writing then (it was 1952) depended almost as much on the didactic and neoclassic vision defended by Bello as it did on the impassioned defense of popular language and verbal inventiveness which Sarmiento sustained. The final paradox is this: as they turn toward the past in search of a tradition which will allow the destruction of another which is more recent, the creators of the rupture tend to choose between positions which in their time were opposed to each other and which time has now neutralized. Like the rival theologians in Borges's famous story, these traditions could reveal that in the eye of God (of the omnipotent present) their differences are minimal, that the sects are eventually merged, that all is one.

The contemporary vision, by contrast, exaggerates the profiles, ignores the similarities, and emphasizes the antagonisms. Thus it is that the vanguard could be ferocious with Darío, that the existentialists abominate Borges, and that many of today's narrators do not tolerate Carpentier. But it also follows that some of the most lucid are capable of recognizing usable material in the immediate past. Thus Cortázar lays aside all parricidal fury in regard to Borges and duplicates (in his style and with his particular perspective) many of his stories, while Severo Sarduy transposes, with maximum structuralist rigor, the marvelous discoveries, the chaotic institutions, and the metaphoric fire of Lezama Lima. In Brazil, the ascetic writing of João Cabral de Melo Neto is not as distant as it might appear from the radical experiments of concrete poetry, and many of the postulates of Mario de Andrade are eventually fulfilled, and in what a dimension, in the vast novels of Guimarães Rosa.

Rupture and tradition, continuity and renovation: the terms are antagonistic but at the same time they are deeply, secretly linked. Because there can only be a rupture with something, a renovation of something, and at the same time in order to create toward the future, it is necessary to return to the past, to tradition. But here, this turn is not a return but rather a projection of the past within the present toward the future. And hence the radically revolutionary element of this tradition of rupture. It should be clarified here that it is not a question of revolution in the sense invoked by the word in political texts. To a great extent, political revolution also seeks to realize itself in a context of cultural revolution, but this context is not generally maintained for very long. The experience of the Russian Revolution, which moved toward Stalinism and the most ordinary forms of directed art (social realism, etc.) is sufficiently explicit. The tradition of rupture is, on the other hand, profoundly revolutionary because it can never be institutionalized and because it is not susceptible to bureaucratic orientation. Even when the poets themselves attempt to reorganize it (as happened in French surrealism, or in some of the ephemeral schools of the Latin American vanguard), the subdivision into sects, the intergenerational polemic and other subordinate forms of rupture eventually impose themselves.

The revolution we are talking about here is a different one: it is the revolution which postulates the questioning of literature by itself, of the writer by himself, of writing and of language by themselves. Revolution which is, by definition, permanent and which cannot be illustrated except as movement.

Since their origins in the Independence movement, Latin American letters have taken on this tradition of rupture (we can talk about literature written in Latin America before its independence, but not about Latin American literature). But this tradition has never been more alive than in the present century and never, since the triumph of the Cuban Revolution politically polarized the culture of this continent, has this tradition been confronted with a greater responsibility to be, and to keep being, authentically revolutionary. That is to say, critical.

QUESTIONING OF THE STRUCTURES

The Rescue of Forgotten Forms

If anything characterizes the literary experimentation of these last years, it is its critical search not only within literature itself (rescue of forgotten forms, negation of the boundaries between genres), but, principally, *outside* of literature. The attitude of questioning justifies these searches and orients many of the discoveries. It is not possible in the present essay to present a complete study of this double search. But some of its clearest manifestations can be pointed out here. One should begin with the rescue of forgotten literary forms because they reveal the extent to which experimentation also signifies a return to the past, an operation of reevaluation and rescue.

Three of the "forgotten" forms which have been rescued by the new literature are: the soap opera serial, the folkloric tale, and anecdotal poetry. In the case of the soap opera serial, probably the most luminous example is provided by the fiction of the Argentine novelist Manuel Puig. Although only one of his novels has been published, *Betrayed by Rita Hayworth*, it is known that Puig has been working for a long time on a second novel, *Heartbreak Tango: a Serial* (which he has finished) and that a third is in progress. Both in *Betrayed by Rita Hayworth* and *Heartbreak Tango*, Manuel Puig sets his fiction on the level of that subliterature intended for "popular" consumption and which has its best-known manifestations in the serial story (radio, television, or printed), in sentimental films, and in the lyrics of popular songs, such as tangos or boleros. With a finely tuned ear for the spoken rhythms of those mass-media forms, Manuel Puig attempts in *Betrayed by Rita Hayworth* to paint a complete portrait of the consumers of those varieties of alienation through fiction. By focusing his gaze on a family in which the mother takes her little son Toto to the movies every afternoon to relieve the tedium of the provinces, Manuel Puig has created a sort of *Madame Bovary* of our time. While Flaubert's protagonist was alienated by the pulp literature of romanticism, Puig's is alienated by radio melodramas, the commercial cinema, and pulp fiction. In *Heartbreak Tango*, in contrast to *Betrayed*, the technique itself is that of a popular pulp serial. Here Manuel Puig has moved entirely into parody. While *Betrayed* (formally, at any rate) follows the tradition of Joyce (*Portrait of the Artist as a Young Man*), of Ivy Compton-Burnett and her disciple Nathalie Sarraute, *Heartbreak Tango* is, formally and specifically, pulp fiction. The external structure of the book, and not just its vision or its speech, reflects the pulp novel as in a mirror. However, as do all parodies that may be respected, *Heartbreak Tango* reveals the exact degree of exasperation which allows a natural distinction between Manuel Puig and, say, *Corín Tellado* [one of the most popular serials in Latin America].

The folkloric tale is, as we already know, at the center of all narration. But the layers and layers of sophistication which Western culture has added to this form, since Cervantes decided to portray not only the Spanish reality of his era in *Don Quixote*, but to reflect the work itself within its own text (an achievement which Michel Foucault has linked to that of Velázquez in *Las Meninas* [Maids of Honor]) has indicated a route which left the popular story, or folkloric tale, far behind. For this reason, it is astonishing that in two of the most surprising narrative constructions of recent years, the popular story comes back into its own. I refer, naturally, to *The Devil to Pay in the Backlands*, by João Guimarães Rosa, and to *One Hundred Years of Solitude*, by Gabriel García Márquez.

At first, the two novels seem to have little in common except their having been conceived and created independently of each other. The lack of communication between Brazil and the rest of Latin America explains how Guimarães Rosa's book, published in 1956 in Brazil, only began to exist for Hispanic-American letters in 1967, the year in which Angel Crespo's translation appeared. This communication gap is widened, in this case, by the difficulties which Rosa's text itself provides the reader. But although Guimarães Rosa and García Márquez created their works with their backs turned to each other, their novels in some ways contemplate and reflect each other.

While Guimarães Rosa centers his interest on the story of a young man who seeks his own identity through the identity of his unknown father (which would relate his novel to Rulfo's *Pedro Páramo*, if they were not so different in other ways), García Márquez centers his novel on the warrior vocation of Colonel Aureliano Buendía and builds the dazzling framework of a family saga around that vocation. While Rosa's whole novel is based on an essentially religious vision (the protagonist thinks he has made a pact with the Devil and has an erotic relationship with a youth who is like a Guardian Angel), García Márquez sidesteps the religious implications of his novel and prefers to establish a metaphysical-aesthetic vision of solitude, understood as both social alienation and cosmic alienation ("the races condemned to one hundred years of solitude," he indicates at the end of his novel). While Rosa tells his story through the protagonist's monologue, García Márquez does not give up his privileges as an omnipotent and ubiquitous narrator: his book is, in a single sweep, the perfect model of authorial writing.

If we make use of a distinction pointed out by Roland Barthes between writing and speech, we could say that while García Márquez writes his book, Guimarães Rosa speaks his. It is clear that the distinction is more apparent than real, as will be seen later. The differences which have just been pointed out between the two books (and others which could be mentioned) do not hide the basic fact that both stem from a tradition of folkloric tale and seek—in different ways, to be sure—not only to renovate it, but also to salvage it. For this reason, both García Márquez and Guimarães Rosa choose as a point of departure one of the standard situations of the popular story. In one case, it is a pact with the Devil, in the other, it is a curse which falls upon the members of a race: a child with a pig's tail will be born if close relations marry. Upon this basic scheme, both Rosa and García Márquez erect structures which reproduce (without mirrorlike duplication) the structure of the folktale.

In the case of Rosa, it is the oral monologue, the confession, the free flow of one who relates what he has seen and heard, as well as suffered. In the case of García Márquez, it is the fable, the tales of the grandmothers, the parable with its inevitable moral. It is not a coincidence that the anecdotal source for both books should be in an experience that has roots in the still folkloric world of the interior of Latin America. If Guimarães Rosa heard the prime material of his novels from the lips of the easygoing *Mineiros* during the days and nights of his practice of rural medicine in the state of Minas Gerais, García Márquez heard from the lips of his grandmother, before he was eight years old, those fabulous tales which many years later would constitute the incandescent material of his stories and novels.

Dissolution of the Genres

The vanguard of the twenties had placed storytelling, or anecdotal, poetry among the poetic relics that had to be left behind once and for all. In a famous condemnation of the literary vices of his time, Borges had declared, around 1925, ultraist poetry's abolishment not only of confessionalism and of the "ornamental gewgaws" (oh, shades of Quevedo and Villarroel), but also of "circumstantiation," that is, of anecdote. Even so, the evolution of his own poetry pulled him more than once toward anecdote ("General Quiroga Rides to His Death in a Carriage" would be a good example), and as for confessionalism, his poetry of the last two decades is a confession, at times inevitably pathetic, of his limited human condition. But now is not the time to point out Borges's contradictions ("It is true, I contradict myself, I am human," he said in a recent interview), but rather to indicate a point of departure. What was anathema in the twenties would be converted into habitual practice during recent years.

It would be easy to trace a line which would pass through the Neruda of some of the *Residences* (I am thinking of "Tango of the Widower"), through the Nicanor Parra of *Poems and Antipoems* (of 1954, do not forget), even through the Octavio Paz of *The Violent Season* (1958), which flows into a poetry of anecdote, a poetry in which "plot" is not systematically excluded, but rather forms part of the poetic creation itself. But instead of outlining a general literary panorama, impossible within the terms of the present essay, I prefer to indicate two distinctly different but complementary paths followed by that poetry which salvages a forgotten form. One path is that of colloquial poetry, which naturally incorporates the anecdotal element into the lyric. In many of the Mexican Salvador Novo's poems, this tone of spoken or conversational verse may already be found, a tone which will be taken up and used in the River Plate area with exceptionally good fortune. In the works of poets as different from each other as César Fernández Moreno, Idea Vilariño, and Juan Gelman, it is possible to recognize a River Plate intonation which rescues the influence of the tango and of popular language, or slang, for poetry. More stylized in the Uruguayan poet, more programmatic and didactic in Gelman, it is probably in Fernández Moreno's last books that the new language, the new form, achieves its richest expression.

Argentino hasta la muerte [Argentine to the Bitter End] has a minimal but consistent plot: it is the experience of the poet who leaves his native land, travels through Europe, and later returns home with a greater recognition of the identity indicated in the book's title, thanks to a formula (quoted with both parodic and emotional intent) of Guido y Spano. Here the external events are minimal, anecdote is almost nonexistent, everything is centered in subjectivity. But the poetic resources of which Fernández Moreno avails himself, the deliberately colloquial tone of his text and his lively spoken language which does not shy away from slang, situate the poem in an existential sequence which is (almost) that of a novel. Hence the predictable connection with storytelling poetry. It is not by chance, then, that this book is continued in another, *Los aeropuertos* [Airports], which offers a new "installment" (or serial segment) of the same existential experience, carrying the persona of the poet another step forward.

The poetry of other poets of that time is more decidedly storytelling. I will mention the work of two poets, one Brazilian and the other Mexican, as examples of this poetic trend. In order to recount the story of one of the victims of the periodic drought in the Northeast, in *Morte e Vida Severina* [Death and Life of Severina], João Cabral de Melo Neto makes use of the basic techniques of verse narrative. His is a story to recount as well as to sing, and in it are summarized (with revolutionary lucidity and precision which make the work more intense) all the themes which many novels and even films of the Northeast have explored in greater detail, although not more effectively. The fact that Melo Neto's poem has been made into a film, and even set to music by Chico Buarque de Hollanda, emphasizes its storytelling quality even more and shows that a "forgotten" form can have an even greater appositeness in our time than the more common forms.

As for *Perséfone*, by the Mexican Homero Aridjis, here indeed is a blurring of the distinctions between novel and short story, on one hand, and lyric poetry on the other. Novel-poem, or narrative poem, *Perséfone* is a text of high poetic quality which develops the theme of sexual love in various temporal sequences. Written after the admirable collection of poems entitled *Mirándola dormir* [Watching Her Sleep], the text of *Perséfone* amplifies to some extent the erotic suggestions proposed by the earlier volume. But now Homero Aridjis is resolutely interested in exploring the more notorious aspect of the narrative. In *Perséfone*, we find not only the pair of lovers, but also the whorehouse owner and the other women, the clients and the exterior world itself which surrounds, enfolds, and determines the characters. Because Perséfone is not the same in the atmosphere of alienated sexuality of the whorehouse as in the security of the room where she closes herself in with the narrator, her lover; she is not the same in the leprous light of the den as in the clear morning light. A novel without sufficient plot, a poem with an excess of narrative elements, *Perséfone* not only illustrates the rescue (and the present-day rewriting) of a forgotten genre, but it also illustrates a new step in present literature; the negation of the explicit boundaries between genres. But this is a topic which requires a separate study. If *Perséfone* oscillates between the novel and the poem, justifying, in its way, Octavio Paz's affirmation that there is no valid distinction between prose and verse, we should be warned that Aridjis's work is one of the many which demonstrate today the impossibility of distinguishing between the different genres of classical rhetoric. The theme is not new, not even in our century, and Benedetto Croce and Alfonso Reyes, in his wake, have already discussed it satisfactorily. What I am interested in indicating here is not the theoretical basis of this discussion, but rather its practical application to a literary reality which is more evident every day: genres have not disappeared altogether, but their boundaries continue to be modified and to be blurred into invisibility, producing works which do not fit into *any* single category.

How, for example, should Borges's *Dreamtigers* be classified? It is a book of prose and verse, it contains pages of prose written with the rigor of poetry, and the material itself is elusive and metaphorical; poems of unredeemed prosaism which could perhaps be improved by a terse prose; short stories which are (indifferently) in verse or prose. But, even better, each page of the book corresponds to a genre which classical rhetoric does not recognize but which is the only genre which justifies the magical lucidity, the vertiginous awe of the reading. The book is a "confession." For Borges, in the twilight of a career as a literary experimenter in the three principal genres (the poem, the essay, the story), the definitive form is that of the confession.

But perhaps the most astonishing example of this superposition and contamination of genres which characterize present literature is that provided by some experiments conducted in Buenos Aires by Basilia Papastamatíu. Her free texts, which are collected in the volume *El pensamiento común* [Common Thought] (1965), and especially her "Lectura de *La Diana*" (in *Mundo Nuevo*, no. 8, Paris, February 1967) shows how far one can go in an exploration of literary forms which leads to a true disintegration of the rhetorical categories called *genres*. In her "Lectura de *La Diana*," the celebrated poem by Montemayor, the Argentine writer not only inserts fragments, conveniently dislocated and extrapolated, from the classical text, but she contaminates them with their own poetic developments: developments which are simultaneously a critical commentary on the text, a parody, a surtext and an antitext, but also an autonomous work of singular fascination. Here the pre-text (*La Diana*) stimulates a genre, poetry, to evoke its counterpart: criticism, but this criticism is not effected through the usual approach of the gloss or discursive exegesis, but rather through the oblique approach, no less fertile, of the *collage*, of parody, of mirrorlike reflection, critical and creative at the same time.

In the theater, a search through these same possibilities is also evident. If the school of the absurd (which has among us such interesting adherents as Isaac Chocrón, Jorge Díaz, José Triana, and Jorge Blanco) still seems too tied to a text, whether or not this is conceived of as prime material for a ritual spectacle, the other line of experimentation clearly points to the elimination of the rhetorical distinctions between genres while at the same time it indicates an assimilation of nonliterary expressive forms. In the way of "happenings," both Marta Minujin in Buenos Aires and her compatriot Copi in Paris have been developing a theatrical activity in which the basic element of drama, the word, is unimportant even if it does not disappear altogether in the face of the primacy of the elements of spectacle. Reestablishing the decisive value of the word, the theatrical group directed by the Argentine Rodríguez Arias has produced in *Drácula* a text which is a parody of the silent film and also a parody of the parodies of the silent film, as well as an experiment which attempts to create a theatrical structure which depends almost exclusively on the very formalized elocution of an essentially *narrative* text. For what Rodríguez Arias is doing in *Drácula* is to dispossess the theater of its aspect of verbal combat or gymnastics. Its agonists are not agonists at all: they do not struggle, but rather they limit themselves to receiving information about events which take place offstage or which will occur offstage, or to commenting on this information in the most passive way possible. That is to say, if Aristotle could define drama as the representation of action by action itself, while the epic represents action by words, this is epic theater, although in a more literal sense than that suggested by Brecht. In reality, the achievement of Rodríguez Arias (and here I do not speak of the ultimate quality of the spectacle, which is something else) is to have intuited that in this era of total questioning of genres, theater as represented action needed to give way to theater as a commentary on (or merely gloss of) action. In this sense, his work is authentically experimental and opens a new way which is even more provocative than that of mere "happenings." In these, action replaces the word, and this separates them definitively from literature.

Concrete Poetry and Technology

If "happenings" finally return the varied forms of spectacle (without excluding erotic exhibitionism or orgiastic ritual) to theater, certifying in this negative way the contamination of literature by the other arts, in a reverse manner, concrete poetry proposes to integrate into literature arts which are obviously exterior to it but which, in one way or another, can benefit it and enrich it. I refer to the plastic arts and to music.

This is not the occasion for a history (brief but already abundant) of a movement which in a little more than a decade has swept across the poetry of five continents like a forest fire. It is sufficient to point out that it has one of its sources, and its most intense center, in Brazil. Although it appears almost simultaneously in various countries (in Italy with Carlo Belloli, in Switzerland with Eugen Gomringer, in Sweden with Oyvind Falström, in Brazil with the Campos brothers), there is clearly a mysterious predestination at work which causes this movement to be marked by the languages of the New World: while Gomringer was born in Bolivia and wrote his first concrete poems in Spanish, Falström spent the first three years of his life in São Paulo. Thus even those poets who later carried out their experiments in the context of other languages, by their origins seem to be marked by the Latin American destiny. Their spiritual roots in the New World would please Juan Larrea with their surreal symbolism.

It is not my intention, however, to create a basis for an absurd national-ization of concrete poetry. By its own nature, concrete poetry is decidedly universal and transcends not only linguistic boundaries, but also the boundaries between the arts. When the Campos brothers and Décio Pignatari trace the genealogy of their experimentation, they invoke precisely Anglo-Saxon poetry (E. E. Cummings, as well as Pound and Joyce), but they also invoke the films of Eisenstein and the music of Webern. On the other hand, the name itself by which they have chosen to identify their group, *Noigandres*, is a mysterious word which comes to them from the Provençal troubadour Arnaut Daniel by way of Ezra Pound (*Cantos*, 20). Thus it is legitimate to emphasize the largely Latin American and specifically Brazilian origin of this movement, as long as we do not fail to stress its internationality. Because it is Latin American, it is international, we would have to say, forcing the paradox.

The diffusion of concrete poetry, beginning with the isolated experiments by Belloli in Italy or Falström in Sweden, which will later be systematized and coordinated from Switzerland and Brazil by Gomringer and Max Bunse as well as the Campos brothers and Décio Pignatari, also reveals another characteristic hallmark of contemporary Latin American literature: its internationalist vocation which is only the other side of the coin of that modernity which Darío pursued and which hallucinated Huidobro, that modernity which Octavio Paz has stressed as the final quality in his admirable exposition of the Mexican (and, in part, American) character in his *The Labyrinth of Solitude* ('1950). We Latin Americans are now for the first time contemporaries of all men, Paz proclaimed then. The evolution and diffusion of concrete poetry has permitted the demonstration of this.

But there is here, in this experiment which is simultaneously visual, verbal, and auditory, something more than a new international poetics. In the first place, concrete poetry accepts the challenge of technology and instead of disowning the new industrial revolution, it proposes to use it in the service of poetry. This zeal has (like all enthusiasms) its tradition. It is this that Huidobro sought, in the wake of Apollinaire, of Dada, of the surrealists, and even of futurism, although for reasons of mere strategy of schools, he often denied these sources and parallels. What Huidobro sought, that raising up of technology through the exaltation of space and of velocity, that transformation of the poet into a parachutist of imaginary space, and of which his *Altazor* (1931) is an impassioned testimony, is what the concrete poets have proposed systematically.

However, the famous lack of communication between Brazil and the rest of Latin America has kept the concrete poets of São Paulo from thoroughly taking advantage of the Huidobran experience. Instead of beginning with *Altazor*, they have remade the trail followed by the Chilean poet, drawing on precisely the same sources and repeating (in curious parallel at times) a part of his trajectory. On the other hand, they did not need to look back at the vanguard poetry in the Spanish language because in their Modernism, the Brazilian poets had the necessary antecedents for this type of exploration. But while Huidobro's experiments were disorderly and were based upon a powerful poetic intuition which totally lacked discipline and was even opposed to any exigent theoretical formulation (Huidobro's famous manifestos are a chaos of the ideas of others, with brilliant and polemical sentences, but with little aesthetic substance), the poets of the *Noigandres* group would distinguish themselves by their capacity to systematize their searches, to classify their discoveries, to continue their experiments not only in the field of language, but also in those of typography, of the plastic arts, and of the audiovisual media. The result is therefore much more complete and complex than that achieved by Huidobro. While the Chilean poet saw the possibilities of a systematic application of technology to poetic creation, while he intuited that the disintegration of language (as it is practiced at the end of *Altazor*) can be the point of departure for a new aesthetics of verse, it was left for the poets of the *Noigandres* group to explore these paths right down to their last real consequences.

The poem-object, the history of which is so long that antecedents may be found in Chaledean or Greek poetry, was certainly not invented by Huidobro (as he allowed his distracted disciples to believe), but what the Chilean poet did indeed perceive was the possibility of making poem-objects that would transcend the technological limitations of previous poetry. This is what has been done by Augusto de Campos, Haroldo de Campos, and Décio Pignatari. With the method of visual *collage*, Augusto de Campos composes in *Olho por olho* [An Eye for an Eye] an illustration of the famous proverb which is graphic and verbal. But a textual analysis of this poem (which consists of a pyramid of eyes, as in the barbarous Chaldean sacrifices), an examination of each of its components and of their interrelationships permits one to see that the poem contains a commentary (essentially verbal) on the contents of the proverb. The eyes of politicians like Fidel, of stars like Marilyn Monroe, of the poet Pignatari, alternate with fingers, lips, and even teeth, giving the proverb an extraliteral dimension. In the same way, when Décio Pignatari plays with the four letters utilized by *Life* for its title, not only does he compose an exciting typographical sequence, but he also introduces a spatial discontinuity which allows the reconstruction, from within, of the word and liberates symbolic meanings: the superposition of the four letters in a single space creates an ideogram which is equivalent to the sign of the sun, that is, of life.

These and other examples which could be mentioned show clearly, in my judgment, that concrete poetry proposes to explore not only all of the verbal qualities of the poem, but also its vocal and visual possibilities to an extent which had not even been dreamed of by the very literal designers of object-poems (like Francisco Acuña de Figueroa or Lewis Carroll, or even Apollinaire in his first *Calligrammes*). Technology, as it has been revealed by certain concrete poets who are also typographers, or musicians, or plastic artists (as in the case of the German-Mexican Matthias Goeritz), does not limit but rather liberates energies. If McLuhan was in error when he proclaimed the death of the book in his truculent prophecies, he probably was not wrong when he pointed out that the book, as object, as a reading machine, only offers one of the possibilities of literary communication.

Beginning with this conviction, the concrete poets undertake to extend the limits of the page and appeal to color (like Haroldo de Campos in *Cristalfome*; like Pignatari in a satire of the Coca-Cola slogan *Drink Coca-Cola*, which uses as a base the intense red of the company which manufactures the product, and the same typography as its ads), or seek in records, in recordings, new paths for poetry. Even the reading of a book does not have to be done in the conventional way: instead of beginning with the first page, it is possible to begin at the end, as in the Semitic cultures; instead of reading the book, it is possible to leaf through it rapidly to *read* the movement of the letters on the nearly blank pages, as happens in *Sweethearts* (1967) by Emmett Williams, the North American poet and theoretician. All these forms, and many others which could be mentioned, call into question poetry's habits of communication. Not the poetry itself which, on the contrary, benefits from being presented in such a form that the reader is obliged to undertake a much more intense operation of decodification.

It is not by chance, then, that a poet as mature and centered in his poetic concerns as Octavio Paz should have adopted in his most recent poems some of the experiments of concrete poetry in order to apply them to his own adventure in creation-communication. Thus in the great poem *Blanco* [Blank] (1967), there are pages on which the poem is separated into visual sectors by means of a simple typographical artifice: each line is written in two different typefaces which divide the verse into two typographical hemistichs. The reading of the two sectors can be done according to the common lineal method, in which case one has Poem A, or by reading first the hemistichs in roman type and then the hemistichs in cursive, in which case one has poem B; and even by inverting the previous order, first those in cursive and then those in roman, in which case one has poem C. The three poems fuse into a single one which includes all three and which is the poem that Paz wishes to communicate. By this simple artifice, the reading of the poem is intensified and the reader is obliged to delve deeply into a text which is not totally accessible at first glance.

A more recent experiment of Paz's is that of the *Discos visuales* [Visual Disks] (1968), poems written on two round disks which rotate one on the other, by a simple manual mechanism. When static, each poem draws a figure, but when the lower disk is made to turn, other texts appear which were hidden by the first figure and which are like the intertexts which must be deciphered in an ordinary poem. This small mechanical invention stimulates not only the possibilities of a circular reading (since one always returns to the first figure, which is the last, etc.), but it also presupposes a dynamic reading in movement. At bottom, this experiment, like those of concrete poetry, proposes to emphasize something which can never be stressed enough: poetry is an art of movement, a dynamic art. Poetry, as we know, is produced in time; it is an auditory structure which the invention of print has subjected to the page giving it the false appearance of a static object. By means of the visual experiments of concrete poetry, or of recorded sound on records, poetry not only returns to its oral tradition, but it is also liberated (visually, too) from static. This is what Apollinaire wanted with his *Calligrammes*, which wander all over the page, and even before him, this is what Mallarmé (the father of them all) desired when he gave value to space in "Un coup de dés" in the double sense of visual space and sonorous space (silence). This is what poetry has always proposed. It is comforting to take note that on the road toward a more imaginative alliance with typography or the tape recorder, that is to say, on the road toward the acceptance of technology, poetry recovers its most ancient magic.

THE LANGUAGE OF THE NOVEL

But it is in the novel that all experimentation flourishes most. For that reason, it is important to examine, albeit rapidly, the evolution of the Latin American novel of this century in order to see, across this span of time, the simultaneous work of the forces of experimentation and of tradition, the rupture toward the future as well as the impassioned rescue of certain essences.

What at first attracts the attention of the observer is the coexistence of at least four generations of narrators; four generations which it would be easy to separate and isolate in watertight compartments but which in the real process of literary creation are sharing the same world, disputing succulent fragments of the same reality, exploring unpublished avenues of the language, passing back and forth their experiences, techniques, trade secrets, and mysteries.

It is not difficult to group these four sets of writers according to the generational method which in the Spanish language has had such distinguished expositors as Ortega y Gasset and his disciple Julián Marías. But here I am less interested in emphasizing the rhetorical category of generation than the pragmatic reality of those four groups as they are seen in action. The generational series are a Procrustean bed and there is always the danger, if they are not manipulated with great subtlety, of establishing the appearance of a very orderly and even rigid process which separates literature into harmonious periods and provokes synoptic overviews. these various generations which tend to confront each other in the manuals from the extreme ends of a vacuum share in reality one space and one time; they intercommunicate more than is thought, they often have influence on each other, back and forth across the current of time.

On the other hand, belonging to the same generation is not a guarantee of similarity of vision or of narrative language. How can one not notice, for example, that even though the Peruvian Ciro Alegría and the Uruguayan Juan Carlos Onetti were born within a few months of each other, the first is an epigone of the great novelists of the land (epigone soon bettered by a narrator of the next generation, José María Arguedas), while the second is a forerunner of the novelists concerned with narrative experimentation, who concentrate their vision particularly on the alienation of men in cities? This seems obvious now and even a child can see it. But in 1941, Alegría and Onetti competed for the same prize in an international competition and no one is ignorant of who won.

It seems better to me, for that reason, to speak of groups rather than of generations. Or if I speak of generations, let it be understood that they do not occupy watertight compartments and that many of the most original creators of the new Latin American novel escape from, more than belong to, their respective generations. With these warnings, let us see what the generational panorama says to us.

Good-bye to Tradition

Around 1940, the Latin American novel was represented by writers who constituted, without any doubt, a great constellation: Horacio Quiroga, Benito Lynch, and Ricardo Güiraldes in the River Plate had their equivalents in Mariano Azuela and Martín Luis Guzmán in Mexico, José Eustacio Rivera in Colombia, Rómulo Gallegos in Venezuela, and Graciliano Ramos in Brazil. Represented there is a valid tradition of the novel of the land or of the country dweller, a chronicle of his rebellion or submissions, a profound exploration of the·links between this man and an enslaving nature, the elaboration of myths which are central to a continent which these authors still saw in its Romantic excesses. Even the most sober of them (I am thinking of the Mexicans, of Graciliano Ramos, of Quiroga) did not escape a heroic categorization, an archetypal vision which converted some of their books, and especially *The Vortex, Doña Bárbara, Don Segundo Sombra*, into romances (in accordance with the rhetorical categories of Northrop Frye) rather than into novels. That is to say: in books whose realism is deformed in such a way by the mythological conception that they escape the quality of documentary or testimonial which they wanted to possess.

It is these very masters who are turned against by the generations which began to publish their more important narrations from 1940 on. A first group would be represented by such writers as Miguel Ángel Asturias, Jorge Luis Borges, Alejo Carpentier, Agustín Yáñez, and Leopoldo Marechal, among others. They, and their equals whom I cannot mention here without turning this essay into a catalogue, are the great renovators of the narrative genre of this century. I should clarify that I include Borges here (just as I included Quiroga) despite the fact that his truly creative work has taken place only in the short story, because any serious consideration of the narrative genre in Latin America seems impossible to me without a study of his work as a truly revolutionary short-story writer.

In the books by these writers, a critical operation of the greatest importance is effected. Turning their gaze toward that literature of myth and impassioned testimony which constitutes the best of the work of Gallegos, Rivera and company, Borges, just like Marechal, Carpentier, Asturias, and Yáñez, attempts to show the obsolete rhetoric that earlier novelistic reality contained. While they criticize it, and even reject it in many cases, the above-mentioned authors search for other alternatives. It is not by chance that their work is strongly influenced by the vanguard currents which, in Europe, allowed the liquidation of the heritage of naturalism. If, during his formative years in Geneva, Borges passed through the experience of German expressionism and through the double reading of Joyce and of Kafka, to open out in Spain into ultraism and the reading of Ramón Gómez de la Serna (that great forgotten writer), Carpentier and Yáñez, as well as Asturias and Marechal recognize, on different levels but with equal eagerness, that dazzling French surrealism.

Latin American narration comes out of the hands of these founding fathers profoundly changed in its appearance and also in its essence. Because they are, above all, renovators of a vision of America and of an American concept of language. This aspect is not usually noticed in the work of Borges (who is still categorized by critics as a cosmopolitan without recognizing that only someone born in a land of immigrants and educated in the various foreign languages used in Buenos Aires could allow himself the luxury of being cosmopolitan; but let us go on); this aspect that is usually denied in the work of Borges, which is so important for the definition of a cosmo-vision of Buenos Aires language, is perfectly clear if we consider the work of Asturias, permeated by the language and imagery of the Maya people as well as by ardent antiimperialist rebellion. It is also extremely clear in the case of Agustín Yáñez, who shows Mexico how to see its own face, and, above all, its superimposed secular masks; and it is indisputable in the case of Leopoldo Marechal, voluntary creator of an "Argentine" novel, *Adán Buenosayres*; and it is also extremely obvious in the case of Alejo Carpentier, in whom the entire Caribbean and not just Cuba appears metamorphosed by the poetic vision of its past, its present, and even its time without time.

Whether they wish it or not, the first books by these founders produce a rupture with the linguistic tradition and with the vision of Rivera and Gallegos which is so profound and complete that after their appearance it is no longer possible to write novels in America in the old way. It is true that when these novels go out into the street, there are very few who actually read them in all their incandescence. But the few readers of the forties are the great minority of today. It suffices to say that Borges published *A Universal History of Infamy* in 1935; that *El Señor Presidente* [The President] dates from 1946; that *The Edge of the Storm*, the decisive novel of Augustín Yáñez, is from 1947; that Leopoldo Marechal published his ambitious, excessive novel in 1948; and that Alejo Carpentier caused astonishment with *The Kingdom of This World* in 1949.

The books which these narrators will publish later—from Borges's *Ficciones* to Marechal's *El banquete de Severo Arcángelo*, [The Banquet of Severo Arcángelo], including Asturias's *Men of Maize*, Yáñez's *The Lean Lands*, Carpentier's *Explosion in a Cathedral*—could be, and surely are, more mature, more important, but here I am not interested in dealing with the theme from this purely evaluative point of view but rather in indicating what those books which have made the rounds of the American lands in the forties signify as a definitive rupture with a linguistic tradition and a narrative vision as well.

The Narrative Form as Problem

The fertile and renovative work of this first constellation was produced almost simultaneously with that of the following generation and which, to give a few examples, we could call the generation of João Guimarães Rosa and Miguel

Otero Silva, Juan Carlos Onetti and Ernesto Sábato, José Lezama Lima and Julio Cortázar, José María Arguedas and Juan Rulfo. Once again it could be shown that these are not the only writers but that only these can be mentioned in my brief study. Once more there is a need to indicate that although these writers are united by certain things, the work of each is personal and untransferable to a maximum degree. But what I am interested in stressing now is what unites them. In the first place, I would say, it is the mark left on their work by the masters of the previous group of writers. To give a single example: what would *Hopscotch*, that quintessentially Argentine novel which *Hopscotch* is beneath its French patina, be without Macedonio Fernández, without Borges, without Roberto Arlt, without Marechal, without Onetti? I must add that Cortázar himself is the first to recognize this multiple filiation and sometimes he does it on the pages of the novel when he transcribes notes made by his narrative alter ego, the ubiquitous Morelli, or in certain discreet homages which constitute episodes of an indisputably Onettian or Marechalian origin.

The visible influence of foreign masters like Faulkner, Proust, Joyce, and even Jean-Paul Sartre also unifies the narrators of this second group. In this matter of influences, there are curious blendings. I will cite the case of Guimarães Rosa who has always denied Faulkner's influence on his novels. He even said to me one day that the little he had read by the Southern novelist had prejudiced him against it; that Faulkner seemed to him unhealthy in his sexual attitude, that he was sadistic, and so forth. And nevertheless, in his great and unique novel, the traces of Faulkner seem conspicuous in the intensity of the monologue, the vision of an impassioned and mythic rural world, mysterious blood ties, and the ominous presence of a divinity. The explanation is a simple one, however. It is no longer necessary to have read Faulkner directly to have been subjected to his influence, to breathe in his atmosphere, even to inherit certain of his stylistic manias. Faulkner's work could reach Guimarães Rosa, very invisibly, through other writers (like Sartre) whose work he had indeed read and admired.

But it is not the influences, recognized and almost always admitted, that best characterize this group, but rather a concept of the novel which through whatever differences there are between one work and another offers at least a trait in common, a minimal common denominator. While the previous group of writers innovated little in the external structure of the novel and was almost always content to follow the most traditional molds (perhaps only *Adán Buenosayres* aspired, with evident success, to create a more complex spatial structure), the works of this second group have been characterized, above all, by their attack on the novel form and their questioning of its very basis.

Thus, in the interminable epic-lyric monologues of the oral narrators of Brazil's interior, Guimarães Rosa has sought (as has already been mentioned in another part of this study) the model for his *The Devil to Pay in the Backlands*. In the meantime, Onetti has created, in a series of novels and stories which could be collected under the general title *The Saga of Santa*

María, a River Plate universe which is dreamlike and real at the same time, with a plot and texture which are very personal, despite the recognized debts to Faulkner. In some of the novels of this *Saga*, above all in *The Shipyard* and *Juntacadáveres* [Corpse-gatherer], Onetti has brought the most subtle refinements to narrative construction, interpolating a literary facsimile of terrifying irony into the reality of the River Plate. This narrative world is related in essence (not just by accident) to that of the Venezuelan Miguel Otero Silva in *Casas muertas* [Dead Homes], and to that of the Argentine Ernesto Sábato in *Sobre héroes y tumbas* [On Heroes and Graves]. As for Juan Rulfo, his *Pedro Páramo* is the paradigm of the new Latin American novel: a work which takes advantage of the great Mexican tradition of the land novel but which metamorphoses it, destroys it, and recreates it by means of a very profound assimilation of the techniques and vision of Faulkner. Dreamlike, too, like Onetti's work, oscillating dangerously between the most unadorned realism and unlimited nightmare, it is so far Rulfo's only novel and its appearance is an important landmark. José María Arguedas is less of an exterior innovator, but his vision of the Peruvian Indian, wrought from within the Quechua language itself, definitely liquidates the well-intentioned folklorism of Latin American intellectuals who do not speak Indian languages.

Two centrally important novels by Julio Cortázar and José Lezama Lima are of an even more revolutionary order because they attack not only the structures of narrative, but those of language itself. In more than one sense, they represent the culmination of the process begun by Borges and Asturias; and at the same time, they open a totally new perspective: a perspective which allows a lucid and precise evaluation of the most recent narrators. In *Paradiso*, Lezama Lima achieves magically what Marechal has proposed rationally with his novel: the creation of a *summa*, a book whose very form is dictated by the nature of the poetic vision which inspires it; the completion of a story of *costumbrista* appearance which at the same time is a treatise about the heaven of childhood and the hell of sexual perversions; the tracing of a chronicle of the sentimental and poetic education of a young man from the Havana of thirty years ago, which is converted through the metaphoric dislocation of language into a mirror of the visible world and, above all, of the invisible. The achievement of Lezama Lima is without equal. He has given us a monument which only now, with great deliberation and without haste, it is possible to begin to read in its totality.

Cortázar's *Hopscotch* seems easier, at first glance; it is a book which benefits not only from a rich River Plate tradition (as has already been indicated), but also from that monstrous broth of cultivation which is French literature and, in particular, surrealism in all of its mutations. But while Cortázar makes use of these advantages, Lezama on his island of thirty years ago seemed to be lost in a vast library of mismatched volumes worm-eaten by errata; while Cortázar seems to have written *Hopscotch* from the very center of his intellectual world, Lezama Lima began to write his *Paradiso* in what was one of the more peripheral peripheries of Latin America. The truth is that

Cortázar pulls away from that apotheosis of culture that is Paris in order to negate all culture, and that his book wishes to be, above all, a *resta*, not a *summa*; an antinovel, not a novel. Toward this end, he attacks what is novelistic, although he takes care to preserve, here and there, the novel itself. The narrative form is called into question by the book itself which begins with instructions to the reader on how it is possible to read it; which then suggests to the narrator a classification of readers into female readers and accomplice readers; and which ends by closing him into a circular and infinite experience, since chapter 58 leads to 131 which leads to 58 which leads to 131, and so on until the end of time. Here, the *form* itself of the book—a labyrinth without a center, a trap which closes cyclically about the reader, a serpent which bites its own tail—is another means of emphasizing the profound and secret theme of this exploration of a bridge between two experiences (Paris, Buenos Aires), a bridge between two muses (la Maga, Talita), a bridge between two existences which duplicate and reflect each other as in a mirror (Oliveira, Traveler). It is a work which duplicates itself in order to question itself better. It is also a work about the duality of being Argentinian, and, even more profoundly and vertiginously, about the double which lurks in other dimensions of our lives. The *form* of the book merges with what used to be called its *content*.

The Great Novel-Making Machines

What this group of writers transmits to the next is, above all, a consciousness of external novelistic structure and a sharpened sensitivity to language as the prime material of narrative. But the working out of both is almost simultaneous and parallel. The relative tardiness with which Guimarães Rosa, Lezama Lima, and Julio Cortázar published their masterpieces causes these novels to appear after many of the more important works of the group I am describing now. Here the generations overlap and the influence is more of coexistence and direct intercommunication than of inheritance. It will be sufficient to say, I think, that this third group of narrators is made up of such writers as Carlos Martínez Moreno, Augusto Roa Bastos, Clarice Lispector, José Donoso, David Viñas, Carlos Fuentes, Gabriel García Márquez, Salvador Garmendia, Guillermo Cabrera Infante, and Mario Vargas Llosa, all writers who simultaneously pay attention to external structures and to the creative and even revolutionary role of language. Not all of these novelists are obvious innovators, although some of them are right up to the furthest limit of total experimentation, as in the case of Cabrera Infante. But Donoso, for example, has followed the riverbed of traditional narrative and has concentrated his inventiveness on exploring the subterranean reality that is beneath the stucco coatings of the Chilean *costumbrista* novel. The same could be said of Carlos Martínez Moreno in Uruguay, of Salvador Garmendia in Venezuela, and of David Viñas in Argentina: the exploration of reality leads them into expressionism and even to caricature. Related to them, although in a certain sense more experimental, is Augusto Roa Bastos, author of *Son of Man*, who enriches naturalism with techniques of fantastic narration in order to produce a work of violent humanitarian denunciation.

But the majority of the narrators of this third group are efficient builders of novel machines. While Clarice Lispector in *The Apple in the Dark* and *A paixão segundo G. H.* [The Passion According to G. H.] finds in the *nouveau roman* a stimulus for describing the arid, tense, metaphysically nightmarish and exitless worlds that are those of her persecuted characters, Carlos Fuentes utilizes all the experimentation of the contemporary novel to compose complex, difficult works which are simultaneously denunciations of a reality which is savagely painful to him and expressionist allegories of a country that is his, a mythopoetic Mexico of superimposed masks which has very little to do with the surface of present-day Mexico, but which is its best allegorical representation. Mario Vargas Llosa for his part makes good use of the new techniques (chronological discontinuity, interior monologues, plural speakers and points of view) in order to orchestrate adeptly some visions of his native Peru which are very modern and traditional. Inspired simultaneously and harmoniously by Faulkner and the novel of chivalry, by Flaubert, Arguedas, and Musil, Vargas Llosa is a narrator of great epic scope for whom events and people continue to matter terribly. His renovation is definitely a new form of realism, a realism which abandons the Manichaeanism of the protest novel and which knows that time has more than one dimension, but which never makes up its mind to lift its feet from the solid, tormented earth.

It is not these great young writers, already recognized as masters by the critics of this decade, who have taken advantage of the more anticipatory aspects of the work of the two preceding groups of writers, but rather authors like García Márquez and Cabrera Infante, who have appeared later in time, but who have already produced works of singular importance. It is possible to recognize, both in *One Hundred Years of Solitude* and in *Three Trapped Tigers*, without any possible doubt, the relationship with the linguistic world of Borges or of Carpentier, with the fantastic visions of Rulfo or of Cortázar, with the international style of Fuentes or of Vargas Llosa. However, these connections (ultimately superficial, after all) are not what really matter in these extraordinary books.

Both novels depend upon a strictly lucid vision of the fictitious character of all narration. They are, above all, formidable verbal constructions, and they proclaim this in a subtle, implicit way, as in the case of *One Hundred Years of Solitude*, in which the traditional realism of the novel of the land seems to be contaminated by fable and myth, served up in the most brilliant of tones, impregnated by humor and fantasy. But they also proclaim their fictitiousness in a militantly pedagogic way, as in *Three Trapped Tigers*, which, in the wake of *Hopscotch* and with even more constant novelistic invention, installs in its very center the negation of its "truth," creates and destroys, and ends by demolishing the carefully made fabric of its own fiction.

While García Márquez seems to adapt the teachings gathered simultaneously from Faulkner and the Virginia Woolf of *Orlando* (a book which

Borges translated into Spanish) to the creation of that imaginary Macondo in which Colonel Aureliano Buendía lives and dies, a warning is in order: we should not let ourselves be fooled by appearances. The already illustrious Colombian narrator is doing something more than recounting an infinitely enchanting fable of inexhaustible humor and enfolding fantasy: with the most insidious of persuasions, he is erasing the tedious distinction between realism and fantasy in the body itself of the novel, in order to present—in a single sentence and on the same metaphoric level—the narrative "truth" of what his fictional entities live and dream. Rooted simultaneously in myth and in history, trafficking with episodes worthy of *A Thousand and One Nights* or of the most archaic part of the Bible, *One Hundred Years of Solitude* only achieves its full coherence in this profound reality of the language. All of which is not even noticed by the greater part of its readers, who are seduced by the enchantment of a style which has no equal in its fantasy, in its rapidity, or in its precision.

The operation practiced by Cabrera Infante is more scandalously flamboyant because his whole novel only makes sense if it is examined as a linguistic-narrative structure. In contrast with *One Hundred Years of Solitude*, which is recounted by a ubiquitous and omniscient narrator, *Three Trapped Tigers* is told by its characters themselves, or rather one would have to say by its speakers, since it is a matter of a collage of voices. An evident disciple of Joyce, Cabrera Infante is no less an admirer of Lewis Carroll, another great manipulator of language, and of Mark Twain, who discovered (before many) a tone of voice for his characters' dialogue. The linguistic structure of *Three Trapped Tigers* is composed, from the title on, of all the possible meanings of a word, and sometimes of a phoneme, of the rhythms of a sentence, of the most unheard of verbal puns. Disciple of those masters but, above all, disciple of his own ear, Cabrera Infante has brought to the body of his novel things which do not come from literature but rather from films or from jazz and Cuban music, integrating the rhythms of Cuban speech with those of the most creative music of this time or with those of the art whose visual persuasion has colonized us all.

When I say that in García Márquez or in Cabrera Infante the concept of the novel as a linguistic structure predominates, I do not forget (naturally) that in *One Hundred Years of Solitude* and *Three Trapped Tigers* the "contents" are of enduring importance. How could anyone not notice that the demented course of violence in Colombia is perfectly depicted, both superficially and in its vertiginous depths, by the magic hand of García Márquez? How could anyone fail to recognize in that Havana of the sunset of Batista's power, in which those sad tigers agitate, a society which is breathing its last, a candle on the verge of burning out or which has just been extinguished as Cabrera Infante evokes it in his book? Of course. It is obvious. But what makes *One Hundred Years of Solitude* and *Three Trapped Tigers* the singular creations they are is not their testimonial evidence which the reader can find in other books as well, books which are lesser achievements and purely extraliterary.

What distinguishes these two works is their devotion to the cause of the novel as total fiction.

The Vehicle Is the Journey

With García Márquez and Cabrera Infante, just as with Fuentes who would reveal himself in his last extremely complex novel, *A Change of Skin*, we enter the dominion of the fourth and, for now, extremely new generation of narrators. It is still not possible to say much about them in detail because almost all of them have published only a first novel, although they are already working on another or others. But I will take advantage of the quality of novelty, of newness, which is etymologically implicit in the word *novel*, to mention some names which seem to be to be of indisputable importance. Above all, in Mexico, Cuba, Brazil, and Argentina, there are a great many young narrators who, at the present time, commit the act of narration with the maximum possible latitude and without respecting any law or apparent tradition, except that of experimentation. Their names are Gustavo Sainz, Fernando del Paso, Salvador Elizondo, José Agustín, José Emilio Pacheco, in Mexico; in Cuba, on and away from the island, but in the Cuba which is united by its literature, are Severo Sarduy, Jesús Díaz, Reinaldo Arenas, and Edmundo Desnoes; in Brazil, their names are Nélida Piñón and Dalton Trevisan; in Argentina, they are Néstor Sánchez, Daniel Moyano, Juan José Hernández, Manuel Puig, and Leopoldo Germán García. It is impossible to speak of them all, and this enumeration already looks suspiciously like a catalogue. I prefer to run the risk of being in error and to choose four from within this number.

The more visible ones or, at least, those who have already produced at least one novel, which distinguishes them from others, are Manuel Puig, Néstor Sánchez, Gustavo Sainz, and Severo Sarduy. These four are united by such an acute consciousness that the most intimate texture of narrative is neither in the theme (as the romantic narrators of the land novels pretended to believe, or perhaps did believe) nor in the external construction, nor even in the myths. It is, very naturally for them, in the language. Or to adapt a formula which has been popularized by Marshall McLuhan: "The medium is the message." The novel uses the word not to say something in particular about the extraliterary world, but rather to transform the novel's linguistic reality itself. This transformation is what the novel "says" and not what is usually discussed *in extenso* when a novel is talked about: plot, characters, anecdote, message, denunciation, protest, as though the novel *were* the reality and not a parallel verbal construction.

This does not mean, of course, that through its language the novel does not allude naturally to extraliterary realities. It does, and is popular for this very reason. But its true message is not on this level, on which it can be exchanged for the speech of a president or a dictator, for the minutes of a committee meeting or the notes of the nearest parish priest. Its message is in its language.

Since the idea of a language of the novel seems to me to be of primary importance, I am going to insist a little more on this aspect. When I speak of a language, I do not refer exclusively to the use of certain forms of language. In literature, language is not synonomous with a general system of the *tongue* [lengua], but rather synonymous with the *speech* [habla] of a specific writer or a specific genre. The language of the Latin American novel is made up, above all, of a profound vision of the reality around it, a vision which owes fundamental components to the work of essayists and of poets, demonstrating yet again the artificiality of the rhetorical separation of the genres. Thus, how can the searing mark of Martínez Estrada not be recognized on that entire parricidal generation which surges up in Argentina around 1950? How can one not notice the style and even the very words of Octavio Paz in so many key passages of Carlos Fuentes's novels? In this incorporation of the work of essayists and poets into the creation of a narrative language, the Latin American novel has demonstrated its maturity. But here I wish to indicate one further step in this process: the novel, by questioning its structure and its texture, has called its language into question and has converted the theme of narrative language into the theme of the novel itself. This, which has been seen in Cortázar and in Lezama Lima, in Cabrera Infante and in García Márquez, can be seen (even more clearly) in the new narrators.

Thus it follows that in a book like *Betrayed by Rita Hayworth*, by Manuel Puig, the most important aspect is not the story of the boy who lives in an Argentine provincial city and who goes to the movies with his mother every afternoon, nor is it the narrative structure which uses Joyce's interior monologue of excessive importance, nor the dialogues without explicit subject which have been popularized by Nathalie Sarraute. No. What really matters in Puig's fascinating book is that *continuum* of spoken language which is simultaneously the vehicle of the narrative and the narrative itself. The alienation of the characters by the films, which the title indicates and which is manifested in the smallest details of their behavior—they only talk about films they have seen, they project themselves into cinematographic episodes cut from old films, their values and their speech itself derive from the movies, they are the new prisoners of the Platonic cave created in the whole world of today by the filmmaker—this central alienation is not only recounted by Puig with irresistible humor and an extremely fine sense of parody. It is also recreated in each reader's personal experience by the alienated language used by the characters, a language which is almost a facsimile of those soap opera radio serials, now on television instead, or of photo-novels. The alienated language makes the alienation of the characters explicit: the alienated language is alienation itself. The medium is the message, and also the massage, as McLuhan himself indicates with his usual enjoyment of puns.

In *Nosotros dos* [The Two of Us] and *Siberia Blues*, Néstor Sánchez duplicates, although from a perspective which is more Cortazarian and in the French style, Cabrera Infante's effort to create a structure which is, above all, auditory, sonorous. He, too, is influenced by popular music (the tango in his case) and by the avant-garde cinema. But his narrative texture, his medium, is even more complex and confused than that of Cabrera Infante, in which an atrocious British lucidity finally governs all delirium and in which the withholding of an important segment of the "reality" (the passion of two characters in *Three Trapped Tigers* for the same woman) is, above all, a sign of narrative modesty. But in Sánchez, tension and ambition sometimes flow in excess. When he hits the mark, he achieves the creation of a single narrative substance which mixes presents and pasts, all and each of the characters, in order to stress that the only central reality of that world of fiction, the only one accepted and assumed with all of its risks by the narrator and his characters, is that of language: glass which is sometimes opaque and which at other times becomes invisible in its sheer transparency. In his novels, not only is the author of *Hopscotch* (for whom Sánchez has a devotion which sometimes takes the form of mimetism) present, but there may also be found the visual and rhythmic, simultaneously uniform and serial, world of Alain Resnais and Alain Robbe-Grillet in *L'Année dernière à Marienbad* [Last Year in Marienbad].

Gustavo Sainz comes to the same material through the medium of an apparatus almost as trivial in today's world as windmills in Cervantes's: the tape recorder. His novel, *Gazapo*, pretends to have been recorded live by such a machine. It is no longer a matter of composing a novel on a typewriter, using as secret keys what X said (although attributing it to Y in order to mislead) or switching the head of A onto the shoulders of B by means of the aesthetic plastic surgery in which Proust was an expert. No, nothing like this. Sainz is a child of this technological era and he prefers to pretend that he uses the tape recorder in order to retain everything in the world of the spoken word. His characters themselves seem to be recording what is happening to them (life, as we know, is a continuous and tedious "happening"). But this basic recording is used in its turn to provoke new recordings or to contradict them; or it is used within a story which one of the characters, perhaps the alter ego of the author, writes. The recording of the novelistic reality within the book itself, as well as the recording of the book, participates in an identical verbal and auditory condition. Everything is words, in the long run. As in the second *Don Quixote*, in which the characters discuss the first *Don Quixote* and even the apocryphal adventures which Avellaneda invented for them, Sainz's characters pass through their own recorded novel over and over again. They are prisoners in the spider web of their own voices. If all of these more or less apocryphal planes of the narrative "reality" of this novel are valid, it is because the only "reality" the "characters" really "live" is that of the book. That is to say, the reality of the word. Everything else is questionable and is questioned by Sainz.

I have deliberately left until last the narrator who has forged farthest ahead in this type of exploration. I refer to Severo Sarduy, who has already published two books: *Gestos*, which pays tribute to a certain form of the *nouveau roman*—the tropisms of Sarraute—but who already reveals an eye and an ear of his own; and *From Cuba with a Song*, which in my opinion is one of the decisive works in this collective enterprise concerned with the creation of a language of its own for the Latin American novel. (A third novel, *Cobra*, is in the process of being written; in the fragments published in magazines, it is possible to see that it confirms what is said here about its author.)

What *From Cuba with a Song* presents are three episodes of a prerevolutionary and essential Cuba: one of the episodes occurs in Havana's Chinatown, a limited world of transvestites and riffraff but at the same time a world of profound, disturbing sexual symbols; the second episode shows black and mulatto Cuba, the colored surface of the tropics, in a parodic and satiric story which is simultaneously a cantata (as such, it has been broadcast successfully over the radio in France); the third part concentrates primarily on Spanish Catholic Cuba, that is, on central Cuba. But what the book tells is secondary to Sarduy's purpose: what is important is how he tells it. Because, unifying the three parts, unequal in their extension and in their interest, there is a means which converts itself into an end, a vehicle which is in itself the journey. Here the Havana speech of the author (not of the characters, as in Cabrera Infante) is the true protagonist. His is a baroque language in the profound sense of Lezama Lima and not in that of Carpentier; a language which turns critically and parodically upon itself, as happens also in the French writers of the *Tel quel* group with which Sarduy has had such a fertile relationship. It is a language which evolves during the course of the novel, which lives, suffers, is corrupted, and dies to be resurrected from its own decayed matter, like that image of Christ which in the third part is being carried in a procession in Havana.

With this novel of Sarduy's, as with *Betrayed by Rita Hayworth*, the works of Néstor Sánchez, and Sainz's *Gazapo*, the theme of the Latin American novel which had been opened to question by Borges and by Asturias, which had been developed astoundingly and from different magnetic fields by Lezama Lima and Cortázar, which is enriched, metamorphosed, and made into a fable by García Márquez, by Fuentes, and by Cabrera Infante, now reaches a true delirium of simultaneously prosaic and poetic invention. It is the subterranean theme of the newest Latin American novel: the theme of language as the place (space and time) in which the novel "really" occurs. Language as the unique and final "reality" of the novel. The medium which is the message. It is also the theme of Brazilian concrete poetry, of the dynamic and visual experiments of Octavio Paz, of experimental theater, of all of Latin American literature in its double search for a *terra incognita* and for a (new) tradition.

4 / The Baroque and the Neobaroque

SEVERO SARDUY

It is legitimate to transpose the artistic notion of the baroque to literary terrain. These two fields offer remarkable parallelism from various points of view; they are equally undefinable.

A. MORET, *El lirismo barroco en Alemania*

THE BAROQUE

From its birth, the baroque was destined for ambiguity, for semantic diffusion. It was the great irregular pearl—in Spanish *barrueco* or *berrueco*, in Portuguese *barrocco*—the rock, the knotted, the agglomerate density of rock—*barrueco* or *berrueco*—or perhaps the excrescence, the cyst, what proliferates, both free and lithic, tumorous, warty; even perhaps the name of a student of the Carraccis', excessively sensitive and affected with mannerism— Le Baroche or Barocci (1528–1612); perhaps fantastic philology, an ancient mnemotechnical term of Scholasticism, a syllogism—*baroco*. Finally, for the denotative catalogue of dictionaries, accumulations of codified banality, the baroque is equivalent to "shocking bizarreness"—Littré—or to "eccentricity, extravagance, and bad taste"—Martínez Amador.

Geologic nodule, mobile and muddy construction of clay—*barro*—guide of the deduction or pearl, of that agglomeration, of that uncontrolled proliferation of meanings, and also of that skillful transmission of thought which the Council of Trent needed to counteract reformist arguments. To this necessity there responded the pedagogic iconography proposed by the Jesuits, literally an art of *tape-à-l'oeil*, which could put all possible resources at the service of teaching, of faith, which could reject discretion, the progressive tint of the *sfumato* in order to adopt theatrical clarity, the unexpected carved out of the chiaroscuro and could banish the symbolic subtlety incarnated by the saints, with their attributes, in order to adopt a rhetoric of the demonstrative and the evident, punctuated by the feet of beggars and of rags, of country virgins and calloused hands.

We will not follow the displacement of each of the elements which resulted from this outburst which provokes a true dislocation of thought, an episte- mological cut, the manifestations of which are simultaneous and explicit;[1] the Church complicates or fragments its axis and renounces a preestablished course, opening the interior of its edifice, irradiated, to various possible ways, offering itself in the meantime as a labyrinth of figures; the city decentralizes, loses its orthogonal structure, its natural indications of intelligibility—moats, rivers, and walls. Literature renounces its denotative level, its lineal enunciation; the single center of the stars' orbits, which until then had been supposed circular, disappears only to become double when Kepler proposes the ellipse as the form of this displacement; Harvey postulates the circulation of the blood, and finally, God himself no longer seems to be a central, unique, exterior evidence, but rather the infinite certainties of personal cognition, dispersion, and pulverization which announce the galactic world of the monads.

Rather than amplifying, unavoidable metonymy, the concept of *baroque*, we would like to restrict it, to reduce it to a precise operative scheme, which would not leave interstices, which would not permit the abuse or the terminological freedom from which this notion has suffered recently and very especially among us, but which would codify, insofar as it is possible, the pertinence of its application to present-day Latin American art.

ARTIFICE

If we seek a precise definition of the concept of baroque in the best grammar in Spanish—the one by Eugenio d'Ors—we will see that one notion sustains, whether explicitly or not, all the definitions and is the basis for all theses: it is the notion of the baroque as a return to the primogenial, that is, to nature. For d'Ors,[2] Churriguera "recalls the primitive chaos, voices of turtle doves, voices of trumpets, heard in a botanical garden.... There is no acoustic landscape of more characteristically baroque emotion....The baroque is secretly animated by nostalgia for the Lost Paradise...." The baroque "seeks the ingenuous, the primitive, the naked...." For d'Ors, as Pierre Charpentrat points out,[3] "the baroque is, above all, as is known, liberty, confidence in a preferably disordered nature." The baroque as immersion in pantheism: Pan, god of nature, presides over all authentic baroque work.

With its repetitions of volutes, of arabesques and masks, of sugar-candy hats and glistening silks, the baroque feast seems to us the apotheosis of artifice, the irony and mockery of nature, the best expression of that process which J. Rousset has recognized in the literature of a whole "age": *artificialization*.[4] To call falcons "raudos torbellinos de Noruega" ["sweeping whirlwinds of Norway"], the islands of a river "paréntesis frondosos / al período [son] de su corriente" [they are "leafy parentheses / to the period of its current"], the Straits of Magellan "de fugitiva plata / la bisagra, aunque estrecha, abrazadora de un Océano y otro" ["of fugitive silver / the hinge, although narrow, embracer / of one Ocean and another"], is to point out the artificialization, and this process of masking, of progressive layering over, of mockery, is so radical that in order to "dismantle" it, it has been necessary to use an operation analogous to the one Chomsky calls *metalanguage*.[5] Metaphor in Góngora is already, of itself, metalinguistic, that is, it sets forth an already elaborate level of language, that of poetic metaphors, which, in their turn, are the elaboration of a first denotative "normal" level of language. As he comments upon the Gongorine process of artificialization, the deciphering practiced by Dámaso Alonso includes this process within itself.[6] In this always multipliable commentary—this very text comments now on Alonso's, another perhaps (I hope) will comment upon this one—the best example of this successive wrapping up of one writing by what constitutes—as we are about to see—the baroque itself.

The extreme artificialization practiced in some texts, and, above all, in some recent texts of Latin American literature, would be sufficient, then, to show the existence of the baroque in them. We will distinguish three mechanisms within this artificialization.

Substitution

When in *Paradiso* José Lezama Lima calls a male organ "the stinger of the leptosomatic macrogenitome," baroque artifice manifests itself through a substitution which we could describe on the level of the sign: the significant which corresponds to the signified *virility* has been removed by sleight of hand and replaced by another, which is totally removed from it semantically and which only functions within the erotic context of the story, that is to say, it corresponds to the first in the process of signification.

Formalizing this operation we could write:

$$\frac{\text{Sig̶n̶i̶f̶i̶c̶ant}}{\text{Signified}} \quad — — — — — — — — \longrightarrow \quad \text{Significant}^1$$

An analogous process may be seen in the baroque work, also in the strictest sense of the word, of the painter René Portacarrero. If we look at his paintings of the Flora series, for example, and even at his recent drawings, like the one which illustrates the cover of *Paradiso* (Era edition) itself, we see that the process of artificialization by substitution operates in the same way: the visual significant which corresponds to the signified *hat* has been replaced by a motley cornucopia, by a floral scaffolding built up on a boat and which only in the graphic structure of the drawing can occupy the place of the significant *hat*. We can find a third example—the *démarche* of these three Cuban creators is isomorphic—in the architecture of Ricardo Porro. Here the functional elements of the architectonic structure are replaced at times by others which can only serve as significants, as mechanical supports to the former, by being inserted into that context. For example, a drainage canal is converted not into a gargoyle—which is its codified significant ever since Gothic times and thus customary by now—but into a flute, femur, or phallus; a fountain takes on the form of a papaya, a Cuban fruit. This last substitution is particularly interesting, since it is not limited to a simple permutation but rather when the "normal" significant of the function is expelled and another totally different one is put in its place, what it does is eroticize the totality of the work—novel, painting, or building. In the case of Porro, eroticizing is accomplished through the use of a linguistic astuteness—in Cuban slang *papaya* also designates the female sex.

With respect to the traditional mechanisms of the baroque, these recent Latin American works have retained and sometimes amplified the distance between the two terms of the sign which constitute the essence of their language, in opposition to the narrow adherence of those which support classic art. Aperture, a gap between the namer and the named, and the appearance of another namer, that is, metaphor.[7] Exaggerated distance, the entire baroque is just a hyperbole, whose "prodigality" is not erotic by mere chance, as we will see.

Proliferation

Another mechanism of the artificialization of the baroque is that which consists of obliterating the significant of a given signified but not replacing it by another, however distant this might be from the first, but rather by a chain of significants which progresses metonymically and which finally circumscribes the absent significant, tracing an orbit all around it, an orbit through the reading of which—which we could call a *radial reading*—we can infer it. Upon being implanted in America and incorporating other linguistic materials—I refer to all the languages, verbal or not—upon having at its disposal frequently motley elements that have been brought to it by acculturation, from other cultural strata, the functioning of the baroque mechanism has been made more explicit. Its presence is constant above all in the form of nonsensical enumeration, in the accumulation of diverse nodules of meaning, in the juxtaposition of hetero-geneous units, and in lists of disparates and collages. On the level of the sign, the proliferation could be formalized in the following way:

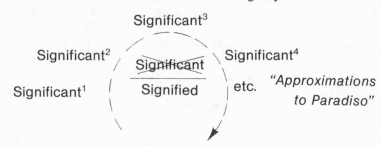

Thus, in chapter 3 of *Explosion in a Cathedral*, Alejo Carpentier, in order to connect the signified "disorder," traces around its significant (absent) an enumeration of astronomical instruments used nonsensically and in the reading of which we infer the reigning chaos: "Placed in the courtyard, the sundial had been transformed into a moondial, marking inverted hours. The hydrostatic balance served to measure the weight of the cats; the small telescope, thrust through the broken glass of a skylight, allowed them to see things, in the nearby houses, which made Carlos, a solitary astronomer perched on top of a cupboard, laugh equivocally."

The visual isomorphism of this mechanism may be found in the "accumulations of the Venezuelan sculptor Mario Abreu.[8] In *Objectos mágicos* [Magic Objects], a juxtaposition of diverse materials—a horseshoe, a spoon, four sticks from a drying rack, four sleigh bells, a brooch, and a key holder—all of them, as in Carpentier, are used in unexpected ways, that is, they are emptied of their functions and what the sculptor succeeds in signifying to us, in codifying by means of the accumulation, is the signified *Cáliz*, without ever presenting us with the normal, denoted significant of *Cáliz*—any form, however metaphorical, of a chalice.

At other times the heterogeneous grouping of "emptied" objects does not lead us, not even in a subtly allegorical way, to any precise signified, that is, the radial reading is *deceptive* in the Barthian sense of the word: enumeration is presented as an *open* chain, as if one element, which would complete the sketched-out sense and conclude the operation of signification, had to be present to close it, thus finishing the orbit traced around the absent significant. Thus in *Manipulorio*, also by Mario Abreu, there is another accumulation. We are presented with six spoons, a glass, and perhaps a plate... but this first nucleus of meaning remains perturbed, that is, it *disappoints* the reading *Preparation of a meal*, for example, because next to these semantically coherent objects there appears an eye superimposed on a symmetrical surface with the shape of an animal hide. The reading leads us only to a contradiction between significants, which instead of completing each other, undermine and cancel each other out. Thus *Banquet / Prophylactic Eye / Primitivism / Rituality /* and so forth, do not function as complementary units of one sense, however vast this may be, but rather as executors of its abolition which, with each new attempt at constitution, at plenitude, manage to invalidate it, retrospectively destroying the sense in bloom, the always unconcluded, unrealizable project of the signification. The enumerations, the brusque and surprising juxtapositions of *Residence on Earth*, by Pablo Neruda, evoke this same reading, as do the semantic constellations—pulverization, dispersion of sound—of the *General Song*:

> Guayaquil, sílaba de lanza, filo
> de estrella ecuatorial,

cerrojo abierto
de las tinieblas húmedas
que ondulan
como una trenza de mujer mojada:
puerta de hierro maltratado
por el sudor amargo
que moja los racimos,
que gotea el marfil en los ramajes
y resbala a la boca de los hombres
mordiendo como un ácido marino.[9]

[Guayaquil, syllable of lance, blade / of equatorial star, / open latch / of the humid shadows / which undulate / like a wet woman's braid: / gate of iron maltreated / by the bitter sweat / which wets the grape clusters, / which speckles the ivory on the branches / and slips onto the mouths of men / biting like a marine acid.]

In the baroque exuberance of *The Devil to Pay in the Backlands*, by João Guimarães Rosa, the two procedures just described are detectable, like oratorical suspenders, but fused in the same rhetorical operation: the signified *Devil* has excluded all direct denomination from the text—substitition; the onomastic chain which designates it throughout the novel—proliferation—permits and provokes a radial reading of attributes, and this variety of attributions which indicate him enriches our perception of the Devil as we gradually become aware of what is happening. To refer to him in any other way would be to add to his satanic panoply and amplify the reaches of his power.

Proliferation, the quintessential metonymic operation, finally gives us the best definition of what all metaphor is, the realization on the level of praxis—of the deciphering process which all reading is—of the project and the vocation which the etymology of that word reveals to us: displacement, transfer, and trope. Proliferation, its sweep foreseen, orbit of abbreviated similitudes, demands—in order to make divineable what it obliterates, to graze the excluded or expelled significant with its periphrasis, and to sketch the absence which it indicates—that transference, that circling around what is missing and the loss of which it constitutes: radial reading which connotes, like no other, a presence, that which in its ellipsis indicates the mark of the absent significant, that which the reading, without naming it, refers to in each of its tacks around, the expelled, that which flaunts the scars of exile.

Condensation

One of the baroque practices is analogous to the oneiric process of condensation: permutation, mirror imagery, fusion, interchange among elements—phonetic or plastic—of two of the terms of a significant chain, the clash and condensation from which a third term emerges which summarizes the first two semantically. Central to Joycism, to all playful work, heraldic shield of the descendants of Lewis Carroll, condensation, and its rudimentary meaning, phonetic permutation, which on the level of the sign, we could formalize in the following way:

Permutation   *Condensation*

$$\frac{(\text{Phoneme}^1 \ldots \overleftarrow{\text{Phoneme}^2 \ldots \text{etc.}}) (\overrightarrow{F^1 \ldots F^2} \ldots \text{etc.} \quad \text{Sig't}^1 \rightarrow \underline{\text{Sig't}^3} \leftarrow \text{Sig't}^2}{\text{Significant}^1 \qquad\qquad \text{Sig't}^2 \qquad\quad \overset{\nwarrow}{\text{Signified}} \overset{\nearrow}{}}$$

Significant^1 Sig't^2 Signified

Signified

Condensation and permutation have found their best exponent, among us, in the work of Guillermo Cabrera Infante—*Three Trapped Tigers, Cuerpos divinos* [Divine Bodies]—in which these forms, these distortions of the form, constitute the plot, the scaffolding which structures the feverish proliferation of words. "The meaning cannot emerge if the liberty is total or nil; the diet of meaning is that of guarded liberty," Roland Barthes has written.[10] In the work of Cabrera Infante the function of these operations is precisely that: of limiting, of serving as a support and as bone structure for the overflowing production of words—for the insertion, which can be prolonged infinitely, of one subordinate clause into another—that is to say, of causing the meaning to emerge there where everything is an invitation to pure play, to phonetic chance, that is, to nonmeaning. Permutations like *O se me valla un gayo* [untranslatable play on words], condensations like *amosclavo* [masterslave] or *maquinoscrito* [typewriter written], to cite the simplest, are used on each page to guard the liberty, which is total these days—rhetoric has disappeared—of the author, and to this "censorship" the work of Cabrera Infante owes its meaning.

This same game of condensation, which in the visual arts was represented classically by the distinct variants of anamorphosis, finds new possibilities today in the incorporation of movement to art (filmic painting and film itself). Through a process of vertical incisions in wood, using three distinct colors to cover each of these depressions, Carlos Cruz-Díez manages to compose three distinct paintings depending on whether the spectator is on the right, on the left, or in front of the panel. The displacing of the spectator—a process in this case comparable to reading—condenses all the plastic units into a fourth element— the definitive painting—which is chromatic and geometrically open.

We have access to the "definitive painting" of Julio Le Parc through condensation, too. The flexible metallic bands which reflect light and constitute the visible support of the painting project various luminous drawings on the back with their movement. None of these instantaneous drawings, which only become unified through perception, constitutes the work, but rather the condensation of all of these reflections and their relationship with the central metallic band, an element which is also animated by a complex movement which resists all reduction to elemental forms. Each reflection is like an ephemeral diagram, an uncrushable "moment" of the work or of its equation: a work the very substance of which is variation and time, the mechanical modulation of a scheme X of multiple articulated variables and their ability to combine themselves without ever revealing the individual elements for an instant.

But, of course, the ideal field for condensation is that of cinematographic superposition: overlayers of two or more images which condense into a single one—that is to say, synchronic condensation—as it is frequently practiced by Leopoldo Torre-Nillson, and also overlayers of various sequences which fuse into a single unit of discourse in the memory of the spectator—diachronic condensation—a frequent procedure in Glauber Rocha.

However, we are not speaking here of a simple artifice of cinematographic writing, as it is encountered more or less in all the authors, but of a certain deliberately stylistic use of this procedure; in Torre-Nilsson the figures which are overlayered have—as in Eisenstein—value, not of a simple linking together, but of metaphor; insisting on their analogies, the author creates a tension between two significants from the condensation of which a new signified emerges.

Similarly, in Rocha it is not simply a matter of a variation of structurally analogous sequences—as in the films of Robbe-Grillet—but of the creation of a tension between very different and distant sequences which an index obliges us to "connect" in such a way that they lose their autonomy and exist only insofar as they achieve fusion.

If in substitution the significant vanishes and is replaced by another, and in proliferation a chain of significants circumscribes the first (and absent) significant, in condensation we witness the "staging" and the unification of two significants which come together in the exterior space of the screen, the painting, or in the interior of memory.

Parody

Commenting upon Góngora's parody of a ballad by Lope de Vega, Robert Jammes concludes:[11] "To the extent to which this ballad by Góngora is a disfiguration [*démarquage*] of a previous ballad which must be read in filigree in order to enjoy it totally, one can say that it belongs to a minor genre, since it exists only in reference to this earlier work." If it refers to the Spanish baroque, this affirmation seems dubious to us already. And if it refers to the Latin American baroque, "painterly" baroque, as Lezama Lima calls it, the baroque of syncretism, variation, and depth, we would succumb to the temptation of amplifying it, but inverting it totally—a baroque operation—and affirming that only insofar as a work of the Latin American baroque is the disfiguration of a previous work which must be *read in filigree* in order to enjoy it totally does it belong to a major genre; an affirmation which will be truer every day, since the references are becoming more vast, as is our knowledge of them, and the works in filigree, which are themselves a disfiguration of other works, are becoming more numerous.

To the extent to which it permits a reading in filigree, to the extent to which it conceals beneath the text—or in architectonic work, plastic work—another text—another work—which this reading reveals, discovers, and opens to deciphering, the recent Latin American baroque participates in the concept of parody, as it was defined in 1929 by the Russian formalist Backtine.[12] According to this author, parody derives from the ancient serio-comic genre, which is related to carnival folklore—hence its mixture of gaiety and tradition. Although it utilizes contemporary speech seriously, it also invents freely and plays with a plurality of tones, that is, it speaks about speech. The substratum and foundation of this genre—whose great moments have been the Socratic dialogue and the Menippean satire—is the carnival, a symbolic and syncretic spectacle in which the "abnormal" reigns, in which confusions and profanations, eccentricities and ambivalences are multiplied, and the central action of which is a parodic coronation, that is, an apotheosis which hides a mockery. The Saturnalian rites, the masquerades of the sixteenth century, the Satyricon, Boetius, the Mysteries, and of course, Rabelais, but above all, Cervantes's *Don Quixote*: these are the best examples of this *carnivalization* of literature which the recent Latin American baroque—and it is not by chance that the carnival is so important to us—has inherited. *Carnivalization* implies parody to the extent to which it is equivalent to confusion and confrontation, to interaction between different strata, between different linguistic textures, to *intertextuality*. Texts which establish a dialogue in the work, a theatrical spectacle the script bearers of which—the performers of whom Greimas speaks—are other scripts; hence the polyphonic character, stereophonic we could say, to add a neologism which Backtine would surely have liked, of baroque works, of the whole baroque code, literary or not. Within the space of dialogism, polyphony, carnivalization, parody, and of intertextuality, the baroque would present itself, then, as a network of connections, of successive filigrees, the graphic expression of which would not be lineal, bidimensional, or flat, but rather large, spatial, and dynamic. Into the carnivalization of the baroque a specific characteristic is inserted, the mixing of genres, the intrusion of one type of discourse into another—a letter in a story, or dialogues in these letters—that is to say, as Backtine pointed out, that the word *baroque* is not only what figures, but also what is figured, and this is the material of literature. Confronted with the intercrossed languages of America—with the codices of pre-Columbian knowledge—Spanish—the codices of European culture—found itself duplicated, reflected in other organizations and discourses. Even after annulling them, or subjugating them, certain elements of the intercrossed languages survived that the Spanish language forced to coincide with elements of its own; the process of synonymizing, normal in all languages, was accelerated because of the necessity to make uniform, on the level of the significant chain, the chaotic vastness of names. The baroque, an overflowing cornucopia, renowned for its prodigality and dissipation—hence the *moral* resistance which it has provoked in certain cultures noted for their economy and moderation, like the French—a mockery of all functionality, of all sobriety, it is also the solution to that verbal saturation, to the *trop plein* of the word, to the abundance of names in relation to the named, to the numerable, the flood of words over things. Hence its mechanism of periphrasis, of digression and detour, of duplication and even of tautology. Verbiage, squandered forms, language which, because of its excessive abundance, can no longer designate things but only other designators of things, significants which enfold other significants in a mechanism of signification which ends by designating only itself, revealing its own grammar, the models of that grammar and its generation in the universe of words. Variations, modulations of a model which the totality of the work crowns and dethrones, teaches, deforms, duplicates, inverts, strips, or overloads until filling all the emptiness, all the space which is available. Language which speaks of language, the baroque superabundance is generated by the synonymic supplement, by the initial "doubling," by the overflow of the significants which the baroque work, the baroque opera, catalogues.

Of course, the work will be properly baroque to the extent to which these elements—synonymic supplement, parody, and so forth—are found situated at the nodal points of the structure of the discourse, that is, to the extent to which they orient their development and proliferation. Hence the necessity of distinguishing between works on the surface of which float fragments, minimal units of parody, as a decorative element, and works which belong specifically to the parodic genre and the whole structure of which is constituted, generated, by the principle of parody, by the sense of carnivalization.[13]

To escape from facile generalizations and from the disordered application of the baroque criterion, it would be necessary to codify the reading of the textual units *in filigree*, which we will call *gramas* following the nomenclature proposed by Julia Kristeva.[14] We will have to create, then, a system of deciphering and detection, a formalized method of decoding the baroque.

At this time, we will venture to propose some elements for a semiology of the Latin American baroque.

Intertextuality

First we will consider the incorporation of a foreign text into the text, its collage or superposition on the surface of that text, an elemental form of dialogue which does not modify any of its elements, which does not alter its *voice*: *the quotation*; next we will deal with the intermediate form of incorporation in which the foreign text is fused with the original, without imposing its characteristics, its authority of a foreign body on the surface, but constituting the most profound strata of the receptor text, tinting its webs, modifying its geology with its textures: *the reminiscence*.

The quotation. Among other baroque gestures, Gabriel García Márquez achieves one of this nature in *One Hundred Years of Solitude* when, in contrast to the homogeneity of classic language, he insists on a sentence taken directly from Juan Rulfo, incorporates into the story a character of Carpentier's—Victor Hugues of *Explosion in a Cathedral*—another of Cortázar's—Rocamadour of *Hopscotch*—another of Fuentes's—Artemio Cruz from *The Death of Artemio Cruz*—and uses a character who evidently belongs to Vargas Llosa, without counting the multiple citations in the novel—characters, sentences, and contexts—which refer to previous works by the author himself. The plastic quotations which Antonio Seguí practices in his recent panels, thus breaking their homogeneity and giving them the forms of a collage, a "loan," or of a transposition, proceed from graphic art—typograhies, various tracings, and so forth—and from the different urban codes—arrows, hands that signal, dotted lines, and traffic signs. The quotations that constitute almost all of the engravings by the painter Humberto Peña come from other plastic spaces—or ones which function as that in graphic structure; anatomical plates which interrupt the drawing of a body with their excessive pertinence and their detailed visceral precision, North American comic-strip-speech-balloons which point out the banality of the emerging sentence.

The detectable quotations in Alejandro Marcos's chalcographics possess tautological insistence as well as parodic. It is the plastic code itself which serves here as the field of extraction, of citable material: perspective, contrast of light and shadow, geometry, all the signs with which conventions denote space and volume and which habit, the same decodification through various centuries, has already naturalized. The signs are used here but only in order to reveal them as arbitrary, as pure formal simulacrum. Citations which are inscribed within the domain of the baroque because upon parodying it, deforming it, emptying it, employing it uselessly or with the aim of misrepresenting the code to which they belong, reflect only upon their own artificiality. Neither distance, nor the scale of objects in perspective, nor volume: everything "fails" here, when only the falsely natural procedures may be found which we employ to give the illusion of them, to deceive, creating the appearance of the flat bidimensional space of the canvas as a "window," that is, as an opening onto a depth. The parodic use of the code to which a work belongs, its apotheosis and mockery—the coronation and dethroning of Backtine—in the interior of the work itself are the best means for revealing that convention, that deceit.

Finally, let us indicate the quotations with which Natalio Galán breaks the serial syntax of his musical compositions by introducing in them, as surprises, some elements taken from country dances, that is, from *habaneras* and *sones*.

Reminiscence. Without cropping out on the surface of the text, but always latent, determining the archaic tone of the visible text, Cuban colonial chronicles—reviews and notices from those years—as well as books and documents—research in periodical libraries—are present, in the form of *reminiscences*—an unadorned Spanish word, recently implanted in America, and of classic origin—in certain fragments of *La situación* [The Situation], by Lisandro Otero. Similarly, it is the reminiscence of the arabesques, of the stained-glass windows and of the colonial baroque ironwork which structures the still lifes of Amelia Peláez; the scaffolding, the bone structure of the painting are determined by the ironwork designs of Creole window gratings and the circles of the *medio-puntos*, although these never appear on canvas except as a formal reminiscence which orients the volumes, accentuates or fades the colors according to the glass circles, and divides or superimposes fruits.

Intratextuality

Under this title, let us group the texts in filigree which are not introduced as allogenic elements on the apparent superficial level of the work—quotations and reminiscences—but which, intrinsic to the scriptural production, to the operation of ciphering—of tattooing—of which all writing consists, participate, consciously or not, in the very act of creation. Gramas which slip, or which the author slips, between the visible traces of the lines, writing within the writing.

Phonetic gramas. On the same level as the letters which provide a meaning in the lineal, fixed, "normal" scan of the page, but forming other possible constellations of meaning, disposed to lend themselves to other readings, to other decipherings, to allowing their *voices* to be heard by whomever wishes to listen to them, other possible organizations of these letters exist. The typographic lines, parallel and regular—determined by our lineal sense of time—to whomever wishes to transgress it, offer their phonemes to other readings which are radial, disperse, fluctuating, and galactic: a reading of phonetic gramas, the ideal practice of which is the anagram, operation par excellence of onomastic hide and seek, of satire which is artful and only perceptible to the initiated, of the laugh destined for the hermeneut; but also the crossword puzzle, the acrostic, the *bustrofedón* [in which lines are read from left to right, and right to left, alternately], and all the verbal and graphic forms of anamorphosis, of double and incompatible points of view, of cubism; forms the deceitful practice of which would be alliteration. Alliteration which proclaims and unfolds, which shows off the traces of a phonetic effort, but the result of which is only to reveal the effort itself. No other reading is necessarily hidden beneath the alliteration, its trail just turns back on itself and what its mask covers is precisely the fact that it is only a mask, an artifice and a phonetic diversion which are its own goal. In this sense, this is a tautological and parodic operation, that is, baroque.

Chromaticism, the cutting play of textures in Portuguese, explored by the Gongorine poet Gregório de Matos, has served as a basis for the phonetic mosaics of Haroldo de Campos's *Livro de ensaios-Galáxias* [Book of Galaxy-essays], alliterations which are extended into mobile pages and which always turn back on themselves, so weak is the "semantic vertebra" which unites them:

> mesma e mesmirando ensimesma emmimmesmando filipêndula
> de texto extexto / por isso escrevo rescrevo cravo no
> vazio os grifos dêsse texto os garfos / as garras e da
> fábula só fica o finar da fábula o finir da fábula o /
> finíssono da que em vazio transvasa o que mais vejo
> aqui é o papel que / escalpo a polpa das palabras do
> papel que expalpo os brancos palpos / ...
> [This use of alliteration is untranslatable]

The title *Three Trapped Tigers* is already an alliteration and one of the characters is even named *Bustrofedón*. The impulse of the writing flows from the attention which is given to the phonetic gramas. If this work—like that of Queneau—succeeds in being humorous, it is because it takes the effort of the gramas seriously. The palindrome "Dábale arroz a la zorra el abad" ["the abbot gave rice to the fox"] has been cited by Cabrera Infante. We recall his commentary on another, popular in Cuba: "Anita lava la tina" ["Anita washes the tub"].

Semic gramas. The semic grama is decipherable beneath the line of the text, behind the discourse, but neither the transgressive reading of its phonemes nor any combination of its marks, of its body on the page, lead us to it. The signified to which the manifest discourse refers has not allowed its significants to ascend to the textual surface: repressed idiom, a sentence mechanically cut out of oral language and which perhaps for that reason does not have access to the page. It is rejected, incapable of emerging from the night of ink into the white space which excludes it, to the volume of the book, but the latency of which somehow perturbs or enriches all innocent reading. Hermeneutics of the signified, *manteia* of the seme, detection of the unit of meaning.

> Todavía en aquel pueblo se recuerda el día que le sacaron Rey Lulo y tú, el mal de muerte que se había ido rápido sobre un ternero elogiado por uno de esos que dan traspiés en la alabanza.
> [In that town they still remember the day when King Lulo and you removed the evil of death which had flowed rapidly over a calf praised by one of those who blunders in praise.]

The popular expression *evil eye*—a malediction provoked in the victim by the praise which the unconscious retainer of evil bestows on it—is "hidden" beneath this sentence from *Paradiso*. Two semantic indicators lead to this idiom: "evil of death" and "blunders in praise." The "repression" which Lezama practices frequently seems exemplary to us: all of baroque literature could be read as the prohibition or the exclusion from the scriptural space of certain semes—in Góngora, for example, the name of certain supposedly maleficient animals—and which discourse codifies by appealing to the typical figure of exclusion: periphrasis. One of the supporting pillars of baroque writing—antipodal to spoken expression—would be the function of concealment, the omission, or rather the use of tacit nuclei of signification, "undesirable" but necessary, and toward which the arrows of the *indicators* converge. The anagram (to which we are led by a semiology of phonetic gramas) and the repressed idiom (to which we are led by a semiology of semic gramas) are the two periphrastic operations which are most easily detectable, but perhaps all language operations, all symbolic productions, conjure and conceal, since to name is no longer to point out, but rather to designate, that is, to signify that which is absent. Every word would have a figure as ultimate support. To speak would be to participate already in the ritual of periphrasis, inhabit that place—like language without limits—which is the baroque scene.

Syntagmatic gramas. Discourse as syntagmatic linking implies the condensation of sequences which reading operates, partial and progressive decipherings which advance by contiguity and refer us retrospectively to their totality insofar as it is closed meaning. This nucleus of signification between quotation marks which is the meaning of totality, is presented to us in baroque work, as the specification of a more vast space, the agglutination of a nebulous and infinite material which sustains it insofar as it is a category and the grammar of which the work proclaims as a guarantee procedure, as an emblem of belonging to a constituted and "major" class.

The reduced practice of this tautology is that which consists in pointing out the work within the work, repeating its title, recopying it in reduced form, describing it, employing any of the known procedures of the "mise en abîme." These tautologists forget that if these procedures were efficacious in Shakespeare or Velázquez, it is precisely because at their level they were not. As Michel Foucault points out, it was a matter of the representation of a more vast content than had been explicitly figured, specifically, in the case of *Maids of Honor*, of that of "representation."[15] The work within the work, the mirror, the *mise en abîme*, or the "Russian doll" have been converted in our time to a clumsy trick, in a formal game which only indicates a fashion and which has conserved nothing of its initial signification.

The form of tautology represented by the syntagmatic gramas is less evident. Here the "indicators," present in the linking of the sequences or in the interior articulations of these, in the major and massive units of the discourse, do not make reference to any other work nor even, of course—ingenuous tautology—to the work itself, but only to the grammar which sustains it, to the formal code which serves it as cement, as a theoretic prop, to the recognized artifice which supports it as the practice of a fiction and thus confers upon it its "authority." In *Adán Buenosayres*, Leopoldo Marechal emphasizes, modulating the most vast units of discourse according to how this grammar configures them, its pertinence to the category *writing / odyssey*. The primary structure of sequence here is, of course, that postulated in Joyce, whose "authority" as a model refers us to the entire Homeric tradition, the tradition of a story the orthogonal axes of which would be "book as journey / journey as book." But the category is never explicit, and only its vastest webs are marked, a universe in expansion, the points-events of which go along configuring possible tracks: readings of a city, of an entire day, or of a book-journey which upon being written down secretly provide this meaning: all meaning is passage. Similarly, the great units of theatrical discourse are those which in the stagings by Alfredo Rodríguez Arias—*Goddess*, by Javier Arroyuelo, or *Drácula*, by Rodríguez Arias himself, for example—function as indices of a space exterior to the play and which guarantee it from their distance and their priority. But in this case the code of authority—which would be that constituted by the explicit theatrical situations—is pointed out negatively. If in these stagings the freezing of gestures serves to underline certain key situations—those which constitute the lexicon of "the theatrical" in the bourgeois tradition: letters containing declarations of love, characters who come out on stage just when someone says that they are awaited, linked calamities, and news which leads abruptly to the "happy ending"—it is precisely to point them out as dead devices. And by enlarging them into the ludicrous through the practice of "slow motion" or "perturbing" them with a contradictory musical accompaniment—Dracula's messages are read against a background of pop music—we are able to make use of them again as nuclei of theatrical energy, as secure terminology, institutionally histrionic. The code is here used as a commonplace, its signs are thus converted into models which parody reclaims by criticizing. It is not a matter, then, of a humorous theater of themes of easy satire which are simple citations of the theater *de boulevard*, but rather of the exposition in explicit terms of a grammar, the parodic enunciation of which, revealing it in its hyperbole, deforming it, makes use of the grammar while at the same time it censures it, crowns it, and dethrones it on the space of the stage, which is carnivalesque for Rodríguez Arias; that is to say, it uses the grammar to practice its apotheosis and simultaneously its own mockery, as every baroque artist does with the lexicon which precedes it.

CONCLUSION

Eroticism

Baroque space is that of superabundance and overflow. In contrast to language which is communicative, economic, austere, and reduced to its function—to serving as a vehicle for information—baroque language takes pleasure in the supplement, in the excess, and in the partial loss of its object. Or rather, in the search, by definition frustrated, for the *partial object*. The "object" of the baroque can be specified: it is that which Freud, but especially Abraham, called the *partial object*: maternal breast, excrement—and its metaphoric equivalent: *gold*, constitutive material and symbol of all baroque—vision, voice[16], a *thing* which is always alien to everything men can comprehend, assimilate from others and of themselves, residuum which we could describe as (*a*)*lterity*, to mark the contribution to the concept made by Lacan, who precisely calls this *object (a)*.[17]

Object (a) as residual quantity, but also as fall, loss, or discrepancy between reality (the visible baroque object) and its phantasmal image (saturation without limits, asphyxiating proliferation, the *horror vacui*) presides over baroque space. The supplement—yet another spiral, that "yet another angel!" of which Lezama speaks—intervenes as verification of a failure: that which is signified by the presence of a nonrepresentable object, which resists crossing over the line of Alterity (A): bi-univocal correlation of (a), (*a*)*lice* which irritates *Alice* because the latter cannot manage to make the former pass through the looking glass to the other side.

The verification of failure does not imply the modification of the project, but rather the contrary, the repetition of the supplement; this obsessive repetition of a useless thing (since it does not have access to the ideal entity of the work) is what determines the baroque as *play*, in contrast to the consideration of the classic work as effort. The infallible exclamation which is aroused by every Churrigueresque or Aleijadinho chapel, every stanza by Góngora or Lezama, every baroque act, whether it belongs to painting or to cake decorating: "What a lot of work!" implies a barely concealed adjective: How much lost work! What a lot of play and waste! What a lot of lost effort! It is the super ego of the *homo faber*, the exist-only-for-work which is here being enunciated impugning the dalliance, the voluptuousness of the gold, the pageantry, the immoderation, and the pleasure. Play, loss, squandering, and pleasure, eroticism as an activity which is always purely playful, which is no more than a parody of the function of reproduction, a transgression of the useful, of the "natural" dialogue of bodies.

In eroticism, artificiality, the cultural, is manifested in the play with the lost object. The objective of the play is in itself and its purpose is not the conveying of a message—that of the reproductive elements in this case—but of squandering in an exercise of pleasure. Like baroque rhetoric, eroticism presents itself as the total rupture of the denotative, natural, direct level of language—somatic—like the perversion which every metaphor, every figure, implies. It is not historic chance that Saint Thomas, in the name of *morality*, advocated the exclusion of figures in literary discourse.

Mirror

Although the baroque game is devoid of any utilitarian aspect, this is not true of its structure. The structure is not a simple arbitrary and gratuitous appearance, a purposeless creation which only expresses itself, but rather the opposite, a reductive reflection of what enfolds it and transcends it; a reflection which repeats its intent—to be simultaneously totalizing and minutely detailed—but which does not succeed, like the mirror which centers the portrait of the Arnolfini couple, by Van Eyck, or like the Gongorine mirror which is "faithful although concave," in capturing the vastness of the language which circumscribes it, the organization of the universe: something in it resists it, opposes its opacity, denies it its image.

But this incomplete being of all baroque on the level of synchrony does not impede—on the contrary; because of its constant readjustments, it facilitates—the diversity of the baroque from functioning as a significant reflection of a certain diachrony: thus the European baroque and the first Latin American colonial baroque present themselves as images of a mobile and decentralized universe—as we have seen—but one which is still harmonious; they constitute themselves as bearers of a consonance: that which they have with the homogeneity and the rhythm of the exterior logos which organizes and precedes them, even if this logos is characterized by its infinitude, by the inexhaustibility of its unfolding. The ratio of the Leibnizian city lies in the infinite number of points from which it may be seen; no image can exhaust this infinitude, but a structure may potentially contain it, indicate it as potentiality—which does not mean even to support it as residue. With its authority and equilibrium, this logos marks the two epistemological axes of the baroque century: the god—the verb of infinite potentiality—of the Jesuits, and its terrestrial metaphor, the king.

On the contrary, the contemporary baroque, the neobaroque, structurally reflects the disharmony, the rupture of homogeneity, of the logos as an absolute. It is this lack which constitutes our epistemological basis. Neobaroque of disequilibrium, the structural reflection of a desire which cannot reach its object, the desire for which the logos has only organized a screen which hides this lack. The vision is no longer only infinite: as we have seen, as a partial object it has converted itself into a lost object. The trajectory—real or verbal—no longer only leaps over innumerable divisions. We know that it yearns for an end which constantly escapes it, or rather, that this trajectory is divided by this same absence around it which it displaces itself. Neobaroque: a necessarily pulverized reflection of a knowledge which knows that it is no longer "peacefully" closed within itself. Art of dethronement and of discussion.

Revolution

Syntactically incorrect because it has received incompatible allogenic elements, because it has multiplied the endless artifice of subordinate clauses until "losing the thread," the neobaroque sentence—the sentence of Lezama—reveals in its incorrectness (false citations, unfortunate "grafts" from other languages, etc.), in its not "landing on its feet," and in its loss of concordance, our loss of the *ailleurs* which was unique and concordant with our image, in summation: theological.

Baroque which, in its action of weighing, in its fall, in its "painterly" language, sometimes strident, motley, and chaotic, is a metaphor of the impugnation of the logocentric entity which until now structured it and us with its distance and its authority; baroque which refuses all restoration, which makes metaphor of the discussed order, of the judged god, of the transgressed law. Baroque of the revolution.

Notes

1. It is a matter of a move from one ideology to another, and not from an ideology to a science, that is, of an epistemological leap, like that which took place, for example, in 1845 between the ideology of Ricardo and the science of Marx.

2. Eugenio d'Ors, *Lo barrocco* (Madrid, i.e., Aguilar, 1964).

3. Pierre Charpentrat, *Le mirage baroque* (Paris: Minuit, 1967).

4. J. Rousset, *La littérature de l'âge baroque en France* (Paris, 1953).

5. Noam Chomsky, *Structures Syntaxiques* (Paris: Seuil, 1969), Chap. 1, n. 4.

6. Dámaso Alonso, *Versión en prosa de "Las Soledades" de Luis de Góngora* (Madrid: Sociedad de Estudios y Publicaciones, 1956).

7. I proposed the elements of a study of the metaphoric mechanisms in *Paradiso*, although not from the point of view of the sign, but from the point of view of the explicitly metaphoric sentence, that which uses the *como*, in "Dispersión / Falsas Notas (Homenaje a Lezama)," *Mundo Nuevo* (Paris, 1968), reprinted in *Escrito sobre un cuerpo*, (Buenos Aires: Sudamericana, 1969). In "Aproximaciones a *Paradiso*," *Imagen*, no. 40 (Caracas, January 1970), Julio Ortega has analyzed this metaphor distance from a superior lexical point of view: the "aperture" between the subject and the predicate.

8. Cf. *Zona Franca* year 3, no. 47 (Caracas, July 1967).

9. Pablo Neruda, *General Song*, part 14, poem 13.

10. Roland Barthes, *Système de la mode* (Paris: Seuil, 1967).

11. Robert Jammes, *Etudes sur l'oeuvre poétique de Don Luis de Góngora y Argote* (Bordeaux: Institut d'Etudes Ibériques, 1967).

12. Michail Backtine, *Dostoevskij* (Turin: Einaudi, 1968), Cf. the summary of this work by Julia Kristeva, *Critique* (Paris, April 1967).

13. In Borges, for example, since the parodic element is central, the quotations, exterior indicators of parody, can allow themselves falsity, can be apocryphal.

14. Julia Kristeva, *Pour une sémiologie des paragrammes*, in *Tel Quel*, no. 29 (Paris, 1967).

15. Michel Foucault, *Las palabras y las cosas* (Mexico: Siglo XXI Editores, 1968), p. 25.

16. Sight and voice = to the partial objects already designated by Freud. Lacan adds these two: cf. course on the *object* (*a*), unpublished, at the Ecole Normale de Paris.

17. On the (a)lterity and the relations between *A* and (*a*), cf. Moustafa Safouan, in *Qu'est-ce que le structuralisme?*

5 / Crisis of Realism

RAMÓN XIRAU

THE VARIOUS TYPES OF LATIN AMERICAN REALISM

It is quite exact but at the same time quite ambiguous to affirm that a crisis of realism exists in contemporary Hispanic-American literature. What do we understand by realism? Since when—if at all—does a crisis of realism exist? Is it really a matter of a crisis or simply of a renovation which is also a return to expressive forms—those of the baroque, for example—which are very typical of Hispanic literature in general and of Hispanic-American literature in particular?

The existence and endurance of a long realistic tradition in Spanish and Latin American literature are undeniable. It is a matter, of course, of the realism which was already manifest in the earthy and physical images of the *Song of the Cid* carried to extremes by the picaresque novel—in America this appeared somewhat tardily in the works of Concolorcorvo and Fernández de Lizardi—and presented throughout the social expressions of the Golden Age Spanish theater. But the Hispanic realism of the Golden Age, although it contains much that is social, is never a sociological analysis. There is little psychology in it and nothing of biology in the scientific sense of the word. This corporeal reality—present even in the mysticism of Saint Teresa—often leaps over the barriers of verisimilitude which were extolled by the French classic writers. Verification and verisimilitude are of little value in Hispanic literature of the classic era. In effect, within this real and plentiful literature, sometimes brutally stripped of its flesh, a kind of desire to violate reality and transcend it is often present. The Cid is real and concrete; let us not forget that, already a mythic hero, he wins his last battle after his death. Sancho Panza is sensible, but he is easily infected by the fantasy and the dreams of Don Quixote. Santos Vega narrates the concrete life of the pampas but, above all, he sings. We know from Ascasubi that Santos Vega was born a singer, "until he died singing." In our tradition a realism of physical presence—and for that reason of Christian tradition—is often manifest, but a realism of facts is infrequent. The Spanish Christs or the popular Christs of Mexico also suffer and bleed; their suffering and their death are incarnated symbols much more than facts.

But is this the only form of realism which appears and reappears in our literature? The answer to this question is, of course, negative. Since the last century, another type of realism has been flourishing, a realism which to a great extent comes from France and which is founded, precisely, on facts. This is the

133

realism of Balzac, Dickens, and Zola. This type of realism tends to be of social and psychological origin, and then sometimes becomes an analysis of customs and *costumbrismo*. The realist school, principally in France, is linked to the philosophical currents of the era. Auguste Comte is a contemporary of Balzac; Zola, the naturalist, is contemporary with the biological stage of positivism.

It is known that Auguste Comte thought of the evolution of humanity as beginning in a theological era—a word which in his writing meant a "magic" era—and to arrive, after passing through the metaphysical era, at the positive state, that is, at the epoch of science, of progress, and of human happiness. In a similar manner, Frazer thought that the evolution of civilizations always follows the same rhythm and the same pattern: from magic to religion, from religion to science. It is not by chance that at the very moment when Comte tried to found a "social physics," the mother of sociology, Balzac was writing "the history of a society" in *The Human Comedy* ("Letter to Hyppolite Castille," in *Complete Works*, 22:361).

The names of Benito Pérez Galdós, Leopoldo Alas, and Pereda in Spain, or of Manuel Payno, Vicente Riva Palacio, Rafael Delgado, Emilio Rabasa in Mexico, of Alberto Blest Gana in Chile, of Tomás Carrasquilla in Colombia, of Eugenio Cambaceres or Roberto J. Payró in Argentina suffice to show the influence of European realism, principally French, on our literature.

Nevertheless, and above all in Latin America, the realistic tradition of a social, psychological, or naturalistic order is of a relatively brief duration and of rather short-term liveliness. In effect, beginning with Martí, Gutiérrez, Nájera, and Rubén Darío, realism—in the very middle of the realist epoch—has already entered into crisis. The Modernists do not seek a description or an analysis of social reality. They seek a harmony which with Darío can be defined as stemming from a double tradition. Darío writes: "If there is poetry in our America, it is in the old things: in Palenke and Utatlán, in the legendary Indian and in the sensual and refined Inca, and in the great Moctezuma on his golden chair; I ask about the noble Góngora and the strongest of them all, don Francisco de Quevedo y Villegas." Aside from the evident French symbolist tradition ("and within myself I say: Verlaine..."), Darío sought in the prologue to *Prosas profanas* two roots: the Indian and that of the Hispanic baroque.

Certainly realism—especially in the novel and to a less important extent in the theater— revives in the twentieth century. The most profound form of a new realism, linked in Mexico to the mural painting of Diego Rivera and José Clemente Orozco, is that of the Mexican novel of the Revolution of 1910. All the novels are about the revolution, although they are not all revolutionary in form or in content. I refer, naturally, to the works of Mariano Azuela—especially *The Underdogs*—and to Martín Luis Guzmán—*The Eagle and the Serpent, La sombra del caudillo* [The Leader's Shadow], and *Memoirs of Pancho Villa*. I also refer to the absurd and joyful novel by Xavier Icaza—*Panchito Chapopote*—to the documentary and Indianist novel by Gregorio

López y Fuentes—*El Indio* [The Indian]—to the novel of classic terseness by Rafael F. Muñoz—*Se llevaron el cañón para Bachimba* [They Took the Cannon to Bachimba]—and to the novelistic and theatrical work of Mauricio Magdaleno—*Teatro revolucionario mexicano* [Revolutionary Mexican Theater]. I also refer to the theater of the Ibsen school, between the naturalistic and the fantastic, of that great writer Samuel Eichelbaum in Argentina, or, somewhat more recently, to the problematic theater, between the documentary and the political, of Roberto Usigli in Mexico. Finally, I refer to the novel of revolutionary intent which finds its best representatives in the Ecuadorian Jorge Icaza—*The Villagers* (*Huasipungo*), *En las calles* [In the Streets]—and in the Peruvian Ciro Alegría—*The Golden Serpent, Broad and Alien Is the World.*

Nevertheless, and despite the indisputable achievements, both literary and documentary, of these three groups of writers, realism is not the principal movement in Latin American literature any more than it is in Latin American painting since the 1930s: let us remember Tamayo, Lam, Mata, and, more recently, Morales, Fernández Muro, Yrrarázabal, Francisco Toledo Soto, Kusuno, and so many others. What predominates, beginning in the twenties and thirties, is a literature which seeks "another" reality without relinquishing the reality in which it has been born.[1]

An apparently valid objection could be made that if we are referring to realism we should include in our discussion the three great novelists of the beginning of the century. Have we forgotten Rivera, Güiraldes, and Gallegos? This question can be answered with another: to what extent is it a matter of realistic writers? Of the three, the one who seems closest to a local, national, and *costumbrista* realism is Rómulo Gallegos. But Pedro Henríquez Ureña has already pointed out that the central theme of *Doña Bárbara* is the struggle against "savage nature" which "makes man savage too." In *Cantaclaro*— Henríquez Ureña writes—"the author shows that he is more confident of the victory of man over his mute enemies and his own excesses" (*Literary Currents in Hispanic America*, Mexico: Fondo de Cultura Económica, 1949). Without a doubt, Gallegos is dealing with a natural and social reality, but it is frequently a reality which tends to be converted into symbols. One must agree with E. Anderson Imbert and E. Florit when, in describing the style and meaning of Gallegos's work, they say: "Artistic impressionism and descriptive realism appear in contrast, both in the themes of his novels... and in the double assault of his style" (*Literatura Hispanoamericana*, New York: Holt, Rinehart and Winston, 1960).

In *The Vortex*, José Eustacio Rivera, as much a poet as a novelist, creates a savage jungle reality—true protagonist of the work—the vigor of which is based, above all, on the metaphoric and imaginative force of an epic poem, real and symbolic.

The work of Ricardo Güiraldes is very different; the influences of the European vanguard movements are already evident in it. His Europeanism, nevertheless, does not remove him from distinct Argentine roots. In *Raucho* Güiraldes shows himself to be, above all, Romantic and almost Rousseauean. It is interesting to note that in this novel already, Güiraldes uses the country and the city as symbols of opposites: of good and evil, liberty and madness, peace and agony. But it seems to me that a more important constant appears from *Raucho* on: that of the cycles. It is not an exaggeration to say that *Raucho*, *Xamaica*, and *Don Segundo Sombra* are, in a certain sense, cyclic novels. In *Raucho* we move from the life of childhood and innocence in the country, to the city, to Paris, and finally, to a return to the innocence of the Argentine land. A similar cycle, although more nostalgic, is in the Jamaican journey.

In *Don Segundo Sombra*, in the words of Borges and Bioy Casares, "the gaucho has become almost elegiac" (Prologue to *Poesía gauchesca* [Gaucho Poetry], Mexico: Fondo de Cultura Económica, 1955, 1:x). Gaucho life has given way to the advance of urban and industrial life. *Don Segunda Sombra* belongs to the almost extinguished era of gaucho life. But who is this gaucho whose name is *shadow*? There is no doubt that Güiraldes tried to make Don Segundo an idealized being, half fiction and half reality. Nevertheless, there is something more than this in Güiraldes's novel. Ciro Alegría has suggested that the novel is more the history of an idea than of a man. Alegría's interpretation is not really acceptable. The fact is that Don Segundo, without ceasing to be a man, is converted into a symbol. He is *also* a symbol, he is *also* an idea. When Güiraldes writes that it is more a matter of an idea than of a man, he refers not so much to a symbol or to an abstract being as to the fact that when the boy sees Don Segundo for the first time, although he sees him only for an instant, Don Segundo appears to him to be a being worthy of admiration; not a being without flesh and blood. In fact, Don Segundo is the model of a moral life. A man of few words, lightly ironic, Don Segundo "understood life."

In *Xamaica* Güiraldes wrote: "Today is always." In *Don Segundo Sombra* the central theme is time. When the two great cycles—the boy and his teacher—separate at the end of the novel, we know that if the lesson has been well learned, the day of today is the day of always. The boy, when he follows the eternal shadow of Don Segundo, has learned to be a man as he enters into contact with the open life of the countryside. His new life as a rancher cannot change this internal person he has learned how to be. *Don Segundo Sombra*, local in its time and place, transcends the circumstance in which it takes place upon being converted fundamentally into a work of moral import.

EMPHASIS ON THE IMAGINARY AND THE FANTASTIC

During the first years of World War I, the great movements of rupture were born in Europe; what Octavio Paz has repeatedly called the "tradition of rupture" and Harold Rosemberg, very appropriately, "the tradition of the new." Dadaism, futurism, and the futurist manifesto, surrealism and the first surrealist manifesto, suprematism, and finally, ultraism in Spanish literature and soon in Argentine literature. It is not necessary to describe here that moment in which our literature is truly reborn. A search for the union of opposites in the unconscious—a clear presence of German romanticism in surrealism—the necessity of affirming the writer or the artist in general as an absolute creator. The different movements—sometimes the different fashions—follow each other vertiginously, with an accelerated mobility which comes right to the most recent artistic expressions. One of the fundamental aspects of the series of schools, subschools, and different -*isms* is the sense of time. Just as in a large part of modern life and owing to the influence of new technologies upon art and letters, the sense of the future is made more acute. An extreme case of this veneration of the future—a good example also of the denial of the future—is that which is demonstrated by futurism when it seeks the "perpetual motion machine" only to find, in the works of Marinetti, Carrà, and Boccioni, that perpetual motion is supreme static.

The movements which begin in Europe are echoed in Latin America until they blend and establish orientations of their own: creationism, ultraism, stridentism....In all of them, there is an element of play. In the best representatives of each, there exists a deep necessity to create new realities which transcend the everyday world. Many are the writers who appear in the twenties and with them—especially if we see the unity of purpose and of style of Spanish and Latin American writers—a new Golden Age of our literature is born. In Hispanic America participants in this movement of renovation are Neruda as well as Borges, Villaurrutia as well as Vallejo, Huidobro as well as José Gorostiza, Westphalen as well as Coronel Urtecho, Lezama Lima as well as Octavio Paz.

In this study I will discuss the meaning of the new Latin American literature in two stages. The first will be symbolized here by the work of Vicente Huidobro, Pablo Neruda, and Jorge Luis Borges; the second, principally, by the works of Octavio Paz, Julio Cortázar, Carlos Fuentes, Gabriel García Márquez, Juan Rulfo, and Lezama Lima.[2]

Three Great Adventures

Vicente Huidobro, Pablo Neruda, and Jorge Luis Borges represent three of the great adventures—three of the great fountainheads—of the new literary spirit. The first of them, the necessity of founding an absolute creation; the second, the attempt to unite magic, subconscious revelations, and revolution; the third, the necessity of creating a world which is fantastic, desired, and impossible.

Vicente Huidobro began to develop his ideas about poetic creation when, in 1913, he founded, in answer and as a challenge to Rubén Darío, the magazine *Azul*. Nevertheless, his first poetic ideas were more of an announcement of nonconformity than clear expositions of a personal theory.

As early as 1914, Huidobro writes in his manifesto *Non serviam*: "We have sung to Nature (which matters not at all to her). We have never created our own realities, as she does or did in times past, when she was young and filled with creative impulses." Twice in his manifesto he mentions the word *creation*. Huidobro announces his future poetic ideal. In 1916, when he gives a lecture at the Ateneo Hispano of Buenos Aires, he affirms: "The entire history of art is nothing more than the history of the evolution of the man-mirror into the man-god." The poet has been the imitator of nature. From now on he will be the creator of new poetic realities which stem from the spirit and not from the world. "To make a poem just as nature makes a tree"—such is the intention of creationism. Huidobro, now living in Paris, knowing and sometimes imitating Apollinaire, makes a place for himself in the vanguard of French literature. Huidobro's vanguardism, however, differs from futurism and surrealism. He does not believe, with the futurists, in the novelty of the poem of gymnastic feats, of slapping blows, of thumping fists ("Let Mr. Marinetti go read the *Odyssey* and the *Iliad*"). He does not believe, with the surrealists, that the expression of the subconscious through automatic writing can be a source of poetic creation because poetry is an act of thought and "the word *thought* already implies control." In the tradition of Mallarmé, of Rimbaud, and of the early Rilke, Huidobro believes in poetry as absolute creation. Like them, and above all like the Mallarmé of "Igitur" and of "Un coup de dés," he thinks we should abolish reality in order to re-create it. The poet is converted, in effect, into the "man-god."[3]

Let us see how the destiny of the poetry of Huidobro is fulfilled, that is, his concept of the world, in the most ambitious and perhaps the most beautiful of his poems, *Altazor*.

Altazor is a poem which fits into a category of contemporary poetry which tends to convert itself into the epic of consciousness and of subjectivity. In this sense *Altazor* is similar to St. John Perse's *Anabase*, Eliot's *The Waste Land*, Ezra Pound's *Cantos*, Valéry's *Narcisse*, or José Gorostiza's *Muerte sin Fin* [Death Without End]. The theme of *Altazor* is death. Right from the first stanzas, we are present at a fall into a space which the poet declares empty:

> Altazor morirás…
> …Cae
> cae eternamente
> cae al fondo del infinito
> cae al fondo de ti mismo.

> [Altazor you will die… / …He falls / falls eternally / falls to the bottom of the infinite / falls to the bottom of you yourself.]

The fall of Altazor is an internal fall, a collapse of the soul. Not an abstract soul; concretely, and also solipsistically, it is the soul of Altazor-Huidobro:

> Justicia que has hecho de mí Vicente Huidobro
> se me cae el dolor de la lengua y las alas marchitas.

[It is just that you have made of me Vicente Huidobro / the pain of my tongue and of my shriveled wings falls from me.]

Nevertheless, Huidobro tries, in direct imitation of Whitman, to be the voice of the universe. Faced with nothing, faced with emptiness, faced with the extinct world, the poet wants to jolt himself with "blasphemies and cries." For an instant, he feels proud in the world created by his imagination: "Soy todo el hombre" ["I am all man"]. The poet wishes to feel terrestrial, immoderate, and human. It seems that the poet has succeeded in fusing himself with the very heart of reality: it is as much his own being as the world he creates. The emptiness seems to be annulled:

> Soy desmesuradamente cósmico
> las piedras, las plantas las montañas
> me saludan las abejas y las ratas
> los leones y las águilas
> los astros los crepúsculos las albas
> los ríos y las selvas me preguntan.

[I am immoderately cosmic / the rocks the plants the mountains / the bees and the rats greet me / the lions and the eagles / the stars the dusks the dawns / the rivers and the forests ask me.]

But the poet knows that this world is *his* world, that this reality is *his* creation; he knows that nothing exists except his hallucinated lucidity as a visionary without an object of vision. He wants to become the All, and he wishes this ("the nostalgia of being clay and stone or God"), he leaves open the possibility of anguish, "anguish of the absolute and of perfection." The poet can no longer believe in the truth of his world. He is left only with the play of images and of sounds: "la golonniña, la golongira, la golonlira, la golonbrisa, la golonchilla."[4] The moment of death has come. The world "is slowly becoming petrified." The death of God leads to the death of man; the poem annuls poetry and annuls philosophy in the same way that Gorostiza's *Muerte sin Fin*—very much like Huidobro's *Altazor*—denies the world, denies plants, animals, and inert beings, denies the poet who denied the world created by him.

In a very general sense, four forms and four contents may be discerned in the poetry of Neruda. The first is constituted by the sometimes playful, sometimes nostalgic romantic poetry, represented by the *Twenty Love Songs and a Song of Despair* of 1934. The second—certainly the most personal—begins with *Residence on Earth* and reappears in the *Elementary Odes*. The third is found in the epic spirit of the *General Song*; the fourth in the poems of a political and propagandistic nature: *Residence on Earth III* and a good part of the *General Song*.

If we limit ourselves to the two styles or epochs of greatest value, vigor, and influence, we must refer to the first *Residence on Earth* and to the *General Song*.

Residence on Earth was written during an era when surrealism had made itself felt in Spanish-language poetry. It would be easy—and not altogether false—to consider *Residence on Earth* as a surrealist poem. What attracts Neruda to surrealism is a type of writing which delves into the unconscious: oneiric writing and that of oneiric temptations. In effect, it is almost always impossible to distinguish dream from reality in *Residence on Earth*. The principal symbols used by Neruda (exhaustively analyzed by Amado Alonso in *Poesía y estilo de Pablo Neruda*) fit into the general category of the "material concretization of the immaterial" (Amado Alonso), those of roses, bees, doves, swallows, bells, grapes, the elements, sex, dampness, rain. All these symbols, to repeat it with Amado Alonso, are "forms of the objectification of the subjective and of the subjectification of objectivity." It was necessary to point out these elements. If we generalize a little more, we will be led to say that the poetry of *Residence on Earth* mixes, in a manner which recalls what the Stoics called *total blending*, the external and the internal, the subjective and the objective, and that this total blending takes place in the material. This Neruda, who believes in the existence of a single substance, and in a sort of communion which is above all a fusion in the total "density," underwent a spiritual crisis which led him to change his methods and style. This crisis began before the Spanish civil war, but became particularly evident after that war, when Neruda became a member of the Communist party. He changed into a social—sometimes pamphleteering—poet and eventually became the epic poet of the *General Song*. The *General Song* also reveals the writer who is pledged to certain ideas, the writer of actions and words, the civic poet. Most of all, it reveals the poet of the land—the poet of the Hispanic-American land—who does not commune with nature but rather contemplates it in order to paint vast and splendid frescoes.

Close to surrealism at the beginning, Neruda becomes a poet who is capable, in his best moments, of singing a kind of monism of living matter, of extolling a total unity of the organic universe.

The universe of Jorge Luis Borges presents two opposite and complementary faces. The first, fantastic and fictitious, is offered to us, above all, in the essays and "fictions";[5] the second, principally, although not exclusively, in the poems.[6]

Borges has declared his "incredulous and persistent fascination with theological difficulties." One of his characters, Buckley, "disbelieves in God, but wishes to demonstrate to the nonexistent God that mortal men are capable of conceiving the world."[7] The inhabitants of Tlön have rigorously applied the phenomenalism of Hume without forgetting the central ideas of *The World as Will and Idea*. The reality of Tlön is never objective. Whatever we know about it is given to us in a "series of independent acts." As in the nominalism of Hume—or of Occam—the world is reduced to a series of impressions which, when associated, form general ideas. Psychic mechanisms, reduced to the "mental chemistry" of which Taine spoke, make the spirit a vacuum where ideas have no relation to any real referent. So it is in

"Tlön, Uqbar, Orbis Tertius." The logical consequence of this radical (and "played") phenomenalism is: the world is reduced to nothing. The universe is reduced to a mere series of words, or as Borges prefers to say: "Perhaps universal history is the history of the various restatements of a few metaphors" ("The Sphere of Pascal"). This nominalism permits Borges to deny the objective world. It also permits him to replace theology and metaphysics by his fantastic fictions which acquire the value of reality. What we could call the *fantastic metaphysics* of Borges can be reduced to a few propositions:

1. The world is unreal or merely subjective. "There is the classic example of the doorway which existed while a beggar visited it, but which was lost from sight when he died" ("Tlön, Uqbar, Orbis Tertius").
2. The world is a metaphor. Examples abound, such as that already quoted from "The Sphere of Pascal"; the wall of China as desired isolation.
3. The world as a single unit. But can personal identity exist if everything is the same, is one?
4. Time does not exist. Various refutations of time are in *Discusión* [Discussion], *Historia de la eternidad* [A History of Eternity], and *Other Inquisitions*.

These propositions are not independent of each other: they are united by an idea, which I will explain briefly.

If time is cyclical, chronological time ceases to exist; each instant is eternity eternally repeated. "All men are Shakespeare." A circular world is also a tautological world and, as such, is in a condition of constant doubt. World, plant, earth, and man are reducible to zero. Everything coincides in a hallucinating transfiguration of nullifications and unrestrained growths. The world can be and should be reduced to metaphor. Reality is verbal in the same way that "the greatness of Quevedo is verbal" (*Other Inquisitions*).

In order to negate the world, Borges uses nominalism. To deny it and reduce it to unity, circle, and metaphor, Borges had to refute time. Thanks to this refutation, which is logically possible but vitally improbable, Borges establishes his fictions. The time we refute is the time we live in. My acts negate all refutation of time; my life affirms me as temporal.

To deny temporal succession, to deny the self, and to deny the astronomical universe are apparent desperations and secret consolations. Our destiny (as opposed to the hell of Swedenborg and the hell of Tibetan mythology) is not terrifying because it is unreal; it is terrifying because it is irreversible and made of iron. Time is the substance of which I am made. Time is a river which carries me away, but I am the river; it is a tiger which devours me, but I am the tiger; it is a fire which consumes me, but I am the fire. The world, unfortunately, is real; I unfortunately, am Borges (*Other Inquisitions*).

The circular ruins disintegrate; the fictions collapse, even when they endure in their astonishing, dreamed beauty. We are faced with life and, from within life, we know that life is death.

Nevertheless, in Borges's poems we frequently find a way of confronting reality which is very different from that of the essays and fictions. Borges's poetry sings of the neighborhoods on the outskirts of the city. There where Buenos Aires becomes the countryside, the poet feels that he is located on the city limits of life. A life of sensitivity and a life of hope. The city opens to the wide pampa, to the open spaces of a concrete and tangible pampa, in harmony with the senses. Borges no longer encounters the Pascalian horror of the vacuum. He finds his land, humble, sacred:

> Ví el único lugar de la tierra
> donde puede andar Dios a sus anchas.

[I saw the only place on earth / where God can walk at his ease.]

The vision of the outskirts of Buenos Aires is opposed to the vision of the fictions. The land is now tenderness and innocence:

> Olorosa como un mate curado
> la noche acerca agrestes lejanías.

[Sweet-scented as a dried herb / the night approaches rustic distances.]

And the pampa, for Borges as for Güiraldes, like the country and the mountains of Rousseau, is the image of natural goodness:

> Pampa
> Eres buena de siempre como el Avemaría.

[Pampa / You are good as always like the Hail Mary.]

In a reference which seems directed to the Borges of the fictions, to his own dreams of a world which is magic, unreal, and "consoling," Borges writes: "As while we think we are praising existence, we are praising sleep and indifference...only living exists."

The Borges of the fictions, of the essays, may be contrasted to the Borges who lives, probably religiously, in the land where it was his lot to be born. Destroyer of chronological times, creator of magical spheres, founder of beautiful and fallible eternities, he is also the poet of the real and simple land, the admirer of José Hernández, of Hilario Ascasubi and of Evaristo Carriego.

A Search for Meaning

While in Huidobro we witness the attempt at an absolute creation, in Neruda we find penetration into a dreamed and physical matter. While in Borges we see the coexistence of two parallel realities (fantasy and the world of the poet's senses), in Octavio Paz we find a search for meaning which transcends history without renouncing it.

The experience of solitude serves Octavio Paz as a point of departure, just as it served the poets of the *Contemporáneos* [Contemporaries] group—José Gorostiza, Xavier Villaurrutia, and Salvador Novo. The surrealist experience—even when Paz is not in agreement with automatic writing—also serves as a starting point. In fact, in his poetry and in his essays, Octavio Paz goes beyond solitude and the experience of the surrealists.

In *The Labyrinth of Solitude*, Paz defines solitude as "the nostalgia of space." Effectively, space centers us, the body that we are in the presence of things that are. That which is external does not belong to the world of solitude. It belongs, rather, to this world that Paz defines as "indifferent to the vain quarrel of men." But when the subject absorbs the world and makes it part of its own spirit, things themselves and the space which contains them disappear; all is diluted in the passing subject ("there is always an air of transience") which contemplates its own self and of which the world is simply a metaphor.

Society is an original and originating experience for Octavio Paz. But Paz himself writes, in *The Labyrinth of Solitude*: "Universal history is now a common task. And our labyrinth is that of all men."

For Octavio Paz, solitude is not a goal, but a point of departure in a movement toward communication, communion, and community. In order to know the meaning which these words have in Paz's work, it is necessary, first, to answer two questions: What is the origin of human solitude? Which are the privileged expressions which allow us, even within our solitude, an authentic participation in the community of all men?

Paz conceives of man as an initially complete being. But this total being is almost always presented to us as divided, fallen, and broken in its center. Half beings, incomplete, and wounded by time, we search for the "lost half" which we must find if we wish to be complete men. The fulfillment of our being is manifested in four privileged experiences: the poetic image, love, the sacred, and the meaning which resides where the verbal or intellectual senses do not reach.

The poetic image appears as a revelation or, as Octavio Paz says in *The Bow and the Lyre*, like an epiphany of our unity which is above and beyond all contradictions. "The poet," Paz writes, "names things; these are feathers, those are stones, rough, hard, impenetrable, sun yellow or moss green: heavy stones. And the feathers, feathers: light." When the poet says "the stones are feathers," "the image is scandalous because it defies the principle of contradiction. When the identity of the opposites is enunciated, the foundations of our way of thinking are attacked" (*The Bow and the Lyre*). In our daily life—and in our logical thought as well—we distinguish between "one" and the "other." What the poetic experience tells us is that the "one" *is* the "other," that oppositions have ceased, that we are in open communication with ourselves and with the world around us. Thus Octavio Paz can write that poetry is "an entrance into being."

Paz's poetry contains images of destruction, solitude, and death. Mixed in with them, a culmination of them, Paz achieves images which are symbols of this unity and of this recovered communion. At its zenith, the sun does not allow shadows or alterations. All is presence. Thus in "Himno entre ruinas" [Hymn Among Ruins]:

> Coronado de sí el día extiende sus plumas,
> ¡ Alto grito amarillo,
> caliente surtidor en el centro de un cielo
> imparcial y benéficio!...
> ...Todos es dios.

[Self-crowned the day extends its plumes, / Loud yellow cry, / hot fountainhead in the center / of an impartial and beneficent sky!... / ...All is god.]

Similar to the poetic experience and, like it, unifying, are the experiences of love and the sentiment of the sacred. In love "all that is tied to the earth by material love...rises and soars" (*The Violent Season*). And here, as in the image, we return to the experience of the unity of opposites:

> todo es presencia, todos los siglos son este presente.

[all is presence, all the centuries are this present.]

In love we live "with pronouns intertwined." The *I* now can only realize itself in the *you* and the *you* acquires full meaning in the *I*. We are finally *us*. In love, more than in any other human experience, we find and we are "the lost half."

The experience of the "other shore," of the sacred, is of amorous origin and poetic nature. Like love, the sacred presents itself first behind ambiguous and even contradictory guises: it attracts us and it repels us. But beyond the contradictions, once the sacred has become experience, once we have passed through the "somber portal," "the experience of the other" culminates in the communion which is "the experience of the one."

In Octavio Paz's recent work—principally in this extraordinary poem which is called *Blanco*, and in the essays of *Conjunctions and Disjunctions*—a new experience gives us the sense of community. In part this experience—based on a cyclic time Paz has offered since *Sun Stone*—is a union of opposites in the eternity of the eternal return, Venusian cycle of the pre-Cortesian religions. But Octavio Paz finds the true revelation, the true epiphany, in a silent meaning which is beyond words, in a poetic existence which without a doubt has its roots in his work but which revealed itself especially during his years in India. The real meanings are beyond our senses. Is this the unreality of the primogenial experience? It is not so in *Blanco* where the basis is the Spirit. From cycle to cycle, from eroticism to word, from love to earth, from word to flower, from earth to flower and word.

El espíritu
Es una invención del cuerpo
El cuerpo
Es una invención del mundo
El mundo
Es una invención del Espíritu.

[The spirit / Is an invention of the body / The body / Is an invention of the world / The world / Is an invention of the Spirit.]

Octavio Paz, in whom poetry is never disembodied, in whom poetry often acquires social tones and intonations, is essentially the poet and the writer of the "conversion" to another reality which is more real than the reality of appearances. Paz tells us that life has meaning if we are capable of thrusting ourselves out of our very selves in order to find ourselves again in others. Is this a form of self-knowledge? It is more; it is to spill ourselves out into the world and convert into what we truly are:

Y el río remonta su curso, repliega sus velas, recoge
sus imágenes y se interna en sí mismo.
(*The Violent Season*)[8]

[And the river flows back upstream, refolds its sails, gathers up its images and retreats into itself.]

Reality, Fantasy, Image, and Myth

From among recent narrators, I select those who are most concerned with the problem of reality and fantasy. My insistence on the work of Rulfo and Lezama Lima is due as much to the value of their respective works as to the fact that they present, like few other writers, extreme cases in which fantasy and reality fuse to the point of forming a unique and total world.[9]

The work of Julio Cortázar intermingles humor, fantasy, irony, psychological analysis, impressionism, and, in recent years, social concerns. *Hopscotch*, Cortázar's best novel, multiplies perspectives and windows to living and dreamed characters. *Cronopios* and *famas* are certainly beings from another world, from an imaginary world, but they are, above all—a recollection of Swift?—a satiric anthill view of our world transformed into fantasy. Paris slogans of 1968 give *Ultimo round* [Last Round]—in its first floor section—touches of reality and of a surreality which sprouted in the atmosphere of those revolutionary days. Mysterious disappearances often recall the "Great Game" of René Daumale, Gilbert Lecomte, and Sima. A sentence of Lenin's in *Ultimo round* anchors journeys around the world, eighty days and rounds of oneiric boxing in Cortázar's last work: "We must dream, but only under condition of believing seriously in our dreams, of examining real life with attention, of confronting our observations with our dream, of scrupulously fulfilling our fantasy." Preoccupied by the critical situation of modern man, Cortázar writes: "Incapable of political action, I do not renounce my solitary vocation of culture, my obstinate ontological search, games of imagination on its most vertiginous planes; but all this does not revolve around itself, no longer has anything to do with the comfortable humanism of the Western mandarins. In the most gratuitous things I could write, there will always be a desire for contact with the historical present of man, a participation in his long march toward that which is best in himself as collectivity and humanity" (*Ultimo round*).

At a similar crossroads, with greater political intent, is the work of Carlos Fuentes, as established in its criticism of Mexican life as in the "sacred zones" of myths. Carlos Fuentes began his career with a collection of stories—*Los días enmascarados* [Masked Days]—which owed as much to surrealism as to Gothic tales. A similar fantastic tradition may be found in the beautiful short novel, *Aura*. In *Where the Air Is Clear* and *The Death of Artemio Cruz*, Fuentes writes critical, satirical, and revolutionary literature. In his more recent novels, and especially in *Sacred Zone*, Fuentes interweaves reality and fantasy. Whence the mystery? In the very appearance of things, in their evidence, in the clarity of fantasies, in the visible. We are part of a world of mutations and of transfigurations. Not only does the novel lack development in the traditional sense of the word; what happens is that "nothing develops, everything is transfigured." Fuentes writes—I don't know if he is consciously acting *El gran teatro del mundo* [The Great World Theater]—"Do you also think we are acting?" Is it acting that we see in Ulysses, Telemachus, the Eumenides, Claudia, baroque frescoes, Artemio Cruz, the exaggerations of *Where the Air Is Clear*, and in men and gods? This question has only one definitive answer. Fuentes writes: "All this could be a performance—a rehearsal—of something" (*Sacred Zone*).

Gabriel García Márquez's *One Hundred Years of Solitude* is an extraordinary novel. Jack Richardson has written: "[García Márquez]...whose art...is epic at a time when so much of what is interesting in literature belongs to the idiosyncratic and consciously complex—("Gabriel García Márquez, Masterwork," *New York Review of Books*, 14, no. 6 [1970]). We come to the end of the novel. Aureliano Buendía discovers that the entire novel was written by Melquíades, one of the gypsies who appear at the beginning of the novel in the thoughts of the first of the Buendías. We read: "Aureliano could not move. Not because he was paralyzed by amazement, but because in that prodigious instant he witnessed the revelation of the definitive keys to the parchments that had been ordered in the time and space of men: *The first of the race is tied to a tree and the last is being eaten by ants.*" We know conclusively that the entire novel is a vast, tragic allegory of the human condition. It is also something more specific: the history of a whole family that passes from innocence to destruction; the creation of a mythic place—the center of the world as in all magic histories—which is Macondo; the fall of men; the exploitation and the corruption of a concrete town in Spanish America; and the presence of the woman—woman-mother, mother-founder—called *Ursula*. *One Hundred Years of Solitude* is the novel of a land and of a family, of the earth and of the men, of the progressively infernal cycles which lead from paradise and innocence to death. Magic predominates in the novel; a magic made of earth and dreams which is also myth and legend more than it is history. Perhaps what is most extraordinary about *One Hundred Years of Solitude* is its capacity to narrate with a realism which is precise and sometimes abstract until reality is transformed into legend without legend losing the physical directness of reality.

It would be unjust not to mention a few of the narrators of the new generation here: we think of Mario Vargas Llosa, in whom may be discerned the influence of Faulkner—as in other novelists of Hispanic America—and who reveals, above all, a powerfully imaginative style in which, as in Fuentes, and García Márquez, social themes and imaginary forms are mixed with a preponderance, in Vargas Llosa, of the social; we think of José Donoso, a writer of a strict classical style and romantic vocation who has given us, in his novels and fine short stories, psychological analysis as well as exaggerated violence recounted with an elegance that few recent writers manage; we think of Cabrera Infante, a writer who, influenced by Joyce, is concerned like few others with the linguistic structure of his work; among the youngest writers, we think of Juan García Ponce, Vicente Leñero, Gustavo Sainz, Severo Sarduy, Salvador Elizondo, Néstor Sánchez, and many others whose works are filled with promise.

Nevertheless, two novels, more than any others, express the problem of the relationship between reality and fantasy: *Pedro Páramo*, by Juan Rulfo, and *Paradiso*, by José Lezama Lima.

Juan Rulfo has published only two books: *The Burning Plain and Other Stories* and the novel *Pedro Páramo*. Rulfo's style, both in the stories and in the novel, fuses popular language with the poetic. In his work the fantastic and the real are blended to such an extent that on some occasions reality and fantasy are practically indistinguishable. All of his work is shaped by the common denominator of solitude and death. In "They Gave Us the Land," a group of men tries, very realistically, to live in a desert, and they find themselves condemned to poverty and death; in "Tell Them Not to Kill Me" we witness the violent killing of an old man by the son of someone he killed thirty-five years before; in "Luvina" we are in a town where the only thing that exists is the wind. "Talpa" recounts a prilgrimage. But who are the pilgrims? Tanilo, who is on the point of death, his wife and his brother, who is his wife's lover. We know that they are dragging Tanilo through mountains and valleys and dusty roads so that he will die faster. In "Anacleto Morones," idolatry and black humor live side by side.

It is true that all of Rulfo's stories refer to realities that are physical, historical, or social. But they are all written in the first person, and they all acquire a confessional tone as though the characters had to flee from their solitude and communicate it to their readers. Rulfo's stories tend to "happen" in the present, and in almost all of them, sometimes repeatedly, the word *memory* appears. At crucial moments of their lives, characters must remember the past, just when they would most like to forget it.

Time is closed in all of Rulfo's work. The future is hermetically sealed. Only the present remains. In this lies the deep sadness of Rulfo's stories; and in this, too, their fatalism. In a word, when only the present matters, when the present can no longer open into the future, destiny presides over all because liberty implies the possibility of a future. Rulfo's characters, determined by what they have done, are immobile in the face of their destiny. With the exception of the funny story "Anacleto Morones," there is never an exit in Rulfo's tales.

The negation of time when time is made into a pure past is only partial—except in the case of "Luvina"—in Rulfo's stories. The radical negation of time, on the other hand, is found in the marvelously real and imaginary novel, the precursor of so many recent novels (including, perhaps, that of García Márquez), *Pedro Páramo*.

What is the plot of *Pedro Páramo*? In the classic sense of the word, the novel does not have a plot. It has been said that what happens in *Pedro Páramo* could take place during the course of years, months, or instants. Here the divisions of time lack importance because at the moment the novel begins, the characters are already dead. In the first version of his novel, Rulfo had used the provisional title *Los murmullos* [The Whispers]. In reality, it is a novel made of echoes, of resonances. It is a novel of a rockbound past in which the characters were (when?) real and of physical substance; *Pedro Páramo* is the novel of a fantastic memory, magic and real. The appearance of the novel—and of Juan Rulfo's stories—is realistic; its true substance is that of a dream.

It is naturally unjust to consider Lezama Lima only as the novelist of *Paradiso* (1968). Lezama Lima is part of a tradition of Western literature which has its first masters in Juan Ramón Jiménez and Valéry. Since his youth, Lezama has been as interested in Cuban life and literature as Emilio Ballagas, Alejo Carpentier, or Nicolás Guillén, even when his work does not seek direct inspiration in Afro-Cuban or Afro-Caribbean poetry. A founder, together with Rodríguez Feo, of the magazine *Orígenes* [Origins]—around which forms the group of great Cuban writers of today: Cinto Vitier, Eliseo Diego—Lezama, ever since "Muerte de Narciso" was written in 1937 when the poet was twenty-seven years old, has been one of the best poetic voices in the Spanish language. "Muerte de Narciso" [Narcissus' Death], a poem which is hermetic, difficult, precise, and as hard as rock crystal, participates in the "return to Góngora" which was initiated by Alfonso Reyes, and Dámaso Alonso, the Spanish poets of the twenties. The same return, which becomes increasingly personal and also more and more baroque, appears in *Enemigo rumor* [Enemy Rumor], *Aventuras sigilosas* [Stealthy Adventures], and in the mature and clear book entitled *Dador* [Giver]. Lezama's essays, which are sometimes ultrabaroque, present a theological-poetical vision of literature and of life.

Particularly distinguished among them are " Sierpe de Don Luis de Góngora" [Descendants of Don Luis de Góngora], "Las imágenes posibles" [Possible Images], and the difficult book—"only the difficult is stimulating," writes Lezama Lima—which is *La expresión americana* [The American Expression].

How can Lezama Lima be placed? Eminently as a poet; as a baroque poet, and as a Catholic poet. Any reading of *Paradiso* which does not take these dimensions of Lezama Lima's work into account will be superfluous or, at the least, superficial.

In *Suma de conversaciones* [Summation of Conversations] (Armando Álvarez Bravo, prologue to *Orbita de Lezama Lima*, Havana: Colección Orbita, 1966), Lezama's poetical-religious intent is clearly expressed. Poet of metaphor and of image, Lezama Lima is the poet of the carnal nature of both. The image is presented as the "reality of the invisible world"; the metaphor, made of opposing tensions, leads to similarites. The poetic world is a world made "in image and resemblance"; it is also the *creation* of images and resemblances. Poetry is thus the revelation of divinity. How can the truth and the veracity of the images and the "resemblances" between the universe of man and God be proved? Lezama Lima, more Augustinian than Thomist, more Patristic than Aristotelian, renounces proofs. A man of faith, close to Tertullian, Lezama knows that there is no proof other than the rich cargo of images and resemblances which man has constructed and which man continues to construct: from the fabulous eras to the fables of the present. The words of Tertullian should be applied—and Lezama Lima does this—to his poetry: "It is true because it is impossible." And Lezama Lima comments: "From this sentence we can derive two paths or poetic methods: the credible because it is incredible (the death of the Son of God) and the true because it is impossible (the Resurrection). To man existing-for-death, which Heidegger announced in *Being and Time*, Lezama substitutes—incredibly; that is, as a question of imaginative faith—man as "existing for the resurrection."

This is the *universe*—seldom is this word used as exactly as it is here— which unfolds in swirls, metaphors, and narrations in *Paradiso*, a work which is laboriously written and perfectly elaborated. It would be useless to attempt here to untangle all the references, allusions, processes, and procedures of this paradisiacal and infernal novel, of this novel which above all transmutes the infernal, the evil of the world, into the living flesh of the image of the resurrections. *Paradiso* is one of these great summas which Lezama sought in *La expresión americana*. Based upon the details of life in Havana during the first decades of the century, *Paradiso* narrates innocence and violence, ingenuousness and sexual deviations, delves deeply into evil, depravation, and horror, mocks history and substitutes myth in its place. But here it is a matter of a believed and believable myth, a myth which is the truth of history. Supremely luminous curves, fruits of the tropics, and gnostic discussions (after all, are not the two most agile, sometimes the most destructive, characters in the novel named Frónesis and Foción?) enrich this altarpiece made of filigree and depths, this altarpiece where luminous Saint George becomes Saint George-the-Almost-Malignant in order to be reborn as the luminous Saint George. The characters of *Paradiso* incarnate in their images and particular resemblances in order to incarnate finally in the Image and the Resemblance of totality. At the end of the novel, it turns back on itself, it returns us to its tides, to its mournful and salvaging games, to a human condition which is fallen and recoverable: "The Malignant One will find himself then on the day of the Last Judgment, faced with the Resurrection." The Saint George of light will have triumphed over the darkness of the Saint George who was hideously imagined by blind Manichaean wills.

Lezama Lima does not renounce this reality; as a man, and without believing in absolutes of history, science, progress, or existence, he knows that life is of this world. But the historical reality, the reality which is credible because it is visible, is only real because of that which is incredible and silent, because of That One toward whom images point.

THE "OTHER" REALITY OF CONTEMPORARY ART

It is easy to see, in some of our best writers of today, that what was understood as realism (*costumbrismo*, local and localist literature, documentary literature) is clearly in crisis in Latin America. If we consider especially the poets—in whom realism is seldom a decisive factor—we would have to count the majority of great Latin American poets of this century among the inventors and discoverers of imaginary worlds. In fact, we would have to so count most Latin American poets throughout the course of Hispanic American history. Among the discoverers of "another" reality—imaginary, fantastic, or surreal—are López Velarde, Gabriela Mistral, Delmira Agustini, Alfonsina Storni, Baldomero Fernández Moreno, Mariano Brull, Alfonso Reyes, César Vallejo, Xavier Villaurrutia, José Gorostiza, Coronel Urtecho, Carrera Andrade, Westphalen (with the Spaniard Larrea the only two authentic surrealists in Spanish language poetry), Molinari, González Lanuza, Francisco Luis Bernárdez, Cintio Vitier, Ida Gramcko, and Alí Chumacero. Among the youngest are José Emilio Pacheco, Homero Aridjis, Roberto Juarroz, and Alejandra Pizarnik.... All poetry tends toward the image which Vico already saw as a reduced myth. All poetry tends toward myth. What is a myth? Few answers seem to me as clear as J. J. Bachofen's already classic one: "Myth is the exegesis of symbols. It develops in a series of apparently interconnected actions which the symbol incorporates into one unit. Myth is like a philosophic discourse in that it divides the idea into a series of connected images and allows the reader to deduce the ultimate consequences." In other words, myth—like the image in Paz or in Lezama Lima—places us on the limit of the sayable, on the shores of silence, on the brink of the meanings which words establish without completely saying them. All images, all myths, are allusive. The language which the majority of the great writers of Hispanic America use today is a language where poetry is the true motor and in which the end pursued may be—even when incorporated, even when corporeal—magic or religious.

Rather than referring to recollections of surrealism or to a continuation of the *-isms* of the twenties, it is necessary to speak of a literature—also of a painting, of a sculpture—which those movements made possible. Art which is not contented with describing reality but which searches, beyond actions and customs—and often making us see customs and actions more clearly, always without abandoning the reality which gives birth to art—for the underlying basis for these manifestations.

American reality, the "American experience," as Lezama Lima calls it, is revealed in the present writing of Latin America as both clearly localizable— Macondo, for example, could not be physically or imaginarily other than where it is, in an American space—and as universal.

I risk the following hypothesis. Claude Lévi-Strauss distinguishes very clearly in *The Savage Mind* between religion and magic. The first consists in the "humanization of natural laws"; the second in the "naturalization of human actions." A good part of Latin American literature, the value of which must be judged principally, of course, from a literary point of view, is inclined toward magic or religious interpretations without this implying necessarily that the writers of Hispanic America hold one or another particular belief. The tendency which, very generally, may be called *religious*, is presented partially in the works of Borges, Huidobro, Paz, and, above all, in the work of Lezama Lima; the magic tendency appears, perhaps principally, in Neruda's *Residence on Earth*, in the marvels of *One Hundred Years of Solitude*, in the distanced actions of Fuentes's last works. More religious or more clearly magical, the writers of Latin America, as was seen by Reyes, by Edmundo O'Gorman in relation to the history of the conquest, live a reality which is at least to some extent "invented" and discovered day by day. The role which they have assumed is precisely that of continuing to invent and discover this reality which is in the process of being made, of being constructed, and which they help to build.

In 1932 Alfonso Reyes wrote in *A vuelta de correo* [By Return Mail]: "The only way of being successfully nationalistic consists in being generously universal, because a part is never understood without the whole. Of course, knowledge and education must begin with a part; thus 'universal' is never confused with the elimination of the particular. Latin American literature of today is aiming vigorously toward this rooted universality."

Notes

1. Since, in any case, Joyce's *Finnegans Wake* is only half intelligible without a certain knowledge of Dublin life and of the oldest Irish traditions.

2. Every selection of authors is somewhat arbitrary. I believe, nevertheless, that the authors I choose here—without ignoring the importance of others—clearly represent the very general tendency which leads, by diverse routes, to the search for "another" reality, sometimes of a magic nature, sometimes of a mythic nature, sometimes of a religious nature. Thus, the authors briefly analyzed here represent both works of indubitable intrinsic value as well as basic tendencies of our literature. The reader who wishes to find an adequate general introduction to the principal Latin American writers of this century can turn to the different literary histories, to specialized monographic studies, and finally to the works themselves: the ones which really matter. For my part, I try to find the diverse symptoms and diverse paths followed by a literary search which does not limit itself to a realism of facts alone.

3. The idea of man as a divine being has antecedents in gnostic thought. In more recent times we have it in what Proudhon called the *antitheistic tradition*; in Feuerbach, for whom man is the only god of man; in Max Stirner, for whom the subject is unique; in the idea of a happy future when humanity will be adored (Saint-Simon or Comte). It is also the idea stressed by the poetic intention of Mallarmé when he thinks of writing "The Book"—a perfect and absolute book. Huidobro coincides with Mallarmé in desiring the poem to be absolute and in declaring it impossible.

4. Untranslatable play on related sounds based on *golondrina*, "swallow." Translator's note.

5. In addition to the vanguard movements, many writers of this era are influenced by Kafka, Joyce, and Proust. In Borges's writing the roots are, principally, English. His universe, sometimes comparable to Kafka's, seems little influenced by Kafka himself.

6. As well as in the poems, this other aspect of Borges's work is apparent in his studies of gaucho poetry, recently: *El compadrito*, in collaboration with Silvina Bullrich.

7. Borges has not declared affinities with Unamuno. They are obvious and Borges's work recalls the man desired by and "dreamed" by God—Unamunian theme par excellence—as often as the Unamunian "realities of fiction which are a fiction of reality."

8. For a detailed analysis of the relationships between cyclic time, revolution, participation, and meaning, see my book: *Octavio Paz: sentidos de la palabra* (Mexico: Joaquín Mortiz, 1970).

9. A certain tendency to fantasy may be found also in the Latin American theater of today, a genre which is altogether much less developed than poetry, fiction, and the essay. Since Conrado Nalé Roxlo, a lyric quality has come into the Argentine theater, a quality cultivated in Mexico by Xavier Villaurrutia. The recent theater of Carlos Fuentes poses problems similar to those in his novels. The "documentary" theater of Vicente Leñero is more testimonial and theological than realistic. The theater of Omar del Carlo in Argentina is also highly imaginative and fantastic.

PART THREE

Literature As Experimentation

6 / Destruction and Forms in Fiction

NOÉ JITRIK

SELF-QUESTIONING IN THE ORIGIN OF CHANGES

> Por entre mis propios dientes salgo humeando
> dando voces, pujando,
> bajándome los pantalones...
> Váca mi estómago, váca mi yeyuno,
> la miseria me saca por entre mis propios dientes
> cogido con un palito por el puño de mi camisa
> (César Vallejo, "La rueda del hambriento")

[The Hungry Man's Rack]

[From between my own teeth I emerge steaming / yelling, shoving, / dropping my pants... / My stomach empty, my intestine empty, / poverty pulls me out from between my own teeth / caught with a toothpick by the cuff of my shirt]

There is no doubt about it: in this poem, Vallejo is describing an aspect of his harsh existence, he is poetically elaborating concrete moments of his true physical "hunger," a dimension which the whole world, metaphorically or not, can recognize without difficulty. But he elaborates, that is, he transforms, although it may be only through the act of intonation: his discourse is weaving, burdened, pathetic. What he elaborates is even more transformed: an image which depicts a birth scene, that of his "autogenesis" (emerge, shove, yell, pull out, but of himself, to be his own belly; all these verbs compose a movement, the flow of which is mixed with that of another movement, that of undressing, and as the two are interwoven, they give body to the idea that existence is granted by degrees; the second image constitutes itself based on the renunciation of the first, existence is owed to a belly which is external and hence dressed: to undress, then, is to be born). Hunger and poverty are the midwives, that needy pair certainly ensconced in a social platform, but this does not limit the scope of the event: what is being born now finally has identity (my own teeth), occupies a place in the world, and possesses the fragility of that which depends on a "toothpick." This is the only materiality possible for man, this concrete-precarious being. Polemically, Vallejo pulls us away from positivism, reign of the rotund, proud, homogeneous affirmations of being.

All this seems certain: here Vallejo pours out his tormented lucidity as well as his questions about "man" (the underlying content of all interrogations, even the most scientific), but he also asks himself about the man who is doing exactly what he is doing in interrogating himself, that is, he asks about the poet who protagonizes the system of questions which is poetry. He is creating figuratively here (and in other poems) what people have been creating since antiquity, a poetic art, but with the direction of its course corrected, shifting the emphasis toward the poet, trying to pinpoint the initial moment in which the word is formulated in him; this moment is linked with the image of birth, is possible in the concrete fragility of the self.

We can see all this from another angle: that image contrasts with all the sure, compact, and unbreakable images which the "great poets" of Latin America in the style of Chocano, Lugones—or Neruda?—had been proposing; the "great poets" had no reason to tremble at the fragility of the self, nothing pushed them to see this quality in themselves, unthinkable in any case within a certain historical context, not authorized by the thought of time; in effect, societies without gaps between global structure and groups, without distinctions between the collective awareness of a group and individual consciousness, although laden with conflicts, they had to engender men who could only believe in what they saw and in facts—variable, no doubt—which proceeded from the coherent external organism. By virtue of his suffering, rebellion, and lucidity, Vallejo is already a child of another time; lacerated by contradictions, he represents a new type because on one hand he has internalized the structure, on the other hand because everything that is breaking down externally resounds in him through experiences that reorient him, that comprise his identity: he is not only a product of his time, but also an example and an interpreter. His poetic world is engendered by this crossing of lines that represents his relationship with the world; for him, the "initial moment" resides here: for this reason, perhaps, all of his writing seems like an eager pursuit of himself in the pursuit of the word; the questions make this crossing of lines immediate, dramatize it, and this finally makes way for the poetic form, the system of personal signs, the writing of them. Very well, to this dramatization upon which the "initial moment" depends, I wish to give the name of *self-questioning*, a term which designates not only a philosophic or moral attitude, but also the virtue this attitude has of converting itself into form. Inversely, the form, demanded, placed in tension, brings us closer to the self-questioning as a nuclear producer, a zone which characterizes both a poet and a literature, as well as both an era and a social system.

At the time of the *Poemas humanos* [Human Poems], there are more than sufficient reasons why particular certainties move us, but it is also necessary to say that Vallejo's poetry is the result of a critical process which begins before his time in Latin America and continues after him. There are essential differences between the *before* and the *after*: the *before* contains a trace of self-questioning which occurs in isolated and limited cases, usually related to the critical system of the vanguardism of the first decades of the century; the *after* presents a generality which links different experiences and which probably confers one of the intense justifications for what we call "contemporary Latin American literature." But Vallejo is not an exclusive example of this process, nor its only axis: if I take him as a point of departure, it is because he is a privileged representative and because self-questioning seems to run through his work with a coherence not found in other poets or writers. This wealth promises a description and an analysis of *form* which would throw light on the nature of his self-questioning and, in the meantime, on some of the principal meanings which organize it. This is not the occasion for an analysis, although before leaving the vast field of suggestions which stem from Vallejo's work, I wish to recall one of Coyné's conclusions which is related to all this. He is referring to language and observes in it a capacity for essential transformation; it is a field in which the transformation which all his poetry implies can be fully realized: "Vallejo does not receive language as a wealth already formed which he would try to utilize in the best possible form, but rather as something he sees born and die before his eyes, endowed with a disquieting existence, as disquieting as existence itself. The poet does not inherit an idiom which is already complete with its code of uses and meanings, he struggles with elements which erupt only to later disappear and which he tries to retain when they escape him, or to exhaust when they obsess him."[1] This field seems central here, but it is not exclusively in it that the symptoms of self-questioning are manifested prior to Vallejo, just as it is not necessarily in it that the consequences of a self-questioning that develops afterward are manifested; the forms which can be recorded in the present appear as so extremely diversified that this diversity is a part of the calculable wealth; thanks to this diversity, Latin American literature has made its great qualitative leap. Thus, just as the great Vallejo experience takes place in what we can call the *zone* of literature, other experiences, especially narrative, are occurring in specific zones, in various sectors in which self-questioning exercises its generative capacity. Those sectors also define literary accomplishment and to recognize them is to depart from the analysis of the narrow and purely verbal category of *style*, so recurrent in traditional criticism.

NEW CONCEPT OF THE FUNCTION OF THE WRITER

But self-questioning is not only a productive nucleus which disappears within the form it produces; we also recover it in this form and whenever it appears it introduces us to a double perspective, that of a world whose knowledge is becoming dubious and, on the other hand, that of an author who transmits correlatively similar doubts about his own capacity to know. Very well, if we refer this double perspective to a formal field where it should produce results, the transformations produced reveal a violent confrontation with traditional Latin American realism, even to the point of its destruction and, correlatively, the accentuation of what we can call the treatment of the literary *word*, even above the value placed upon the contents. This is arrived at by diverse approaches which resemble each other in their mechanics, which are set into motion by self-questioning. It is worth considering here, through an analysis of what has occurred in specific narrative sectors or elements, how it is possible to have achieved the total change which has taken place.

Around 1910, by virtue of the principal work of Roberto J. Payró, and even more particularly, around 1914, after Manuel Gálvez embarks on the realistic, classic, Franco-Russian novel, but thanks also to the work of Mariano Azuela and Rómulo Gallegos among others, realism consolidates its empire and, ideologically, is synonymous with social criticism, with combat against privilege; the realist project, consequently, puts the whole society on trial and needs to inventory it in order to fulfill its mission; the success with which it achieves this varies; suddenly, descriptions of atmospheres and of problems seem attractive; suddenly, the immediacy of accumulated objects makes these detailed presentations impassable. Not only does the novel take on that task, and approach it from that perspective, but the theater and poetry do too. Good documentary evidence remains of a Latin American social era and of a certain philosophy, as well as of a literary attitude weighted with ethical meaning, but no matter how well realized these productions may be, as in the case of some of Gálvez's novels, one nevertheless feels a quality of externality in the sense of a gap between the novel and the reader; realism is affirmed in its power to reproduce reality, that responsibility makes it reveal the deformations and aberrations of that reality, to show it is to denounce it, is to oblige the reader to take sides; the reader condemns or absolves, as the realist wishes, but for a cause that is not his own because so much has been pared away; for example, one can consider that while to be an illegitimate child is certainly something terrible and reveals a problem or a social evil, since not all readers are illegitimate children they can choose sides, sympathize with the unfortunate one, without their consciences being affected at all.[2] The fundamental contradiction of the realism of Gálvez, like that of Gallegos, and above all like that of the social and Indianist novel, is that it pursues a contact with the reader through successive identifications which should culminate in the sympathetic adhesion of the reader; the reader, on the contrary, can only be a spectator, at best compassionate in relation to the situations which are depicted, but fundamentally unchanged; the theme may have affected his ethic sense, but the literary word has not captured him in his totality, has not obliged him to strip, as Vallejo wished, in order to make him be born from his own fragility.

I think that throughout the entirety of Latin American social realism the same contradiction and its effect, which I would call *mentalism*, may be seen, but the importance of this observation rests on the fact that the system of identifications which gives form to the realist system depends on the characters; yes, of course it depends on the theme, too, but the possible combinations do not go beyond these two elements which ultimately fuse together.

Very well, at the peak of the era of realism, without avoiding its fundamental exigencies, it is possible to say that the work of Horacio Quiroga implies a radical differentiation.[3] Quiroga, too, after all, presents characters and concentrates the effect he seeks in their behavior, but what matters is the situation they are in and which they must develop or discern. The difference begins to be seen: when the center of greatest emphasis is the character, the character is converted into a hero, into a being who is exceptional in one way or another, whether for his virtues or his vices; instead, Quiroga begins his work of transformation by generalizing this character in that, on one hand, he is not classified through description and, on the other hand, what happens to him, and what occasions the story, could happen to anyone (a snakebite, a sunstroke, a criminal act); in a second stage, he renders him helpless before external events and, in the meantime, moves him onto a symbolic plane on which the snake which bites the Indian is less important than any human challenge, than any work or any reflection about what leads a man to confront a risk. Through these characters the reader is affected in another way, from within, by a risk which he cannot but share because it forms part of his own system of relationships with the world.

A displacement is thus produced: the hero, prestigious for his personal qualities or for his origin or for his peculiarities, also fulfilled an accessory but representative function: to show that his selection involved the intervention of a criterion well rooted in the real, a criterion, certainly, belonging to the author, who through the chosen characters appears to us homogeneously, affirmatively, with just the same distance as the readers will have between themselves and what is described or narrated. But in contrast, when he generalizes the hero, when he takes away his exceptional qualities in deference to a more all-inclusive situation, the author is diluted in him, it is easier for him to project himself in the blurred personality traits, if there is a risk to express, he will be the first implicated, this character who is required for what he will live through will be, above all, a possible form of his consciousness.[4] And this displacement has another consequence which is still more important: the author will also manifest in this way his dissolution into the whole which, in its turn, has entered into dissolution: a character, then, will be a form of his search, his configuration will be consequently an experiment in the double sense of literary configuration and self-recognition; the author will wish to see in those others—his possible doubles—how they are affected by the relationships he has with the world. In this manner we are face to face with a change in the function of the writer: for Horacio Quiroga, an isolated case from 1907 until 1925, the only possible course is to ask himself incessantly, above all for himself as a way of recovering something lost and fragmented, his reality and that which is external to him, only capable of dazzling in its inaccessibility and precariousness. In the elaboration of the question, he produces his writing: in the struggle to get the interrogatives out, he gradually finds his forms.

THE CHARACTER

I think that from all this a new attitude toward the character can be deduced: perhaps it is only sketched in Quiroga's stories, but it is evident that it is developed paroxysmically afterward. And it is understood that similar responsibility has fallen on the character: it is the element in narration as we know it which represents the maximum intelligibility of what is being narrated; in the extent to which the story is being told by one human being to others, it is the most precise structuring element, it is what activates the anthropomorphic relationship which governs all the actions of man. But "the" character is, in turn, innumerable characters, and their respective forms vary in accord with conditions of application of the anthropomorphic projection just mentioned; in this way, it would be possible to trace a history of the form of the character whose moments of evolution or of change would surely coincide with the moments of change in the narration itself. We can see this in present Latin American literature: what gives it a new aspect has a close relationship to what has changed in the concept and function of character. It is clear that this topic merits a study of its own, which would be very useful since it has not even been sketched out; I leave it here, however, in order not to lose track of the description of the concrete process of change in the concept and function of the character in our contemporary literature.

Returning to Quiroga, I want to say that if his characters represent a kind of dissolution into generality, that does not constitute a unique case but rather a particular aspect of a more widespread tendency. I will refer to this as I recall the reflections and essays of Macedonio Fernández in his *Museo de la novela de la eterna* [Museum of the Novel, the Eternal], the book which inaugurates the great change in the conscious orientation of Latin American literature in this century. Its intent is too vast and complex to be fully summarized here: I emphatically advocate reading it, and for my part, I am going to examine only one of its ideas. It is about his observation that it would be an "author's pretension" to select a character who is a "genius" because this would assume that the author is one; a pertinent observation because an imagination does not exist which is not comparable to the object it is capable of imagining; in addition, if the character is conceived in accord with norms of verisimilitude, the mechanism of identifications on which verisimilitude is based must function: character-author, character-reader, reader-author. Not being a genius, but without altogether failing to be one—who can affirm this?— Macedonio thinks of a character who would be a "perhaps-genius?," that is, that its form is that of a conjecture in itself, an unverifiable possibility. This imprecise field prolongs the author who has conceived of it and includes him since he has emerged from it. It may be noticed then that Macedonio has retained something of the verisimilitude and of the identifications, but it may also be seen that this leads him to conjectural models: he does not wish to keep copying that which is real; these models reside in the imaginary and he depends on these norms both when he conceives of NEG, the Non-Existent Gentleman, and when he composes his curious catalogue: characters who, before agreeing to be included in the novel, ask if they will be allowed to leave it, characters who do not agree to take part because they have to watch some milk that is on the stove, characters from other novels, characters who say good-bye and leave, and so forth.

But if the creation of a "genius" character would be an unacceptable "pretension," what is the creation of imaginary characters? It is the following of models which are also imaginary—let us recall that the identification continues—which may be found there where the imagination can give them a form. And if identification subsists, the author is pulling out of himself his own quality of the imaginary, his conjectural substance. On one hand, this implies a radical rejection of anything which imposes on the self, that is, the affirmation of liberty; on the other hand, that conjectural substance creates models, sustains an activity based on itself which is translated—by virtue of its liberty—into an infinite number of operations: it doubles itself, divides itself, reproduces itself, projects itself. Each of these, or the combination of several, opens the way to possible forms of characters, and all those that reach that level organize themselves so that the conjectural substance which is in their origin may manifest its meaning. This organization constitutes a superior entity and is in the consciousness of the author; even more than that, the author is an author because his objective is to produce this organization. We arrive, then, at a conclusion: the author presents himself, through Macedonio's texts, as an organizer; the result of his work is the new form which is interpreted and manifested by this circuit which goes from self-questioning to his theory of the novel.

Undoubtedly, we will encounter this theme of the writer as organizer farther on, when we need to refer to the idea of montage, central in the structure of contemporary literature; I prefer to continue discussing the character, whose history of variants and evolutions has barely been sketched out. I wish to refer now to the novels of Juan Carlos Onetti, in which the Macedonian criticisms of the "real" consistency of the character seem to be prolonged and transformed; beginning with *La vida breve* [The Brief Life], Onetti involves his characters in permutations; the protagonist of that novel, Brausen, while he engages in a certain type of action and describes thoughts that isolate him, lives another life under another name in the apartment next door to his; meanwhile, he writes a movie script whose protagonist, Díaz Grey, is a new version of himself, this time imaginary; this episode—a novel within the novel—is narrated in the third person, but in the last chapter the first person is imposed as though Díaz Grey had prevailed over his imaginer. The three characters are interchangeable, they are not just diverse, divided aspects of a single one, they are Rimbaud's phrase, "Je est un autre" ("I is another"), with such force that they eliminate the distinctions between reality as imagined by the author and the imposture and imagination of the character. These transfers create a complex structure upon which are outlined an assembly of actions whose anguished imprecision seeks an outlet; this impulse is generalized, and the whole novel becomes a search, thus acquiring a detective-novel tone.

In this way, Onetti develops a scheme which appears in Borges's stories almost paradigmatically: to question oneself, to seek oneself, to project oneself into others in order to find an answer or a solution, are aspects of the enigma-investigation balance that Borges formulates with a purity stripped of history in the stories/bibliographic notes or, most of all, when presenting a purely causal account which does not make the constitution of the investigative movement less necessary.[5] In this movement the characters change skins just as if that which they seek were obsessively their identity. The man who dreams in "The Circular Ruins" is the dream of another, in the same way that in "The Shape of the Sword" or "Theme of the Traitor and the Hero" A turns out to be B and even this is obscure, even whether A is A and B is B, as though nothing could be determined, as though the result of the investigation would involve us in a new enigma for which we are given no key. This mechanism of dissolution, repeated and characteristic in Borges, is less habitual in Onetti, but also less mechanical, although beginning with *La vida breve* and especially in *Una tumba sin nombre* [A Nameless Grave], it is made ever more refined and dramatic, as though each time there were less distance between the narrative structure and the fundamental question which is aimed, there is no doubt about it, primarily at himself.

Generalized, imaginary, interchangeable characters, the solutions are many and to list them all would require a detailed inventory; let it suffice to add the fabulous solution in Gabriel García Márquez's novel, *One Hundred Years of Solitude*, characters who go on and on, slimmed down in their consistency but reappearing in their descendants like reflections of themselves, and the conjectural solution in Alberto Vanasco (*Sin embargo Juan vivía* [Nevertheless Juan Lived]) and in José Emilio Pacheco, whose novel *Morirás lejos* [You'll Die Far Away] is a kind of culmination, in my judgment, of the whole process I have tried to define. Let us see how these two last authors proceed.

Vanasco proposes a story in the second person and in the future tense, which implies a kind of order, given by the narrator, of existence; the characters thus constituted depend on a specifically organizing will and are presented as figures whose history—that which unfolds—is a hypothesis without confirmation: "Tomorrow morning you will get up early" is a phrase which condenses the whole manner of storytelling. Pacheco begins his novel with a situation, a character who is sitting in a park and another who watches him through a window; we do not know who they are or what they are doing, but the narrator begins to conjecture and each stage of the conjecture (twenty-seven of them) has to do with reality, on one hand because all the possibilities can be verified, on the other hand because to imagine them and formulate them is to awake them all, to set going a system in which the only thing that is inadmissible is the distance between the two characters and, still more, the distance between author and narrators. From this an idea of fusion emerges which, given the nature of the conjectures, is immediately moral: we are not innocent of any crime, not even of those we have not committed. The original questions, even those in which identity itself is put on trial, do not imply a historically evasive attitude but rather an involvement which is perhaps more profound than that proposed by the realism of the conscience which is affirmed and proclaimed as being without boundaries or barriers.

THE "CHARACTER-AUTHOR" RELATIONSHIP

It is clear that the modifications which this concept of the character presents do not exhaust all the modifications which characterize present Latin American literature; I repeat, character is only "one" element among many and each in its way, some more or less than others, has been gradually varied, stimulated, or placed in tension, all beginning with the same profound attitude of self-questioning which is like the eye of the hurricane, originator of all changes. There are not too many of these "elements" but enough to allow a certain number of combinations, each of which produces a text. It is useful to list the elements: Characters (C), Storytelling Procedures (P), Theme (T), Descriptions and Explanations (DE), Rhythm (Rh), Language Employed (LE).[6] Very well, given these elements, the combination / T DE C Rh LE / will yield a very different text than the combination / C LE DE T / and each one of these combinations (the order of the elements is indicative of their emphasis within each combination) configures or describes a novel; this means, correlatively, that every novel—existent or possible—owes its particular form, its identity, to a certain disposition of elements which can be analyzed and described. But it is also necessary to say that the combination is brought about thanks to a certain organizational energy which doubtlessly stems from language, of which the novel is a manifestation or result. In this way, *combination* is equivalent to *organization*. Very well, the combinations are made, consequently, according to models provided by combinations which organize language; thus it is possible to homologate both levels, which allows the understanding that, given certain elements, the combinations—the novels—are innumerable. (In language, beginning with a certain number of sounds, an infinite number of sentences may be composed, or, as Humboldt proposes in regard to grammar, a finite system of rules engenders an infinite number of superficial and deep structures connected in an appropriate manner.)[7] But each combination presents one or various elements which are more developed than others, thus the definitive form of the novel resides in or depends on that reinforcement: it may be better understood or better visualized when the predominant element is understood: in this way, we can say that the form of the psychological novel, for example, has as its organizing center the "element" characters (*Los siete locos* [The Seven Crazies], by Roberto Arlt); in the social novel, on the other hand, the organizing element is the theme (*The Time of the Hero*, by Mario Vargas Llosa, or *Los dueños de la tierra* [The Owners of the Land], by David Viñas), while in a novel like *Paradiso*, by José Lezama Lima, the originating explosion may be found in language in its pure state, what he tells builds on the tensions which appear in a language which is awakening and the "novel" is essentially a work based on a certain language, with all the other circumstances, characters, storytelling procedures, and so forth, as accessories.[8]

There is no doubt that this idea of the combinations of elements as figures of the organization of the novel offers us an amplification of criteria to draw us closer to the transformations which have taken place in the form of present Latin American literature, beginning with the nucleus we are calling *self-questioning*. Although it would not be vain to reflect a little more on the "character," we do not wish to leave aside the fact that this, like the other "elements," has a genesis and a history and has produced diverse results in accord with the conditions of its application.

The novel, as we just said, is anthropological fundamentally on its semantic level (messages and meanings which come from man and return to him) but also, for the same reason, it is anthropomorphic both because of the meanings it mobilizes and because the character—who represents man within the novel—is the mobilizer: it is he who provokes the linguistic concentration from which a recognizable form is composed. In his turn, if the reader understands this form it is because he shares a way of being with the characters—because both participate in the same system—he identifies with them because through them the signs which reside in the text become decipherable to him. On his side, the author constructs his characters following the effective or virtual pattern which he knows in people, he singularizes them by respecting, varying, and denying certain models, the selection of which surely constitutes the first stage in the genesis of a novel. Very well, the precise determination of this moment offers us a field of describable analysis: in the first place, the selection of models is indicative, why certain ones and not others (military in Vargas Llosa, employees in Benedetti); in the second place, it is important to specify what is done with the models, that is, what characters are obtained; in the third place, one must see from what perspective they are shown to be developing and acting. This last step proposes, in its turn, two possibilities: (*a*) it reveals them from within their own consciences, it makes us believe that the author is part of that internal world that he is articulating; (*b*) it reveals them from an outside, external point of view, like someone who is describing. If he chooses (*a*), fusions are facilitated or, at the very least, it is difficult to maintain distance; if in effect he does not maintain it, if the fusion does occur, what he is doing is telling about himself through the chosen figures, that is, he chooses himself as a model; if he selects (*b*), the outside point of view can create a distancing which is so great that the selection of the model can lose its meaning since the character thus shaped, singularized in this way, will be too separate from him and therefore, from the reasons which impelled the author to choose him.

These extreme positions indicate the limits which can detain a critique which wishes to take into account all of the elements which intervene in the production of a text, ranging from the form of the characters to the motivation of the author, but more important still is the fact that at both these extremes, all construction of characters in present Latin American literature is debated: the extremes of total fusion and impersonal distance are both snares and they must be struggled against. Of course, there are enriching qualities within each of the extreme positions, but the solutions of compromise between interiority and objectivity are more common, the balances between a vigorous realism and the consciousness which describes itself. In my opinion, this last is the more adequate alternative if it is accompanied by a distancing sufficient to permit a transformation of the model into a character; if not, it is often the refuge of monotonous personal confessions presented through interior monologue. An approach to the characters through external description should not be blocked off either, but on condition that the outside layers should be penetrated and that the model should be transformed according to the author's necessities. Of course, all this does not mean to say that a rigorous isolation at either of the extreme positions cannot provide results or really effective presentations: for example, the strict nineteenth-century or thirteenth-century objectivity with which Gabriel García Márquez (*One Hundred Years of Solitude*) exhibits his characters does not impede, but rather favors a complex ordering by means of which he shows, in a kind of impressive fresco, the principal traditional Latin American types and conflicts (the model followed), and, on the other hand, through the confused genealogy which he works out, he leads them to the plane of myth (the transformation of the model).[9] There is, of course, a verbal richness which corresponds to an imagination which is out of the ordinary, but the transition from stereotypes to mythical characters is produced by virtue of the insistence on presenting them from the outside, as pure actors, up to the point where they simply exceed themselves, they begin to have a significance for the reader which is far beyond the terms in which they are described. Mario Vargas Llosa, in *The Green House*, employs the same strategy although he presents it in a technically more complex way: the characters are analyzed by an almost objective point of view which registers what they are doing and saying without inflections; the zone of the narrator's distance is created by this mechanism and the characters, left on their own in this way, begin to gain ground and convert themselves into figures who, in their disembodiment, represent situations, types, paradigmatic climates, a little like the images of the church which are so expressive in their bareness. At the other extreme, José María Arguedas (*El zorro de arriba y el zorro de abajo*[10] [The Fox Above and the Fox Below]) proposes a character who not only speaks in first person, linking himself with the narrator, but who even bears the author's name to indicate this character-author fusion: the distance has totally disappeared but because this character has a place on the fringe of literary convention, the model is transformed and the character draws apart from the author, transcends him and is generalized.

In general terms, we can point out that the existence of extreme positions, with the accomplishments and limitations of each, justifies attempts at equilibrium, as we can observe in Carlos Fuentes's *A Change of Skin* or David Viñas's *Los hombres de a caballo* [Men on Horseback]. In the way the characters of the two novels are presented, both extreme tendencies seem to be taken into consideration and an evident effort made to achieve a synthesis: certainly the characters are both seen from the outside and from within, but the desire to integrate the two perspectivies is evident, more than just an overlapping of the two points of view, a point in which the reader passes from one to another as in a continuum; of course, this is a complicated objective: people like Fuentes himself (*Aura*), Cortázar (*Bestiario* [Bestiary]), Bioy Casares (*Historia prodigiosa* [Prodigious History]) have tried to resolve it through the fantastic; all these attempts are extremely interesting, but they have limitations because if it is a matter of showing characters who are their inside and their outside at the same time, removing them from mere verisimilitude, especially Latin American verisimilitude, if it is a question of avoiding the above-mentioned dangerous extremes, the venture into the fantastic appears to reduce the whole problem to a question of semantic inverisimilitude, which produces a new partialization.[11]

NARRATIVE PROCEDURE

The other element I wish to consider in its variations is the storytelling procedure. Let us begin by recalling that for traditional realism the unity of the account resides in the point of view from which it is told: it is the realistic eye which analyzes what is external to it, orders it, forms it into hierarchies and gives it meaning. This vision is delegated to a narrator who, presuming to be objective, tells in third person about everything around him; the narrator is a convention, it is he who connects the two levels, the real and the imaginary; he is distinguished from the author in that it is he who narrates from within the story while the author writes, does a job, a real activity. The convention is necessary because the separation must be maintained and, on the other hand, the story must be moved along according to human and real laws of narration. Now then, the boundaries within which the "objective" eye operates are equally conventional and necessary: since what the eye sees is told to us in such a way as to seem true, the time in which the eye gathers its information is arranged so that it seems true (generally it is arranged in a lineal and chronological manner) and the space, conceived as a pure frame or a pure perspective, is presented as a continuum which moves out from the eye and returns to it as the only way of being perceived and understood. I think that the sensation of flatness, of lack of relief, which the realistic novel produces is due to this; the three conjoined conventions are directed at the reader so that he must respond in a single way, coincident with the initial "point of view."

But realism is not "the" realism but rather a series of realistic approaches and in each of them the limited basis may be reduced, sometimes because the relationships between time, space, and vision are not necessarily and mechanically confluent but are occasionally fragmented and dialectic, other times because experimentation may appear there, too, if not in all three elements then in one of them separately. A single example would be the "avant la lettre" objectivism of Antonio di Benedetto,[12] a description of a situation from the point of view of the objects themselves, as though the perspective were theirs and not that of an external person, an objectivism which is an essentially realistic effort but the effect of which is not superficial, probably because the displacement of the point of view disconnects the relationships, breaks up the asphyxiating conjugation. The experience of di Benedetto is exemplary and shows, above all, a certain framework within which many other trans-formations are possible; one of the more important ones is the first person narrator who, in the traditional Renaissance bourgeois novel, was only tolerated within a story related in the third person: this new procedure takes upon itself a new perspective and formalizes it, announces that the "eye" that tries to get back into the characters and leap again from there to the external perspective is another, less conventional if you wish; in any case if this novelty does not fail on one hand to ratify the very principle of verisimilitude (since this new version would be more efficacious and "true"), on the other hand, it shows that the instruments must adapt. Let this conclusion serve to emphasize the critical range of a new procedure.

I think that in Macedonio Fernández one must seek the first systematic inflection of the procedures. From what point of view is his *Novela de la eterna* told? Not from the point of view of someone who presumes to see and know everything from the outside, but clearly from within the story itself; Macedonio makes all the turns and twists imaginable to ensure this modification: the speaker—the narrator—covers various planes simultaneously, moves around everywhere, carries on dialogues with the characters without being one himself, admonishes the author, permits the insertion of readers into the conversations between characters, selects and eliminates or invents characters as he wishes. The narrator assumes, then, explicitly, stridently, the whole selective role, the "omniscience" of the traditional narrator but, on the other hand, like the author, as an organizer, he convokes real elements to give form to an imaginary world; the narrator, within the story, is the one who unifies elements which would appear in total disorder if they were not placed into contact and relationships and if they were not given a meaning. The consequences are important: the valuation of the narrator as a fundamental element of the story and, correlatively, the destruction of the homogeneity of the narrator who locates himself outside the story. This does not mean to say that Macedonio invented a new type of narrator, nor even a new method, but that emphasizing its function, categorizing it, helps to clarify the meaning of its variants in the subsequent process.

The lines initiated on a purely trial basis by Macedonio continue in Latin America, in most cases without knowledge of this formidable focus of renovation; Borges, on the contrary, his great heir, constitutes an excellent example of what a conscious and imaginative application of Macedonio's teachings could have produced. But the greatest continuity resides in the appearance of novelists and short story writers who exasperate the search for new narrator functions and new procedures. Of course, in this sense too, one must distinguish between the pure experimenters and those who accept the experiences of others and generalize them. In the first category, I will mention Alberto Vanasco and Vicente Leñero, in the second, Juan Rulfo and Guillermo Cabrera Infante.

We have already spoken of *Sin embargo Juan vivía*: its second person narrator and its future tense accomplish two purposes: to show how the narrator is the organizer of the action and how all the action is hypothetical. Let us add that compared to the usual verb tense in which a story is told, the indefinite indicative tense, time of completed actions, of things which can be measured and referred to, the future tense seems fragmented and heterogeneous, revealing what resides in the imagination or in critical reflection rather than the results of pondering: the story stops being something which is told in order to become something which is being constructed. The classic functions of the narrator are clearly forced here: surpassed, demanded, and placed on another level they express both the insigificance of systems created by a glance which vainly classifies things it cannot manage to see or tell about, as well as a proposal to work on a basis of fundamental nakedness. Procedure and history are thus homologous: when history loses a burden which has become drudgery, procedure shakes off its burden in the same way, its weight of everything inherited and asphyxiating in literature, whatever impedes literary creation in literature.

Leñero, in *Los albañiles* [The Bricklayers], blurs the outlines of his characters and an atmosphere of "anything is possible" is established, which does not mean "anything at all" but rather new frameworks, systems which are not necessarily based on the yeses and the nos which regulate our knowledge.

Of course these conclusions are schematic and even hasty (this must be pure conjecture for some) and it would be risky to apply them to the totality of Latin American literature, but this does not keep us from understanding that behind the extreme experimentation a circuit is established which goes from the initial self-questioning, passes through the field of formal modification, to reach zones where problems of knowledge are debated which only well-developed methodologies can attempt to formulate specifically. I think that the following reflections of Chomsky's can be applied to what the present Latin American narrative is seeking: "It does not seem surprising to me that at this particular moment in the development of Western thought there should have existed the possibility of the birth of a new psychological science, a psychology which begins by undertaking the following problem: the definition of many possible systems of knowledge and of human belief, the concepts in terms of which those systems are organized and the principles which justify them."[13] It is possible that the general meaning of our analysis brings us closer to this perspective; it would be necessary, in any case, to establish the particular passages in at least the most representative works; even as a hypothesis this far from trivial framework would come to be the essential condition of its expressive wealth—in its turn a condition, in the best cases, of the awakening of the world of the readers—but, even more, it would convert the Latin American novel into a force of transformation on the level of thought and consciousness which are part of the general irrepressible Latin American movement toward the creation of new forms, that is, its revolution.

In reference to the second category, we can say that Juan Rulfo's *Pedro Páramo*, for example, presents a story with clear antecedents: it belongs to the tradition of the Latin American rural novel, the subspecies social novel, the most important aspect of which is the description of the barbaric charac-teristics of country life and the denunciation of cruelties, injustices, and exploitation. As a social novel of the land, it presents its explicit contents through a conjunction of procedures which do not intend to diminish the subject but rather to transcend it while taking it on fully: the theme is fundamental here but as a basis upon which the procedures build up and interweave the meanings. In this way, an original first-person narrator permits the appearance of another, also in first person; when this intervention is concluded they cross back and forth (Juan Preciado and Eduviges), making it seem that two planes are also intercrossed, time and notion of reality, one alive and one dead; the first narrator dies and the story goes on anyway; then there is a voice in third person which picks up an incident again and develops it: the portrait of Pedro Páramo, the description of the atmosphere and the prolix revision of the Mexican myth of death begin to take form through all these narrative levels which do not provide different focuses of one reality but simply complementary views, accumulated facts which, since they come from different perspectives, atomize any overall vision and reconstitute the object in an instant, as in a pointillist painting. The theme and the characters oblige us to think of Mexican muralism, but the gamut of procedures applied leads us to pointillism: the intercross is enriching, the adoption of certain techniques allows us to imagine that behind the traditional content, more effectively presented, there is also a thought process occurring on all the levels of reality and not limited to the denunciation, which, of course, is important in itself.

As for Cabrera Infante's *Three Trapped Tigers*, to the description of the

Havana night and the conflicts, adventures, or sexual and intellectual problems of a group—a common theme in urban realistic literature—a diversity of procedures is applied which could probably be reduced to only one: the juxtaposed accumulation of stories and thus of narrators. A center of action is immediately distinguishable, thanks to those narrators who constitute a group, certainly, where no single point of view is given more emphasis than others; they all begin by telling about themselves—confession—and take turns as protagonists, revealing not so much a tendency to equalize the characters— which happens, too—as a principle, that there is no difference between narrator and characters, that the functions are interchangeable. It would seem that a new role is attributed to the narrator: on one hand it is he who tells the story, it is not possible to understand the story without him; on the other hand, he has the same consistency and matter as the characters. Let us go back to a conclusion that had appeared to us with great clarity when we discussed Macedonio: the narrator belongs to the system as substantially as any of the other elements, characters, and theme, which were recognized as indispensable in all narrative architecture. But we also see how experiences which amplify their scopes can be integrated into a scheme, the final purposes of which are not totally new. The significance of these appropriations cannot be anything but positive: the instrument in all its parts is renovated, its greater richness removes it from insignificance and extinction.

VISION, TIME, SPACE

To recapitulate: the narrator is an "element" which takes on form beginning with an organizing vision which, in its turn, is situated in a perspective; consequently, there is a reordering of time and space, those primary categories of all perspective. What I called *procedure* of storytelling will consist, then, both of the treatment of the vision (the narrator) and of the treatment of time and space. Well then, the sign of the modifications effected in the area of the narrator is the fragmentation and the permutability of the visions; what has occurred with time and space in the Latin American narrative gives even greater emphasis to this tendency; the use of a linear time or of a space as ambient has been subjected to a harsh attack, the consequences of which may be measured in the changes produced. We can already observe this in Rulfo's novel where the story, as it advances through a very complex system of backward motions, breaks temporal lineality: a segment narrated to a certain point, then a new beginning which includes the initial point of the first segment, then new development of the first segment at the point where it was abandoned, then new movements backward when certain characters appear. The result is a mesh of lines which do not dilute an action which is meaningful from a historical point of view but which propose, above all, an experience of time treated as an object of consciousness, incrusted in a memory, fixed like an engraving or like a traumatism the causes of which are being investigated. Backward movement, retellings and fragmentation are forms of the recuperation of that memory, a treatment which is similar to that of psychoanalysis and, like psychoanalysis, to the extent to which they configure an object, they create a space, the novelistic location where the whole recuperative attempt takes place. This space is equally discontinuous, and it is not the field of an appropriative vision as in the old rural novel; it is open and it is expandable and it permits the eviction from its folds, as an act of action-doing, of the image which is being narrated, but at the same time it permits it to transfer into other consciousnesses, those of the readers; the image is made objective in this way and is shown in its essential meanings, present and verifiable reality becomes the "dead life" or, rather, the alternation of the living and the dead which are not only in the novelistic theme but also in the world which has provided the author with models.

I think there is no present Latin American fiction which does not move in both dimensions in this way. Including the fiction which seems most to respect the classic norms, like that of Gabriel García Márquez (*One Hundred Years of Solitude*) where the story begins at a specific moment and ends years later, the events are entangled, the actions of the characters are intermixed, the activity of some affects others who suddenly awake from strange oblivions and abandonments and a zone is created which is blurred, hazy, even cyclic, thanks particularly to the names which repeat, as if the passing of time were hindered by the lack of differentiation. To limit this analysis, I wish to recall that the cyclic is, above all, the result of a cumulative movement, as though there were no rationality but only necessities; in this way, the house of the Buendías and Macondo itself go along growing explicitly, but their clear outline dissolves and we no longer know the form of either one or the other. Perhaps they fuse with the swamp they came out of thanks to will power and to the founding energy of the myth of incest? Space is thus in *One Hundred Years of Solitude* a product of time, and it superimposes itself, like the acts of men, upon real space: the story is the expression of this work, simultaneously heroic, mythic, and useless.

These new ways of treating narrator, time, and space indicate the interest of the change which they have produced in the total physiognomy of Latin American fiction. And through the most successful novels and stories there surges, too, the image of power being exercised, the power of transformation. I think that Julio Cortázar's *Hopscotch* clearly displays evidence of this aspect. In this text, the three instances of the procedure appear beneath the common sign of a fragmentation which includes the very presentation of the material: the recommended two ways of reading, one ordered in accord with a certain plot thread but discontinuous in terms of pagination, and another in accord with the pagination but discontinuous in terms of the plot line, immediately offers the image of a sought rupture which is presented as a criticism of all criteria of composition, or at least of the usual criteria or of those which try to adapt themselves to the (supposed) exigencies of the reader's ability. It is obvious that *Hopscotch* is a declaration of boredom with a rhetorical manner of organizing the story, each of its fragments breaks the law of a beginning, a middle, and an end, just to mention a very general principle. And this does not mean a lack of development of the themes, but rather a development which the reader must complete through his narrative memory but also through his own power of creation, since what is being demanded of him is the very fusion of his intelligence with the given text. The basic contents of the text, the conflicts which are dramatized there, are in a certain way common enough but the fragmented form in which they are ordered expresses the fragmented manner in which they are lived in reality: disorder and fracture are the answer to an appearance of knowledge, a rebellion against the repressive order of intelligibility which may not be questioned, of logic which does not rise up against itself, of truth which contents itself with the image it once had of itself.

But everything that *Hopscotch* endeavors to discuss is a culmination of a process, expresses necessities of rupture which cannot be channeled through a social order in which culture is used repressively to impose and sanction that which is well finished, that which is already known; *Hopscotch* is composed, thus, as much of previous experiences which Cortázar uses to advantage as it is of lessons which other writers extract, and of later evolutions of Cortázar himself. And if *Hopscotch* is the proof of the power of transformation I referred to earlier, the later works of Cortázar express what comes after the technical upheaval which it implies. All of this opens an important door, an aspect which cannot be dismissed.

DESTRUCTION OF TECHNIQUE: MONTAGE

Hopscotch has certainly indicated many paths for the fiction which it follows and which follows it. This is due, above all, to the liberties it takes with narrative procedures. Beginning with *Hopscotch*, all matters of story organization are classified hierarchically, a theoretical and practical field begins to be justified. But let us be more exact: neither themes nor situations and, in this case, probably not even characters are really new, they belong to the standard Rio Plate repertory; what is new is the procedural liberty which permits the articulation of new meanings on top of contents which are to some extent old. This liberty, I repeat, is manifested in a fragmented external form which definitely has critical content: the fragmentation breaks up a way of story-telling which pretends to be homogeneous and the manipulation of which, the secrets of this manipulation, confers an undeniable power which is deposited in the writer, who is the one who possesses the ability to tell the story with impeccable technique. Because of this power, the writer is considered as a special representative of the species, he is not a laborer nor a producer, he is a "creator." This image is still widespread today and it is hard to dispute it, although its diffusion is the responsibility of a social organization, a system or a group of systems which are also the ones who determine it: the writer thus made sacred will be a privileged agent of a culture to which he gives meaning through the exercise of his power; in addition, the writer practices his craft as a model destined to fascinate other writers as well as readers and those hybrids called *critics*; the masterly technique, which provokes the most reverence when it is most perfect, unites these three poles and seems to constitute the cipher of intelligibility: the more I admire and recognize a great technique, the more I identify myself with it, since I am capable of appreciating it, and the more power I give myself on the Olympus of outstanding human abilities. The fascination, then, is almost a necessity, the cement which fills in a system's chinks, the form in which the father god manifests himself as he orders the existence of his children, wishing to prolong himself in them by means of his paralyzing majesty.

But the "technique" is not atemporal but rather historic; after centuries of search it finds its institutional moment in the bourgeois era and afterwards its irrepressible disintegration in the beginnings of the twentieth century. What happens then is not on the order of a replacement of "one" technique by "another," but rather that the idea itself of "technique" loses its appeal and begins to be pushed off its pedestal, the demythification begins, the true hero of the bourgeois novel, the author, is dispossessed of his halo and he is offered, in exchange, the great field of the experience of fiction: experience of forms but also of the body itself whose consistency—not to speak of its efficacy—is put dramatically into play. In this way, Joyce—to give only one example—displaces the organizing nucleus of his work, removes it from its grand task and installs it in the narrative elements themselves; *Finnegans Wake* will be a montage constructed upon the worldwide paradigm of the words. Joyce proposes to delve into the sonorous mass which the whole culture has managed to accumulate in order to seek an organization there which the great technique cannot even manage to understand.[14]

Late, perhaps, for Latin America (but Macedonio in 1920 had already understood it), the fragmentariness of *Hopscotch* makes a similar attempt at the destruction of "technique" as supreme power: the broken mirror is the first thing seen as the result of multiple experiences; behind it, or after having united the fragments and having understood the fragmentation, new planes are established: the principal one is that of the organization in the form of "model" which is arrived at, a model which does not impose itself nor conclude since its intelligibility is not presented "in itself," but instead projected into the deciphering ability of the recipient who finishes it, adapts it, connotes it, internalizes it, rejects it, lives it. As Cortázar says, the reader stops being "female" and acts.

In this moment—essentially destructive—the idea of the montage of a model is a concrete alternative, a possibility of getting away from the fascinating pressure of technique, installed in the consciousness like a censuring and correcting superego. But the idea of montage is also useful for something else, it serves to denounce the relationship which can exist between culture, form, and individual: montage is a system or a group of systems of structures which are mobile, alterable, physically (sonorously) and significatively replaceable which tend to sustain themselves upon concepts of fluidity and mobility; this scheme is homologous to the cultural scheme, its organization has an echo in the organization of social acts, the individual sees his creative power exalted as well as his simultaneous social poverty in the same way as the organizer and the reader of the literary word do. Well then, the attack on "technique" as power, fragmentation as result and montage as method constitute a circuit which depends upon a previous critical impulse: to exploit reason, to investigate thought and knowledge, to try to arrive at the root of totality in an attempt to shatter appearances and conventions. Is this objective attained? In any case, in the attack on technique there is a culmination of the system and the ability to annul, with a new efficacy, the efficacy of technique: what begins to matter is the richness of the montages (and of the models) and no longer the "art" of extracting great results from fixed rules. It is not surprising, then, that the "literary genres" also enter into a vertiginous liquidation and that *Hopscotch* is not a novel,[15] just as the different languages and organizations are intercrossed, intermixed, and transferred back and forth and integrated into new units. In this way, in *Hopscotch*, thought and reflection are dramatized novelistically; poetry impregnates, composes, and defines what is novelistic in *Paradiso*; music guides the composition and the rhythm of *Siberia Blues* by Néstor Sánchez or of *Three Trapped Tigers*; linguistic theories shape the novel in Sarduy's *From Cuba with a Song*; the language of films, finally, is a model for all kinds of texts which is not strange at all since in films, montage is a necessary structural category, films cannot be understood without montage.

The liberation from the oppression of the genres is probably a fatality no one decided on deliberately but, be that as it may, it means the possibility of regaining a liberty without which writing is merely repetition. Regaining it or feeling it for the first time? Let us take into account that this repetition, for us, was by epigonic addition, that is, by mimicry of foreign accomplishments, our old problem of dependence, if you wish, our mental and economic under-development. But there is something more: to liquidate the oppression of the genres is also to find a way to move about in the vacuum which the exercise of liberty promises (a vacuum which disconcerts, anguishes, or confuses readers who, if they reject, reject the loss of the norms and who, if they applaud, applaud the lack of limits, the confusion) but not to many authors who in this way permit themselves to reduce the organization of their messages to the original zero.[16] We will have to see, too, what the "liberty" of the writer means within a context without liberty, if it is an irritating pretension or if it is an ability to sublimate, which speaks of a certain primordial health in societies which are for so many reasons suppressed, weakened, demolished, and alienated.

The forms achieved through that liberty and the comprehension of its significance have a common point of contact which resides in the reading process which offers an opportunity for reflection which theater foreshortens and even prohibits. Yet it is in the theater where the results of the destruction of the limits of genre are probably most evident, and where almost all that is left of the old percept is the idea of spectacle; characters also remain, or actors and certain motives, but these elements are more resistant in what we continue to call the *novel*: perhaps in the same way in which Joyce is at the source of what is now current in narrative, in the theater one must refer to Artaud and the "living theater" as the founders of this dissolution of theatrical relationships by virtue of which text, theme, authors, lights, costumes, and spectators constantly emerge anew from nothing, everything is unforeseeable, what matters is the central point of the theatricality. Beginning with the destructive movement already under way the ground under foot is progressively more secure, the ability to formalize functions, it is as though new instruments, which correspond to a new way of understanding reality, were constituting themselves to give a new physiognomy to literature. A constructive attitude, finally, which is at the end of the circuit and by virtue of which we have returned to an affirmation—again—of "technique," that which was born as dissolution of procedures is now being proposed as a new system of procedures. In Cortázar himself we can observe the transition: *Hopscotch* was the broken mirror, fragmentation; *La vuelta al día en ochenta mundos* [Around the Day in Eighty Worlds] is, on the contrary, an accumulation of separate texts, a collage which clearly formulates its theory in *62: A Model Kit*: the montage enunciates the laws which lead it to the form and which it could not refuse to obey in the same way that the "happening," at first an open expanse of pure senses, falls back on certain principles ("lack of mediation, direct communications with objects and people, a short distance between spectator and spectacle")[17] of a sort it cannot desert because to do so would be to convert itself into something else, losing its significative and significant outline.

Flux and reflux in relation to "technique," restoration of its force. Is this necessarily negative? Can it not be the second stage of an investigation? A stage justified in the process, although less brilliant or obstreperous than the first because it reveals less a violent experience of elemental vacuum than a laborious search for stabilized criteria, the consecration of instruments whose solidity is the proof of their representative achievements, once experimentation is exhausted. Fuentes's last novel, *A Change of Skin*, illustrates this change; it would seem that there is a desire to institutionalize—to consecrate— the return to technique which comes after the liquidation of "technique": the novel is organized, visibly, on a basis of the confluence of a group of new procedures—as in a kind of fresco of techniques—that can affiliate with each other, tell of each other, define each other, and verify each other in their efficacy; for that reason, they appear well adapted, comfortably inter-connected, coherent, manipulated with the assurance of the already established and, thus, they subordinate themselves to the story, they serve the purpose of semantic enlightenment. But they do not undertake to express any particular attitude in themselves: once more the world is told about and judged, but the manner of telling does not in itself add a word to what is being said by the contents of the theme and the actions of the characters.

This is surely the stage which Latin American literature should be going through right now: a stage full of acquisitions, of certainties, and of achievements but also of contradictions and of dissatisfaction since it is no mystery for anyone that the triumph of a literature is only a metaphor of the triumph of a culture and a people and that in Latin America the culture and the peoples—except insofar as Cuba is concerned, in my opinion—are still a long way from this triumph which awaits them around some historical corner. And if self-questioning has intervened as an engendering nucleus in the constitution of this metaphor which has stimulated us and brought us out of isolation, since the social and cultural reality have not changed—and even if they were to change—self-questioning will continue to play a role in the stages ahead of us: will cause new forms to be produced, new ruptures and reconciliations and with all this our literature will continue to create models for our new reality. Latin American literature will not stop asking questions, as in one way or another the Arguedas just cited suggests to us; those questions—and in Arguedas it is clear that they are directed primarily at himself but that upon being formulated they are pulled from within in order to put them into an all-inclusive perspective—which are becoming form and the form which is becoming interpretation.

DIALOGUE

Apart from this productive mechanism, I wish to call attention to what I think is an explicit formulation of self-questioning: it is the dialogue, the characteristics of which as seen in the contemporary novel offer themselves as an index of more general effects.

Dialogue is, of course, a common structure in narrative but what stimulates this observation is the frequent occurrence of this structure extrapolated from action and proposing to elucidate questions of an intellectual order. The basic scheme is this: two or more characters begin to talk about any circumstance, generally irrelevant, and almost immediately, instead of examining their relationships or pouring out classic confidences or contriving a new situation, they establish the limits, scope, and repercussions of sometimes arduous philosophic questions. The verifiable generalization of this type of dialogue tends to constitute the proof of the opening of the contemporary novel to criticism and thought; consequently, there are a great many examples, although I think that the principal ones, which I will confine myself to citing, are provided by Leopoldo Marechal's *Adán Buenosayres*, *Hopscotch*, *Paradiso*, and *Three Trapped Tigers*.

But if this "form" is significative, it is so above all because at first sight it seems to be an antinovelistic vice in accord with models which inform the good "technique" based on equilibrium and the clarity of the functions. Seen from this angle, a mechanism like the following one is incomprehensible and even disqualifiable, but what matters to me is its articulation: once unchained, the conversation is unsuppressible and the theme—I said this already—is intellectual; at times, however, conflicts or situations linked to the world of the story are mentioned, are suggested as keys to comprehension (a secret tie is established between conflicts presented by the story and a transcendent intellectual problem) but these points are touched on rapidly, there is a monotonous return to the almost Socratic relationship in which the final disciple is naturally the reader; an impulse of enlightenment predominates, of answering questions formulated by a historical consciousness which takes on the weight of what preoccupies an era. On the other hand, self-questioning, as I have been describing it, undoubtedly crosses over this discussion but is embodied in cultural problems, it is not closed into an individual experience. We also observe that the link between this type of dialogue and the total structure of the mentioned novels is weak, so that it is difficult to establish causal relationships; what more often appears is a group of characters endowed with the capacity to examine which hierarchizes the novelistic ambient in terms of the problems which are analyzed and understood: the characters thus endowed demonstrate the authors' necessity to show how they can confront and even state the complex problems of culture in their full meaning; the characters are their intermediaries and, through the contents of what they discuss, they try to transmit their own ability to deal with these matters which preoccupy them, that is, Latin American culture in its totality.

Very well, why that generalized preoccupation? What in Latin American culture occasions the explicit consideration of its problems? On one hand, I think, Latin America during the last few years has been living in a time of access to universality, which necessitates restatements on all planes and levels; on the other hand, one must take into account that for Latin Americans universality is situated very specifically in European culture; if this backdrop exists, the necessity to become equal, to become separate, to leave behind, to better comprehend what European culture comprehends, and to enjoy having a place within Western culture are causes which, if they do not produce, at least justify this use of dialogue which, seen from this perspective, channels this vast updating. The great model-source has not yet become the interlocutor, it makes its presence felt so far only through its distant approval or disapproval, without any direct communication: dialogue is a form of demand to Europe, it is to ask Europe to end its silence but meanwhile the word it asks for is drowned out by that pair of incessant dialoguists. But the public that reads these dialogues is Latin American: it is this public whose attention is being sought and for whom questions are exhibited which it may or may not have thought about; thus the author, through the dialogue of his characters, really has a dialogue with Europe, makes himself a translator for Latin America, brings them up to date.

This returns us to a common present Latin American situation: the appeal to Europe, then the slow, laborious, anguished digestion of the food it has asked for but which has often been refused it, many times simply superimposed and not at the service of our needs. In this situation which still continues, the self-questioning which we have observed becomes the new form of questioning which has always gone on although now, clearly, the consequences of that attitude, because they deal head on with perplexity and are not afraid to take it on, are infinitely richer and encourage our literature to continue its process of change. This does not impede the mentioned novels from expressing such emotions as a nostalgia for Europe, a resentment of rejection, a desire to overcome the antimony and a showing off of accomplishments for Europe's benefit. And while the intellectual dialogue serves to allow us to comprehend the long perpetuation of this conflict, a leitmotiv of Cabrera Infante's novel opens this dimension even more for us: it is the theme of translation, which reappears incessantly and with which the book concludes. To translate well is something, a value, says an "intellectual" character in reference to Novás Calvo, but also *traduttore traditore.* there is an unresolved dilemma between an impoverished folkloric language which is at best picturesque if it is transcribed directly (hence the appreciation of the baroque effort of Carpentier which elevates and mythifies it), a copied language which always seems artificial and false (hence the inoperativeness of the Mujica Láinezes and the Victoria Ocampos) and a language which is adapted—or translated—which represents the only possibility of universalization (hence the general respect for Borges, great forefather of the current language). Dialogue filters this problem and the novel opts in general for this third alternative. It follows then that we should ask: is this how *all* the contemporary writers solve this dilemma? When the third solution is adopted, are the problems of our cultural specificity resolved by this? Are we succeeding, by virtue of the concrete forms which we have attained through that third solution, in having Europe speak with us, in having Europe really be an interlocutor, so that we can finally stop trying to attract its attention, directly or indirectly? These are questions which need new analyses, openings which would lead us to investigate and attempt to understand problems which are more than literary. It is sufficient to say, for now, that the meanings which have been restored in Latin American literature led to the thresholds of such investigations; they lead up to them and go right through the doors, since, in their turn, they are the consequence or result of a mechanism which has permitted them to arrive at a stage of form: *self-questioning*.

Notes

1. André Coyné, "César Vallejo y su obra poética," in *Letras Peruanas* (Lima, 1957).

2. I refer to Monsalvat, a character in *Nacha Regules*, shaped in Tolstoian fashion according to the pattern of the mystic bastard.

3. Cf. Noé Jítrik, *Horacio Quiroga, una obra de experiencia y riesgo*, 2d ed. (Montevideo: Arca, 1967).

4. Carlos Fuentes, *Mundo Nuevo*, no. 1 (Paris, 1966): "What is happening is that when the North American capitalist world superimposed itself on the feudal and semifeudal structures of Latin America, the writer lost his place in the elite and became submerged in the petite bourgeoisie...He became a true writer."

5. See my essay "Estructura y significación en *Ficciones* de Jorge Luis Borges" in *El Fuego de la especie* (Buenos Aires: Siglo XXI Argentina Editores, 1971).

6. In my book, *Procedimiento y mensaje en la novela* (Cordoba: Universidad Nacional, 1962), I try to make evident the existence, genesis, and comportment of the "elements," but I concern myself fundamentally with the procedure of the story, the five possibilities of which I examine in detail.

7. Cf. *Change*, no. 1 (Paris, 1968); Noam Chomsky, "Linguistique et étude de la pensée:" "Using Wilhelm von Humboldt's terminology from the beginning of the nineteenth century, a grammar should make *infinite use of finite means.*" And Jean-Pierre Faye, referring to Chomsky: "And which makes us enter into the very generation of language by itself: capable of generating an infinite number of sequences with a finite number of elements, of generating 'unheard of concepts'."

8. Cf. Julio Cortázar, *La vuelta al día en ochenta mundos* (Mexico: Siglo XXI, 1967): "Why not accept that the characters of *Paradiso* always speak *from the image*, since Lezama projects them from a poetic system, which he has explained in multiple texts..."

9. Cf. Propp, "Le transformations des contes fantastiques" in *Théorie de la littérature* (Paris: Seuil, 1966).

10. There is a preview segment of this novel in *Amaru*, no. 6 (Lima, 1968).

11. Cf. *Communications*, no. 11 (Paris, 1968), various articles about verisimilitude.

12. Antonio di Benedetto, "El abandono y la pasividad," in *Declinación y ángel* (Mendoza, Argentina: Biblioteca Pública San Martín, 1958).

13. N. Chomsky, "Contributions de la linguistique à l'étude de la pensée," *Change*, no. 1 (Paris, 1968).

14. Cf. Jean-Pierre Faye, "Montage, production," *Change*, no. 1 (Paris, 1968).

15. Cf. David Lagmanovich, "Rayuela, una novela que no es novela pero no importa," *La Gaceta*, Tucumán, Argentina, 29 March 1964.

16. We can call this *literarity*, that is, the tendency to produce a form based on certain verbal material.

17. Cf. Roberto Jacoby, "Contra el happening," in *Oscar Masotta y otros "happenings"* (Buenos Aires: Jorge Alvarez, 1967).

7 / Antiliterature

FERNANDO ALEGRÍA

ANTINARRATION

Against Lies

The antiliterature I refer to is a revolt against a lie which is accepted socially and venerated in place of a reality. This antiliterature begins by demolishing the forms and erasing the boundaries between genres, giving language its true values and taking on with sincerity the burden of the absurd which is our heritage. The blasphemous, as well as the irreverent, the insulting and even the obscene are ways of giving man a clear view of the mirror which reflects his image. More than forms of protest, they are acts of commiseration and of solidarity in anguish. The antiliterature of the twentieth century is, thus, an allegation against the falsification of art and an attempt to make this art into a reason to live, outlive, and resolve the absurdity of the human condition by accepting it right down to the dregs.

Two facts may be deduced from this statement: first, antiliterature presents an image of the contemporary world as a chaos and of man as a victim of reason; second, the fruits of this image constitute an act of external and internal violence. Without a doubt, a historical development in this art has been produced which, in the long run, will turn out to be revolutionary.

"How can anyone hope to put order into the chaos which constitutes that infinite and formless variation: man?" This question was asked by Tristan Tzara in his *Dada Manifesto* of 1918 in order to give voice to a dogma: chaos *is* the reason for existing. Thus the first part of the antiliterary dichotomy acquires its accelerated movement within a closed orbit. The Dada protest is not revolutionary. At any rate, it is not so in the political sense which it will have in André Breton's *Second Surrealist Manifesto*. Tzara accepts chaos as a reality within which the work of art will function without consideration of its social effects. The surrealists give antiliterature a theoretic base and an analytic method. An art is not destroyed as a premise in order to be replaced by another. Breton opens a floodgate in the rationalist concept of artistic creation, and through this floodgate flow, with the force of an immense tidal wave, the contents of a collective memory and a creative subconscious. It is of great importance to emphasize this function of the surrealist manifestos. They are a liberating force, they cut the cables of the human balloon and throw out its sandbags, they make the interlocutors independent, they give language a single continued action in which the powers of the night are freed, and they assault institutions, they implant antimagic, that is, the functional exercise of reality in dreams.

Considered thus, the surrealist manifestos help to explain the subsequent evolution of antiliterature. One could say that if Breton gave a leap into the depths of man, antiliterature gave another leap to the surface of reality. It removed the ritual apparatus and its dogmatic insistences from surrealism; it liberated it in its turn and put surrealism in tune with a simultaneously luminous and violent disorder.

Of what does the *anti-* of Brecht's theater, of Genet's fiction, and of Prevert's poetry consist? A revolt against a form of speech or against an attitude and a form of acting? That *anti-* is a revolution against a type of society which speaks in lies, which feigns an ethic, and which murders to survive. On a literary plane, this revolution re-creates the forms of expression, naturally, but this is not what really matters, (just as the important thing in a revolution is not the dynamiting of a government palace, the Congress, and the law courts). The revolutionary artist rips out the seams of institutional art not because he must follow a certain program, but rather out of personal necessity. In the process he sees himself and judges himself. It is *his* revolution.

The critics who observe the aesthetic event will fix certain coordinates and will play with them; they will examine a new concept of time and will apply it rationally to the development of fiction, as well as to the theatrical "happening"; they will seek symbolic projections, they will believe again in Romantic irony and will establish principles for a reinterpretation of the epic and of the *romanzo*, as well as of the comic novel; they will create capricious diagrams of time and space to explain how the story enfolds man and moves the surrounding world. All this will create a critical superstructure which, in the best cases, those of privileged critics, will appear to us as an ingenious mobile floating over a literature which takes pleasure in its contemplation.

This criticism lacks immediate meaning in the functioning of antiliterature at the midpoint of our century. The fiction of Burroughs, let us say, for example, like Arrabal's theater or Ginsberg's poetry, imposes a chaotic action (no longer simply a chaotic enumeration) with a sui generis concept of its structure. The same may be affirmed of the theater of Jorge Díaz or the films of Alejandro Jodorowski.

The Latin American Novel

Latin American antiliterature, nevertheless, produces a type of self-criticism which could well be considered marginal to the phenomenon I am alluding to; that is, the literary work which bears within it its own self-negation, its well-constructed time bomb. This is the case of *Hopscotch*, Julio Cortázar's antinovel. The important thing here is that, in addition to the antiliterary phenomenon, we are given the theoretical speculation which defines it and justifies it. Let us examine the case of *Hopscotch*. Against what is Cortázar rebelling? What does he propose as his ideal novel? He is rebelling basically against two things: first, against a form of narration which corresponds to a false concept of reality (that form which Cortázar calls *Chinese egg roll*); and second, against a language which, chewed over and ground down into excrement, finally saps the strength of literary expression. Cortázar proposes an "open" novel, made of fragments which, in their simultaneity, will give an authentic image of reality.[1] The irony of this intended scheme, what transforms *Hopscotch* into the negation of its affirmation, that is, into an antinovel, is in the fact that the author of this venture is not Cortázar, but a character, Morelli, who is submitted to a mercilessly critical scrutiny. The self-criticism is, in reality, the reverse of the novel which Cortázar really intended to write: the story of the characters la Maga and Horacio. Cortázar, like an eccentric malefactor, leaves conspicuous clues everywhere: Gide, Gombrowicz, and Borges. Joyce, Kafka, and Pound are in less obvious places. And, despite himself, Sábato.

Hopscotch satirizes Spanish *costumbrista* narrative as well as Latin American regionalist or Creole narrative. It could also have included the "poetic" novel which, in a certain way, represents the culmination of a descriptive and illusionist rhetoric. On the other hand, we should take notice of the abyss which separates *Hopscotch*, the antinovel, from the so-called magical realism of Carpentier and from the Indianist surrealism of Asturias. We should take notice, I say, because it helps to distinguish between the roots of Latin American literature. At first glance we could believe that in Asturias and in Carpentier we find certain constants of the antinovel, since neither one nor the other is a novelist in the traditional sense of the word.

Alejo Carpentier, who began his fiction as an ethnologist and folklorist (¡*Ecué* Yamba-O!, 1933), discovered only later a vein which accommodated his hallucinating vision of reality: the historical adventure at the margin of all chronology and enfolded in baroque language. He achieved the "transcendence" and "universality" which seemed so desirable to the mid-century novelists by means of symbolisms, particularly in *The Lost Steps* (1953) and *Explosion in a Cathedral* (1962). To the extent to which Carpentier detached himself from immediate reality, experimented with the concept of time and dared to monologue lyrically, he seemed to coincide with some of those on the forefront of antiliterature. For example, he coincided with the Spaniard Ramón Sender (*The Sphere*, *The King and the Queen*). However, Carpentier does not dynamite the edifice of his baroque structure. On the contrary, he seems to stylize it more and more. And in stories like "El acoso" [Manhunt] and "Journey Back to the Source," we see the growth of his interest in creating patterns of indirect but functional arrangement.

Miguel Ángel Asturias, on the other hand, uses a chaotic movement in his Indianist fiction while at the same time disdaining the "established" mechanisms of the regional novel. But this does not represent a deliberate attack on a literary tradition: Asturias's unhampered exuberance is poetic and follows an order imposed by his ritual acceptance of Mayan mythology. There is nothing in his fiction which, once it is put together, is taken apart; nothing which loses its meaning within a primitivist concept of the world, and nothing which unexpectedly deflects its social intention.

It is necessary, then, to seek other relatives for Cortázar: writers who have sought the opening in the story through which time flows freely, that is, through the pores of an amorphous reality in the process of accumulating its disorder. I think of a Chilean writer known by very few: Juan Emar (his name was Pilo Yáñez, but he preferred the *j'en ai marre*). His books, *Un año* [One Year] (1934), *Ayer* [Yesterday] (1935), and *Miltin* (1935) are a scandalous mockery of the realistic and *costumbrista* novel: the novelistic material is surrealist, heroic, and comic; the language represents the mechanical routine of the Chilean *petit bourgeois* and his scatological outbursts, and it is also based on the strategic use of the leitmotiv. He adorns language and then immediately reduces it again. The tale is assembled but never within the story itself; on the contrary, Emar tells how a novel cannot be told. His humor is insulting, eccentric, and not in any way symbolic. Nevertheless, Emar, so lively, sophisticated, cruel, and daring, is, in truth, a primitive—an antinovelist with very little language at his disposal. I mean to say, an expert swordsman without a sword. He fought with the hilt and a battered piece of iron. Well endowed with words, he would have been an heir of Sterne. In addition, he had the ability to analyze the aesthetic basis of his disorder and, with a deep thrust, to lunge to the heart of the greatest Chilean critic of his epoch: alone. This thrust missed. But I am referring to the intention, not to the bloody deed which was not consummated. Juan Emar, with his self-destructive instinct and his cannibalistic sympathy for his characters, not to mention his cubist approach to the patriotic customs of his fellow countrymen, as well as his knowledge of the world as an apple, four squares of a universal quadrangle (an image lucidly interpreted in the illustrations made by his wife) beautifully preceded the "omissible chapters" of *Hopscotch*. But he was not the only one.

Leopoldo Marechal would have understood Juan Emar's game, and feeling it insufficient, would have urged him to reflect in the revolving mirror of his epoch in order to achieve that simultaneity of space, time, and action which is the mark of *Adán Buenosayres* (1948). The "comic" novel, that is, the novel as a mask of the man who has lost himself in contradictions and who falls continuously into traps of his own predilection, is for Marechal a preconceived form, while for Juan Emar it was a way of living from day to day which never ceased to surprise him. It cannot be said that Marechal opens the novel nor that he turns it around (as happens in *Ayer*), but instead he converts it into movable images of a Romantic epic and satire.[2]

The fiction of Juan Carlos Onetti, on the other hand, constitutes a fascinating case of antinovel because it opens in depth, rather than in extension, which is the case of *Hopscotch*. Onetti's action is produced in a space halfway between immediate reality and an emotive and intellectual superreality. He prefers the invisible corridor in which the characters know one another by intuition, although the places where people simulate understanding each other also form part of the world of his creation. If it is possible to conceive of a type of novel in which the heroes intercross without looking at each other, or confessing, or even introducing themselves, in which they do nothing and, nevertheless, provoke a horrendous catastrophe and are submerged in an undefined and irrevocable perdition, that will be Onetti's antinovel. It is different from Marechal, Emar, and Cortázar in that there is no play. Although he knows the rules of the game, he prefers to get tangled up in them. He stumbles past them and searches out the mortal spring which they conceal, that is, the reason for their falsity and for their sinister power.

Paradiso (1966), by José Lezama Lima, also gives the impression of opening into depths. I think, however, that this is only an impression. In the hands of Lezama Lima, the novel breaks apart. It simply falls by its own weight. I do not see a literary mechanism in *Paradiso*, nor a narrative system, nor a linguistic organization. Instead, I see a slow explosion, with lots of dust and things and beings in the air, something like a monumental circus tent which begins to collapse, cutting cables, trapezes, bars, and stairs, with falling chairs and jugglers, animals, wardrobe keepers, and equestrian princesses, clowns of island ancestry, family musicians, cooks, and supporters of slavery. I also see a record-breaking crowd and, after its very slow collapse, the movement under the shapeless canvas of a beast which is collective, unnamed, and eager to match his hunger of murky depths against that death in the sawdust. *Paradiso* is an open novel in the sense that a ball is open, that is, the novel opens toward the outside, floating in the universe which is created by words as they resound, are prolonged and remain in man as they are converted into things and into signs of a useless and beautiful time. A sexual time and a belly which thinks, a slow-moving eye which peruses the past, examining man's anxiousness to eternalize himself on paper and in stone, a mouth which consumes the skin of God ceaselessly and hands around and around the family napkins and the rings which gradually get lost, the friendships of dance and of poetry—all this, counted up, is an antinovel; sung, it would be an opera.

It can be concluded, then, that the Latin American antinovel is an attempt to disassemble narrative in order to make it fit into the disorder of reality.[3] It is also a critical self-vision of this attempt and a heroic affirmation, that is, comic, of the absurdity of this and any metaphysical attempt to which man puts his hand.

ANTITHEATER

When this anarchy and its surrounding chaos are transformed into pure action, without speculations or justifications, without reservations or condescensions of any kind, we do not then speak of antinarrative but rather, as the critics say, of the "theater of the absurd," of antitheater, of "happening," of castration and universal love. Referring to a young Chilean dramatist, I said this some time ago:

> In this complex world of contradictions, rebellions, anxieties, triumphs, and failures in which our young writers move, more questions are phrased than answers and as many blows are given as received; falsity and bourgeois conventionalism are attacked by the weapon they deserve: the absurd and the irrational. Civic regimentation is met by the image of ruin, of abuse, of the cruel destruction of innocence, which are the hallmarks of our contemporary pseudoculture. There is a great dance of death on the stages of the modern world. and this dance does not wait for the Last Judgment to confuse the dead and the living: it moves off the stages, it goes beyond the theatrical sets, it invades the orchestra stalls and flows out into the town squares in order to parade the shames of man, to mock his false dignities, and to reveal the secret conclaves where the garments of vice, betrayal, and hate are sewn. The public goes to applaud its nightmares, to request an encore of the artist who insults it: it is not a matter of a catharsis but rather of the intensification of anxiety through the recognition of dishonor, that is, in the feigned act of death.[4]

This probably can be applied to the frontal attack that is conducted today against the armchair-man by authors like Virgilio Piñera in Cuba, Abelardo Castillo, Osvaldo Dragún, and Dalmiro Sáenz in Argentina, Menén Desleal in El Salvador, Alejandro Jodorowski in Mexico, and Jorge Díaz and Jaime Silva in Chile.

This antitheater is the most enduring flower of Dada. It coincides with the antinovel in its eagerness to negate forms and to involve directly the reader or spectator. It coincides with antipoetry in its skill at projecting violence.

Here is an art which has always been ruled by laws and formulas, directly or tacitly accepted. Today the boundaries between actor and spectator have been erased. The theater filled out, it exceeded its customary limits, it hung up movie screens, sent its people running around the orchestra, the balcony, the gallery, and the separating walls; it liquidated the unities and the curious idea of an "illusion of reality"; it discarded the plot, and the knot was untied, the denouement was stretched out into infinity; the directors and prompters talk to their relatives who have remained outside the prompter's box. Dance, concert, natural death, crime, orgasm, and projectiles are meaningful elements of an action which can lead to the destruction or the re-creation of history.

Antitheater is an individual act. It is only collective if the spectator is infected, if he is drugged and struggles on the same plane with the actors who make up the company. The antitheater, consequently, is a duel to the death, that is, a forum without time limits. Everyone contributes, some more and some less, to the liquidating of the last vestiges of the last art which pretended to be a copy of life. Opera is sung antitheater. Antitheater put an end to tragedy, drama, and comedy, replacing them in classic proportions by the absurd, the bourgeoisie, and violence. Antitheater, like the antinovel and antipoetry, is comic, controls emotion by means of drugs and herbs and uses the stage sets so that the heroes can jump to their deaths through the window. That is, it does not control emotions but rather converts them into acts, incites man to jump through the window or, if he feels like it, to laugh. It does not have principles nor does it need special settings. In antitheater all the world is a stage. It provokes revolutions.

ANTIPOETRY

Antecedents

For the first Latin American antipoets, Pablo de Rokha and César Vallejo, for example, the revolution of language did not constitute a formal phenomenon; it is not a matter of readapting language to a new concept of poetry (creationism). It is a matter of putting an end to the poetry which agonizes in death throes, drowned in words, and returning to the poet the right to express himself as a person, not as an organ-grinder, a dictionary, or as a spirit of the air, returning to him the right of conversation, the right to violate society and to violate himself.

The right to conversation begins to be given to Latin American poetry by Ramón López Velarde and not Lugones or Herrera y Reissig or José A. Silva because these writers came down to their front porches, sat around the breakfast table, or appeared in their beds with a certain Latin, classic, popularly patrician spirit. López Velarde avoids any recognition of the conflict described by González Martínez in his famous sonnet. He does not wish to speak of swans or of owls. Instead, he refers to his cousin Águeda. The first contribution of López Velarde to the basis of the antipoets is: he narrates rather than singing or describing. He explains with irrational reasons, with which he produces an antimelody. His poetry sounds of prose. The effect is deceptive. López Velarde arranges his conversation artfully and the product is almost craftsmanship. But not quite.

The second contribution of López Velarde to the basis of the antipoets is humor. He is not sarcastic, only tenderly ironic, if irony can be tender (cf. *La suave patria* [The Gentle Fatherland]). It is not only his homeland which López Velarde softens: he also softens poetry, takes off its corsets, its topknots, its makeup, and its ribbons (the precious stones were already taken off by other postmodernists), loosens its stockings, and unties its shoes. He is the delicate disorganizer of the end-of-century mannequin. López Velarde proceeds with a smile on his lips, from a distance, without involving himself. His colloquial tone, his light touch, and his provincial elegance accomplish more than the antiswan sonnet to put an end to the choral societies of Latin American poetry.

As Vicente Huidobro affirms in *Altazor* (1919), "Here lies Vicente, antipoet and wizard." What Altazor was this to declare such a thing? Formed in the tradition of modernism, Huidobro in his first epoch used a language of extremely clear goldsmithery, essentially ornamental, of Parnassian origin and romantic tonality. However, in an emotional response to an integral vision of the revolution in European art, he changed suddenly. He discovered the value of colors, of internal rhythms, the melancholy of a reality which is always suggested, never directly expressed, the technical value of the image and the false economy of the metaphor. That is, he sought the shadow of symbolism to put out the tropical light of Darío, he cut the world into pieces and reordered it with cubist calligraphy, the result of which was the invention of a new rhetoric and a dynamic preciousness made now not of allusions to the surroundings, but of superpositions, collages of the reality characteristic of his epoch. Huidobro did not come to terminate poetry but to repair it. He was not, in truth, an antipoet. He was, rather, antidescriptive, antisentimental, antipossessive, and antimetric.

Prepared by his readings of Bergson, Baudelaire, Mallarmé, Verlaine, Rimbaud, Apollinaire, as well as witness of the Armistice and of Dada, acquaintance of Picasso and Arp, Huidobro is surely the most characteristic—certainly the most brilliant—of the vanguardists of the Spanish language. Consequently, the exclamations of *Altazor* are equivalent to the ars poetica not only of creationism, but also of ultraism, stridentism, futurism, and the other *isms* of the twenties.

In Argentina, Lugones had developed an approach to reality which he considered Creole. His language, however, did not correspond to this reality, and his image of it would come out sounding literary, superimposed on the complex of classical allusions which served him as a pedestal. Macedonio Fernández and Jorge Luis Borges do not avoid this eagerness for linguistic polishing or the use of the mechanism of surprises, both inherited from postmodernist vanguardism. The case of Borges is more serious because he feels an Argentine reality which he cannot meaningfully express: he alludes to it and encircles it stylistically, but he does not manage to speak for it, since the language of that reality does not form part of his experience. Neither Lugones, then, nor Macedonio Fernández, nor Borges, will be the precursors of an antipoetry, only sharers of a Creolism which in contrast to Modernism sounds beautifully real. One must read César Fernández Moreno to feel that an antipoetic attitude is not only a literary revolt of a vanguardist nature and an inclination to uglify, but a coming to terms with an individually untransferable human condition.

Two Precursors

In 1916 Pablo de Rokha said in a poem entitled *Genio y figura* [Genius and Figure]:

Aún mis días son restos de enormes muebles viejos.

[My days are still relics of enormous old furniture.]

And as a form of conclusion, he added:

El hombre y la mujer tienen olor a tumba.[5]

[The man and the woman have the smell of the tomb.]

Speaking thus, plainly and directly, De Rokha began to hammer at poetry with an intention which was certainly very different from López Velarde, from Huidobro and his ultraists. Naming things was an immediate necessity for him. The name of animating content, in his case a content of tremendous passion, became for De Rokha the setting in which the poetic crime took place. De Rokha penetrated Chilean reality from above, from beneath, and from the sides; he represented the first surrealist attack in our midst and used a language which, all of a sudden, gave reality to the antipoetic attitude of the vanguardists. De Rokha would say later that he wrote "como roto, como medio pelo" ["like a pauper, like a drunkard"]. In truth, he wished to say that he destroyed rhetoric among us with the only valid weapon: the language of a broken-down humanity and universe, a language which cannot be learned, which he bore as a mark of his birth.

Published in 1927, *U* is his key book which proves what I am saying. Here De Rokha goes along leaving inscriptions which represent a direct violence against bourgeois society and against the man who is comfortably settled in it. He strips poetry of all artifice, except one: grandiloquence. To arrive at his inscriptions, it is necessary to cut out explanations, exclamations, repetitions and oratory. What remains is astounding: once the myth of a beautiful poetry is decapitated, language is liberated; the power of popular language and the intuitive, not analytic, faculty of conversational speech is recognized; the hybrid value of scatological vocabulary is accepted, its visceral humor as well as its primitive social echo; and then an aggressive condemnation of the cultural apparatus in which man finally castrated himself appears. These are some of the inscriptions to which I refer:

A Dios se le rompieron los neumáticos.
En verdad, hermanos, en verdad
la hora de las cosas peludas
llegó
llegó
la hora de las cosas peludas
dicen los crucificados.

Las mujeres son problemas con pelitos.
El animal de ladrillos se pone condones illuminados.

Los idiotas artificiales
humedecen los muros únicos del manicomio.
La araña cría pelos y se transforma en filósofo.

El marrueco de la filosofía
se abrocha con tres botones y un testículo.[6]

[God's tires went flat. / It's true, brothers, it's true / the hour of the hairy things / arrived / arrived / the hour of the hairy things / say the crucified. Women are problems with little hairs. / The brick animal puts on illuminated condoms. / The artificial idiots / dampen the unique walls of the insane asylum. / The spider breeds hairs and is transformed into a philosopher. The Moroccan with philosophy / fastens his pants with three buttons and a testicle.]

These buttons are a sample. De Rokha, like Sabat Ercasty and Armando Vasseur, felt himself to be a cosmic individual, a mover of masses, a poet-mountain. On this plane he goes on extending himself until he has organized his system of images and has affiliated it militantly with a Marxist position. Then he stops being an antipoet, and his task becomes that of national reconstruction and revolutionary agitation.

In 1918 César Vallejo said, still a follower of Darío:

Hay golpes en la vida, tan fuertes...yo no sé!
golpes como del odio de Dios...[7]

[There are blows in life which are so strong...I don't know! / blows like the hatred of God...]

Vallejo personally met God, not like De Rokha with a stone in his hand, but rather as a neighbor meeting another neighbor. Vallejo's eye was strong and well on the way to being cruel. He says:

La tumba es todavía
un sexo de mujer que atrae al hombre.[8]

[The tomb is still / a woman's sex which attracts man.]

The language of Vallejo, modernist in *The Black Riders*, breaks the conventional logical restrictions, adopts a free association of images, and continues in a bitter conversational tone to confront the false face of the world, spitting in it, hitting it, and distorting it. This face, of course, is the reflection of a mask which Vallejo puts on with his hat of thorns. Thus the process is, at bottom, one of self-destruction without rebellion.

Vallejo rides on the shoulders of Christ as he recounts human miseries in language which is plain, stripped down, and bleeding, revealing its wounds and those of its companion, howling in a low voice, involved in the chaos it produces, not in the revolt. The commiserating tone is enfolded in trivial colloquial forms: it is one of his ways of deflating the poetic balloon. Sex, death, commandments, friendships, country of origin, and family lose their institutional look and meaning in poetry; they are converted into very concrete forms of his suffering, his solitude, and his anger; they are marks on his face and on his body. They are wounds and scars lacking ornamentation. He says:

> Éste ha de ser mi cuerpo solidario
> por el que vela el alma individual; éste ha de ser
> mi ombligo en que maté mis piojos natos
> ésta mi cosa, cosa tremebunda.
>
> Por entre mis propios dientes salgo humeando,
> dando voces, pujando,
> banjándome los pantalones...
> Váca mi estómago, váca mi yeyuno,
> la miseria me saca por entre mis propios dientes,
> cogido con un palito por el puño de la camisa
> Una piedra en qué sentarme
> no habrá ahora para mí?[9]

[This must be my solid body / which my individual soul watches over; this must be / my navel in which I killed my native lice / this my thing, tremendous thing. From between my own teeth I emerge steaming / yelling, shoving, / dropping my pants... / My stomach empty, my intestine empty, / poverty pulls me out from between my own teeth, / caught with a toothpick by the cuff of my shirt. / Won't there be a stone / for me to sit on now?]

This is Vallejo's antipoetry; a pendulum which, as it moves, erases itself, a constant negation of the deed in the moment when this deed hits man, a contrast of existence and nonexistence. It is Vallejo's own method of self-destruction: to negate poetry by affirming it, to affirm life by negating it with extreme sarcasm and bitter brutality. It is the necessary expression of someone who has discovered the mechanisms of the trap and awaits the moment when it will snap shut, not about to betray it by hurrying it.

Latin American Antipoetry

Nicanor Parra, speaking of traps, conceives of the modern world as a monumental sewer in which rats and men are hunted. Before arriving at this conclusion, he says:

> De sus axilas extrae el hombre la cera necesaria
> para forjar el rostro de sus ídolos.
> Y del sexo de la mujer la paja y el barro de sus templos.[10]

[From his armpits man extracts the wax necessary / to mold the face of his idols. / And from the sex of the woman, the straw and the clay of his temples.]

This sex and these temples immediately establish the line which unifies the antipoetry of Parra and that of Vallejo and De Rokha. In order to come to the conclusion that the world is a sewer, Parra makes a prior ordering and synthesis of vices, crimes, lies, hypocrisies, and swindles. He exhibits each of these as immobilized and pathetic, as in an ancient comedy of errors. The antipoetic line reaches its greatest tension. Parra perfects the signs of destruction. His gift for synthesis allows him to define human anguish in the exact measure of its inefficacy and impotence.

Parra uses an everyday language mixed with pedagogic formulas and sayings of popular wisdom; it is his war horse, the same one used by any anonymous person who is hiding his desperation as he converses. His way of expressing himself is sarcastic, full of a rage which does not burst out in blows, but rather in gestures, words and movements, and which hangs in the air, threatening but useless. His most recriminating poems have become frozen in time and are like posters stuck up on certain walls of downtown buildings, courthouses, and public libraries. I refer to "The Viper," "The Trap," "*The Vices of the Modern World*," and "*The Individual's Soliloquy*."

After that, Parra had to carry antipoetry to its extremes, converting his prayers into axioms, key sentences which represent the direct concretion of the philosophical absurd and of social anarchy. He has arrived, then, at a mural poetry, not the subtle, distilled kind that the ultraists pasted on the walls of the big city, but an activist poetry which is written violently on the wall in a mood of defiance.

I insist that Parra isolates himself and burns his bridges and fills in the trenches around him. Within his poetry, Parra is like a frenetic woodcutter, axe in hand, cutting and destroying even the last vestige of his tree of life. Soon nothing is left. He was never as alone as now when antipoets are appearing everywhere and holding out their arms to him. In the expositive tradition of antipoetry, the inclined plane where it opens and extends to humanity like a hide stretched out on the floor, where the needle holes are marked and a canvas is spread underneath to catch the blood, Parra marked definitive patterns.

I think that Gonzalo Rojas, Ernesto Cardenal, César Fernández Moreno, and Roque Dalton unquestionably accompanied him. Among others.

It is already obvious in 1948 when his book *La miseria del hombre* [Man's Misery] appears, that Gonzalo Rojas does not wish to fight only in the white armor of Chilean surrealism: chaotic enumeration, the act which disintegrates, the cumulative process of an ornamental anguish. Instead, he attacks certain basic aspects of the human condition with weapons that are characteristic of antipoetry: the non sequitur, the everyday phrase, sarcasm, and formulas of dogmatic reasoning. Rojas squeezes the poetic object, concentrates on seeking the seed, and then opens it, extends it, extracts consequences. He is a friend of definitions, and in them he finds the most provocative of his antipoetry.

> Entre una y otra sábana o, aún más rápido que eso, en un mordisco, nos hicieron
> desnudos y saltamos al aire ya feamente viejos, sin alas, con la arruga de la tierra.

> Uno está aquí y no sabe que ya no está,
> dan ganas de reírse
> de haber entrado a este juego delirante.
> Dios no me sirve. Nadie me sirve para nada.
> Soy, pues, el Perro que adivina el porvenir:
> profetizo.[11]

[Between one sheet and another, or even more rapidly than that, in a bite, we stripped ourselves / naked and leaped into the air already hideously old, without wings, with the wrinkle of the earth.

One is here and does not know he is no longer here, / they make one want to laugh / at having entered into this delirious game. / God is no use to me. No one is any use to me. / I am, then, the Dog who foresees the future: / I prophesy.]

A poem like "¿A qué mentirnos?" is already a decisive proclamation to round out Rojas's final intention. Like Parra in "The Vices of the Modern World," who goes over and over the achievements of man and is finally left with only a louse on his necktie, Rojas, too, sees humanity as an incessant, heavy, bloody, sad, headlong fall into the coffin, a kind of silent movie, speeded up, repeated into infinity. To say this with sonority and anguish, with defiant sarcasm, is the mark of his antipoetry.

The antipoetry of César Fernández Moreno contrasts with the sacred and blasphemous oratory which is prolonged from Pablo de Rokha to Gonzalo Rojas. Fernández Moreno avoids anything that might delay him: reflection as much as pronouncements. He speaks with extreme velocity in the agitated monologue of someone who recounts a movie plot and in telling it, contradicts himself, makes mistakes, goes back, jumps ahead, and makes flying commentaries. To be the antipoet that he is, Fernández Moreno needed to rewrite his biography and the history of his country. As he learned to lack respect for Argentina, he found himself face to face with himself:

> así soy de todas esas maneras
> español francés indio quién sabe
> guerrero campesino comerciante poeta perhaps
> rico pobre de todas las clases y de ninguna
> y bueno soy argentino.[12]

[so I am in all those ways / Spanish French Indian who knows / warrior peasant businessman poet perhaps / rich poor of all classes and of none / and well I am Argentine]

Fernández Moreno describes the place before tourists took the photos and military geographers made the maps, in its domestic portion of chaos, beyond the marbles and boulevards, the stadiums and the beaches, the casinos and the barracks. His roll of film is always spinning along, and it never ends. His antipoetry is a bazaar. It is also a player piano and a neighborhood biography. Fernández Moreno's antipoetry is closely related to the novelists Sábato and Cortázar. Like Cortázar, he plays with changing the sounds of language:

> disculpen si les hablo así alelado
> el hielo me hiela la lengua
> igual siglo glitando
> las malvinas son algentinas
> así me lo enseñaron en la escuela...[13]

[forgive me if I speak to you thus tongue twisted / the ice freezes my tongue / but I kleep shlouting anyway / the Malvinas are Argentina's / that's what they taught me in school...]

Like Sábato, he is always tracking. His ear is to the ground to hear the pulses from far and wide across the country which is still not awake. Fernández Moreno fights. The political current runs through his antipoetry like an underground train which, during moments of crisis, emerges and sounds its whistle at the open stations. There are no formulas or countersigns. Only exclamations, some mural propaganda, memories of the Spanish civil war, of Peronism, and vague plans for the moment of truth. But throughout poems and antipoems, there is always a voice, even, firm, remembering certain anniversaries right on time, some names, and the hands of people that are in the process of being raised. this voice never sounds of oratory; on the contrary, when it is most serious, it is least eloquent; when it is most emotional, it is most spare, hard, and clipped. Fernández Moreno is conscious of the chaos he is creating and of the action which will be its consequence.

Argentine antipoetry, like that of other Latin American countries, has picked up speed in recent years seeking the vanguard where it will make its final attack. Of Fernández Moreno's "newsreel" there remains, at times, the speed, but not the control of the voice. The verse falls now like a brick into water. The anguish is more immediate: it comes from the very real prison, close at hand, of a city slum or shantytown, of an obligatory exile. The revolt is not announced or analyzed: it is produced. The language of solitude is the same as that of a family in debt, of a prisoner, of a striker, or of wounded people in the First Aid Station. This language does not have a literature that converts it into memory. It is immediate reporting, with scabs and scars. The curious thing is that the voice sounds like a chorus on one side and on the other like the world. The sound of demolition is general and the dust which remains floating in the air hides the sun. The writing is unique.

From the outside one can follow this movement through key publications: *El escarabajo de oro* [The Golden Beetle] in Argentina, *El corno emplumado* [The Plumed Antler] in Mexico, *G. B.* in Sausalito, *Kayak* in San Francisco, *La pájara pinta* [The Game of Forfeits] in El Salvador, *El techo de la ballena* [The Whale's Ceiling] in Venezuela, and *Fire* in London.

The light which Víctor García Robles seeks in his antipoetry (*Oíd mortales* [Listen, Mortals], 1965) is found by hacking away with a hatchet at the great sacred shadows around him. He pounds on the daily mold where neighbors gather to divide up the bones of a student. But where he hammers enthusiastically is in his poem "Sepa lo que pasa a lágrima viva y con malas palabras." The title is an exact summary of the poem: a counterpoint of tears and curses. It gives me a real sense of what the new generation feels as it runs throwing rocks in front of embassies and imperialist companies, ripping trees and benches out of town squares, exploding bombs, and ending up in police wagons under a rainfall of nightsticks. The speech in front of the newspaper stand brings tears to my eyes. The young Argentine poet says:

> pero la radio no dice: Se aprobó la reforma agraria,
> por la radio no dicen los nombres de los presos políticos,
> por la radio no dicen quién mató a Satanowsky y a Ingalinella,
> por la radio no dicen una mierda,
> meta boleros y preguntas y respuestas,
> los diarios son lo mismo, para qué carajo sirven los diarios,
> nos engrupen sobre oriente,
> nos engrupen sobre occidente,
> las revistas nos distraen con unas cuantas minas en pelotas.[14]

[but the radio doesn't say: Agrarian reform was approved, / on the radio they don't give the names of the political prisoners, / on the radio they don't say who killed Satanowsky and Ingalinella, / on the radio they don't say shit, / they put on boleros and questions and answers, / the newspapers are the same, what the hell are papers good for, / they lie to us about the East, / they lie to us about the West, / the magazines amuse us with a few naked chicks.]

García Robles names what he must: the city slums, Loeb, Shell, Standard Oil, aircraft carriers, the liberating revolution and he draws his conclusions. The poem "Atenti Primavera" succinctly establishes the direction of this poetry: García Robles does not accept being alone, he does not shut himself up to dissect himself, nor to flagellate himself, nor to look for lime. On the contrary, his antipoetry grows like a huge plant in a neighborhood flowerpot. Consequently, it seems that in this case antipoetry stripped poetry in order to discover a new way of speaking to man about justice and love, a way the *virtuosi* had betrayed, disguised, denied, and buried. This is not a new way, then, but the only true one, reborn.

This makes me think of the Nicaraguan poet Ernesto Cardenal whose work is one of the most direct and violently antirhetorical expressions I know. Cardenal not only has dismantled the *preciosista* language of Central American Modernism and postmodernism, he also terminated the myth of the creative image, exiled the metaphor, and incorporated the popular voice. His symbols are like a dark curve seeking the Indian past. Not even in his great poem " El estrecho dudoso" [The Doubtful Strait] (1966), where the historic and the geographic are continually enfolded in surrealist effects and where there are frequent mystic absences and brief visions, like flashes of light over the Mayan lake, does Cardenal lose sight of the immediate surroundings that are extended like a trap at his feet. This externalism is never decorative, it is not even representative (as an objective image of reality), and it does not function to situate each thing in its place, but rather the opposite: its dynamism derives from the disorder of the real world, from the absurdity and the anger which serve it as a foundation, and, above all, from the essential love of life and man which constitute his transcendent bond.

Cardenal is a rough and dissonant antipoet who tries to light an internal flame in the prosaic in order to provoke other lights around it: he is a namer of things and of beings, a confuser of history, a transmuter. He behaves with impetuous revolutionary force. His best lines are attacks directed at anyone who molests him and dirties his life on his solitary island: imperialism, Fascist violence, the military dictatorship, the Coca–Cola above the face armed with knives and amulets. Cardenal discovers in material objects a truth which is not necessarily beautiful, but which must become transcendent when breathed upon by common man. This is the root of his antipoetry.

Cardenal, like García Robles, Jitrik, and Szpunberg, like the Colombian J. Mario, the Cubans Heberto Padilla and Carlos Rodríguez Rivera, the Peruvians Antonio Cisneros and Carlos Germán Belli, the Ecuadorian Carlos Ramírez Estrada, fights on the plane of social revolution with weapons conquered in the antiliterary revolution: he uses antipoetry to unmask, attack, and purify—antipoetry at the service of the revolution.

Involved in this enterprise with Cardenal is Roque Dalton, the Salvadorian who has done most of his writing in Mexico and Cuba. In his first books Dalton moves in the midst of surrealist roots seeking luminosities and rhythms in familiar, regional, and routine allusions. The tone of voices possesses a noble, tragic quality. The image dismantles, spins countries, people, schools, and churches; a youthful tenderness seeks its expression. Dalton's accent awakes echoes of other poetic worlds in which the adolescent searches for the nocturnal sun. He pulls in that imaginist net, however, and hides it beneath social recrimination which is as strong and as aggressive as Cardenal's. His revolutionary experience as a student, his imprisonments and exiles, the girls who shared with him the clandestine movement in America and Europe, his family background, the faces of colonels and policemen, the green Banana Mafia, and the blockade of imperialist rifles in Santo Domingo throng through his antipoetry, and what was in Mexico a somber youthful ballad (*La ventana en el rostro* [The Window in My Face], 1961) is suddenly converted into imprecation, yells, and anticipation of the approaching combat. From Cuba, Dalton denounces his homeland in angry tones:

> Patria dispersa: caes
> como una pastillita de veneno en mis horas.
> ¿ Quién eres tú, poblada de amos
> como la perra que se rasca junto a los mismos árboles
> que mea? ¿ Quién soportó tus símbolos,
> tus gestos de doncella con olor a caoba,
> sabiéndote arrasada por la baba del crápula?[15]

[Disperse homeland: you fall / like a tablet of poison on my hours. / Who are you, populated by masters / like the bitch who scratches herself right by the same trees / she pees on? Who tolerated your symbols, / your ladylike gestures which smell of mahogany, / knowing you steeped in the spittle of crapulence?]

He takes the lid off history as off a spoiled stew:

> Hernán Cortés era un sifilítico iracundo
> hediondo a cuero crudo en sus ratos de holganza
> vengador de sus bubas
> en cada astrónomo maya a quien mandó sacar los ojos.
> Hombre hecho a las fatigas de los piojos
> a los humores del vómito perla del agrio vino...[16]

[Hernán Cortés was a syphilitic irascible / stinking of rawhide in his moments of leisure / avenger of his pustules / on each Mayan astronomer whose eyes he ordered put out. / Man made for the weariness of the lice / for the humors of the pearly vomit of the sour wine...]

Dalton addresses God with the cynical, tired, compassionate voice of the antipoets. He takes notice of flies, consecrates Vallejo, and crucifies himself in an implacable self-portrait pinned up by an arrow next to the bloody faces of his father and mother.

Health and Agitation

Reading Dalton, Cardenal, Fernández Moreno, Parra, Rojas, and García Robles, thinking about De Rokha and Vallejo, one begins to draw the following conclusions: antipoetry, which has been an anarchic attitude, an anti-rhetorical blow, found a direct and violent language and began to return to man the reality which he had lost, not giving it in installments, like peddlers, but all at once. The internal violence was converted into an attack on and punishment of contemporary society; the anguished metaphysic, into a confrontation between neighbor and neighbor, one might say a face-to-face encounter with a God who is considered to be worried, boxed in, on the point of dying under the concerted assault of subjects and objects in revolt; the father has returned seeking the rib of his son, who hides it; the woman becomes open like a tomb, engrossed in policies, wills, pills, and impotence. The fly buzzes over the scene of the crime.

Now then, the most recent antipoetry, that which follows the Cuban Revolution, introduces certain operational changes in this system of violence: the fly does not disappear, but becomes a sign of bourgeois pestilence and of international flight. God descends from the cross and gets on his motorcycle and sings, smokes the good golden herb of Acapulco, jingles his little bells, and confronts the police. Violence is turned against the imperialist establishment, against local robbers, the neo-Fascist barracks, the embargo of the conscience, and toward agrarian reform. The Third World has been born. One, two, three Vietnams. From the surrealist sunset, antipoetry has been pulling out tools and the components of a time bomb. Meanwhile, the period of Molotov cocktails goes by. The antipoets no longer negate themselves. They make signs from one country to another, they take the crossbar off the door, they give their cudgel blow. They distribute health and agitation.

Notes

1. Julio Cortázar, *Rayuela* (Buenos Aires: Sudamericana, 1963), pp. 452 and 500.

2. Cf. Leopoldo Marechal, *El banquete de Severo Arcángel* (Buenos Aires: Sudamericana, 1965).

3. Cf. Antinovels like *Three Trapped Tigers* (1967), by Guillermo Cabrera Infante, *Los niños se despiden de la miseria* (1968), by Pablo Armando Fernández, *El garabato* (1967), by Vicente Leñero, among others.

4. Fernando Alegría, *Literatura chilena del siglo XX*, 2d ed. (Santiago de Chile: Zig-Zag, 1967), pp. 117–118.

5. I quote from *Antología 1916–53* (Santiago de Chile: Multitud, 1954), p. 9.

6. Pablo De Rokha, op. cit., pp. 63–65, 67–68, 71, 75.

7. I quote from *Poesías completas, 1918–1938*, second edition, (Buenos Aires: Losada, 1949), p. 23.

8. C. Vallejo, op. cit., p. 61.
9. *Ibid.*, pp. 94, 98. Turn to the essay by Noé Jítrik for an analysis of this text.
10. Nicanor Parra, *Poemas y antipoemas* (Santiago de Chile: Nascimento, 1954), p. 141.
11. Gonzalo Rojas, *Contra la muerte* (Santiago de Chile: Universitaria, 1964), pp. 14 ff.
12. C. Fernández Moreno, *Argentino hasta la muerte* (Buenos Aires: Sudamericana, 1963).
13. By the same poet, *Los aeropuertos* (Buenos Aires: Sudamericana, 1967).
14. Víctor García Robles, *Oíd mortales* (Havana: Casa de las Américas, 1965), p. 137.
15. Roque Dalton, *El turno del ofendido* (Havana: Casa de las Américas, 1962).
16. *Ibid.*, p. 85.

8 / The New Criticism

GUILLERMO SUCRE

CRITICISM AS CREATION

Although obvious, it may be said again: criticism is essential to literary creation. Not only does it form a part of it, but it also makes it possible. But criticism is something more than a method or a way of knowing. Just as literary function cannot be reduced to its pure, expressive techniques and there is always a dimension of it which transcends them, in the same way, criticism cannot be confined to a mere exercise of investigation. All great criticism supposes, of course, a method, just that this method is a personal relationship with the work it examines. And behind every method, there also exists a system of ideas, but these do not operate as permanent categories: they function in particular reference to the work and to the experience of it. In principle, critical activity is inherent in the very nature of man. Impulse or action, man is also a reflective pause; his true being is defined by this tense equilibrium of opposites. "All living," affirmed Alfonso Reyes, "is being, and at the same time, a pulling away from being. The pendular essence of man moves him from act to reflection and confronts him with himself at every moment." The great Mexican writer also added: "Criticism is to be conditioned. Poetry is to be conditioning. They are simultaneous, since only theoretically is poetry prior to criticism. All creation is infused with poetic art, and thus every creator carries creation with him."[1]

Simultaneous with creation, criticism does not crystallize however, except in its last phase: in the relationship of the already created work with the reader. And we know that this relationship is not an external one, that is, the work does not reveal its meaning or meanings except in contact with a scrutiny which actualizes it. It is the movement from potential to true presence—a presence which is continually a possibility. For Borges, the aesthetic act is the imminence of a revelation which does not materialize.[2] Critical vision is the search for this revelation. In its present and in its discourse, this vision is multiple just as the nature of the work itself is multiple. A single way of reading a poem or a novel would be impossible and would even be the death of all aesthetic creation. If poetry, as Antonio Machado pointed out, is the word in time, criticism is the scrutinizing vision in time: succession and change, like the very work itself. Its absolute is the instant, but the instant which carries with it a whole context of correspondences and relationships. Thus, criticism is not only a method of suggestive reasoning, as Poe wished, it is even more. It is "a force of reminiscent reasoning," as Lezama Lima defines it today.[3]

The poet is recognized in the simple act of making the reader an "inspired one," Valéry said. It would not be arbitrary to propose that efficacious criticism may also be recognized as that which is most inspired. That is, criticism which upon receiving the poetic message (this should not be confused with thesis or aberrations of propaganda) not only clarifies it and illuminates it profoundly, but makes it more resonant at the same time. Thus, perhaps the foundation of criticism is creation. "Poetry and criticism are two forms of creation, and that is all," concluded Alfonso Reyes in an analysis of the topic.[4] And even before him, an essayist like Rodó expressed a similar point of view: "The specific attribute of the critic," he wrote, "is a force which is not essentially different from the power of creativity." Formulated at the beginning of the century, this concept could serve as the beginning of modern Latin American criticism. And it is just this in many senses. Rodó tends to liberate criticism from that impoverishing need to affirm or deny the values of a work, and allows it, rather, to participate in them. If the work—he reminds us, although still with a certain nostalgia for naturalism—is the world perceived through an individual temperament, the important thing is that he sees that the work in its turn must pass through another temperament's contemplation in order to reveal its intimate nature. For this reason, for Rodó, criticism carries in it "a germ of activity and creative originality which only differs in degree from those which constitute the genius of the artist."[5]

What kind of creation is criticism? one might still ask. Of course, it is not the same kind as poetry. In effect, criticism only lives on the works of others, although it is also true that it makes them live. It is not an autonomous (*autotelic*, Eliot would say) activity like poetry. Criticism is creation, then, not of the same type as that of poetry, but perhaps, yes, of the same structure. No poetic work is a creation ex nihilo either; if the poet confronts the blank page , as Mallarmé described (did not Darío himself suggest the same thing in his poem "La página blanca?" [The Blank Page]), we know that this innocence is impregnated by a tradition and by a memory. Finally, the inspiration of the poet is his memory and the continuous adventure of this memory in relation to language. In a similar manner, the critic confronts a blank work, I mean to say, he confronts a work which would say nothing or would say very little if we were only to consider it literally and were not to convert it—or to actualize it—into its true symbolic and multiple nature. Is this not, perhaps, the vision which leads a poet like Octavio Paz to entitle one of his last books *Blanco*? It would no doubt be vain to seek another implication in this name which would not be what Paz considers to be the true nature of poetry and criticism, and even of the world. His book is certainly a blank [*en blanco*] book. All the procedures which Paz employs in it (from the typographical characters, the arrangement of the text, the space on the pages, even the images themselves) lead us to this evidence: it is a book which is and is not written and in which the word is and is not spoken. It is, then, a call to the reader, converted in his turn into a poet, to make him say what it contains. But what the reader says is in some way implicit in the discourse of the poet.

But would it not be excessively presumptuous of criticism to claim to be the vision which confers existence on the work? And on the part of the poet who accepts it, would it not also assume a dismissal of his high creative powers? Perhaps neither one nor the other. Let us begin with the latter. Now, as never before, the creator has become conscious that his language has lost singularity and all rigid semantic connotation; he is conscious, too, that any vision of the world is now undergoing rupture and fragmentation, that is, its coherence is in perpetual motion. Not a compact unity but a conjunction of relationships. Thus, his work is presented not as something already made and established ahead of time, but rather as something being made right under our eyes; his language is above all a search for meaning. For this reason, Borges always tends to weaken the notion of authorship. There is no paternity because the work is a continuous making and remaking. The author does not have the last word. But neither does the critic. In effect, the critic does not presume to impose a static and eternal code of references; he knows, on the contrary, that his comprehension of the work is not only unique but also personal, and he even undertakes it as an adventure. What he does is restore to the work its original character as an open work, that is, he restores its inclination to be what it really is: reality and unreality of a world by means of the word. To understand a work without petrifying it or taking it apart, does that not make it live all over again? Furthermore, the true critic makes it visible within a conjunction of works. In that sense, his task is also a creative one. It is not that he invents the work, obviously, but, as Octavio Paz maintains, "he invents a literature (a perspective, an order) based on the works." Paz himself carries this idea to its extreme consequences when he adds: "In our era, criticism establishes literature. While the latter constitutes itself as a criticism of the word and the world, as a question about itself, criticism conceives of literature as a world of words, as a verbal structure. Creation is criticism and criticism, creation."[6]

But in order to invent that perspective and that order of which Paz speaks, the critic cannot depend upon pure erudition. It is true that what we could call among ourselves *university criticism* has produced profound research efforts. These efforts may constitute the elements of a future science of literature. However, they are not really criticism as such. They may lack an intensity of imagination and of deciphering power. The most efficacious criticism, for Eliot, was that which was based upon facts. But what are the facts of a work of literature? It is not possible to think of the criteria of objectivity and of verisimilitude. There are no univocal events in literature. There are only forms which are symbols, signs which are symbols. And as such, they must be interpreted. As Alfonso Reyes warned, no mathematical equation or fixed relationship exists between poetic language and what it communicates to us;

that relationship changes for each reader. It follows, Reyes concluded, that "the study of the literary phenomenon is a phenomenology of a fluid entity."[7] In another of his texts, he stated: "If all perception is translation (the light is not light, the table is not a table, etc.), this is even more true when the filter is the artistic sensibility."[8] In effect, only because of the bitter aftertaste of positivism (of extreme causality) can one believe that all interpretation is merely arbitrary fabrication or a way of eluding the reality of a work.

The true critic continues to be a translator and an interpreter, as Baudelaire conceived of it. But as he interprets and translates, he illuminates the very being of the work. Then, it does not seem possible to speak about a work if one does not speak from it. The critic's purpose is not to discover the work—says Roland Barthes—but to cover it with his own language. In fact, the intuition of the critic is not a show of inventiveness; when it is efficacious, it is in synchrony with the intuition which made the work possible. It is also true that certain present criticism is dominated by such a mania for interpretation that not only has the spontaneous aesthetic pleasure of the work been lost, but also the concept of its very nature. This is what Borges denounced a long time ago as "the superstitious ethic of the reader": that is, to submit the emotion which the work communicates to a kind of analysis, inhibitory and even fetishist, of its various parts. Thus Borges sustained: "There are no longer any readers left, in the ingenuous sense of the word, since they have all become potential critics."[9] More recently, this has been pointed out by Susan Sontag in her book *Against Interpretation*. But, of course, what Borges and the North American writer are against is a certain type of interpretation, a type which Borges would call *ethical superstition* and which Susan Sontag, in her turn, denounces as *humanistic superstition*, that is, the subjection of art to purely intellectual meanings to the detriment of its sensory reality, of its formal power. But both writers, at bottom, assume a manner—a new manner— of interpreting a work. It is evident, for example, that if the criticism of Borges manages to illuminate that which is essential and inherent in creation, it will not for this reason cease to be a very particular personal view, which makes all it sees "Borgian." And not because Borges is—as Eliot called the artist critics—a *practicing critic*. If we think of a pure critic like Emir Rodríguez Monegal, we find that at the very base of his criticism, which is imminently and fundamentally attached to the texts, there is a more or less constant line of interpretation; that is, profound psychology, symbolic biography. This interpretation returns us, in its turn, to a personal perspective, or rather to Rodríguez Monegal's own internal search. By internal search, I also mean aesthetic and symbolic. One of the ambiguities of criticism is inherent in this: it lives on the *I* of the work and on the *I* of the one who contemplates it, it lives on the work as object and on the solitary decision of a subject which experiences it.

There are interpretations of interpretations. And, in addition, to not take them on—within and not outside of the work—could lead to two equally negative risks: that of falling into pure impressionism, or that of submitting to

the canons by which traditional criticism has lived and which Roland Barthes
has already denounced effectively enough in his book *Critique et verité*. These
canons, as we know, are verisimilitude, objectivity, and thus, the asym-
bolicness of a work. A critical perspective based upon these canons would
definitely have to begin by recognizing a kind of authority, of reality that is
external to the work or of total literalness. But everything is interpretation,
Barthes warns us, since the work is a universe of symbols and a coexistence of
multiple meanings. Thus, he also invokes the famous sentence by Rimbaud
concerning the meaning of *Une saison en enfer*: "J'ai voulu dire ce que ça dit,
littéralement et dans tous les sens."

Only in this way does criticism assume both the rigor and the adventure
implicit in all works based on language; that is, it postulates a method, and that
method only takes into account the changing reality of the work itself. For this
reason, if criticism is analysis (and comparison, as Eliot wished), it is also
passion, a profound identification with the work, even when this identification
finally implies an opposition. What is Proust's *Contre Sainte-Beuve* but the
most radical and also the most subtle reproach of criticism based only on pure
intelligence, which seemed to be faithfully represented by the author of
Lundis? And is it not admirable, at the same time, that this book of Proust's
should be basically the preliminary meditation on the meaning of his great
novelistic creation? That is, Proust intuits the reality of his own work by also
intuiting the reality of criticism and of art. Thus, on the aesthetic plane, his
book is fully valid today; it also reveals, yet again, that it was not Sainte-
Beuve—the professional critic, the critic of facts and of objectivity—who
really established modern criticism in France. Does not this destiny belong,
rather, to a poet like Baudelaire? Beyond his limitations or prejudices, it is
evident that Baudelaire's criticism was not only the most efficacious and
enlightening of his era, but also that which has contributed the most to the
knowledge of modern art. And Baudelaire proposed only a criticism which was
"partial, impassioned, political, made from an exclusive point of view,"
although he specified luminously: "but from a point of view which opens
horizons as much as possible." Thus, and today there is no doubt about it,
passion is for him the domain of both lucidity and imagination, the alliance of
critical reflection and creative impulse. For this reason, when Baudelaire
defines poetry (speaking of Poe), he excludes all sentimentalism and proposes
a new emotiveness: the passion of the imagination. This alliance marks all
contemporary art and thought; that is, both are essentially subjective. Thus,
the criticism that still presumes to be scientific is the least scientific of all and
sustains itself on the basis of principles (objectivity, verisimilitude, judgment,
etc.) which also turn out to be hypocritical now: they promote the contrary of
what they postulate. The new criticism, on the contrary, when it defines itself
as subjective is certainly more sincere and efficacious; when it assumes its own
risks, it enlightens the very destiny of all literary labor: a perpetual adventure to
decipher the world by means of the word. And it is thus that Baudelaire's

attitude evokes a response today, like an echo, in Roland Barthes's perspective. "A systematized subjectivity," he writes, "that is, *cultivated* [relative to culture], and submitted to the immense pressures which emerge from the symbols themselves of a work, has perhaps more opportunity to approach the literary object than does an objectivity which is uncultured, blind in respect to itself, and which takes refuge behind the letter as behind a natural state."

The interpretation of a work and invention of literature itself, criticism is thus also, and above all, a writing. I do not mean a knowledge of how to write "well," nor do I allude to matters of punctuation and syntax, ironically evoked by Borges who, apart from this, did not encourage negligences either. It is a matter of something which is perhaps more significant: a knowledge of how to intuit the real play of all writing, that of inventing itself while it invents the world. In this, writers and critics gradually merge. Eliot establishes a difference between practicing critics and pure critics; this difference still appears to revolve around a notion of possible objectivity or of amplitude in favor of the pure critic. For this reason, this distinction is perhaps inadequate today, not so much because that notion has become less valid nor because it has been perhaps the practicing critics (from Baudelaire to Eliot himself; from Borges to Paz, among us) who have penetrated most profoundly into the work of art. But above all, it is because the writer and the critic are confronting a same reality: language. "There are no longer poets or novelists: there is only writing," points out Barthes. This means, as Barthes himself explains, not only that the activity of the critic is centered in language, but that his true objective, just like that of the poet or the novelist, is to reveal the symbolic nature and the constitutive ambiguity of that language.

In fact, it is not true that the poet or the novelist has original material which is the world. Their true material is language; they see the world only through words. "In the beginning of literature there is myth, and also in the end," writes the mature Borges.[10] And we know that all mythic creation begins in the word. "The true experience of the poet is above all verbal," says Octavio Paz in his turn, "or if you wish: all experience, in poetry, immediately acquires a verbal tonality."[11] Paz himself explains how this characteristic has especially defined modern literature, ever since romanticism. Certainly, it is a distinctive characteristic of the modern poetic consciousness. Not even a poet as renovative as Góngora went so far as to propose a criticism of the meaning or of the sense of the word. In contrast, Paz notes, writers like Mallarmé or Joyce (we could add Cortázar, among us) are a criticism and sometimes an annulment of the meaning. This effort supposes a double movement: the destruction of the language and its new creation at the same time. The poet should cede the initiative to the words, suggested Mallarmé. It is not the dismissal of the poet, obviously, but rather the greatest possible acceptance of his true creative energy: that energy which words communicate to him. It follows that all is inverted in modern literature: it is not the ideas (basis or foundation) which make the words (form), but rather the inverse, because everything is language. The poet proposes and language disposes. "The form secretes its idea, its vision of the world," as in Paz's synthesis of this topic.[12]

Well then, criticism will remain at the fringe of true aesthetic creation if this sense of modern literature is not taken into account. It is not a matter now of a criticism of authors, but rather of works and texts. Behind each author there is a language, not an *I*. Following Valéry, Borges proposed a history of literature where no names would appear, only works. Octavio Paz even proposed a tradition which would not be a succession of names, works, and tendencies, but rather a system of meaningful relationships based on language. It is this consciousness of language—as interrogation and problem—which finally constitutes the new criticism. A work is made up only of words, and there is no objectivity outside of words, but only among them, in the text itself which is configured by them. And even this objectivity is a changing one: words communicate among themselves in order to reveal their meaning, but they also communicate with someone who upon receiving them modifies them in some way. The sincerity of criticism is to assume this risk of language. It is not a matter, then, of the critic writing "well." The important thing is for him to achieve, with all lucidity, something that has also been emphasized by Barthes: criticism is a language which speaks fully of another. Fully, with all the powers of the word, with its ambiguity, its multiple energy, its discourse and its silence, with its erotic force, too. Criticism is erotic insofar as it is based upon the pleasure of language. This pleasure does not at all diminish its lucidity; on the contrary, it introduces an even more stimulating relationship with the work and with the world.

CRITICISM IN LATIN AMERICA

Does a critical perspective in the terms we have just described exist in Latin America? This is the question we are interested in examining from here on. Until now, we have only formulated an approximate—and perhaps theoretical—description of such a criticism. But the reader will have noticed that that description is based continually upon the thought and creative experience of Latin American writers. Does this not already provide proof of the existence of such a criticism?

In a book published in 1957, Enrique Anderson Imbert analyzed the situation of Latin American criticism at that time.[13] From a sociological but also aesthetic point of view, that analysis began by indicating the negative aspects of our criticism. He mentioned, for example, the disproportion between "an enormous critical production of generally slight value, and the literary production itself. "In this type of criticism," sustains Anderson Imbert, "there is some of everything. Naturally, what abounds is irresponsibility. In general, opinions are set forth that are not backed up either by a concept of the world or by a scale of values. In the best of cases, from these capricious opinions it is possible to extract the rudiments of a very superficial critical position: dogmatic, hedonistic, and impressionistic." Nevertheless, his analysis becomes more optimistic at the end. "Despite what has just been said," he concludes, "there is good criticism in Hispanic America. We have among us some brilliant critics who would do honor to any culture."

More recently, Octavio Paz expressed a more radical attitude toward the same topic—more radical and perhaps more oriented within a new concept of criticism. His ideas are therefore essential in this discussion. Is not Paz himself one of the founders of modern criticism among us? Paz observes that we have lacked both a way of thinking and a system of doctrines such as that capacity which criticism has to situate a literary work in its intellectual space, that is, in that space where works encounter each other and dialogue among themselves, thus making a literature possible. "Criticism," he affirms, "is what constitutes that entity which we call literature and which is not so much the sum of the works as the system of their relationships: a field of affinities and oppositions."[14] From this perspective, which we essentially share, it is evident that Hispanic-American criticism has not been truly effective; rather than illuminating the literary works and their aesthetic-cultural context, it seems to have oriented itself toward mere information or external description.

But Paz's position is doubly significant: by denying the existence of that criticism among us, he is formulating and constituting it—or rather, as we will see, rescuing it—from realities and concrete data which, until now, have been submerged in our critical thought. Thus, their negation is converted into a beginning of affirmation. And it is what has also occurred in our own literature: it has really been born of its self-questioning, of its consciousness of its abandonment or of its anachronism.

It is true that Latin American criticism, in general, has not nourished itself on its own thought, nor has it known how to serve as a basis for our literature, as Paz points out. It has been, rather, an external criticism, impressionistic or vaguely sociological; rarely has it structured itself upon a true vision of the world or around a notion of literature as the aesthetics of language. Perhaps it could be maintained, as an extenuating circumstance, that criticism of this type also corresponded to a literature which was equally external, which believed in the literary work as a reflection, document, or testimony of reality. But that is only extenuating and very precarious because, in the first place, criticism does not have to be the echo of the literature it deals with, although it is fair to recognize that a close relationship between the two is inevitable (criticism is also historical). On the other hand, not all of our literature emerges from a concept which we could call *ingenuously realistic*. With the Hispanic-American Modernist movement, beginning at the end of the nineteenth century, a new creative perspective was established. That perspective represented an essential change; that is, its renovation of poetic language certainly implied a different way of conceiving of creation itself. And although it is true that no critical system emerged which corresponded to Modernist aesthetics, what matters is that for the first time there is a tendency to contemplate the literary work as a creation of language. Rodó, Blanco Fombona, Sanín Cano, García Calderón, and others initiated this change in critical perspective. And theoretical contributions by the creators of Modernism themselves were not lacking. Rubén Dario or Jaimes Freyre, for example, not only renovated and enriched the poetic rhythm and the structure of the poem, but they also formulated ideas about the topic; and the same could be said of Lugones in respect to the metaphor. It is perhaps the first moment in which the relationship of creation and criticism grows closer and more intimate.

Certainly, it is not this which Paz questions. His ideas deal primarily with the existence or nonexistence of a coherent critical concept on all levels; he does not deny individual contributions. But perhaps it is these contributions which count today, mainly because they have not been so isolated and also because they are the ones which have influenced the new literature. There has been a radical change in our own creative literature. It is not only a matter of a move from a realistic or testimonial literature to a literature of real imagination and of liberated language. There is a fact which is probably even more fundamental: the Latin American writer has become conscious that even more than a world to express or to take inventory of, what he has in front of him is a world to found. He has become conscious of what Paz himself has called "the literature of foundation" and which, in different but not contradictory terms, has been described by other Latin American writers, too: Carpentier, Lezama Lima, and Cortázar.

I am not going to summarize all of Paz's thought in regard to this, but I do think it is indispensable here to emphasize some of his points of view. Like all literatures, ours is constructed against a reality. But the reality against which our literature is erected—Paz affirms—is a utopia; that which was created by European thought about America at the time of the discovery. The utopia crystallizes in the name itself that condemned us to be a new world, that is, a world just being born and yet to be formed. Were we really? The paradox of this utopia was that actually it founded itself on anachronistic structures: those which came to us from a certain peninsular tradition. For this reason, our literature enters into modernity only when it begins to break with this anachronism, when it begins to really realize the utopia. The Modernist movement's rupture with peninsular Hispanic literature had an even wider significance: the negation of a past, a search for the new and for a universal tradition. It followed that Modernism should initially have been a literature of evasion and rootlessness; but, at bottom, it had a higher objective: to recover our reality as a new world based, this time, on our own invention. Thus the literature of evasion is progressively converted into a literature of exploration and return. Rubén Darío, says Paz, is the universal spirit who rediscovers Hispanic America, and with this is established a significant difference from the

Spanish writers of his era: the Spanish writers discover the world beginning with Spain (did not Unamuno even say that it was necessary to "Hispanify" Europe?). But the literature which followed Modernism was also a literature of rootlessness, of adventure in the universe, which only later would discover America. Think, for example, of the poetry of Vallejo, of Neruda, of Enrique Molina. The so-called Brazilian Modernism of the twenties, with Mario de Andrade, Manuel Bandeira, Jorge de Lima and Drummond de Andrade, also illustrates this double movement toward the universal and the American. The work of Borges himself, in Paz's perspective, "not only postulates the nonexistence of America, but also the inevitability of its invention." Thus, our literature is an effort to found reality, an enterprise of the imagination. To found a world, Paz concludes, is simultaneously to invent and to rescue the real. "Reality recognizes itself in the imaginations of the poets; and the poets recognize their images in reality. Rootless and cosmopolitan, Hispanic-American literature is both a return and a search for a tradition. Upon seeking it, it invents it."[15]

Consequently, anyone who denied the existence of critical thought among us was, in fact, formulating it laterally. Paz's ideas cast light on the nature of the new Latin American literature on a level which includes the aesthetic and goes beyond it. Or in other words, it is an aesthetic conceived within a true image of the world; that image is radically Latin American, but it is based on the traditional *Americanisms*.

It is not difficult to find resonances or analogies of Paz's ideas in present-day Latin American literature, both in fiction and in criticism. But they are also very apt in reference to writers of Paz's own generation and even earlier. Is this not, perhaps, the best sign that, in the essentials, a coherence in our attitude toward literature does exist? Borges, for example, has emphasized many times that the tradition of the Latin American writer is multiple, and for this reason, it is not a simple synthesis, but a true creation. Asked what the Argentine tradition is, Borges has answered in an essay: "I believe that our tradition is the whole of Western culture, and I believe, too, that we have a greater right to that tradition than do the inhabitants of other Western nations." Although Borges is referring particularly to his country in this essay ("El escritor argentino y la tradición"), it is evident that he is discussing—and he says so in several passages—a general South American theme. He recalls the participation of the Jews and the Irish in Western culture, a participation governed by a double movement: they act within and also outside that culture. This double movement has allowed them to be groups with their own creative originality. And then Borges affirms: "I believe that the Argentinians, South Americans in general, are in an analogous situation; we can handle all the European themes, handle them without superstitions, with an irreverence which can have, and already has, fortunate consequences."[16] Likewise, in this essay, as in all of his writing, Borges deals not only with the theme of tradition, but also with that of literature as invention. He breaks with the customary idea of determinism, which had so dominated in our literature. For him, even the supposedly popular literature, gaucho poetry, is something more than the simple reflection of a reality: it, too, is an intentional verbal creation, it is "a directed dream," like all art.

Literature as an enterprise of foundation (Paz) or as verbal creation (Borges), are these perspectives not also related to Lezama Lima's reflections about the image or about the imaginary eras? In effect, for the Cuban writer literature is based on "a concept of the world as image," and also "on the image as an absolute, the image which knows itself to be an image, the image as the last of the possible histories." Lezama Lima has a vision of the image which is both aesthetic and metaphysical. As for the aesthetic, the incantational power of the poem crystallizes in the image, it is the final vision which assures the metaphoric body, the infinite relationships which are evoked by the poem. And the metaphysical, the important thing in the image is not the realistic illusion (although it does not reject resemblance), but rather its capacity to marvel, and in the act of marveling, the possibility of embodying the world and its secret connections. For this reason he affirms: "No adventure, no desire where man has tried to conquer a resistance, has begun without a resemblance and an image; man has always felt himself to be a body that knows it is an image, because the body upon accepting itself as a body, verifies taking possession of an image."[17] The image is, then, substituted for nature, but in this substitution, a way is opened for all the possible relationships with culture and with the images created by it. It follows thus that the aesthetic of Lezama should be an aesthetic of intuition; he completely rejects the facile causal relationship in order to seize hold of the creative synthesis. It is also an aesthetic of form, in which nature, through the action of the metaphoric subject, is converted into "landscape." The essential things in this aesthetic are, therefore, the structures and the language connections. As Severo Sarduy has clearly pointed out, speaking of Lezama's fiction, "But the cultural exactness of [his] metaphors matters: what they activate are relationships, not contents; what counts is not the veracity—in the sense of identification with something nonverbal—of the word, but rather its dialogic presence, its mirror."[18] In the same sense, for Lezama, the dialogue between man and nature makes of the latter a space in which natural and cultural entities are conjugated which mutually metamorphose themselves in order to create a new reality: the vision. On the other hand, the image governs the relationship of man and nature, but also that of man and history. We do not know history, finally, except through the dominant images of each era; history is the myths which embody it. The "imaginary eras" are the time of man.[19]

VARIOUS TRENDS IN THE NEW CRITICISM

The vision of literature as an autonomous world, with its own laws and structures, of the work as a symbol and imaginary incarnation of the real, is what has given a new tone to Latin American criticism. The trend is not recent, although it is more general in recent times. Among its initiators, one must immediately mention—how could one not?—Alfonso Reyes. His admirable work of erudition always provides clear evidence of the sensitivity and the critical view which were capable of capturing the true movement of creation. It could be no other way. He was also one of the most lucid creators of our literature. It is true that part of his critical effort is limited to erudition and to exegesis; comparable to the erudition of another master, Pedro Henríquez Ureña, Reyes's was perhaps more refined and, although scattered at times, it leads to a synthesis where aesthetic experience prevails: in that experience one also feels the personal adventure, the passionate search. His counterpart, for that reason, among us, would be Borges. In addition to a writing style which is careful, ironic, and capable of great subtleties, they both share the concept of art as form and as play: a form which is converted into the very essence of creation, a game which comes to imply the fullest reality. The parallel could be extended, but perhaps that is sufficient. Many of the things which could be said about Reyes are also true for Borges, and inversely. They are kindred spirits, and they are at the beginning of our modernity. But I still want to emphasize some of the aspects of Reyes's critical thought, which is one of the most coherent in Latin American literature. It is expressed above all in two fundamental books: *La experiencia literaria* [The Literary Experience] (1941), and *El deslinde* [The Boundary] (1944). In the latter, while Reyes did not really formulate and systematize a theory of literature, he did establish its basis. With penetrating rigor, he knew how to mark the boundaries [*deslindar*] between the orbit of literature and the other activities of the spirit, without forgetting the interconnections between them in the meantime. In the first book Reyes begins, as I have indicated already, with the idea of literature as form, as language, although not only in the manner of stylistic or philological criticism. Poetic language, for him, is based on the three planes of the idiom (grammatical, phonetic, and stylistic), and it is the one which best makes use of them and deepens them. But it is equally a creation which is irreducible to these planes. Truly, the poet forges himself in a struggle against language; poetry is a transcended word: a language within the language, as Valéry proposed. "Hence," says Reyes, "its essential procedure; catachresis, which is a describing in words of that which has no words to describe it." This explains both his vigilance and his passion for form: "The poet," he adds, "should not trust himself too much to poetry as a state of soul, and instead he should insist on poetry as the effect of words."[20] Literature is finally a creation, "an imaginary occurrence" whose validity does not reside in a supposed correspondence with the real, but in the word itself. This validity is in its own context. Like the Greek Sophists he quotes, Reyes considers "the serious acceptance of the deceptions of art as an index of human dignity." This statement seems to imply, in turn, that it is the attitude of the reader—in the last instance, also that of the critic—which makes a reality of this acceptance: the reality of the unreal. That in itself is memorable. If we think of all the emphasis on verity and the sociologizing prurience which have fogged up our traditional criticism, Reyes's thought reveals to us what a radical change he postulates. Like that of Borges, Reyes's thought marks the line of *partage* not only between two critical perspectives, but even more, between the two creative attitudes.

Reyes and Borges—we repeat—are the beginnings of our modern literature. And there is a fundamental fact in this; both of them emphasized the *imminence* of the literary work and, thus, of criticism itself. The various trends later manifested in Latin American criticism have, at least, this common denominator. Thus, they all gravitate around a dominant value system: literature as creation of forms and imaginary worlds, literature as the constitutive principle of the real, and not as a reflection of it. That is, these trends have broken with the causal relationship between literary work and reality, literary work and society, literary work and history. That relationship—reciprocal and dialectic—is now perceived on an aesthetic plane. Even the new criticism with a historical or sociological basis (which among us has its finest antecedents in Gilberto Freyre, Martínez Estrada, and Picón Salas) is very far from the positivist or determinist concepts of the past. This is so because, first, it does not cover over the ideology on which it is based; second, because it does not tend to speak in the name of a "truth." Rather it seeks to constitute the nonobvious values of an era in the profound relationship with what the work simultaneously says and does not say. It is not criticism which wants to be simply "involved," but which aspires, instead, to discover how a concept of the world and the consciousness of a society are developed within the literary work. It is a criticism which, in this sense, situates itself within the new sociology of culture in the manner of Lukács, Adorno, and Goldmann.[21] But what should be pointed out, even within this type of sociological criticism, is that it does not lose sight of a fundamental fact: the meaning of a work is not provided by the ideas it contains, but by the totalizing vision which the writer has of the world, and finally, by its behavior in terms of its own language. What we would call *moral* both of the writer and of the critic resides in this deference to the powers of language.

Linguistic studies and the stylistic criticism which was derived from them are to be found in the beginnings of our new criticism. If to some extent this approach tends to seem academic or university oriented today, its primordial virtue cannot be ignored: that of having explored, with an aesthetic sense, the linguistic nature of the word. One of the first—or perhaps the first—to practice this stylistic criticism was the Chilean Yolando Pino Saavedra in his book *La poesía de Julio Herrera y Reissig* [The Poetry of Julio Herrera y Reissig] (1932). But it had its center of formation and influence in Buenos Aires, around the Spanish critic Amado Alonso. This literary approach has contributed not only to renovate our criticism and propose a proper method, but also to illuminate the reality itself of the literary object: its formal reality. In such a sense, at least, it is a first attempt at what today constitutes structuralist analysis. It is revealed as this in the critical works of Raimundo Lida, Angel Rosenblat, María Rosa Lida, Ana María Barrenechea, and Enrique Anderson Imbert. A book by this last writer, *Crítica interna* [Internal Criticism] (1961), might be said to summarize the essential characteristics of this critical approach. But it is perhaps the study by Amado Alonso, *Poesía y estilo de Pablo Neruda* [Poetry and Style of Pablo Neruda] (1940), which continues to be the most representative of the method; in many ways, it is still also one of the best books of criticism in Latin America. Later, other critics have followed this line of approach. Among them are: Aberto Escobar, Orlando Araujo, and Jaime Alazraki. Another of the most representative is the Brazilian writer Afranio Coutinho, a renovator of criticism in his country and very close to the concepts of new criticism.

But while stylistic criticism revealed the formal and even structural nature of the work, it seemed to come up against a limitation: it did not fully translate the open character of the work, the multiplicity and the changing energy of its language. At the heart of its analysis, not only did it respect a certain notion of objectivity, but also the semantic stability of the poetic word. For this reason, without rejecting the contribution of stylistics, but rather incorporating it, a critical approach appears which is all-inclusive, which apspires to incorporate into its visions elements of linguistics as well as of other sciences of the spirit (e.g., anthropology, psychoanalysis, sociology). Thus, the aesthetic phenomenon tends to be seen as a totality because this totality is provided in language itself, in language as a system of connections. This new critical focus has various modalities, even on its highest levels.

Octavio Paz and Lezama Lima practice a criticism which we could call that of the *great correspondences*. The literary work is illuminated not only in its own text, but also in a wider context: dialogue with other works, with a living tradition. The literary work is thus a true bundle of relationships, and the task of the critic is to reveal the projections and connections of its plot. It is no longer a matter of singularizing a language, and through this language the "personality" of the author, but rather of eliciting, from the work itself, a more universal presence which transcends itself incessantly. It is this approach which has allowed Octavio Paz, for example, in his book *Cuadrivio* [Quadrivium] (1965), to renovate the view which our traditional criticism had of Rubén Darío or of López Velarde. His analysis obliges a new reading of these poets and perhaps of all Latin American poetry.

In effect, the Darío and the López Velarde who appear in Paz's book are poets who are almost unpublished, creators of a tradition, but included in a wider one which illuminates them and gives their works a new resonance. Darío, in a tradition of cosmic and esoteric symbolism; López Velarde, in the erotic tradition begun by Provençal poetry. But in addition to its purely aesthetic value, all of Paz's criticism, like that of Lezama Lima in his book *Analecta del reloj* [Analect of the Clock] (1953), has the great virtue of knowing how to place the Latin American in a universal context. This is accomplished without falling back on the sad expedients of the influences (that lowly detective work, of which Borges speaks) or of the so-called criticism of sources, so common in our traditional criticism. This is criticism based not on external notions, but on the styles and on the systems of thought. In this sense, the critical work of Cintio Vitier and of César Fernández Moreno should be considered here. The first writes a book entitled *Lo cubano en la poesía* [What Is Cuban in Poetry] (1958). The nature of its concept is already given in the title—not the desire to propose a "Cuban" poetry, but rather to show a country's contribution to universal creation. Fernández Moreno makes a similar effort in his book *La realidad y los papeles* [Reality and Papers] (1967). Even when his vision of modern Argentine poetry tends to configure itself around certain national categories, these, nevertheless, are also seen in the context of a universal and aesthetic perspective. Fernando Alegría in regard to Chilean literature, Enrique Pezzoni in regard to the Argentinian, and Wilson Martins in regard to the Brazilian also assume a perspective of universality. Thus, the important characteristic of the new Latin American criticism is its effort to transcend localism and narrow value judgments. There is a growing consciousness that the Latin American world is part of a wider spiritual order.

Imminent criticism, too, but which tends to elucidate other meanings (psychoanalytic, philosophic, etc.) in the text, is that which has been written by Emir Rodríguez Monegal, Ramón Xirau, Rafael Gutiérrez Girardot, Marcial Tamayo, Adolfo Ruiz-Díaz and Néstor García Canclini. The first is perhaps one of the most complete and penetrating critics of present Latin American literature. In his essays about our contemporary novel (still not all collected in book form), he has known how to point out what is distinctive about this fiction and what separates it from the realistic tradition. But above all his book about Neruda (*El viajero inmóvil* [The Stationary Traveler], 1966) reveals the merit of his critical method. This method applies the concept of depth psychology, that is, the analysis of the text as the actions of a symbolic and imaginary self, created by the work itself. This method involves not the search for the biography of the author behind the work, but the search (according to the ideas of Ezra Pound) for the poetic persona. But in this effort, Rodríguez Monegal not only reads in the text but also in the life of the author. For this reason, his interpretation of Neruda's poetry—especially *Residence on Earth*—is so different from Amado Alonso's. While for Alonso it is a hermetic poetry, for Rodríguez Monegal it is an open poetry, an existential adventure. Xirau, Gutiérrez Girardot, Marcial Tamayo, and Ruiz-Díaz (these latter two, at least in the book they wrote together, *Borges, enigma y clave* [Borges, Enigma and Key], 1955) are oriented toward the illumination of the philosophic implications of the literary work. But the philosophic aspect in them appears like a horizon; the true space is constituted by the formal reality of the work. It is essentially, then, an aesthetic criticism. Although they do not especially practice criticism, but rather formulate a philosophic and theoretical consideration of the aesthetic phenomenon, writers like Wilson Chagas and Vilém Flusser of Brazil are outstanding. And Brazil has produced some of the richest aesthetic thought in Latin America in recent years. It is not merely by chance that one of our most renovative poetic movements, that of concrete poetry led by Augusto de Campos, Décio Pignatari, and Haroldo de Campos, should also be a very precise theory about language.[22]

There are other critical tendencies more difficult to see in terms of definite trends. These contributions are valuable to the extent to which they continue to operate with an imminent vision of the literary work. Some are oriented markedly toward the sociological context, incorporating other perspectives, too, like Ángel Rama, Emmanuel Carballo, Luis Harss, and Noé Jítrik. Others give priority to aesthetic analysis: Alfredo Lefebvre, Cedomil Goic, Jaime Concha, José Manuel Oviedo, Saúl Yurkievich, Manuel Durán, and Luis Leal.

Among the youngest, if any tendency stands out in greater relief than others, it is that of structuralism. Severo Sarduy is the first and the one who best represents this approach. His book *Escrito sobre un cuerpo* [Writing on a Body] (1969) is an admirable example of lucidity and of reading ability. But one must also take notice of Julio Ortega (*La contemplación y la fiesta* [Contemplation and Celebration], 1968) and José Balza. To these three we owe some of the most perceptive analysis of our new fiction. Some of Sarduy's essays also tend to propose a new form of critical writing: a combination of textual analysis and of marginal commentary which not only includes the critical level as such, but also the critic's asides, his pauses, his mental processes at the very moment of writing. The stance of the writer who creates and watches himself create, which is so dominant in the best of our literature (Borges, Paz, Cortázar, and Sarduy himself) is matched now by that of the critic who analyzes and watches himself analyze. If the writer's gaze diverts him temporarily from the current of creation and turns it into criticism, the critic's—which is double and perhaps for that very reason—diverts him from pure analysis and plunges him into creation itself, that is, it makes his relationship with the literary work a living and unique experience.

Perhaps the future of criticism and of the essay lies not in the judgmental evaluation of the values of a literary work, but rather in their embodiment in the double perspective of analysis and of participation. In addition to having written excellent critical essays in his early years, the Cortázar of maturity also seems to announce this new form of critical writing. I refer to *La vuelta al día en ochenta mundos* [Around the Day in Eighty Worlds] (1967). This book not only contains perceptive observations about Latin American literature and even real critical texts, like the one dedicated to Lezama Lima; it not only includes, like Borges's essays, a special ability to desecrate culture by restoring humor and irony to everything it touches upon; it not only manages to combine and confuse the most diverse levels: confession and pure analysis; but it is also a book in which language itself is converted into a kind of critical system: language as the most radical adventure of thought. Although it is autobiographical as well, perhaps what counts most in it is its impersonal vision. And being in some way a book of essays and of criticism, its undertaking is to make all relationships with literature and the world problematical: to learn—as in the Jules Verne text he quotes—the lessons of the abyss. Is this not what, at heart, all new criticism undertakes?

Notes

1. Alfonso Reyes, *La experiencia literaria, Obras completas*, vol. 14 (Mexico: Fondo de Cultura Económica), 1962.

2. Jorge L. Borges, *Otras inquisiciones* (Buenos Aires: Emecé, 1960).

3. José Lezama Lima, in *Analecta del reloj* (Havana: Orígenes, 1953).

4. A. Reyes, *La experiencia literaria*.

5. José E. Rodó, *Proteo, Obras completas* (Madrid: Aguilar, 1967).

6. Octavio Paz, *Corriente alterna* (Mexico: Siglo XXI, 1967).

7. Ibid.

8. A. Reyes, *El deslinde, Obras completas*, vol. 15 (Mexico: Fondo de Cultura Económica, 1963).

9. Jorge L. Borges, *Discusión* (Buenos Aires: Emecé, 1957).

10. Jorge L. Borges, *El hacedor* (Buenos Aires, Emecé, 1961).

11. O. Paz, *Corriente alterna*.

12. Ibid

13. Enrique Anderson Imbert, *La crítica literaria contemporánea* (Buenos Aires: Gure, 1957).

14. O. Paz, *Corriente alterna*.

15. Octavio Paz, *Puertas al campo* (Mexico: Universidad Nacional Autónoma de Mexico, 1966).

16. Jorge L. Borges, op. cit., cf. note p. 6.

17. Lezama Lima, *Analecta del reloj*.

18. Severo Sarduy, *Escrito sobre un cuerpo* (Buenos Aires: Sudamericana, 1969).

19. José Lezama Lima, *La expresión americana* (Havana: Instituto Nacional de Cultura, 1957).

20. Alfonso Reyes, op. cit., cf. note p. 1.

21. A good example of this type of sociological analysis, especially applied to Latin American literature, may be found in the magazine *Aportes*, no. 8 (Paris, April 1968), an issue prepared by

Rubén Barreiro Saguier and to which Fernando Alegría, José Guilherme Merquior, Iber H. Verdugo, and Guillermo Yepes-Boscán also contributed. Equally representative of this trend are the Brazilian writers Otto María Carpeaux and António Cândido, who have done important work in this field.

22. Cf. Augusto de Campos, Décio Pignatari, and Haroldo de Campos, *Teoria da poesia concreta* (São Paulo, 1965).

PART FOUR
The Language of Literature

9 / Beyond Exclusive Languages

HAROLDO DE CAMPOS

CRISIS OF NORMATIVITY

The tendency toward a strict literary demarcation of the genres, toward a precise elaboration of a canon of the genres, is a natural corollary of the regimentational and normative concept of language, characteristic of classicism. We owe to the Czechoslovakian structuralist Jan Mukařovsky a very exact study of that problem, entitled *Aesthetic of Language.* "A period in which the tendency toward the aesthetic regulation of language arrives at its culmination is generally called *classic*, and this tendency in itself is labeled classicism.... Classicism, the culmination of the aesthetic perfection of the language, manages to arrive at the strictest obligatoriness and at the greatest generality of the norm." In a line from the famous "Thesis of 1929" of the Linguistic Circle of Prague of which Mukařovsky, as we know, was one of the founders, he distinguishes linguistically various functional forms, such as intellectual and emotional language, pattern-language (standard) and colloquial, written and spoken language. Each of these forms has its own rules, and the aesthetic norms are different in each "functional dialect." The norm thus fulfills, in the words of the Czech theoretician (who, be warned, is only describing and not making value judgments about the phenomenon), the role of a true custodian of the "purity" of a determined form of language or of language in general. Classicism, by definition, tends to the exact delimitation of the diverse functional dialects. Mukařovsky refers to the opinion of Buffon, in *Discours sur le style*, according to which "those who write as they speak write poorly, although they may be speaking well." The canonic theory of the genres is nothing more, then, than the projection of this attitude into literature, since "each literary genre also represents a certain functional branch of language."

Our era witnesses exactly the opposite side of the coin, with the vertiginous dissolution of the law of the genres and their division into linguistic compartments. Romanticism constituted, in this sense, a revolution against the predominantly prohibitive character of the classic aesthetic norms and manifested itself above all—always according to Mukařovsky, who focuses particularly on the French example—in the field of lexical studies, where there was discrimination between noble words [*nobles*] and low ones [*bas*], these last being excluded from the pattern-language.

Once the rigid intemporal typology had been surpassed, with its absolutist and prescriptive propensities, the theory of the genres thus comes, in modern poetics, to constitute an operational descriptive instrument, endowed with historic relativity, and which does not have as an end the imposition of limits on the free manifestations of textual production in its innovations and various combinations, and where the idea of genre as an imposing category is dissolved, and concomitantly, the notion of a language which would be exclusive to it, which would serve it as a distinctive attribute, is also made relative.

But the theoretical reflections about the theory of the genres which are possible today, equipped as we are with new perspectives, do not represent anything other than the metalinguistic aspect of a revolution which is already known in the field of the language of literature, in its "praxis," one can say. We have already spoken of the romantic questioning of the prohibitory inter-dictions of classicism. Within romanticism itself we can distinguish, however, with a view toward Modernity, those romantics we can call *extrinsic* (e.g., Lamartine, Vigny, Musset, and Hugo), as well as the *intrinsic* ones (the line which runs from Novalis to Poe, which in France produces a Nerval and comes, through Baudelaire, to symbolism and to modern poetry). These last writers, much more than the first, made an aesthetic of rupture of the aesthetic of their poetry and succeeded in carrying their disagreement with classic rhetoric's code of possibilities through to the very materiality of their language.

As the North American critic Edmund Wilson already observed in his study of symbolism, modern poetry is finally, to a great extent, a result of the foreshadowing contribution of "some romantics who, in certain ways, carried romanticism far beyond where it had been taken by Chateaubriand or Musset, or Wordsworth and Byron, and they become the first precursors of symbolism and later were placed among its saints." A reevaluating and rectifying critical intervention was even necessary to enable some of the more important of the romantics we are calling *intrinsic* (Novalis, Hölderlin, Nerval, and even Poe) to occupy the place which they have today in literary history.

"MASS-MEDIA": ITS INFLUENCE

A decisive point in the process of the dissolution of the purity of the genres and of their linguistic exclusiveness was that of the incorporation into poetry of elements of prosaic and colloquial language, not only in the matter of vocabulary, especially emphasized by Mukařovsky, but also in respect to the syntactic patterns. Because of this, beginning with the premises which can be traced, for example, in a Heine, in a Gautier, the *colloquial-ironic* line of symbolism (thus called by Edmund Wilson) of a Corbière and of a Laforgue develops, which in contemporary times informs the *logopeya* of an Eliot or a Pound.

Linguistically, that problem may probably be seen as a conflict related to that which the structuralists of Prague, in the "Thesis of 1929," called "modes of linguistic manifestations," that is, the *oral manifestation* and the *written manifestation* and, in the second place, the "alternating language with interruptions" and the "continuous monologue language." The determination and the measurement of the association of those modes, together with the functions of language, that is, with the diverse functional dialects, is the problem which the signers of the thesis set for themselves here. Concentrating specifically on *literary language*, the linguists of the Prague Circle observe that their characteristic features are represented above all in continuous language and particularly in written material. Spoken literary language is less different from popular language, although it keeps clear limits or distinctions in regard to it. Continuous languages (in public discourses, speeches, etc.), keeps itself at a greater distance. Closest of all to popular language is the alternating and discontinuous language (conversation) which constitutes, in the Prague exposition, a series of transitional forms between the canonical forms of literary language and popular language.

Undertaking the problem of the relationship between the *primitive genres* (those of popular or oral literature) and those of *developed literature*, Wellek and Warren (*Literary Theory*) refer to the opinion of the Russian formalist V. Schklovsky, for whom the new forms of the art are simply the canonization of inferior (infraliterary) genres. And Victor Erlich, in his basic *Russian Formalism*, shows how the members of that renovating critical school paid special attention to the *hybrid genres*, autobiographies, letters, reports, and pamphlets, and to the products of popular culture which live a contingent existence on the periphery of literature, journalism, vaudeville, gypsy songs and police stories, to explain through them the innovations of authors like Pushkin, Nekrasov, Dostoevski and Blok.

The "hybridism of the genres," in the context of the Industrial Revolution which began in England during the second half of the eighteenth century, but which reaches its peak with the birth of big industry in the second half of the nineteenth century, comes to be blended with the hybridism of the media, and will be nourished by it. The appearance of big newspapers has a fundamental role in the course taken by literature. Discontinuous and alternating language, characteristic of conversation, will find its natural channel in the simultaneity and fragmentariness of the newspaper. The importance of the newspaper did not escape Hegel or Marx. Hegel pointed out that the reading of the newspaper had come to be, for our era, a kind of morning philosophic prayer; Marx, reflecting on the impossibility of the epic in our time, as it was conceived of by the classics, uses a beautiful paranomasia to express that, amid newspapers, speech and fable, story and song (*das Singen und Sagen*), the Greek muse could finally no longer make herself heard. And Mallarmé who saw in the press the "modern popular poem," a primary form of the ultimate encyclopedic book of his dreams, is inspired by the techniques of visual spatialization and by the headlines of the daily papers, as also by musical scores, for the architecture of his constellational poem "Un coup de dés" (1897). This poem, only a little over ten pages long, may be considered, justly, a kind of epic of the new times, a synthetic and dense epic of the critical spirit in struggle with Chance and meditating on the very possibility of poetry, whose death or crisis Hegel had prophesied.

Marshall McLuhan has attempted to interpret, very suggestively, this conflict of the media. For the Canadian theoretician—who is considered by many to be only the controversial "prophet" of the electronic age, ignoring that he is a profoundly erudite scholar of the works of Joyce and Pound, of Poe and Mallarmé—the big newspapers, especially since the invention of the telegraph and its influence, with the form of a kaleidoscope of news items, in the style and the format of newspapers, draws closer to oral culture, which is not lineal but synesthetic, tactile, and simultaneous. The apparent paradox is explained by a phenomenon of hybridization, of intercrossing. Thus, the alphabetic Guten-bergian beginning, with its unity of point of view and its lineal chain, is surpassed precisely when, with its culmination in the daily newspaper, the telegraphic medium merges with it and from the two a hybrid form is born. "The hybrid or the encounter of two media is a moment of truth and revelation, from which the new form is born.... The moment in which the media encounter each other is a moment of liberation and of rescue from boredom which they are accustomed to imposing on our senses." Sustaining that the principle of hybridism is a technique of discovery and creation, McLuhan—who projects the influence of the popular press onto Mallarmé and Joyce, and who compares a modern newspaper to a surrealist poem—sees Edgar Allan Poe as the great pioneer in this field. He writes that:

> The kaleidoscopic image of TV was announced by the popular press which was developed together with the telegraph. The commercial use of the telegraph was begun in 1844, in North America, and a little earlier in England.... Artistic empiricism often anticipates science and technology by one or more generations. The significance of the telegraphic kaleidoscope in its *journalistic* mani-festations did not escape E. A. Poe. He knew how to use it in two notable creative forms: the symbolist poem and the detective story. These two forms demand of the reader a do-it-yourself-type participation. By presenting an incomplete image or process, Poe involved his readers in the creative process, in a way which Baudelaire, Valéry, T. S. Eliot and many others admired and endeavored to follow.

THE PROCESS OF DESTRUCTION OF THE GENRES

A Precursor

This introduction was somewhat extensive but necessary. It did not lead us away from our specific objective; on the contrary, it will permit us to enter more fully into the background of this objective, provided with a wealth of ideas which will facilitate our meaningful reading of the Brazilian—and by extension Latin American—literary space which it is our purpose to analyze.

What would be the situation of Latin American literature, within the problem of a surpassing of the canon of the genres and their exclusive language?

We know that our poetic romanticism—the key moment, as shown already, for the consideration of the modern aspects of the problem—is a late-flowering and imitative romanticism, fully dependent on the European models and not on the intrinsic models, still forgotten in their countries of origin, but rather, primarily, on the extrinsic paradigms (Hugo's oratory, Musset's sobbing intimacy, Lamartine's tearful religiosity). If Valéry is so inflexible with the French writers who were so admired by our romantics ("l'oeuvre romantique, *en général*, supporte assez mal une lecture ralentie et hérissée des résistances d'un lecteur difficile et raffiné"), how could we, without detriment to critical objectivity, be more benevolent and complacent with our own authors? Unless we want our evaluations to have a merely local value and we do not aspire to the more exigent tribunal of *universal literature* where they would not have validity because of their artificial criteria, we should not be so complacent. They would be provisional evaluations, fruit of an indulgent awareness, which would relegate our literatures to the condition of being mere "protectorates," that is, *minor literatures*, subject to a permanent rule of aesthetic guardianship. The Latin American critic, above all at the present time when our literatures have taken their place on the world stage, cannot have two souls, one for considering the European legacy and another to deal with the particular circumstances of his literature. He must consider them both with the same awareness and the same rigor, and only this exemplarily radical attitude can bring about the reexamination of our literary historiography, which even though it is recent, is not free of clichés of sensibility, of unreflective and monotonous repetitions of preconceived judgments which cannot withstand a firmly based analysis. We are living in the era of the compression of information and of rapid communication, when Marx's and Engels's prediction becomes a daily reality: "The intellectual works of a nation become the common property of everyone. National narrowness and exclusiveness become more impractical every day, and from the variety of national and local literatures, a universal literature is born."

On the other hand, we do not believe that there is a relationship of symmetrical correspondences between artistic development and technological progress. "Nothing more erroneous," affirms Roman Jakobson, "than the widespread notion that between modern poetry and medieval poetry there is the same relationship as between the machine gun and the cross bow." In a letter sent to Conrad Schmidt in 1890, Engels sustains that philosophy belongs to a determined domain of the division of labor which supposes an intellectual documentation transmitted by predecessors who serve him as a starting point, which explains why economically backward countries can eventually offer an original contribution in this field. The same thing can be said of literature, by analogy, it seems to us.

Thus, it would not constitute a contradiction of what was previously said about our romanticism if we were to discover that a poet of our second romantic generation (born in 1832) is a precursor of the vanguard directions in universal poetry. The new perspective offered us by modern poetry and criticism, within this same programmatic rigor which makes us reject as worthless the division into major and minor romantics proposed by traditional Brazilian historiography, permits us, in compensation, to recognize the geniality of a poet declared marginal by his contemporaries precisely because his language surpassed the threshhold of comprehension of his time. This poet is Joaquín de Sousa Andrade, "Sousándrade," as the poet liked to be called, with his two family names united and accented on the antipenultimate syllable, in order to give it a Greek sonorousness and the same number of letters as in Shakespeare's name.

In the literature of the Spanish language, after the fury of the "Golden Age" had passed, it was necessary to wait until Modernism came along at the end of the last century (1880–1910) to find a new era of creative eruption, there being nothing in the intermediate time except "timid spots of green" (Bécquer, Rosalía de Castro) which are comparable to Coleridge, Leopardi, or Hölderlin, nothing at all like Baudelaire. That is the opinion of the Mexican poet Octavio Paz, one of the most perceptive and up-to-date Latin American critics, in his study of Rubén Darío. Huidobro said the same kind of thing, polemically: "After the Golden Age, Spanish letters are a desert, until Rubén Darío comes along."

Sousándrade is a contemporary of Baudelaire. His first book, *Harpas salvajes* [Savage Harps], where there are already poetic marvels worthy of Fernando Pessoa, appeared in 1857, just like *Les fleurs du mal*. In that book, we find a type of meditative-existential poetry which is related to the expression of Novalis and Hölderlin and which also has affinities with Leopardi's *Idilli*. But Sousándrade's decisive work is the poem *Guesa*, the first cantos of which were published in 1867, and the last edition of which, still incomplete, includes thirteen cantos (London, 1888). It is a poem with a Pan-American theme, inspired by a legend of the Muysca Indians of Colombia, collected by Humboldt (*Vue des Cordillères*, 1810).

The Guesa was a child who was stolen from his parents and selected to fulfill the mystic destiny of Bochicha, god of the sun. Educated in the temple of the god until he was ten years old, he was supposed to then repeat the ritual pilgrimages and, finally, to be sacrificed to the divinity when he was fifteen. In a circular plaza, tied to a column, the Guesa was killed with arrows shot by the priests [xeques]. His heart was torn out as an offering to the sun, and his blood was collected in sacred vases. Sousándrade identifies his personal destiny as a poet with the predestination of a new Guesa, but beyond this individual drama of a *poète maudit*, explicable in terms of the *mal du siècle*, there is a strong historical-social motivation: the poet hypostatizes his destiny in that of the American Indian exploited by the white conqueror. On one hand, he condemns the forms of oppression and corruption of the powerful, combating colonialism and satirizing the dominant classes (nobility and clergy). On the other hand, he advocates the Greek-Inca republican model, taken from Plato's utopian social republic and from the Incas' community system, or perhaps from a free interpretation of early Christianity. The poet travels through the Americas, and the poem forms without a strictly logical thread, with the autobiographical looseness of someone who reconstitutes memories of diverse times and puts them together as he remembers them. The culminating moment is the episode of the "Inferno of Wall Street" which takes place at the New York Stock Exchange, during the 1870s. (Sousándrade, during this period, lived in the United States). The poet is impressed by the contradictions of the republic which he is going to discover in his own paradigm of the era, the North American republic ("the young country of the vanguard"), whose revolution against the metropolis became a fount of inspiration for the colonized peoples of the continent. Like Ezra Pound later, obsessed by the idea of a "financial inferno," Sousándrade perceives the evils of rising capitalism in its very center of operations, Wall Street, and criticizes them scathingly. And in view of this, under the pressure of new contents, he tries out new formal solutions. Before Mallarmé, whose "Un coup de dés" dates from 1897, and more radical than Poe, whose poetry, in many aspects, is even conventional, he is inspired by the telegraphic composition of the newspapers. The episode of the "Inferno" is in itself a kind of synthetic theater, put together through a process of a montage of events, with news items taken from newspapers of the era, historical and mythological fragments, quotations, biting commentaries, all in compressed dialogues, in a discontinuous style, studded with polylingual words and phrases. The poet is perfectly explicit about his technique of composition. In 1877, referring to the canto of *Guesa* where this episode is found, he notes: "In canto VIII now, the author retained the proper names which were taken for the most part from New York newspapers and the impression that they produced in him." But let us see the first of the 176 stanzas which make up the "Inferno of Wall Street":

> (El Guesa, habiendo atravesado las Antillas, se cree libre de los xeques y
> penetra en NEW-YORK-STOCK-EXCHANGE;
> la voz de los desiertos:)
> —Orfeo, Dante, Eneas, al infierno
> Bajaron; el Inca ha de subir...
> =*Ogni sp'ranza lasciate,*
> *Che entrate...*
> —¿Swedenborg, hay mundo por venir?

[The Guesa, having crossed the West Indies, thinks himself free / of the *xeques* and enters the New York Stock Exchange; / the voice of the deserts:) /

—Orpheus, Dante, Aeneas, descended to hell; / the Inca must ascend... /
=*Ogni sp'ranza lasciate*, / *Che entrate...* / —Swedenborg, is there a world to
come?]

The poet, in the "person" of Guesa (the "Inca"), fleeing from the *xeques*
("priests"), enters the inferno of Wall Street. Only he, coming geographically
from South America, through the West Indies, ascends to the infernal places ⌐
instead of descending to the subterranean world, as Orpheus, Dante and
Aeneas did. A second voice, identified by an equals sign, repeats Dante's
warning, inscribed on the entrance of hell, but in a form which is incomplete,
fragmented, and adapted to the dimensions of the stanza. The first voice (a
"Voice which clamors in the desert") answers calling Swedenborg (Swedish
theosopher and visionary, 1688–1772) and asking about the possibility of a
more just world. In the work of Sousándrade, that isolated Latin American
patriarch of vanguard poetry, the dissolution of genres is effected in a manifest
way. His *Guesa* escapes the usual classifications. The poet himself found that
his poem was not dramatic, nor lyric, nor epic, but that it was rather closer to
narrative. *Poem-novel* it was called by one of his contemporaries, Joaquín
Serra. If the poem is epic, it is not so in the traditional sense of the genre, but
only in the sense that it "includes history," as Pound desired. It is a matter, as
in the case of the North American poet's *Cantos*, of a *plotless epic*, of an epic
of memory, which includes narrative (in the manner of Byron), lyric, and
dramatic elements in the same design. Because of its theme of continental
scope (e.g., the critic Silvio Romero observed: "Of our poets he is, I think, the
only one who concerns himself with a theme gathered in the Spanish
republics"); because of the baroqueness of its language; for its character as a
lyric-biographic-ideological *summa*; because of its landscape-depicting
passages, and because of its legendary and historical preoccupations,
Sousándrade's poem anticipates another modern effort to renovate the epic or
the long poem, the *General Song* (1950) by Pablo Neruda.

Modernism and the Vanguard in Latin America

In Spanish America, the era of that rupture of the idea of genres and their
linguistic exclusivism—above all in respect to the great categorical divisions
poetry and *prose*—is indicated by the *Modernism* of Rubén Darío and his
companions. That Spanish-language Modernism (which, chronologically,
corresponds to Brazilian Parnassianism and symbolism, although not always
in a way which is aesthetically symmetrical), had its innovative characteristics
very well summarized by Octavio Paz:

Verbal reform, Modernism was a syntax, a prosody, a vocabulary. Its poets
enriched the language with borrowings from the French and the English; they
overused archaisms and neologisms; and they were the first to use the language of
conversation. On the other hand, it is frequently forgotten that in the modernist

poems a great number of American and Indian words appear. Their cosmopolitanism did not exclude either the conquests of the French naturalist novel or
the American linguistic forms. A part of the Modernist lexicon has aged just as
the furniture and objects of *art nouveau* have aged: the rest have entered into the
mainstream of speech. They did not attack the syntax of Spanish; rather, they
gave it back naturalness and avoided Latinizing inversions and emphasis. They
were exaggerated, not overpresumptuous; often they were pretentious, never
stuffy. Despite their swans and their gondolas, they gave Spanish verse a
flexibility and a familiarity which was never vulgar and which would lend itself
admirably to the two trends of contemporary poetry: the love for the unusual
image and poetic prosaicness.

   A second and more definitive stage of this same process is constituted by the
vanguard, by the creationism-ultraism promoted in Spain and in Hispanic
America particularly by the activity of the Chilean poet Vicente Huidobro,
who already in 1917 published *Horizon carré* (Paris) in French, and the next
year, in Madrid, *Ecuatorial* [Equatorial] and *Poemas árticos* [Arctic Poems],
in Spanish, as well as another two books in French, *Hallali* and *Tour Eiffel*
(this last illustrated by Delaunay). The role of Huidobro in Spanish-language
poetry of this century seems similar to that of Rubén Darío toward the end of
the nineteenth century: "Because if Rubén Darío came to put an end to
romanticism, Huidobro has come to discover the senility of the nineteenth
century writers and their archetypes, in imitation of which the youth of today is
becoming adept, unfortunately, like the students of drawing who practice
copying the hands and feet of classic statutes." (Casinos-Asséns, 1919).
Huidobro incorporates into his poems the blank space of the Mallarméan page,
the typographical devices of Italian futurism, freely manipulates the elements
of reality in a fragmented syntax, starred with "polypetal" images in which
suggestions of the everyday and of the mechanical world are not lacking, as
well as technico-scientific jargon, of which the poet makes use in his effort to
"humanize things." ("Something vast, enormous as the horizon, is
humanized, is made familiar, filial, thanks to the adjective *square*.")
   The importance of Huidobro as a poet and as a theoretician of poetry is
essential for anyone who wants to consider the problem of the renovation of
poetic resources in Hispanic America. Meditation on his example would
salvage a good part of present-day poetry from the rhetorical compulsion, the
unorganized torrential flow of genitive metaphors, which is the tardy heritage
of French *surréalisme* (and of all surrealism which is coextensive with it).
Instead, there would be a greater understanding of the problems of the poem's
construction as an object made of signs, as a semiologic entity: "I will tell you
what I understand by a created poem. It is a poem in which each constitutive
part, and all of it considered together, reveals a new event, independent from
the external world, unconnected from any other reality than its very own, since
it takes its place in the world as a singular phenomenon, separate and distinct
from all other phenomena" (Huidobro).

Modernism in Brazil

Brazilian Modernism—a literary movement which corresponds to creationism-ultraism—lacked the radical aesthetic of the Hispanic-American
vanguard, and it included no single writer who was comparable to Huidobro.
Octavio Paz expresses this opinion in an article published in the literary
supplement of the London *Times* (14 November 1968). We permit ourselves
here to disagree with this point of view, although Paz's article is a remarkable
assessment of the literary problem of our continent and contains truly
illuminating observations on the topic. Brazilian modernism of 1922 was
simply later in time than the similar European movements (the first manifesto
of Italian futurism is of 1909). But two major figures stand out in it, Oswald de
Andrade and Mario de Andrade (not relatives, despite having the same
surname). They made contributions of great inventive power to both poetry
and prose, which decided the future of Brazilian literature. Oswald contributed
with his *Brazilwood* poetry (1925–1927); with his novels or *inventions* as he
preferred to call them (*Memórias sentimentais de João Miramar* [Romantic
Recollections of João Miramar], 1924, *Serafim Ponte Grande*, 1933); with
his explosive manifestos (*Manifiesto de la poesía palo-brasil* [Manifesto of
Brazilwood poetry], 1924, *Manifiesto antropófago* [Manifesto of Anthro-
pophagy], 1928); and with his revolutionary theater (1933–1937). Mario
contributed with his poetry (beginning with *Paulicéia Desvairada* [Crazy
Paulicéia], 1922); with his novel or *rhapsody*, *Macunaíma* (1928); with his
theoretical and polemical writings (the "Extremely interesting Preface" of the
Paulicéia; and with the essay of Modernist poetics, *A escrava que não é
Isaura* [The Slave Who Is Not Isaura], 1925).

The *Brazilwood* poetry of Oswald—its name taken from the rosewood the
exploitation of which by the Portuguese constituted our first "export
product"—is characterized by its reduced language, its extreme economy of
means, and by the surprising intervention of the direct image, of the colloquial,
of humor. However, in contrast to the Mexican José Juan Tablada, a
fascinating transition figure between Modernism and the vanguard who,
around 1917, writes the first haiku in Spanish, Oswald, in his poem-capsules
that tend toward the concision of Japanese poetry, does not reveal any
indication of oriental exoticism: they are capsules of live language, caught in
daily living, endowed with lyric high voltage and frequently with critical
perspicacity, just as later—at the end of the thirties—Brecht would do with his
elliptic poems, whose interconnections are left to the reader to decipher.
Mario, in his turn, practices a poetry which is *polyphonic*, of simultaneous
voices, less naked than that of Oswald but, like his, marked by the
discontinuous rhythms of modern civilization and by the spontaneity of spoken
speech (Brazilian Portuguese, with "the wealth of all its errors" rather than the
pedantic language of the "purists" of Lusitanian precept). In both cases, the
limits between poetry and prose are erased in a way which is so disorienting
that the contemporaries of "old-fashioned" mentality no longer manage to

recognize these productions, which to them seem to be the fruit of "paranoia" or "mystification." If it is true that this poetry received the stimulus of the European vanguards (futurism, Dadaism, surrealism; Oswald, like Huidobro, lived in Paris with painters and poets associated with cubism; Mario was an untiring reader of the European experimentalists and, even, of Huidobro himself), it is no less true that in these loans there was a kind of assimilation which was very different from that which characterized the previous literary periods. There was something in our midst which could be called *congeniality* in relation to the new experiments, and which could be explained only partially by the process of rampant industrialization in cosmopolitan centers like São Paulo. António Cândido explains the phenomenon:

> In Brazil the primitive cultures are mixed together with daily life or are still living memories of a recent past. The terrible audacities of a Picasso, a Brancusi, a Max Jacob, a Tristan Tzara, were, at bottom, more coherent with respect to our cultural heritage than to theirs. The familiar customs of Negro fetishism, of the *calungas* ("dolls"), of the votive offerings, of folkloric poetry, predisposed us to accept and assimilate artistic processes which in Europe represented a profound rupture with the social medium and spiritual traditions. Our modernists, then, found out rapidly about the European vanguard art, learned psychoanalysis and molded a type of expression which was both local and universal, reencountering the European influence through a plunge into Brazilian detail.

It was what Oswald theorized about under the name of *anthropophagy*, that is, the nonpassive acceptance which takes the form of a critical devouring of the European contribution, and its transformation into a new product, endowed with its own characteristics which, in its turn, came to have a new universality, a new capacity for being *exported* to the whole world (thence the name of Brazilwood poetry, as we indicated earlier).

In prose, the renovation reveals itself with the creation of works which are no longer limited by the traditional concept of novel (the "finished" novel, the "well-made" novel of nineteenth-century realism). Oswald's *Miramar* is a kaleidoscope of 163 fragments which are supposed to be mounted cinematographically in the spirit of the reader and where a chapter can be a Brazilwood poem, a piece of postcard or a simple humor line ("My mother-in-law became a grandmother"). Finished a year after the appearance of Joyce's *Ulysses* in 1911, Oswald's book is included in the antinormative trend of the contemporary novel. And Oswald intensified even more his processes of scenic disconnection and parodic humor in *Serafim Ponte Grande*, a Rabelaisian farce which António Cândido defined as a "satiric summation of capitalist society in decadence" and which another critic, Mario da Silva Brito, considered to be "the sauciest book in the Portuguese language." Between these two books, influenced by the first and influencing the second, Mario de Andrade published his *Macunaíma*, which, although it distinguishes itself from the traditional model of the novel (Mario called it *rhapsody*), and like Oswald's books is profoundly parodic in theme and in language, retains specific characteristics which make it a singular work in the basic trilogy of Brazilian Modernist prose. In 1928, in Leningrad, Vladimir Propp publishes his *Morfológuia Skázki* [*Morphology of the Story of Magic*], which was to have such importance for contemporary structural analysis of fiction. The Slavic scholar establishes the invariable elements in the field of the Russian folktale in order to indicate the basic functions, which can be acted out by various characters, but the inalterable linking together of which constitutes a unitary compositive scheme, always repeated, with one or another variation. In that same year, providing evidence of a singular affinity of structural imagination, and making a symmetrically inverse sweep, to phrase it that way, Mario published his superfable, created through the combination of interchangeable elements of a corpus of legends which he had preliminarily analyzed and selected for his narrative purposes. As in the case of Sousándrade's *Guesa* (which was unknown to Brazilian Modernists), the guiding theme of *Macunaíma* is Pan-American, drawn from legends of Amazonic America that were collected by Koch-Grünberg (*Von Roroima zum Orinoco*, 1916). According to the critic Cavalcanti Proença, Mario "chose the name of *Macunaíma* because it did not belong only to Brazil but exists in Venezuela, too. And the hero, finding his own consciousness, feels it to be that of a Hispanic American, and he makes himself comfortable within this inclusive awareness." Etymologically, *Macunaíma* means "The Great Bad One." Mario makes him a hero without a definite character, a kind of prototype of the Brazilian (and, by extension, of the Latin American) in search of his national character and of his ethnic identity. The book moves along in a satiric tone, not in accord with any logical or psychological principle, but in agreement with that order of necessity and syntagmatic causality which is provided by the original structure of the congeneric tales. The author gives *coloratura* to the connective interwovenness of the story by including variants taken from other legends, from popular stories from different regions of Brazil, in addition to including contemporary elements and social criticism (e.g., the giant Piaimán, from the *taulipangue* mythology, with whom Macunaíma fights, is at first a Peruvian peddler who robbed his talisman from him; later, he is an Italian immigrant who has gotten rich in São Paulo). The language of Macunaíma becomes compounded, a kind of mixture of the heterogeneous Brazilian languages, with archaisms, regionalisms, Indianisms, Africanisms, and popular slang expressions.

No More Boundaries between Poetry and Prose

The rarefaction of the boundary markers between poetry and prose, with the introduction, in the novel, of construction techniques from the poem, has been already affirmed by the contemporary writers (who followed Proust and Joyce) as a transmitted heritage, a peaceful acquisition. "Perhaps the most important heritage which this line of poetry leaves us in the novel is the clear awareness of an abolition of false frontiers, of rhetorical categories. There is no longer a novel or a poem: there are situations which are seen and resolved in their own verbal order," declares Julio Cortázar (*Situación de la novela* [The State of the Novel], 1950). The same writer, in an earlier work (*Notas sobre la novela contemporánea* [Notes on the Contemporary Novel], 1948), after establishing a distinction between *enunciative language* and *poetic language* (which recalls Jakobson's distinction between *cognitive* or *referential* function and *poetic* function of the language), sustains that, in the great traditional novels, there was an interference of these two forms but that this happened without the breakdown of the rationalist "aesthetic order" of the novel. In the contemporary novel, "only the death of the novelist would show the relapse of enunciative language—revealing the entrance of a nonpoetic situation and reducible for that reason to a mediatized formulation." And he concludes, "But to continue speaking of the 'novel' no longer has meaning at this point. Nothing remains—formal adherences, at most—of the ruling mechanism of the traditional novel. The step from aesthetic to poetic order necessarily signifies the liquidation of the generic distinction novel-poem."

We would like to describe that attitude—again using terms of Jakobsonian linguistics—as a continuous turning of the writer toward the materiality itself of the language (the *poetic function* is that which turns toward the material aspect of the signs) even when it is, apparently, making up that which conventionally would be called prose. In contemporary Brazilian literature, after the notable precedents of the 1922 Modernism, such an attitude produced the introspective lyricism of Clarice Lispector (*Perto do coração selvagem* [Near the Savage Heart], 1943, the first and still the most successful of her books) to culminate in Guimarães Rosa's *The Devil to Pay in the Backlands* (1956). In Spanish-language American literature, the peak, in our opinion, may be found in *Paradiso* (1966) by the Cuban Lezama Lima. Both *Grande Sertão* and *Paradiso* are baroque books: neobaroque, really. Rosa's because of its constant inventions of vocabulary, its innovative syntactic qualities; because of the lexical hybridism (which goes from archaism to neologism and to the montage of words); the oxymoronesque confrontation of barbarity with refinement (the metaphysical *sertão*, setting of the ontological adventures of the Yagunzo-Fausto, torn between God and the Devil); and because of the topos of "prohibited love," "perverse love" (Diadorín, the woman disguised as a man, who awakes in the protagonist, Riobaldo, a passion which he cannot confess). Lezama's because of the Gongorine metaphorization of everyday events; because of the marvel of a language which is a fictional scandal to the extent to which he replaces the conventions of the realistic novel "type" with its exigencies of verisimilitude by the multifaceted unity of the author's poetic discourse (a cook or a housewife, in Lezama, express themselves in the same way as a university student or a doctor, as though the author, superpoetizing his prose, were responding thus to the introduction of the conversational into modern poetry); because of the syncretic mysticism; because of the fusion, too, of sophistication and of naïveté (to such a point that it verges on being kitsch at moments); and, finally, because of an amorous theme presented through the topic of prohibited Eros (the ill-fated passion of Foción for Frónesis which culminates in Foción's madness).

"The baroque, [which] is what is interesting about Spain and about Spain in America..." exclaims José Lezama Lima through the mouth of José Cemi (*Paradiso*). Cemi is a character who has many autobiographical qualities (also, perhaps, an intentional onomastic anagrammatization: *Lezama Lima*/EZ-IM/CE-MI). And who knows, perhaps precisely in the baroque, in its transplation to Iberoamerica—when, simultaneous with the *fusionism* characteristic of that style, the mestizo mixtures of different cultures and races in confrontation are being produced—it will be possible to find in embryo form this attitude of nonconformity with the classical heritage of the genres and their correlative literary conventions on the part of the Latin American writer. In respect to this we may refer to Severo Sarduy, author of the new generation, whose book *From Cuba with a Song* (1967) is also one of the most significant manifestations of that neobaroquism which sees the destiny of writing in the "plasticity of the sign" and its character of "inscription."

Trying to characterize his compatriot Lezama's baroqueness of "superposition," Sarduy mentions this commentary by Cintio Vitier about the first Cuban poem, *Espejo de paciencia* [Mirror of Patience] (1608), by Silvestre de Balboa: "What is generally considered an extravagant blunder in Balboa's poem—the mixture of Greco-Latin mythological elements with Indian flora, fauna, instruments, and even clothing (remember the hamadryads in *naguas*, 'under-petticoats')—is what in our opinion indicates his most significant and dynamic quality, what really connects him with the history of our poetry..." It is indeed symptomatic that something very similar may be found in the work of the Bahian Gregorio de Matos (1633–1696), the greatest figure of Brazilian baroque poetry and one of our most contemporary poets (from a synchronic point of view). Gregorio, nicknamed the "Mouth of Hell" for the virulence of his afflatus, carries the hybridization of elements, characteristic of the period, to the very structure of his language, mixing into it, in order to obtain effects of contrast and for the grotesque quality, *tupí* (Indian) and African words, in a jocund operation of linguistic-satiric amalgamation. In this sense, his language, as Octavio Paz has said of Lezama's, is already a "Creole broth," seasoned in the tropics.

The Metalinguistic Dimension

But another factor, no less important, intervenes in modern literature, contributing powerfully to the rupture of the tradition of the genres and to the precise linguistic discrimination which corresponds to it. Here it will be necessary for us to return to Mallarmé and his "*Un coup de dés.*" In that poem, as though in response to Hegel's affirmation that, for the modern spirit, reflection about art always turned out to be more interesting than the art itself, Mallarmé introduced the megalinguistic dimension of the practice of language, a dimension reserved more for the aesthetics and the science of literature than for literature as such. Mallarmé "invented the critical poem" notes Octavio Paz. It is a poem which questions itself about the essence of poetizing, in a very different sense, however, from the traditional versified "poetic arts": what we have is not a recipe book of how to make poetry, but rather a more profound inquiry into the peculiar truth of the poem, an experience of boundaries.

Thus the language of the essay and of the theoretical-philosophic specu-lation ("langage de formulation," to use a term from the Prague Circle thesis) becomes integrated into the poem, which becomes a metalanguage of its own object-language.

Along with this incorporation of a metalinguistic dimension into the literature of imagination, we also find what the Russian formalists called "a stripping of the process" which is nothing other than an uncovering of the very architecture of the work while it is being made, in a permanent self-critical circuit. This can happen in a "serio-aesthetic" way (Edmund Wilson's expression), as in the case of Mallarmé, or in a parodic, ironic, antiillusionist way, as in the case of that extraordinary precursor of the directions of the modern novel, Laurence Sterne, with his *Tristram Shandy* (1759–1767). We know that Victor Schklovsky, in his *Theory of Prose*, in a deliberately polemical analysis, considers *Tristram Shandy* the most typical fictional work of universal literature (the opposite of the usual view of it as exceptional and extravagant) precisely because it bares the structure of the novel, subverting it, "deautomatizing" it for the perception of the reader, who is thus moved to reflect upon the nature of the verbal object which is proposed to him, and to assume an attitude of critical participation in regard to it.

In Latin American literature, it seems to us that this metalinguistic problematization occurred for the first time in the exceptional writing of the Brazilian Machado de Assis, especially in *Epitaph of a Small Winner* (1881), *Philosopher or Dog?* (1891), and *Dom Casmurro* (1899), books which show traces of the influence of Sterne, assimilated, however, and organized in a very personal way. They are novels in crisis, which do not manage to remain within the limits of the genre, scorning customary novelistic development in favor of a continuous ironical-critical author-reader dialectic. After Machado there is a long wait until the Argentinian Macedonio Fernández comes along—"the writer of nothingness," as César Fernández Moreno calls him—before there is a new, and, in a certain way, even more extreme approach to the problem. Macedonio refuses to write programmatically (not only to distinguish between genres, but to make literature into a finished product), and his texts—his "papers"—are the reasoned itinerary of this refusal.

Because he slips spontaneously out of genres and literary categories, or because he creates categories of his own, still unnamed, he is a difficult author, although few have wished to be less difficult than he.... He is difficult, among other reasons, because it is not easy to situate his writings within traditional forms or literary customs.... His manner of expression which is both elliptic and analytic, his text which lacks conjunctive interwearing, to such an extent that sometimes one must read with a microscope in order not to lose the thread or defoliate the crown of thoughts which surround the lineal development of the theme—all this requires the collaboration not of passive readers, but of readers who are as adventurous as the author, reader-coauthors.

Thus, Adolfo de Obieta defines the enterprise of the destruction of literary traditions carried out with metaphysical humor and ironic fantasy by the author of *Una novela que comienza* [A Novel that Begins].

From Macedonio we pass along to Jorge Luis Borges, his most complete successor, consummate master of literature as metalanguage and the most distinguished figure in Latin American literature today, for his wide readership and universal influence (even, and this is especially significant, in the renovation of the techniques of the European novel: the French *nouveau roman* renders him open tribute). For Borges, the "librarian of Babel," there exists no practical difference between the essay and literature of the imagination, between his "inquisitions" and his "fictions." Themes like that of the single anonymous atemporal book which summarizes all books and is the work of a single author, reimagined through the ages—a Mallaréan theme par excellence—are central in his prose as an essayist or as an author of works of fiction. It is deliberately tautological writing, haunted by leitmotiv: the labyrinth; the garden of the forking paths; the circular ruins; the rediscovery of precursors by retrospective anachronism; the deciphering of a divine message inscribed in the spots of a jaguar; and the glimpse of the momentary face of God in a poet-translator (Fitzgerald) whose supreme skill can only be explained because he is a hypostasis of the poet-translated (Omar Khayyam). Such motifs can be interpreted as a single and vast metaphor (it is what Eliot says of the *Divine Comedy*): a metaphor about writing and about the writer who, at a certain moment, is written when he thinks he is writing. A story such as "An Examination of the Work of Herbert Quain" (from *Ficciones*) is para-digmatic in this sense. Written ironically in the manner of a critical study (*in memoriam*), it consists of the perceptive and erudite analysis—with structural outlines and even footnotes—of the work of an experimental writer who never existed (but who could be Borges himself). It is an example, too, of the Borgesian love of a brief text and of his search for a style which is neutral, transparent, almost impersonally precise and elegant (Borges "has made an effort to make his mechanisms so subtle they have become invisible," observes Luis Harss in *Into the Mainstream*). A style, precisely, that eliminates the boundaries between literature as a work of verbal art and criticism as a metalanguage mediating that language-object. It is thus that that adversary of the baroque—who considers verbal games an extravagance for the young and who sustains that Spanish does not lend itself to very complex linguistic inventions, of the Joycean type (cf. interview with G. Toppani, *Il Verri*, no. 18 [1965])—comes to be, nevertheless, one of his own circular paradoxes, an Alexandrian in residence in Buenos Aires, who prefers the geometry and the ellipsis of *mannerism* (as the term is understood in the rigorously technical sense that Curtius and Hocke give it) to the proliferations of the baroque.

And thus we come to Julio Cortázar, who evolves from a novel which is still *costumbrista*, *The Winners* (1960), ventilated by magical-realism, to the admirable *Hopscotch* (1963). Of the latter, Luis Harss says: "*Hopscotch* is the first Latin American novel which takes itself as its central theme, that is, which contemplates itself in full metamorphosis, inventing itself at each step, with the complicity of the reader, who becomes part of the creative process." In addition to a normal reading (chapters 1 to 56), *Hopscotch* allows a second combinatorial reading on the syntagmatic axis, seeming thus to be the embodiment of that fictitious book *April March*, a "regressive and ramified" novel, which engenders other novels, attributed by Borges to his character-persona Herbert Quain. Octavio Paz, recognizing Macedonio Fernández's premonitions, rightly includes Cortázar's book in the modern family of "open works" and points out: "*Hopscotch* is an invitation to play the risky game of writing a novel." In the book there is an apparently collateral protagonist, the old writer Morelli, who has something in him of Poe, of Mallarmé, and of Joyce, and who is a kind of "portrait of the artist as an old man." A prospective portrait, which repels the author (who, as a man fascinated by the practice of life, and also *engagé*, denies the idea that the world exists in order to end up in a book), but, at the same time, irremissibly seduces him. Between the other chapters and, above all, in counterpoint with the lyric-amorous-obsessive plot which is central in *Hopscotch* (the triangle formed by Oliveira and his double, Traveler, and La Maga/Talita), this character weaves his revolutionary theory of the novel in filigree. It is the theory of an "unwriter" who rebels against the discursive logic of narrative and literary language, who considers the descriptivism of the realistic novel to be a thing of the past ("music loses its melody, painting loses its anecdote, the novel loses its description") and who summarizes thus the intention of his work: "My book can be read however anyone pleases. *Liber Fulguralis*, mantic pages, and so on." In later books— in *62: A Model Kit* (1968) but above all in the collected writings of *La vuelta al día en ochenta mundos* (1967) and *Ultimo round* (1969)—Cortázar seems to persevere in that which he defined self-ironically as "little Hamletlike steps within the very structure of that which is narrated." Now, just as with Borges, there remains no distinction between essay and fiction; both function as sidewalks for the same life-experiencing and investigative stroll. ("Much of what I have written is ordered under the sign of eccentricity, since I never admitted a clear difference between writing and living.") In *La vuelta al día*, he innovates in the very physical form of the book object, with the introduction of a dialogue on three levels between the text, the typography, and the illustrations (the layout). In *Ultimo round*, the influence of newspaper pagination and the simultaneity of the reading leads to the material divisions of the book into two articulable segments (first floor and main floor).

Also important in Cortázar is the embarkation upon the metalinguistic dimension through parody (sometimes in the diction of the characters, or sometimes in the treatment of the most diverse textual materials, ranging from scientific explanations to the eccentric memoirs of provincial visionaries). Morelli wants to attempt the *roman comique*, like Oswald and Mario de Andrade did, each in his own way. And at this point, when the manifestation of parody in the novel should be seen as a dialogue between texts or an *intertextuality* (a term which the semiologist Julia Kristeva coined based on Mikhail Bakhtin's studies of Dostoevski and Rabelais), we cannot fail to mention another recent Latin American work which enters fully into this dialogical or polyphonic parodic space where the "elevated" genres and their linguistic exclusivities are corrupted, where literature is subjected to a profound poularizing "carnivalizing" (Bakhtin) process. We refer to *Three Trapped Tigers* (1964) by Guillermo Cabrera Infante, whose verbal *féerie* (joined to the montages of words of Huidobro's *Altazor* and to the "gliglical" of certain of Cortázar's passages) seem to contradict Borges's skepticism about the playful capacities of the Spanish language. We saw, then, how in Latin American literature the metalinguistic eruption produced the contamination of fictional prose by the critical essay, corroding, on this other side, the dogma of the "purity" of the genres. A similar process can be traced out in poetry.

From Oswald de Andrade to Carlos Drummond de Andrade and João Cabral de Melo Neto, in Brazil, from Huidobro to Octavio Paz and even Nicanor Parra in Spanish America that line of the poem about and/or against the poem is drawn: of the poem as a message to the second power, as a supersign, whose significant questions that signified of its first message (or its very process of significative production).

Oswald writes texts like *Biblioteca Nacional*, a poem which consists of the simple enumeration of the titles of books found on a shelf of a provincial library: it is metalinguistic humor, parody again. This same humor, and also the *serio-aesthetic* attitude of Mallarméan root (which is the other side of the coin of the problem of metalanguage) are found in Drummond: in a personal anthology the poet calls the second attitude *contemplated poetry*. In Cabral, who descends from Drummond, it is the machine itself of the poem which is put together and taken apart incessantly with a rigorous geometrical precision (*O Engenheiro* [The Engineer], 1945; *A Psicologia da Compasição*, [The Psychology of Composition], with the *Fábula de Anfión* [Fable of Anfión] and the *Antiode*, 1947; *Una Faca só Lâmina* [A Knife Only a Picture], 1955, etc.).

In Spanish-speaking America, the Chilean Huidobro, herald of the future, sketched, as early as 1916, this true program of semiological investigation of the poem object:

> Por qué cantáis la rosa, ¡ oh Poetas!
> Hacedla florecer en el Poema.

[Why do you sing the rose, oh Poets! / Make it flower in the Poem.]

(The Brazilian João Cabral, at the end of the 1940s, would say even more synthetically: "flower is the word *flower*"). The pole of humor prevails in the "antipoems" (1954) of another Chilean, Nicanor Parra, with his antilyricism, his antidecorativism, his criticism of rhetorical devices, his ever more accentuated stripping down. But in Octavio Paz the metalinguistic posture will reach its summit: first in a brief composition like "Las palabras" (from *Puerta condenada* [Condemned Door], 1938–1948), made up of ironic ambiguity and life-experiencing ferocity, in that "hour of truth" in which poet and poem seem to measure their strengths reciprocally. Later in *Blanco* (1967), an unfoldable poem, visual, of multiple readings, where, in our opinion, the Mexican poet achieves the culmination of his itinerary, managing to respond in terms of his own poetic practice to the perceptive theoretical meditation which he has been developing around Mallarmé's "Un coup de dés" and the future of poetry (as witnessed by the beautiful essay "Los signos en rotación," 1965).

Concrete Poetry

It is possible to say that, at the present time, a series of manifestations of what we have agreed to designate as literature pass beyond the traditional contours of that concept, just as do the categorical ideas of poetry and prose (not to speak of genres and their linguistic exclusivities), and point toward a new and more adequate concept of *text*. "The concept of text," writes the German philosopher Max Bense, "has a more ample aesthetic reach than the concept of literature. In addition, a text is rooted much more profoundly in the realm of doing than literature and does not permit the marks of production to be erased from it so easily, exposing the still unfinished forms and the interforms and revealing the multiple gradations of the transitional states. Its function as an amplifier of the concept of literature resides precisely in this circumstance." And he adds:

> The concept of style is adequate for literature; that of structure, for the text, that is, in the second case language enters, essentially, into the domain of Microaesthetics.... Prose and poetry are concepts which characterize something which can be made into a language which presents itself as finished, when its forms are known and given and can be consumed and spent. The text is something which is made with language, and thus of language, but something which, at the same time, modifies, amplifies, perfects, breaks, or reduces the

language. The text is always an informative report in the language about the language and only this.

Here we should consider the case of *concrete poetry*, which is precisely one of the forms of textual production which have been, particularly, the object of Bense's theoretical reflections.

The international movement of concrete poetry began in the early 1950s with the simultaneous, but independent, work of the Brazilian *Noigandres* (later *Invención*) group of São Paulo, and of the Swiss poet Eugen Gomringer (born in Cachuela Esperanza, Bolivia, of a Bolivian mother). The first evidence of the movement, in world terms, was the Brazilian exposition in 1956, in the Museum of Modern Art of São Paulo.

Octavio Paz says of Brazilian concrete poetry, in the previously mentioned London *Times* article: "It is impossible to find among the young poets of Spanish America anything comparable to the Brazilian *Invenção* group...In 1920 the avant-garde was in Spanish America; in 1960, in Brazil."

Brazilian concrete poetry originated in a critical meditation about forms. It attempted to synthesize and carry to extremes the experiences of international and national poetry. On one hand, there existed the example of Mallarmé, with his visual syntax and his use of the blank space of the page; Pound's ideogramic technique; Apollinaire's theory of the calligram ("il faut que notre intelligence s'habitue à comprendre synthético-idéographiquement au lieu de analytico-discursivement"); Joyce's word montage; E. E. Cummings' typographic gesticulation; the futurist and Dadaist contributions. On the other hand, Oswald de Andrade's *Brazilwood* poetry, with its linguistic reductions and its montage techniques, and also João Cabral's poems, with their constructive rigor, their engineered discipline. But there was also the film (Eisenstein and the ideogramic theory of montage), the music of Webern and his followers, the plastic arts (from Mondrian to Albers and Max Bill and the concrete painters of the *Ruptura* group of São Paulo); and also the newspaper, the poster, propaganda, the world of nonverbal and audiovisual communication.

Concrete poetry is nourished by this intercrossing of media. It proclaims itself to be "spatio-temporal" and "verbi-voco-visual" (using a Joyce expression). Not only the problem of the genres, then, is brought up for judgment, but that of literature itself and that of verbal language. In that radical attitude, in which all the parameters of the poem submit to a general desire for structuring (the semantic, the typographic-visual, the sonorous), there exists as "a suggestion of the basic community of the arts," to make use of what Suzanne Langer says when she takes on the problems of space and time in painting, in music and in literature. The author of *Feeling and Form* says:

> The fact that the primary illusion of an art can manifest itself as an echo, as a secondary illusion in another, gives us a suggestion of the basic community of the arts.... The primary illusion always determines the *substance*, the true character

of a work of art, but the possibility of secondary illusions confers upon it the richness, the elasticity and the ample liberty of creation which make the true work of art so difficult to trap in the nets of theory.

In the same sense, A. A. Mendilow observes (*Time and the Novel*):

> In fact, it is almost possible to affirm that the most significant experiences and innovations made by painters, sculptors, composers, and novelists proceed not only from the total exploitation of the qualities inherent in their instrument of work but rather, above all, precisely from their attempts to transcend it and introduce effects and illusions beyond the strict capacities of the limited instrument.... The degree to which this is effected can probably serve as an index of the progress of an art from a simpler phase to a more complex, more highly organized one.

Voluntarily going beyond the field of literature; presenting its first manifestos in an architecture magazine; organizing the book like a visual object, entirely planned, a portable exhibit of ideograms which function like Japanese *kakemonos*; moving on to the poem-poster and again taking up the example of Mayakovski, of the *agit-prop* and the "Rosta windows" era; finally proposing a general art of language, concrete poetry comes to exercise its influence not only in literary evolution but, in a parallel way, in the techniques of layout and editing of newspapers, magazines, and books, as well as in publicity texts. And since it never abandoned the semantic layer (it never reduced itself to pure sonority or to mere *lettrisme*), it could also propose problems of *engagement*, that is, of a semantic and structurally revolutionary poetry distinguishing itself from "absentism" and from the "purism" of the Swiss line and of other European manifestations of the movement. Accompanying its activities of textual production by an intense theoretical effort and a constant and programmed output of creative translation (which includes, for example, poems by Pound and Cummings, fragments of Joyce's *Finnegans Wake*, poems by Mayakovsky, Jlebnikov, and German and Italian vanguard writers), the adherents of the movement even proceeded to the reexamination of Brazilian literature, rediscovering Sousándrade and reevaluating the Modernism of 1922, challenged by the "neo-Parnassianism" of the so-called Generation of 1945.

But what is even more germane to our present topic is the repercussion which concrete poetry, in itself and in its reexamination of the work of Oswald de Andrade, would have on a field apparently far removed from it, that of popular music. As a public event it can be said that the reevaluation of Oswald culminated in the performance, in 1967, of the dramatic work *O Rei da Vela* [The King of the Candlestick] (written in 1933, published in 1937, but never before performed on the stage), staged by the most creative of the Brazilian theatrical directors, José Celso Martínez Correa, and his group *Oficina*. This production had a great impact on the young composers and singers of the so-called *Grupo Baiano*, directed by Caetano Veloso and Gilberto Gil. Impressed by the Oswaldian "anthropophagy" in José Celso's violent theatrical version, they created *tropicalia*. The poet Augusto de Campos, one of the founders of the movement of concrete poetry and, at the same time, as a music critic, the one who fought most for the *Grupo Baiano* (having dedicated a large part of his book *Balanço da Bossa* [Balance Sheet of the *Bossa*], 1968, to the members of the group), writes:

> Caetano, Gil and their comrades make use of a musical *metalanguage*, that is, of a critical language, through which they reexamine everything that was produced musically in Brazil and in the world, in order to consciously create something new, at first hand. For this reason, their records are an unforeseen musical/literary collage, where everything can happen and the listener, through the course of it, rediscovers everything and relearns to *listen with free ears*, just as Oswald de Andrade proclaimed in his manifestos: *see with free eyes*.

Many of the compositions of the *tropicalistas* demonstrate affinities with techniques and procedures of concrete poetry, developed in a principally oral sense, in a voice-music relationship. Augusto also points out: "Gil and Caetano resurrected an almost dead genre: sung poetry. The Bahians have an acute sensitivity for *altura* (a musical parameter in which, according to Ezra Pound, poets in general are less precise). They achieved great refinement in this rare art which Pound, remembering the Provençal troubadours, calls 'motz el son,' that is, the art of combining words and sound." For that very reason, the concrete poets, without fear of the apparent paradox which existed in that change of field (literature/music) and also in the change of sphere (from the sphere of production or that of limited consumption—as is the case with poetry—to that of mass consumption, as is the case with popular music, presented through records, shows, radio and television) consider Caetano to be the most important poet of the younger generations that followed the movement (and not other poets who are known as "proper" descendants, voluntarily or not, of concrete poetry, and who do not offer the original contribution that the Bahian poet-singer does. Marshall McLuhan shows the function of the typewriter in the recuperation of the oral character of poetry, as a musical *partitura* for the poet, who can thus register all the nuances of his elocution, with the liberty of a jazz musician (and in connection with this he quotes the poems of Cummings and the oral poetry of Charles Olson). Decío Pignatari, another member of *Noigandres*, had already pointed out in 1950: "I feel inclined to believe that the poet made his public out of paper, tailoring it to the image of his song, and making use of all the graphic and typographic resources, from punctuation to the calligram, to try to transpose the oral poem into the written one, with all its qualities." The experience of Caetano and Gil in Brazilian popular music seems to give a new practical dimension to that same problem, changing the techniques of a partitural and typographic poetry back to their oral expression.

With this topic of concrete poetry we bring our study to a close. Truly, here we go beyond the problems of a restricted semiology (verbal language and the literature based on it) to those of a general semiology or semiotics, where the signs Jakobson calls "pansemiotic" and which verbal language shares with other systems of signs, are used methodically and consciously.

10 / Intercommunication and New Literature

ROBERTO FERNÁNDEZ RETAMAR

In 1943, in the preface of the Spanish edition of a book of World War II chronicles, Pablo Neruda wrote: "It chokes me with anger to see the young Aztec, the young Cuban or Argentinian spinning out their theories about Kafka, about Rilke and about Lawrence...."[1] Today, more than a quarter of a century later, occasions to choke on this anger are fewer: today, the young Mexican, Cuban, or Argentinian when speaking of literature would find it in poor taste to omit the mention of a whole tribe of Latin American writers. Which does not necessarily mean, of course, that he is ignorant of Kafka or Rilke. This reveals several things; one of them is that a greater intercommunication on the literary level exists among us Latin-Americans today.[2]

WRITERS OF A SHARED LITERATURE

Evidently, the new Latin American literature has taken on prestige in the eyes of the new Latin American reader: neither the Buenos Aires idioms of *Hopscotch* nor the fabulous Colombia of *One Hundred Years of Solitude* have impeded Mexicans, Chileans, and Cubans from feeling gratitude and pride in regard to these major books of our common tradition. Nor have Cortázar and García Márquez been obliged to write in an abstract, neutral language which would be comprehensible to all Hispanic Americans but appealing to none. Nor have they felt obliged to crowd their pages with the familiar glossaries of folkloric texts. Instead, they have proceeded with the wise, natural ease with which the best literature has always been written, speaking of their own subjects in their own language, and the singular consequence of this has been that the Argentinian Cortázar and the Colombian García Márquez are being read in the various countries of Latin America not as fairly close-by foreigners, but as writers of a same literature, as representatives of what it is now customary to call "the new Latin American novel." They are in the company of the Cubans Carpentier and Lezama, the Argentinians Marechal, Sábato, and Viñas, the Brazilian Guimarães Rosa, the Mexicans Yáñez, Revueltas, Rulfo, and Fuentes, the Peruvians Arguedas and Vargas Llosa, the Uruguayans Onetti and Benedetti, the Paraguayan Roa Bastos, the Haitian Alexis, the Venezuelan Garmendia, and so many others. In order to appreciate better the relative novelty of this situation—that these should be read in Latin

America as Latin American authors—it is useful to recall some of the other times when our literature has been considered as a single unit.

THREE PERIODS OF INTERCOMMUNICATION

Romanticism

Naturally, the first of those times corresponds to that spirit of secession, or at least of autonomy, which had been expressed by Andrés Bello in his *Alocución a la poesía* [Allocution to Poetry] (1823) immediately after the political independence of the continent had taken place, and which would be above all one of the goals of the first Latin American romantic generation. It is not surprising that Bello's text should be the opening selection of *América poética* [Poetic America] (1846), the anthology with which Juan María Gutiérrez wishes to reveal a body of Hispanic-American poetry which is separate from the European (from the Spanish for the time being). The desire was greater than the accomplishment, but it is important to take note of that initial consciousness of integrating one literature into another. Well then, who were the readers of that ambitious anthology? Although we lack a study of the public, of the consumers of literature in Latin America, everything leads us to believe that, during a good part of the nineteenth century, there were hardly more readers than there were producers of literature. The authors, amid illiterate masses which for their part produced and transmitted oral literatures, read each other's writings, and in addition (or above all) they read those greater writers who were the Europeans.

Modernism

If that is the situation, for practical purposes, during that first era, the same cannot be said of the Martí-Rodó period, a period which includes the first literary movement which really began in Latin America and was capable of influencing Europe itself—at least, that part of Europe which was Spain— Modernism. Elsewhere I have wished to contribute to the rectification of the inadequate appreciation of the nature of this movement,[3] an appreciation based only on an aspect of the writing of Darío and other closely related poets, and which does not do justice to men like Rodó and especially Martí. For the time being, it will suffice to point out that the authors of this era, to different extents, of course, do count on a real public which is no longer synonymous with the group of writers themselves, but which is made up above all of a growing middle class from which both producers and consumers of literature are recruited, a phenomenon which will be seen more clearly at the beginning of the century. It is possible that few of the Modernist books (Quiroga's stories, *Ariel*...) enjoy wide distribution (they are predominantly poetry, of more limited consumption), but a high quality press, developed then, makes these authors known from one side of the continent to the other. Some twenty newspapers circulate the chronicles of José Martí, which deeply move the aged Sarmiento and form the prose of the young Darío. Among these newspapers is, of course, *La Nación* of Buenos Aires, a city which immigration has already helped to convert, in Darío's words, into a *cosmópolis*. Darío and Rodó later contribute to *La Nación*. If at first glance the "Palabras liminares" [Preface] of *Prosas profanas* [Profane Prose] seem an answer to *Alocución a la poesía*, seventy years later, saying that no, that poetry has not moved to America and continues to reside in Europe, especially in Paris; if Rodó can say to the author of *that* book that he "is not the poet of America," it would be absurd to detain ourselves with these skirmishes and limit Modernism to that book by a twenty-year-old poet. Darío is also (and why not *above all?*) the author of *Cantos de vida y esperanza* [Songs of Life and Hope], of "Poema del otoño" [Autumn Poem], even of that "Canto a la Argentina" [Song to Argentina] which no Parnassian or symbolist could have written (any more than Lugones's *Odas seculares* [Secular Odes] or *Romances*), and in which the poetry of the *Silvas americanas* [American Verses] moves, on its way to the *Suave patria* [Gentle Fatherland], toward certain hymns of *Tala* [Felling] and above all of the *General Song*. Even in terms of his subject matter and his way of dealing with it, Darío *is* the poet of America: a poet who, when he finally managed for his dreamed-of Paris to become a real Paris, was only to discover that the city, through the beloved mouth of Verlaine, said "*merde!*" to him. Darío is the first poet of America, just as Martí is the first universal figure of the American spirit. The Modernists, in general, are the ones who, having pulled away, paradoxically in many cases and out of aversion for their poor lands, are going to constitute the first group of writers who will fulfill the Bello-Gutiérrez project. Martí's chronicles, Darío's best poems, some of Rodó's essays, Quiroga's stories, certain of Lugones's pages, and many other texts (including the most widely popular, those which gained the largest reading public right up to our times, cutting across class lines and social groups, and which nevertheless we tend to silence today: those of Vargas Vila and Nervo) succeeded in giving the continent its own voice, and knew that inter-communication which some have the temerity to attribute only to the new literature of today.

Vanguardism

Before we come to our own era, we should allude to a third period: that which, for lack of a better name, we designate as that of *vanguardism*. We can speak, as I will again now, of a vanguardist generation, but the characteristically vanguardist phenomenon hardly goes beyond the thirties in this century. But if we abandon the notion of a generation, which continues to produce and even reaches maturity after those years, in order to fix our attention on an epoch, the panorama becomes more complex. As a limited phenomenon, literary vanguardism—like Modernism, but narrower—was a predominantly poetic event: Huidobro had invented his creationism before the twenties and in Europe; Borges carried ultraism from Spain to Argentina in 1921; Maples Arce launched stridentism in Mexico, and Hidalgo began simplism in Peru in the mid-twenties. All of these were poets, and they felt themselves to be ardent vanguardists, although they could hardly explain what that meant, beyond pointing out various ways of dismantling verse and an impoverishing metaphoric fanaticism. Their magazines were for minorities, and some of them so small that, like the mural *Prisma* [Prism], they only amounted to one side of a page. But their intercommunication was substantial, and their influence considerable, much greater than it would seem at first glance. One example among many of this intercommunication is the anthology *Índice de la nueva poesía americana* [Index of the New American Poetry], which appeared in 1926 with a prologue by the Peruvian Alberto Hidalgo—who apparently compiled it—the Chilean Vicente Huidobro, and the Argentinian Jorge Luis Borges. This precocious book assembles, in addition to Hidalgo, Huidobro, and Borges (who would be placed in a hierarchy by time), Marechal, Bernárdez, Pablo de Rokha, Rosamel del Valle, Díaz Casanueva, Neruda, Cardoza y Aragón, Maples Arce ("comrade Maples Arce," as Borges said then), Pellicer, Novo, and Pereda Valdés. As for the second matter, its influence, it would be an error to take into account only their publications for minorities, although these did not lack importance. (Think of *Martín Fierro*, of *Amauta* [Inca Sage], of *Revista de Avance* [Vanguard Review], of *Contemporáneos* [Contemporaries].) The truth is that they frequently assaulted large publications and imposed their criteria from these pages. It happened thus in Cuba, where the late-appearing vanguardist group managed to express itself in the best widely circulated magazine of the country (*Social*) and in the most conservative and established newspaper (*Diario de la Marina*), whose literary supplement it controlled in 1927.

And if we look not only at the limited poetic phenomenon which vanguardism was, but at the entire decade from 1920 to 1930, the situation is much richer: in that decade, Vasconcelos had made Mexico a center of attraction for intellectuals from the whole continent, and had launched the mural painting movement from there, as well as his own messianic words; in that decade, the novels *The Vortex* (1924), *Don Segunda Sombra* (1926), and *Doña Bárbara* (1929) appeared almost simultaneously. Their authors, Rivera, Güiraldes, and Gallegos, belong in terms of their age to the previous generation, that of the poets Luis Carlos López and Baldomero Fernández Moreno. But while these poets found themselves with a defined body of literary work, which they would hardly modify, at the beginning of the twenties, it was only at this point that the novelists, who needed greater maturity, would produce their relevant works. This finally linked them more closely, in some ways, to the next generation, which came to see them then as their elders.[4] The phenomenon was not new or exclusive, and we will see it repeated with narrators of the vanguardist generation itself, like Asturias and above all Carpentier, whose important works will appear after 1940, amid the publications of much younger generations.

Only with difficulty can it be denied that Latin American intercommunication was unknown to the era of the vanguardist magazines, of Neruda's *Twenty Love Songs and a Song of Despair*, the surge of Negrism, of the *Raza cósmica* and *Indología*, of *The Vortex*, *Don Segundo Sombra*, and *Doña Bárbara*, of Henríquez Ureña's *Seis ensayos en busca de nuestra expresión* and Mariátegui's *Seven Interpretative Essays on Peruvian Reality*. It is an era which expressed confidence in everything ours and in which that confidence found echoes, from one end of the continent to the other.

CONSOLIDATION OF THE NOVEL

Nevertheless, while there was a certain amount of Latin American intercommunication in regard to literature during previous eras, there is undoubtedly much more now. Our conviction of the truth of this is reinforced in us by the contrast which our era offers not so much with the situation of Modernism or of vanguardism, as with that of the years which are just prior to the present ones: that "immediate past" so perceptively seen by Reyes as "in a certain way, the enemy." Those years seem to us like years of isolation, of *Balkanization* (a term which was not used then), in which there was considerable fragmentation of the consciousness of Latin American unity and the consequent intercommunication. Even an event of such continental influence as the Mexican Revolution, which at the time had affected all the Latin American countries, seemed to shrink now into a local Mexican event, the commentary of which (and a very lucid one) would be the first version of Octavio Paz's *Labyrinth of Solitude*. In that vein of agonizing persecution of the fragments may be included meditations not about Latin America, but about particular countries, Argentina (Ezequiel Martínez Estrada: *X-Ray of the Pampa*, *Muerte y transfiguración de Martín Fierro* [Death and Transfiguration of Martín Fierro] or Cuba (Cintio Vitier: *Lo cubano en la poesía* [What Is Cuban in Poetry]. They are admirable books, but instead of looking at Latin America (as even Mariátegui's *Seven Essays* and some works that appeared after that do, despite being centered on a single country) they turn their attention to those isolated compartments, and although rejecting the folkloric trap, they want to gather with pain, with illusion, sometimes with anger, the characteristics which permit us to know that we are one, except that those characteristics do not seem continental to their authors any more, but local, national (in countries which sometimes were barely nations). At this time, when we were caught between the anguished rootedness of the present and the rootlessness which turned us, feeling inferior, toward other places which seemed better than ours, the Neruda of those days roars the anathema which we quoted at the beginning of this essay. When he turned to his local magazines, the young Mexican would read *El Hijlo Pródigo* [The Prodigal Son]; the Cuban, *Orígenes* [Origins]; the Argentinian would keep reading *Sur* [South]. Contrasted with this era, our own seems very full, with greater energy than ever, of confidence in the values of our literature.[5]

This is not equally valid for all the genres: it is hardly true, in general, for the theater; it is rarely true for the essay—if we leave aside the political essay to concentrate on the strictly literary one—it is more valid for poetry; and it is valid above all for the narrative, which today is undergoing a development comparable to that which poetry knew seventy years ago with the Modernists or thirty or forty years ago with the vanguardists. It is particularly apt to compare these new Latin American novelists with that first group, the Modernist poets. In fact, the novelists seem to be doing for the novel what the Modernists did for Latin American poetry. To say this is not, of course, to deny that there was a novelistic tradition before them as well as important novelists in Latin America (e.g., Rivera, Güiraldes, Gallegos, Amado, and Alegría.[6] In *Tientos y diferencias* [Approaches and Distinctions], after reminding us that "a great novel may be produced in an era, in a country" without meaning that "*the novel* really exists in that era, in that country," since in order to speak of the novel, a theory of the novel [*una novelística*] must exist," Carpentier adds: "The novel is a late genre. There are countries in the world now, in Asia, in Africa, that, possessing a thousand-year-old poetry, are just barely beginning to have a theory of the novel."[7] Everything indicates that for Latin America this is the hour of consolidation of that "late genre" which only appeared very tardily in America (it has been said with pleasing symmetry that "the last picaresque novel of world literature was, paradoxically, the first Hispanic-American one")[8] and that, after efforts not lacking in value, it is now acquiring that stable configuration which poetry achieved among us many decades ago. Its ratification by the public, as well as a certain homogeneity which we will speak of later, provides proof of this. As does the relationship which the achievers of this *novelística*, this "novelistic theory," maintain among themselves. Carpentier also said that the existence of a Romantic novel is not demonstrated by the presence of *Werther* and *The Man Who Laughs*: "The Romantic novel is defined by the work of various generations of Romantic novelists."[9] It is an articulate and coherent body of work. That is precisely what we encounter with these new Latin American novelists, who already stem from each other: Cortázar from Marechal, from Borges, from Arlt; the early Fuentes from Yáñez, from Carpentier; Vargas Llosa, in part from Arguedas, like Benedetti from Onetti; Pablo Armando Fernández from Lezama and García Márquez. García Márquez himself writes, in *One*

Hundred Years of Solitude, a novel-summa in which his characters intercross with some of Carpentier's, Cortázar's, and Fuentes's—as does his style. What Martí said in 1893 about the Modernists may be said today about these novelists: "It is like a family in America." Of course, it is not a question in any of these cases, or in others which could be cited, of assuming any literary Robinson Crusoeism; these novelists also know, and make use of, what the fiction of other countries has produced. Anyone can point out what they owe to Joyce, Proust, or Faulkner. But there already exists among them (a sign that they constitute a *novelística*) a continuity, an internal tradition comparable to that which poetry had achieved decades ago (e.g., Martí/Darío, González Martínez, Herrera y Reissig, Lugones/Fernández Moreno, López Velarde, Gabriela Mistral/Huidobro, Vallejo, Borges, Neruda, Drummond, Pellicer, Guillén, Roumain/Lezama, Molina, Césaire, Paz, Diego, C. Fernández Moreno, Mutis, V. de Moraes, Parra, Rojas, Cardenal/Melo, Depestre, Adoum, Lihn, Belli, Jamís, Gelman, Montes de Oca, Dalton, Pacheco). It is even worth the effort to point out that those novelists also stem from (one must always be cautious about these lexicalized metaphors) poetry. Some, in an obvious manner, because they are also poets (Asturias, Marechal, Roa Bastos), or primarily poets (Lezama, P. A. Fernández); others, in a less obvious but no less real way. José María Valverde has observed with reason of *The Time of the Hero* that "it is a matter of a 'poetic' novel, in which the present manner of understanding narrative prose among Hispanic American culminates—to their good fortune. Each word, each sentence, is said and heard as in a poem; the hour has come when the boundaries between lyric, verse epic and prose epic are erased."[10] This could also be said of Carpentier, of Cortázar, of Revueltas, of García Márquez, and of many others. Just as the editors of the Mexican anthology *Poesía en movimiento* [Poetry in Motion] (Mexico, 1966) included prose texts by Juan José Arreola, we might well proceed in a similar manner with the majority of these authors. I can say from experience that it is not easy to decide to include certain of Álvaro Mutis's pages in a selection of poetry and to exclude other pages by García Márquez which visibly continue Mutis's. Is it a matter of these authors having finally managed to erase, as Valverde desired, "the boundaries between lyric, verse epic and prose epic?" It is premature to answer this question, and in any case it is not necessary to do so now. In any event, if we also bear in mind that the impassioned meditations of American essayists resound in many of these narrators, nearly all of them essayists of earlier times—a Martínez Estrada, a Reyes, a Mariátegui, a Paz—we cannot help feeling that the consolidation of the *novelística* does not seem to be only that: it seems to be also, alongside a poetry which already has notable antecedents, the arrival of the coming of age of a whole literature. This would be essential to explain the interest of the new Latin American reader in this present literature of Latin America, and also the intercommunication which gives testimony of this event.

SELF-CONSCIOUSNESS, REQUISITE OF WIDE DIFFUSION

And nevertheless, one may ask if this is altogether so: if those present-day readers turned with pride toward our own productions, intercommunicated readers who have now given up the self-deprecating gaze toward the outside world in order to find out what there is that must be read; or if it is not the case, that upon looking toward other countries they now see in them the names of our authors, and upon seeing them there, where previously they were accustomed to finding only the prestigious foreign names, they are incited to read and enjoy their countrymen with the consent and almost with the encouragement of the metropolises. The occurrence would not be a new one: although it is not a matter of the same phenomenon, it could be recalled that in not a few zones of America, like the Caribbean, for example, *negrismo* began to be popular more than forty years ago, not because this was, as it is, a mulatto zone, but because in Europe negrism was fashionable. (Things turned out to be less simple after that.)[11] Today, even readers who are very estranged from certain of Borges's attitudes, for example, have felt a certain candid local pride upon reading the first line of Foucault's *Les mots et les choses* (1966): "This book was born from a text by Borges." It was not only that literary works, that a whole French group such as Tel Quel confessed its filiation with the Argentinian: it was that an important work of thought (even cited as *vedette* by the weekly magazines) had been provoked by him. Apparently, Latin American literature had ceased to be a marginal literature; not only was it talked about in Europe, but things were written thanks to it. Something had happened in this quarter of a century.

A year before Foucault's book appeared, in 1965, Roger Caillois proclaimed in *Le Monde*: "Latin American literature will be the great literature of tomorrow, as Russian literature was the great literature at the end of the last century and North American was the great one from 1925 to 1940; now the hour of Latin America has come. This will be the source of the masterpieces we all await."

Thus far, a hopeful prophecy, based on the present (*"now* the hour of Latin America has come"). A few lines later, this clarification follows: "Latin American writers only know each other when they are popular outside of Latin America. Their respective works, in effect, never cross over the barriers of the Andes, of the equatorial jungles, of the plains. To go from Argentina to Brazil, the cultural route necessarily passes through Paris, New York, or Moscow, and recently, through Havana."

(Havana, for Latin American writers, is the opposite of "outside Latin America." But we will return to this.) More recently, the *Times Literary Supplement* dedicated its issue of 14 November 1968 to Latin American literature. On one of its pages, the headlines of an editorial leap out in big letters: "There is no doubt that the most significant contribution to world literature of today comes from Latin America"; and it is followed by the names of the authors whose books are discussed: Borges and Fidel Castro, Neruda and Che Guevara, García Márquez and Debray.... Examples like this (and they could be multiplied, including those from the United States) are presented as a kind of consecration of a literature. The claiming of this consecrational possibility explains Octavio Paz's opinion when, after ridiculing, in reference to the Latin Americans, a certain "recent and noisy 'critical' activity, almost indistinguishable from the most vacuous forms of publicity," which has now chosen " 'the success of our writers, especially the novelists, outside of Latin America' as its little war horse," he adds:

> In the first place, the word *success* embarrasses me; it does not belong to the vocabulary of literature but to that of business and of sports. In the second place, the vogue of translations is a universal phenomenon and not exclusive to Latin America. It is a consequence of publishers' success, an epiphenomenon of the prosperity of the industrial societies. Everyone knows that publishers' agents make the rounds of the five continents, from the hovels of Calcutta to the patios of Montevideo and the bazaars of Damascus in search of manuscripts of novels. Literature is one thing and publishing is another.

And after this sociological analysis which cannot be dismissed lightly, he adds: "As far as I can see, in order for a work to be well considered among us, it must first receive the blessing of London, New York, or Paris. The situation would be comic if it did not imply a dismissal."[12]

To an extent, we should accept the fact that Latin American literature is read in Latin America is not only proof of the intercommunication that exists, but is also part of a larger phenomenon, although perhaps less than a certain publicity proclaims, that is, that literature is read today in the world. Why? Paz has suggested an answer to us, but we cannot content ourselves with attributing such an event only to publishers' activities. To postulate that criterion, to use the vocabulary of the North American "new critics," would be to incur an *editorial fallacy*. It is difficult to deny that one of the factors in the popularity of the Latin American novel is that it lends itself to a commercialization generally denied to other genres. Narrative, and especially the novel, recounts what is going on, and makes it accessible to a greater number of readers, if they are interested in what is going on. Modern literatures tend to be popularized by their narrative aspect. When Caillois speaks of the vogue of Russian literature at the end of the nineteenth century or that of North America between 1925 and 1940, he is thinking of their respective narrative writings. But it would place too much faith in the power of publishers to go much beyond this. The agents who are scouring "the hovels of Calcutta... and the bazaars of Damascus in search of manuscripts of novels" (which is really touching), have they found those manuscripts in appreciable quantities? Or is there talk today of a popular wave of Hindu or Syrian novels, the way there is talk of the Latin American novel? If the answer, as I fear, is negative, it will be necessary to disbelieve in the godlike efficacy of the publishers, although they do have a great responsibility for the distribution and commercialization of our literature. Let us see things as they are: the publishers have not provoked the popularity in question; they have simply benefited from it, and here or there they have modulated it in favor of certain postures, as occurs in the so visible *boom*, which is only a particular example of the event being considered, an example to which a large part of the explanation proposed by Paz, as well as other similar ones, is indeed applicable, and which assumes the clever taking advantage of a situation along with the presence, too, next to works of real value, of the occasional, inevitable subproducts of such circumstances.

The question to ask is rather: why have the publishers (even European and North American ones, much more powerful than ours) turned to *that* literature, in preference to others. A hurried response to this question would lead us to a *qualitative fallacy*, even less acceptable than the last one: the reason for the interest conceded to Latin American literature could only be a growth in the quality of that literature. Well then, that a high level of quality should be required for a literature is not even a question that needs to be discussed; but that that level should *suffice* for it to be popularized is an indefensible thesis. To begin with, I do not think that anyone seriously maintains that the present authors are qualitatively superior, for example, to the group formed by Martí, Darío, Rodó, Lugones, Quiroga, and González Martínez.

The popularization of a literature needs, of course, qualities like these. But they are a long way from being sufficient. Others are required, especially one essential: the popularization of a literature requires the existence of that literature. And this last, in its turn, requires that there should exist, as a sufficient historical entity, the zone of that which is literature. Although I have quoted them more than once, I cannot resist mentioning Martí's indispensable words again: "There is no literature which is expression, until there is an essence to express in it. There will not be a Hispanic-American literature until there is a Hispanic America." Recently, a structuralist, the Brazilian critic António Cândido, has distinguished between *literary manifestations* and *literature as such*. The first are simply individual works; and the second: "a system of works linked by common denominators, which allow the recognition of the dominant notes of a phase. These denominators are, apart from the internal characteristics (language, themes, images), certain elements of a social and psychic nature, although literally organized, which manifest themselves historically, and make literature into an organic aspect of the civilization."[13]

The two questions are fused together: it is evident that notable isolated Latin American works can exist (like the *Royal Commentaries*, *Facundo*, or *Martín Fierro*) without a real Latin American literature existing, as Martí thought at the beginning of Modernism, a beginning which turned out to be also that of our era. At the same time, through the mere fact of speaking of *Latin*

American literature, a nonliterary radical element has been made to erupt because *Latin American* is not a literary or aesthetic category nor, of course, is it "geographical-sentimental," as Borges would say humorously, and without any basis in reason; it is a *historical* category (to it belong those "elements of a social and psychic nature...which manifest themselves historically," of which Cândido speaks). Mariátegui had already pointed out in his *Seven Interpretative Essays* that "the flowering of the national literatures coincides...with the political affirmation of the national idea," and that "the 'nationalism' in literary historiography is thus a phenomenon of the purest political derivation, foreign to the aesthetic concept of art." Even to speak of *one* single *Latin American* literary work would mean to have passed over, knowingly or not, to the torments of history. This is what Martí perceived in all clarity, and carried to its ultimate consequences: in order for there to be a Latin American literature, there had to be a Latin America. And he undertook to make one, with which, in a movement characteristic of the Third World, he opened the aesthetic adventure to an ontological enterprise of a political basis. This had been intuited, too, by the first romantic generation: it is the Bolivarian spirit which animates it. Just as it is the Martían spirit—or rather, the spirit of which Martí is the forerunner and major spokesman—that animates and consolidates the best of Modernism, a consciousness (not always very clear, except in Martí himself) of what would later be called the *underdeveloped character* of our world, and the beginning of the antiimperialist attitude.[14] It is the radical spirit nourished by the Mexican Revolution of 1910 and by the repercussion of the Russian Revolution of 1917, a spirit expressed articulately by José Carlos Mariátegui, which gives a Latin American sense to the insurgency of the vanguard. In all of these cases, through literature (and not only literature) there is Latin American intercommunication which is really self-consciousness. This is so because such intercommunication—in the first romantics, in the Modernists, in the vanguardists, in our days—is nothing other than the ideal reencounter of a historic unity temporally dissipated in reality.

A WORLD WHICH IS BECOMING STRUCTURED

If in our time Latin American literature is more widely distributed than ever; if the intercommunication of the various Latin American zones reaches a higher level than ever before, this is the natural consequence of the fact that, from the pathetic possibility Martí saw, Latin America is now becoming a dramatic reality, as has been shown during the recent years (the years, of course, of the literary triumph of the continent) of the Latin American revolution which has taken place in Cuba. This advance is incarnated today, exemplified—as previously by Martí, and by Bolívar before that—by Ernesto Guevara. The reasons for the awakening of interest in Latin American literature, and its growing popularity, are the same ones which had led young people of the entire world, for the first time in history, to raise the effigy of a Latin American in the streets of their stupefied cities. It is not strange that advantage should be taken of this unheard-of circumstance by scattering Latin American literary texts widely—sometimes mixing them with openly political texts—when such advantage is taken of the very photographs of that man, enlarged and converted into living-room posters.

It is of the greatest interest to explore this topic, which we are only going to touch upon here: present Latin American literature, in one sense or another, is the literature of the emergence of the Latin American revolution, which for the time being has only triumphed in one country, but whose roots and prospects are widespread. Certainly, it would be too simple and thus easily refutable, to suppose that this implies a mechanical relationship between the two occurrences, that is, between political-social commotion and literature. The situation is much more complex.[15] Just as it was more complex when it was a matter of the French Revolution or of the Russian Revolution in the process of their repercussion on the literatures of other countries, including ours. And it must be more complex now, although it is a matter of a revolution on a fragment of our own historic territory, in a province with which basic cultural elements are shared. Even so, we should not expect that it be only a matter of the presence of certain subject matter directly related to the historical process. Which is certainly not to say that such subject matter is lacking, particuarly in the Cuban writers themselves. In the first place, it is present in the poets, as also happened in the case of the Russian Revolution; then among the narrators: Edmundo Desnoes, *Memories of Underdevelopment*; Jesús Díaz, *Los años duros* [The Hard Years]. Also in the works of writers of other countries in which similar processes have taken place (certain poems by Ernesto Cardenal, Roque Dalton, and even by poets who died in action, like Javier Heraud and Otto René Castillo; Edmundo de los Ríos: *Los juegos prohibidos* [Forbidden Games]; and Renato Prada: *The Breach*); or simply in writers linked in some way to the revolution (Julio Cortázar: "Meeting," poems by Thiago de Melo, Juan Gelman, and René Depestre). However, more than a question of subject matter, it is a question of perspective. From the perspective made possible by the present revolution, Carlos Fuentes presents Mexican society (in *The Death of Artemio Cruz*), Benedetti, the Uruguayan (in *Gracias por el fuego* [Thanks for the Light]), David Viñas, the Argentinian (in *Los hombres de a caballo* [Men on Horseback]), while Julio Cortázar, who had offered a singular multiclass vision in *The Winners* creates in *Hopscotch* the prodigious X ray of a man "obligé de representer un pays" of ours; and García Márquez will dream the history of Macondo-Colombia-Latin America in *One Hundred Years of Solitude*. From that perspective, the Cubans themselves look back at their past: Lisandro Otero, in *La situación* [The Situation]; Miguel Barnet, in *Biografía de un cimarrón* [Biography of a Run-Away Slave]; Pablo Armando Fernández in *Los niños se despiden* [The Children's Farewell].

There remains to be considered, beyond the subjects taken individually, and of the perspectives themselves, the narrative structures and their relationship with determined historical circumstances; studies of this type are presented in essays by Jean Franco and Noé Jitrik, for example.[16] Even if these approaches were multiplied, it would not seem in any way forced to make the most dissimilar texts appear as necessarily linked to the revolutionary process. There will always be a considerable marginal area in which various groups of literary works are situated, ranging from those which, without a real nexus, thrive in the shadow of a kind of industry of the Left (whose exercise and unmasking are at the root of the indispensable polemics which accompany this new literature), passing through those of previous years (upon some of which they cast a curious light) and including the ones which are indifferent or even hostile to that process, but which benefit from it anyway in terms of widespread distribution and maintain unforeseeable relationships to it.

The consolidation of a literary genre assumes, of course, the conquest of a language. (All real literary works assume this.) This was seen with the Modernist poets; it is seen now with the new Latin American novel. But it is important not to confuse the role of this event, forgetting what Della Volpe, with full knowledge of contemporary linguistics, has reminded us of again: "the pertinence of poetry [that is, of literature] to thought in general."[17] The growth and consolidation of a literature are the growth and consolidation of a determined form of thought which finds its adequate expression. The search for this last, in itself, is not *the* goal of a literature. For each author it is a goal in the elementary sense in which a writer is a man who writes, a man who works with the language. But with that language, he says things, in some fortunate cases he manages to say a world of things. "House of the self," Heidegger called speech. And that house of the self, he said, is constructed by thought.[18] The speech of Latin America is saying its self. It would diminish this task merely to point out the obvious merits of the house. The appreciation of Modernism was damaged thus through decades, by the flourishing of its details, and leaving in shadows its *functions*, its great revelations.

In 1941, Jorge Luis Borges wrote: "In contrast to the barbarous United States... this continent has not produced a writer of worldwide influence—an Emerson, a Whitman, a Poe—nor a great esoteric writer: a Henry James, a Melville."[19] This melancholy observation was only partially true; although we may not have had very abundant examples of them, it is not necessarily true that we did not *produce* them (Inca Garcilaso, Hernández, Darío, Martí?): it is that we did not *export* them (to continue with this vocabulary). Both of these observations are beginning to be true to a major extent, in the measure in which Latin America, abandoning its laterality, is unified, entering into the central history which the United States has already entered into, with different goals and origins, when it produced and exported its Emerson, its Whitman, its Poe, its Melville, and its James (who, like Eliot later, was exported altogether). Latin American intercommunication is not the result of the new literature, nor vice versa: both are expressions of a world which is structuring itself, of a continent which is becoming one, in a violent anagnorisis. The young (and those who are less young) are truly beginning to read Latin America, because Latin America is truly beginning.

Notes

1. Pablo Neruda, "Prologue" to the book by Ilya Ehrenburg, *Muerte al invasor. Crónicas de guerra 1941–43* (Mexico: La Lucha de la Juventud, 1943), p. 9.

2. Still within a continental scope, we can understand the term *intercommunication* in two senses: as referring to authors, conscious of aspiring to common goals; or as referring to the readers, who enter into contact through literature. In general, we will use it in this second sense, which also tends to include the first; but since the inverse is not true, we will indicate the distinctions.

3. "Modernismo, noventiocho, subdesarrollo." Essay read at the Third Congress of the Asociación Internacional de Hispanistas, Mexico, August, 1968.

4. Güiraldes collaborated with the Argentinian ultraists, as one of them. A Cuban vanguardist, Juan Marinello, will openly mix those novels with those of his own generation, but considering them as "three exemplary novels," in *Literatura hispanoamericana. Hombres, Meditaciones* (Mexico: Universidad Nacional de Mexico, 1957), pp. 143–163.

5. As it could be thought that I succumb here to the easy temptation to incriminate our immediate past, I wish to recall some words I said in that past, on 11 November 1957, in a lecture at Columbia University: "If we think of the good old days of the vanguard, when the whole continent seemed to feel united by a common spirit, with all the magazines with ingenuous names pointed toward the future—*Proa, Revista de Avance, Contemporáneos*—we cannot help feeling a certain nostalgia upon seeing the disunity and the dispair of our days." "Situación actual de la poesía hispanoamericana," *Revista Hispánica Moderna* (New York, October 1958), and later in the book *Papelería* (Havana: Universidad Central de las Villas, 1962), pp. 26–27.

6. Respectable anthologies of the earlier Latin American novel have even been published: cf., for example, Angel Flores, *Historia y antología del cuento y la novela en Hispanoamérica* (New York: Las Américas, 1959); or *Novelas selectas de Hispano América, siglo XIX*, 2 vols., with prologue, selection, and notes by Salvador Reyes Nevares (Mexico: Labor, 1959). It was also possible to make up respectable anthologies of Hispanic-American poetry before Modernism, from that of Gutiérrez to that of Menéndez y Pelayo, and even that of Calixto Oyuela, who appeared later, but with a pre-Modernist perspective.

7. Alejo Carpentier, *Tientos y diferencias*, *(Ensayos)* (Mexico: Universidad Nacional Autónoma de México, 1964), pp. 5 and 9.

8. Angel Flores, *Historia*, p. 7.

9. Alejo Carpentier, *Tientos*, p. 6.

10. Quoted on the cover of *The Time of the Hero*.

11.   Negrism is born in Europe (in a more or less conscious way) within the artistic vanguard's rejection of the values of capitalist society that is on the way to capitalist expansion. To propose the superior beauty of African carvings implied the deauthorization of the supposed civilizing mission of the white man among the producers of those carvings. The Third World does not only inherit the interest in those forms, which are its own, after all, but it also develops the rebellion implicit in the European option. Thus, there is a consequent link between the interest of Apollinaire and the cubists in African art, and the revolutionary texts of Guillén and Césaire—and even those of Fanon. However, with its tremendous capacity to retain the forms while altering the functions, capitalist society eventually takes over for itself a certain negrism, reduced to ornament (as it will do with a good part of the entire vanguard, ornamentalized).

12.   Octavio Paz, *Corriente alterna* (Mexico: Siglo XXI, 1967), pp. 41–42.

13.   Quoted by Angel Rama in "Diez problemas para el novelista hispanoamericano," *Casa de las Américas*, no. 26 (Havana, October–November 1964).

14.   "Darío's generation was the first to be conscious of this situation, and many of the Modernist writers and poets defended our civilization passionately. With them, antiimperialism appears." Octavio Paz, *Cuadrivio* (Mexico: Joaquín Mortiz, 1965), p. 47. In reality, anti-imperialism has already appeared with José Martí; but it is the younger modernists who take it on later as a collective attitude.

15.   It should also be taken into account that the awakening of the Third World is prior to 1959 (it becomes visible beginning with the Second World War) and that the Latin American revolution is only one chapter in that awakening, one which attracted attention to those marginal zones. This explains why even before 1959, but within the wave of interest in the Third World, there was a beginning of widespread distribution of works like those of Asturias, Carpentier, and Borges. However, these authors, even when published by Gallimard in France, were included in a particular collection created for the purpose (*La croix du sud*, directed by Caillois): the ghetto had still not been broken (see Claude Couffron, "La literatura hispanoamericana vista desde Francia," in *Panorama de la actual literatura latinoamericana*, Havana: Casa de las Américas, 1969). On the other hand, once the process has begun, we can see an effort to absorb the forms and empty them of their substance, which reminds us, taking into account all the differences, of what happened with negrism, for example.

16.   Cf. Noé Jitrik, "Estructura y significado en *Ficciones* de Jorge Luis Borges," and Jean Franco, "El viaje frustrado en la literatura hispanoamericana," *Casa de las Américas*, no. 53 (Havana: March–April 1969).

17.   Galvano della Volpe, *Crítica del gusto*, trans. M. Sacristán (Barcelona: Seix y Barral, 1966), p. 127.

18.   Quotation translated from Martin Heidegger, *Carta sobre el humanismo*, trans. Alberto Wagner de Reyna, published together with *Doctrina de la verdad según Platón* (Santiago de Chile: Universidad de Chile, ca. 1956), p. 223.

19.   Jorge Luis Borges, "Prologue" to the *Antología poética argentina*, edited by J. L. B., Silvina Ocampo, and Adolfo Bioy Casares (Buenos Aires: Sudamericana, 1941), p. 11.

PART FIVE

The Social Function of Literature

11 / Literature and Underdevelopment

ANTÓNIO CÂNDIDO

BACKWARDNESS AND UNDERDEVELOPMENT: ITS REPERCUSSION IN THE WRITER'S CONSCIOUSNESS

The Brazilian writer Mario Vieira de Mello, one of the few who have dealt with the problem of the relationships between underdevelopment and culture, establishes a valid distinction not only for his country, but all of Latin America. He says that there was a marked change in perspective, since until more or less the 1930s the notion of a "new country" prevailed among us, that is, a country which has not yet been able to establish itself but which claims great possibilities of future progress for itself. Without there having been any essential change in the distance which separated us and which separates us from the rich countries, what prevails now is the notion of the "underdeveloped country." The first perspective emphasized the as yet unachieved power and consequent greatness. The second emphasizes the present poverty, the atrophy; what is lacking and not what abounds.

The conclusions which Mario Vieira de Mello draws from that distinction do not seem accurate to me; but considered in itself it is just and it helps to understand certain fundamental aspects of literary creation in Latin America. In effect, the idea of a "new country" produces certain fundamental attitudes in literature, derived from surprise, from interest in the exotic, from a certain respect for the grandiose, and from the hope for future possibilities. The idea that America constitutes a privileged place was expressed in utopian projections, which affected the physiognomy of the Conquest, as Sergio Buarque de Holanda demonstrated in a basic study where he analyzes the transposition of notions and fantasies of a paradisical nature which compose the image of the New World. Pedro Henríquez Ureña points out that the first document which relates to our continent, Columbus's letter, sets the tone of astonishment and exaltation which will be communicated to posterity. In the seventeenth century, the Luso-Brazilian Jesuit Antonio Vieira, mixing pragmatism and prophecy, advised the transfer of the seat of the Portuguese monarchy to Brazil, which would be predestined to accomplish the highest purposes of history, as the seat of the Fifth Empire. Later on, when the contradictions of the colonial statutes led the dominant classes to political separation from the metropolis, the complementary idea arose that America had been predestined to be the land of liberty and thus fulfill the destinies of Western man.

Latin American intellectuals have inherited that state of enthusiasm and have transformed it into an instrument of national affirmation and ideological justification. Literature became a language of celebration and tenderness, favored by romanticism, with the backing of hyperbole and in the transformation of exoticism into a spiritual state. Our sky was bluer, our flowers more luxuriant, our landscape more inspiring than that of other places—as we read in a paradigmatic poem written around 1840 by a Brazilian, Gonçalves Dias, which could, however, have been signed by any of his contemporaries from Mexico to Tierra del Fuego.

The idea of *patria*, of "fatherland," was closely linked to that of *nature* and in part took its justification from this. Both led to a literature which compensated for material backwardness and the weakness of institutions by the supervaluing of "regional" aspects, making exoticism a cause for social optimism. In Rafael Obligado's *Santos Vega*, at the very end of the nineteenth century, nativist exaltation is projected onto what is really civic responsibility and the Argentine poet implicitly differentiates between *patria* (institutional) and *land* (natural), uniting them, however, in the very movement which identifies them:

> ...la convicción de que es mía
> la patria de Echeverría,
> la tierra de Santos Vega.

[...the conviction that / the fatherland of Echeverría / the land of Santos Vega / is mine.]

One of the ostensible or latent assumptions of Latin American literature was this connection, generally exalted, between the *land* and the *patria*—taking for granted that the greatness of the second would be a kind of natural unfolding of the might attributed to the first. Our literatures were nourished by the "divine promises of hope"—to quote a famous line of Brazilian Romantic poetry.

But on the other side of the coin, the discouraging visions also depend on the same associations, as though the weakness or the disorganization of the institutions constituted an inconceivable paradox when faced with the grandiose natural conditions. ("In America everything is big, only man is small.")

Very well, given this causal union "beautiful land—great *patria*," it is not difficult to see the impact of the change of perspective brought about by the consciousness of underdevelopment, a change imposed by the reality of the impoverished soil, the antiquated technology, the appalling misery of the people, their paralyzing lack of culture. the situation is a pessimistic one for the present and problematical for the future, and the only trace left of that earlier expectation of the millennium is perhaps the confidence with which it is accepted that the removal of imperialism will, in itself, bring about the explosion of progress. But in general, it is no longer a matter of a passive point of view. Stripped of exaltation, it is an agonizing perspective and leads to the decision to fight, since the traumatism produced in the consciousness by the verification of how catastrophic backwardness is, stimulates political reforms. The preceding gigantism of a naturist base appears then in its true essence—as an ideological construct transformed into a compensatory illusion. Hence the eagerness for combat which spreads over the continent, converting the idea of underdevelopment into a propulsive force, which gives a new character to the traditional political concern of our intellectuals.

The consciousness of underdevelopment comes after the Second World War and manifests itself clearly from the fifties on. But ever since the thirties there had been a change in orientation, above all in regionalist fiction, which may be considered as a thermometer, given its generality and persistence. This fiction abandons its agreeableness and its *curiosity*, foreseeing or perceiving what there was of masking over in the picturesque enchantment or in the ornamental gentlemanliness with which the rustic man had been treated before. It is not false to say that the novel acquired, from this point of view, a demythifying force which anticipates the awakening of consciousness of the economists and politicians.

In this essay we will speak alternately or comparatively of the literary characteristics in the phase of the agreeable consciousness or backwardness, corresponding to the ideology of "new country," and in the phase of the catastrophic consciousness of backwardness, corresponding to the notion of "underdeveloped country." We will speak of both because they are intimately connected and because in the immediate and remote past we can become informed about the trends of the present. In respect to the method, it would be possible to opt for a sociology of diffusion or for a sociology of creation. Without forgetting the first, I have preferred to emphasize the second which, although it removes us from the rigor of statistics, brings us closer, instead, to the specific interests of literary criticism.

ILLITERACY, CULTURAL WEAKNESS, MASS COMMUNICATION MEDIA, LIMITED LITERARY PUBLIC

If we take notice of the material conditions for the existence of literature, the basic fact is perhaps that of illiteracy which, in the countries that had advanced pre-Columbian civilizations, had been aggravated by the linguistic plurality which still exists. The manifestations of cultural weakness are related to that illiteracy: the lack of means of communication and distribution (publishers, libraries, magazines, newspapers); the nonexistence, dispersion, and weakness of the available public for literature due to the very small number of real readers (many fewer than the already limited number of those who are literate); the impossibility of the specialization of writers in their literary tasks, which in general are accomplished as marginal activities or as mere avocation; the lack of resistance or discrimination in regard to influences and external pressures. The total picture of this weakness is completed by factors of an economic and political nature, such as the insufficient levels of remuneration and the financial anarchy of the governments, in conjunction with educational policies which are inept or criminally disinterested. Except in what refers to the three meridional countries which constitute the "white America" of the Europeans, revolutions have been necessary to change the conditions of predominant illiteracy, as happened gradually in Mexico and rapidly in Cuba.

The above-mentioned traits do not appear automatically or always in the same way, since there are various possibilities of dissociation and combination among them. Illiteracy is not always a sufficient motive to explain the weakness of other sectors, although it is the basic trait of underdevelopment in the area of culture. Peru, for example, is less badly off than other countries in respect to the level of instruction, but it reveals the same backwardness in respect to the diffusion of culture. In another sector, a fact like the development of publishing in the forties in Mexico and Argentina showed that the lack of books was not a consequence only of the limited numbers of readers and of the low purchasing power, since all of America, including the Portuguese-speaking part, absorbed the very substantial printings, especially those of high quality. Perhaps it would be possible to conclude that the bad publishing habits and the lack of communication aggravated the inertia of the public, and that there was an unsatisfied capacity of absorption. This last example reminds us that in Latin America the problem of the public is a unique one, since this is the last group of underdeveloped countries that speak European languages (with the exception of the indigenous groups just indicated), and they come culturally from metropolises which are still underdeveloped today. In these old metropolises, literature was and continues to be a product of limited consumption, compared to that of the developed countries where the public may be classified according to its reading habits and such a classification may be compared to the social stratification of the whole society. However, in Spain and Portugal as in our countries, a negative prior condition exists, which is the number of literate people, that is, of those who can eventually be readers of books. This makes the Latin American countries closer to the virtual conditions of the old metropolises than are the underdeveloped countries of Africa or Asia which speak languages different from the countries which colonized them and where the question concerning which language to use for literary creation presents a serious problem. The African writers of the French language, like Leopold Sedar Senghor, or of the English language, like Chinua Achebe, are doubly separated from their virtual publics and are associated either with the metropolitan publics or with a local public which is terribly limited.

This is said in order to show that the Latin American writer's possibilities of communication, within the general picture of the Third World, are much better than others despite the present situation, which so much limits its eventual public. Nevertheless, it is also possible to imagine that the Latin American writer could be condemned to be always what he has been: a producer for the minorities, although this does not necessarily mean groups of high aesthetic taste, but simply the limited number of the groups interested in reading. In effect, one must not forget that modern audiovisual resources may produce such a change in the processes of creation and in the means of communication that when the great masses finally get some elementary education they will seek satisfaction of the universal needs for fiction and poetry outside of books.

To clarify: in the majority of our countries there are great masses which still have not reached a level of interest in erudite literature, which have immersed themselves in a folkloric stage of oral communication. When they are literate and absorbed by the process of urbanization, they move into the domain of radio, television, comic strips, illustrated magazines, and constitute the base of a mass culture. Thus literacy does not proportionally augment the number of readers of literature, as we understand it here, but thrusts the literate, alongside the illiterate, directly from the folkloric phase into that kind of urban folklore which is mass culture. In the era of catechizing, the colonial missionaries wrote plays and poems, in Indian or vernacular languages, to make the principles of religion and of the metropolitan civilization accessible to their audiences through traditional literary forms, equivalent to those aimed at the educated man at that time. In our era, a reverse catechism rapidly converts the rural man to urban society, by means of communicative resources which include even subliminal indoctrination, imposing upon him values which are dubious and very different from those the educated man seeks in art and literature.

This problem is, in addition, an extremely serious one for the under-developed countries, because of the massive interference of what could be called *cultural know-how* and of materials themselves manufactured by mass culture, which originate in the developed countries, which can not only spread their values by this means, but also act abnormally through them and use them to orient the opinions and the sensibility of the underdeveloped populations in favor of their political interests. It is *normal*, for example, for the image of the Western cowboy hero to be spread or popularized, because independent of value judgments, it is one of the characteristics of North American culture of which the world is aware. In countries with a large Japanese population, like Brazil, the image of the samurai is also popularized in a *normal* manner, above all through the movies. But it is *abnormal* that such images should serve as vehicles for the inculcation in the publics of the underdeveloped countries of attitudes and ideas which cause identification with political and economic interests of the United States or Japan. When we realize that the majority of the comic strips and the illustrated magazines carry North American copyrights, and that a large amount of the pulp fiction (photo-novels, detective and adventure stories) comes from the same source, or imitates it slavishly, it is easy to appreciate the negative effect that these may eventually exercise, as *abnormal* diffusion to defenseless publics.

It should be pointed out in respect to this that in erudite literature the problem of influences (which we will examine later) can have a good or a deplorable aesthetic effect; nevertheless, only exceptionally does this have any repercussion in the ethic or political behavior of the masses, since it reaches a very limited number of people. However, in a mass civilization, where the nonliterary, paraliterary, or subliterary media predominate, like the ones we have mentioned, such limited or differentiated publics tend to become uniform, to the point where they merge with the mass, which receives the influence on an immense scale. And, what is more important, that influence is imposed by means of vehicles where the aesthetic element is reduced to a minimum, and can be mixed with ethic or political intentions which, in extreme cases, can penetrate the entire population.

Since we are an "intervened-in continent," Latin American literature must be extremely vigilant not to be carried away by the instruments and values of mass culture, which seduce so many contemporary theoreticians and artists. It is not a matter of joining the "apocalyptic" ones but of alerting the "integrated" ones—to use Umberto Eco's delicious distinction. Certain modern experiences are fertile from the point of vanguard spirit and of the meshing of art and literature with the rhythm of the time, as in the case of concretism. But it is not hard to realize what would happen if they were to be manipulated politically by the wrong side, in a society of masses. In effect, although right now they present a hermetic and restrictive appearance, the principles upon which they depend, tending toward graphic display, expressive sonority, and syntagmatic combinations of great communicability, can eventually make them much more effective than the traditional literary forms in dealing with mass audiences. For the literary expression of Latin America, there is no advantage in moving from the aristocratic segregation of the era of the oligarchies to the directed manipulation of the masses, in the era of propaganda and of total imperialism.

CULTURAL WEAKNESS AND ITS INFLUENCE ON CREATION

Illiteracy and cultural weakness do not influence only the external aspects which we have just mentioned. The critic is more interested in their interference in the writer's consciousness and in the very nature of creation.

Ideology of the Enlightenment: Aristocratism

In the era we are calling that of "pleasant consciousness of backwardness," the writer participated in the ideology of the Enlightenment, according to which education automatically carries with it all the benefits which permit the humanization of man and the progress of society. At the beginning, education was proclaimed for the *citizens*, a minority from whose ranks were recruited those who participated in economic and political advantages; afterward, for the common people, something envisioned vaguely from afar, less as a reality than as a liberal concept. Emperor Pedro II of Brazil said that he would have preferred to be a teacher, which indicates an attitude similar to that of Sarmiento's point of view, according to which the domination of civilization over barbarity presupposed a latent urbanization, based on education. In Andrés Bello's continental vocation, it is possible to distinguish the political vision from the pedagogic project, and in the more recent group of the Athenaeum of Caracas, resistance to the tyranny of Gómez was identified with the spread of enlightenment and the creation of a literature impregnated by myths of redemptive education, all projected onto the figure of Rómulo Gallegos, first president of a reborn republic.

A curious case is that of the Brazilian thinker Manuel Bomfim, who in 1905 published a book of great interest, *A América Latina* [Latin America]. Unjustly forgotten (perhaps because it depends on antiquated biological analogies, perhaps for the uncomfortable radicalism of its positions), he analyzes our backwardness as a function of the prolongation of our colonial status, seen in the persistence of oligarchies and foreign imperialism. At the end of the book, when everything leads toward a theory of the transformation of social structures as a necessary condition, a disappointing strangulation of reasoning occurs, and he concludes by eulogizing education as panacea. We feel ourselves to be there, in the center of the illusion of Enlightenment, ideology of the phase of hopeful consciousness of backwardness which, significantly, did very little to establish that education.

It is not surprising, then, that the idea referred to, according to which the new continent would be destined to be the fatherland, the *patria*, of liberty should have suffered a curious adaptation: it would be destined equally to be the fatherland of the book. That is what we read in a rhetorical poem, where Castro Alves says that, while Gutenberg invented the printing press, Columbus found the ideal location for that revolutionary technology:

> Quando no tosco estaleiro
> Da Alemanha o velho obreiro
> A ave da imprensa gerou
> O Genovês salta os mares,
> Busca um ninho entre os palmares
> E a *pátria da imprensa* achou.

[When in the coarse shipyard / Of Germany the old laborer / Generated the bird of the printing press, / The Genoese leaps over the seas / Seeks a nest among the palms / And the *fatherland of the printing press* was found.]

This poem, written in the 1860s by a youth steeped in liberalism, is expressively titled *"O Livro e a América"* [The Book and America] manifesting the ideological position to which we refer.

Thanks to it, those intellectuals constructed a vision which was equally deformed in respect to its relation to the dominant lack of culture. When they lamented the ignorance of the common people and desired that it should disappear, so that the fatherland might automatically rise to its destinies, they excluded themselves from the context and considered themselves as an isolated group, really "fluctuating" in a more complete sense than that of Alfred Weber. They fluctuated, with or without a sense of guilt, superior to the lack of culture and the backwardness, sure that these could not contaminate them, nor affect the quality of what they were doing. Since the situation could not accommodate them intellectually, except to a very limited extent, and since their values were rooted in Europe, they projected themselves toward Europe, unconsciously taking it as a standard of reference and considering themselves equivalent to the best there was in the Old World.

In truth, the general lack of culture produced and produces a much more penetrating weakness, which affects the whole culture and the very quality of its manifestations. Seen from the perspective of today, yesterday's situation seems different from the illusion people had of it then, since we can analyze it more objectively now, due to the regulatory action of time and to our own efforts to unmask it.

The question will become clearer when we discuss the foreign influences. In order to understand them well we need to return, bearing in mind our reflections on backwardness and underdevelopment, to the fact of cultural dependency. It is a fact which may be considered natural—given our situation as colonized peoples who either descend from the colonizer or suffered the imposition of his civilization—but which becomes complicated in positive and negative ways.

The cultural penury necessarily subjected the writer to the metropolitan models and to European models in general, establishing a position, an aristocratic one in a way, with respect to the uncultured man. In effect, to the extent to which there existed no sufficient local public, he wrote as though his ideal public were in Europe, thus often disassociating himself from his own land. This gave origin to works which the authors and readers considered highly refined because they assimilated the European forms and values. Although, because of the lack of local points of reference, they did not go beyond being exercises of mere cultural alienation, not justified by the excellence of the achievement—as may be seen in the bazaar quality and the affection of Spanish-language "Modernism" and its Brazilian equivalents, Parnassianism and symbolism.[1] There are valid aspects of Rubén Darío, it is true, as of Herrera y Reissig, Olavo Bilac, Cruz e Sousa. But there are many fake jewels unmasked by time, a lot of contraband that gives them the appearance of being contestants for some international prize for "beautiful" writing. The refinement of the *decadents* and *nefelibatas* became provincial, revealing the erroneous perspective that can be established when the elite, without any kind of base in an uncultured country, does not have the means to face up to itself critically and supposes that the relative distance which separates them signifies an absolute altitude. "I am the last Greek!" the writer Coelho Neto, a kind of industrious local D'Annunzio, declaimed theatrically in 1922 in the Brazilian Academy, protesting against the vanguardism of our "Modernists," who came to debilitate the aristocratic "pose" in art and in literature.

We must remember another aspect of alienating aristocratism, which at the time seemed praiseworthy refinement: the use of foreign languages in creative works. Certain extreme examples were paradoxically comical, such as that of a late fifth-rate Brazilian Romantic, Pires de Almeida, who published, at the beginning of this century, in French, a nativist theatrical work probably composed well before that: *La fête des crânes, drame de moeurs indiennes en trois actes et douze tableaux*.... Nevertheless, the fact is a really significant one when it appears in connection with authors and works of quality, like the eighteenth century poet, Claudio Manuel da Costa, who left an extensive and good body of work in Italian. Or Joaquim Nabuco, a typical example of the cosmopolitan oligarchy of liberal sentiments, in the second half of the nineteenth century, who wrote a play in French about the moral problems of an Alsatian after the war of 1870 (!), in addition to autobiographic fragments and a book of maxims. Various Brazilian symbolists wrote all of their work or part of it in this same language, including one of the important writers, Alphonsus de Guimaraens. Francisco García Calderón wrote a book in French which was very useful in its time as an attempt at an integrated vision of the Latin American countries. Vicente Huidobro wrote part of his work and of his theory in French. I am sure that similar examples could be found in all of our countries, ranging from the vulgar official and academic subliterature right up through works of quality.

All of this did not exist without ambivalence, since on one hand the elites imitated both the good and the bad of the European suggestions, but, on the other, sometimes simultaneously, they affirmed the most intransigent spiritual independence, in a pendular movement between reality and the utopia of an ideological nature. And thus we see that illiteracy and refinement, cosmopolitanism and regionalism, can have intertwined roots in the soil where culture is lacking and the effort to overcome it.

Backwardness, Anachronism, Cultural Degradation

The facts of backwardness, anachronism, degradation, and confusion of values are a more serious influence of cultural weakness on literary production. Normally all literature presents aspects of backwardness, and it is possible to say that the average literary production at any given moment is already a tributary of the past, while the vanguards prepare the future. In addition to this there is an official subliterature, marginal or provincial, generally expressed by the academies. Nevertheless, what attracts our attention in Latin America is the fact that aesthetically anachronistic works are considered live; or the fact that secondary works are acclaimed by the best critical opinion and can survive for more than a generation, when both these categories should have been long since put in their respective places, as things of minor value or as manifestations of purposeless survival. Let us cite only the strange case of the poem *Tabaré*, by Juan Zorilla de San Martín, an effort at a national Uruguayan epic almost at the beginning of the twentieth century, taken seriously although conceived and executed according to models which were already antiquated in the romantic era.

At other times the backwardness is not offensive, and only indicates slowness. This is what occurs with naturalism in the novel, which arrived a little late and lasted until now without any substantial break in its continuity, although it has been modified in its applications. The fact that most of our countries still have problems of adjustment to and struggle with the environment, as well as problems connected with the racial diversity, extended the naturalistic preoccupation with physical and biological factors. In such cases, the weight of local reality produces a kind of legitimization of the influence, which acquires a creative sense. For this reason, when in Europe naturalism was outmoded, among us it could still be an ingredient of quite legitimate literary formulas, such as those of the social novel of the thirties and forties, which could be called *neonaturalistic*.

Other examples exist which are frankly disastrous: those of cultural provincialism, which loses its sense of proportion, granting the type of recognition and admiration to worthless works which in Europe were reserved for excellent books; which still leads to phenomena of true cultural degradation, making spurious works *pass*, in the sense that contraband is *passed*, because of the weakness of the public and the lack of sense of values on the part of the public as well as the writers. See, for example, the routine acceptance of influences which are in themselves dubious, such as those of Oscar Wilde or Anatole France during the first quarter of this century. Or, verging on the grotesque, the real profanation of Nietzsche by Vargas Vila, whose fame in all Latin America reached an audience which in principle should have been immune, on a scale which is startling and amusing. The *profundity* of the uncultured and semicultured creates conditions for these and other blunders.

FOREIGN INFLUENCES AND AMBIVALENCE:
COSMOPOLITANISM AND REGIONALISM

From Dependency to Interdependency

A problem which is interesting to discuss from the point of view of the dependency caused by cultural backwardness is that of the various types of influences, good or bad, inevitable and unnecessary.

Our literatures (like those of North America, too) are fundamentally branches of the metropolitan literatures. And if we put the susceptibilities of national pride to one side, we are going to see that, despite the autonomy which they gradually acquired in relation to those European models, they are still to a great extent reflections. In the numerically dominant case of the Spanish-and-Portuguese-speaking countries, the process of autonomy consisted, to a great extent, in transferring the dependency, so that European literatures other than those of the particular colonizing powers, especially French literature, became the model beginning in the nineteenth century, a process which was also taking place in the old metropolitan centers, Spain and Portugal. Now it is necessary to take North American literature into account, since it constitutes a new focus of attraction.

This is what we could call *inevitable influence*, sociologically linked to our dependency since the Conquest itself and the sometimes brutally enforced transplantation of cultures. Here is what Juan Valera said about this matter, at the end of the last century:

> From this side and the other of the Atlantic, I see and confess, in the people of Spanish language, our dependence on that which is French, and, to a certain point, I think it unavoidable; I do not wish to disparage the merit of French science and poetry in order for us to shrug off its yoke, nor do I wish, in order for us to achieve independence, that we should isolate ourselves and not accept the proper influence that civilized peoples should exercise upon each other.
>
> What I sustain is that our admiration should not be blind, nor should our imitation be uncritical, and that we should take what we take with discernment and prudence. [From "Critical Judgment," about *Tabaré* by Juan Zorilla de San Martín]

Consequently, let us admit with serenity our pleasing connection with the European literatures, since it is not an option; it is an almost natural fact. We never create original expressive forms or basic expressive techniques, in the sense that we mean by romanticism, on the level of literary movements; the psychological novel, on the level of genres; the free, indirect style, on that of writing. And although we may have achieved occasional originality on the level of expressive accomplishment, we implicitly recognize dependency. This is so much the case that the various nativisms never rejected the use of the imported literary *forms*, because to do so would be the same thing as being opposed to the use of the European languages which we speak. What was demanded was the choice of new *themes*, of different *sentiments*. Carried to the extreme, nativism (which in this sense always seems ridiculous, although sociologically comprehensible) would imply the rejection of the sonnet, the realistic story, verse of free association. The very fact that the question has never arisen reveals that, on the profound strata of creativity—those that include the choice of the expressive media—we always recognize our inevitable dependency as natural. And when it is seen in that light, it ceases to be dependency in order to be transformed into a form of participation and contribution to a cultural universe to which we belong, which goes beyond nations and continents, permitting the reversibility of experiences, the circulation of values. Even in the moments when, in our turn, we have influenced Europe, on the level of completed works, not on that of thematic suggestions, what we have returned were not inventions but rather perfected versions of received instruments. This happened with Rubén Darío in respect to Spanish Modernism and with Jorge Amado, José Lins do Rego, and Graciliano Ramos with Portuguese neorealism.

Many consider Hispanic-American "Modernism" a kind of rite of passage, marking a literary coming of age by evidence of capacity for original contribution. Nevertheless, if we alter the perspectives and define the fields, perhaps we will see that this is more true as a psychological fact than as an aesthetic reality. It is true that Darío, and eventually the whole movement, reversing the current for the first time and carrying the influence of America to Spain, represented a rupture in the literary sovereignty which the latter exercised. But the fact is that this reversal was not based on original expressive resources but rather on the adaptation of French processes and attitudes. What the Spaniards received was the influence of France already filtered and translated by the Latin Americans, who in this way took their places as cultural mediators.

This does not at all diminish the value of the "Modernists" or the significance of their achievement, based on a high consciousness of literature as art, not as document, and with a sometimes exceptional capacity for poetic expression. Nevertheless, it allows "Modernism" to be interpreted along the line developed here, that is, as a sociologically important episode in the story of the creative fertility of dependency, the peculiar way our countries have of being original. In the same way, also without innovating on the level of aesthetic form, the corresponding Brazilian movement, which although less valuable is less deceptive since it calls its two stages *Parnassianism* and *symbolism*, indicating very clearly the source from which everyone drank.

A fundamental stage in the overcoming of dependency is the ability to produce first-class works influenced not by foreign models, but by previous national examples. This is evidence of the establishment of an internal causality, which makes the loans taken from other cultures even more fertile. In the Brazilian case, the creators of "Modernism" in the twenties are derived to a great extent from the European vanguards. But the poets of the next generation, in the thirties and forties, descend directly from them—as we can see when we examine the influences on Carlos Drummond de Andrade or Murilo Mendes. These poets, in their turn, inspired João Cabral de Melo Neto, despite the fact that he also is indebted to Valéry, first of all, and then to the contemporary Spaniards. Nevertheless, these excellent poets did not have influence outside their own country, and even less in the countries from which we receive inspiration.

Thus it is possible to say that Borges represents the first case of indisputable original influence, exercised in a widespread and recognized manner upon the countries of origin as a new way of understanding writing. Machado de Assis, who could have opened new horizons, at the end of the nineteenth century, was lost on the sands of an unknown language, in a country then without importance.

Thus even our own affirmations of nationalism and cultural independence are inspired by European formulas; an example of this would be the case of Brazilian romanticism, defined in Paris by a group of young writers who lived there and founded there, in 1836, a magazine which began the movement.

The case of the vanguards of the twenties is an interesting one; they demonstrated extraordinary liberty of expressive procedures and prepared us for a great change in the treatment of the themes presented to the consciousness of the writer. What do these factors of autonomy and self-affirmation consist of, examined from our angle? Huidobro establishes creationism in Paris, inspired by the French and the Italians; he writes his poetry in French and expounds his principles in French, in magazines like *L'Espirit Nouveau*. Argentine ultraism and Brazilian "Modernism" stem from the same origins. That did not keep these movements and their proponents from being innovative, the creators par excellence of the new literature: in addition to Huidobro, Borges, Mario de Andrade, Oswald de Andrade, Manuel Bandeira.

We know, then, that we are part of a larger culture, in which we participate as one of the cultural varieties. On the contrary to what our grandfathers have sometimes candidly supposed, it is an illusion to speak of the suppression of contacts and influences. At a time when the law of the world is inter-relationship and interaction, utopias of originality do not continue to exist in the patriotic sense, comprehensible in a phase of national formation, which conditioned a provincial and umbilical vision.

In the present phase of consciousness of underdevelopment, the question becomes a more complex one. Is there a paradox in this? In effect, the more we find out about the tragic reality of underdevelopment, the more the free man who thinks allows himself to take revolutionary inspiration seriously, that is, he believes in the need to reject the economic yoke of imperialism and to modify the internal structures which nourish the situation of under-development. Nevertheless, he sees the problems of influences with more objectivity, considering them as cultural and social connections. The paradox is apparent and really constitutes a sign of maturity, impossible in the cloistered and oligarchic world of ideological nationalisms. This is so often true, that the recognition of the connection is associated with the beginning of the ability to innovate on an expressive level, and with the attempt to struggle on the level of economic and political development. While the traditional affirmation of originality, with a sense of elementary particularism, led and leads, on one hand, to the picturesque, and on the other, to cultural servility, two diseases of growth, probably inevitable but still alienating.

Since the aesthetic movements of the twenties, the intense aesthetic-social consciousness of the thirties and forties, and the crisis of economic development and technical experimentalism of more recent years, we begin to feel that dependency is directed toward a *cultural interdependency* (if it is possible to use this term without being misunderstood, since it recently acquired such a disagreeable meaning in political terminology). This will not only give the writers of Latin America consciousness of their unity in diversity, but will also encourage mature original works which will be gradually assimilated by other countries, including the metropolitan and imperialist nations. The process of reflection about underdevelopment leads, in the area of culture, to that of transnational integration, since what used to be imitation is changing more and more into reciprocal assimilation.

One example among many: in the works of Vargas Llosa, above all in *The Time of the Hero*, there appears, extraordinarily refined, the tradition of the interior monologue which, belonging to Proust and to Joyce, belongs also to Dorothy Richardson and Virginia Woolf, to Döblin and Faulkner. The latter may have provided certain of the techniques preferred by Vargas Llosa who, in any case, deepened and fertilized them, to the point of making them his own as well. One admirable example: the unidentified character who perplexes the reader, since his voice is juxtaposed to the third-person voice of the narrator and to the monologues of other identified characters, and can be confused with them at various times, and who, at the end, when he is revealed as Jaguar, retrospectively illuminates the structure of the book, stimulating us to reexamine all that we had established about the characters. This technique seems to be a concrete form of the image Proust uses suggestively (the Japanese drawing reflected in the bowl of water), but it means something different, on a different plane of reality. Here, the novelist of the under-developed country received ingredients by cultural loan from the countries which are producers of original literary forms. Nevertheless, he adapted them profoundly to his design, in order to portray his own country's problems, and he made the formula a very personal one. There is no mechanical reproduction or imitation. There is participation in the resources which come to be common property through the situation of dependency, thus helping to make this into an interdependency.

These circumstances seem to be integrated into the critical consciousness of America; one of the most original writers of the present, Julio Cortázar, writes interesting things about the new writing which reflects local fidelity and worldwide mobility, in a recent interview in *Life* (vol. 33, no. 7). And in regard to foreign influences on recent writers, Rodríguez Monegal assumes, in an article in the magazine *TriQuarterly* (nos. 13–14), an attitude which could be called "critical justification of assimilation." Nevertheless, contrary points of view still exist, linked to a certain localism which is associated with the phase of pleasant consciousness of backwardness. According to these voices of opposition, such assimilations are manifestations of a lack of personality and of cultural alienation, as can be seen in an article in the Venezuelan magazine *Zona Franca* [Free Zone] (no. 51), where Manuel Pedro González actually says that the true Latin American writer would be the one who not only lives in his country but also uses its characteristic themes and expresses its particular problems, without an external aesthetic dependency.

It seems, however, that one of the positive characteristics of the era of underdevelopment is the overcoming of the attitude of suspicion, which leads to the indiscriminate acceptance of local themes or an illusion as to their originality. Anyone who fights against real obstacles becomes more tranquil and recognizes the fallacy of fictitious obstacles. In Cuba, vanguard of America in the struggle against underdevelopment, is there artifice or escapism in the surrealist impregnation of Alejo Carpentier or in his complex vision, which is transnational, even thematically, as it appears in *Explosion in a Cathedral*? In Brazil, the recent movement of concrete poetry adopts Ezra Pound's inspirations and Max Bense's aesthetic principles; nevertheless, it leads to the redefinition of the national past, stimulating a new reading of forgotten poets like Sousa Andrade, a precursor lost among the romantics of the nineteenth century; or conveniently illuminating the stylistic revolution of the great *Modernists*, Mario de Andrade and Oswald de Andrade.

From Copying and Regionalism to Superregionalism

Considered as a derivative of backwardness and of the lack of economic development, dependency presents other aspects which have repercussions in literature. Let us reexamine the phenomenon of ambivalence, which manifests itself in impulses to copy and to withdraw which seem contradictory but which can be seen as complementary.

Backwardness which encourages servile copies of anything offered by current fashion in the advanced countries, in addition to their seduction of writers with migration, external and internal. Backwardness which promotes what is most distinctive about the local reality, establishing a regionalism which seems to be an affirmation of national identity, but which can be really an unsuspected way of offering to European sensibility the exoticism it desires, as a distraction, making this regionalism into an acute form of dependency within independence. From the present perspective, it seems that the two tendencies are fused and stem from the same situation of backwardness or underdevelopment.

At its most gross, the servile imitation of literary styles, themes, attitudes, and uses, has a ludicrous or limiting quality of provincialism after serving as mere compensatory aristocratism of a colonial country. In Brazil this is carried to an extreme, with an Academy copied from the French, installed in a building which reproduces the Petit Trianon of Versailles (Petit Trianon actually came to mean, by association, the same institution), with forty members who are called *immortals* and who, like their French models, wear embroidered uniforms, two-cornered hats, and small dress swords. But throughout America, the Bohemian life-style which imitates Greenwich Village or Saint-

Germain des Prés is often a homologous occurrence, under its appearance as innovative rebellion.

Probably no less gross, on the opposite side, are certain primary forms of nativism and literary regionalism which reduce human problems to a picturesque element, transforming the passion and suffering of rural people or of the *colored* populations into an equivalent of pineapples and papayas. This attitude cannot only be equivalent to the first, but can also be combined with it, once it bends over backwards to *serve* up to an urban reader who is European, or falsely Europeanized, the almost touristic reality which he would like to see in America. Without realizing it, the most sincere nativism risks making itself into an ideological manifestation of the same cultural colonialism, which its cultivator would reject on the level of plain reason, and which emphasizes a situation of underdevelopment and consequent dependency.

However, it would be erroneous, from the point of view of this chapter, to offer, as is fashionable, an absolute condemnation of regionalist fiction, at any rate before establishing some distinctions that will allow it to be seen, on a level of judgments of reality, as a consequence of the effect which economic and social conditions have on the choice of themes.[2] The underdeveloped areas and the problems of underdevelopment (or of backwardness) invade the writer's consciousness and sensitivity, making suggestions, building themselves into a topic which is impossible to avoid, transforming themselves into positive or negative stimuli of creativity.

In French literature, or in English, there can be great novels which occasionally take place in the country, like those of Thomas Hardy, but it is obvious that it is only a matter of a setting and that the real topic is the same as in urban novels. In addition, the different forms of regionalism are in themselves a secondary, and in general, a provincial form, amid much richer forms, which occupy the center of our attention. However, in the underdeveloped countries, like Greece and Spain, or in countries that have large underdeveloped areas, like Italy, regionalism can occur as a valid manifestation, capable of producing excellent works, like those of Giovanni Verga, at the end of the last century, and those of Elio Vittorini or Nikos Kazantzakis right now.

For this reason, in Latin America, regionalism was and still continues to be a stimulating force in literature. In the phase of consciousness of a new country, corresponding to a situation of backwardness, it especially lends itself to the decorative picturesque and functions as discovery, recognition of the reality of the country and its incorporation into the body of possible literary themes. In the phase of underdevelopment, it functions as prediction and then as consciousness of crisis, motivating documentation and political concern, through the feeling of urgency it imparts.

In both stages we see a kind of selection of thematic areas, an attraction to certain remote regions where groups marked by underdevelopment live. They can undoubtedly exercise a negative seduction upon the city writer through their picturesqueness of dubious consequences, but, apart but from this, in general, they are the really problematic areas, which is significant in literatures that are as in touch with living reality as ours are.

This is the case of the Amazon region, which attracted Brazilian novelists and short story writers right from the beginning of naturalism in the 1870s and 1880s, at the height of its picturesque phase. The Amazon basin is material a half century later for José Eustacio Rivera's *The Vortex*, which is halfway between picturesque and the denunciatory (more patriotic than social); and this region is an important element in Vargas Llosa's *The Green House*, a product of the recent phase of high technical consciousness, where the picturesque and the denunciatory are recessive facts before the human impact which makes this book a universal work of literature.

It is not necessary to enumerate all of the other literary areas which correspond to the panorama of backwardness and underdevelopment, like the high Andean plains or the Brazilian *sertão*. Nor is it necessary to describe the situations and living conditions of the Cuban, Venezuelan, and Brazilian Negro in the poems of Nicolás Guillén and Jorge de Lima, in Alejo Carpentier's *Ecué Yamba-O*, Rómulo Gallegos's *Pobre negro* [Poor Black Man], Jorge Amado's *Jubiabá*. Or if you wish, the man of the prairies—*llano*, *pampa*, *caatinga*—object of a persistent compensatory idealization which began with the romantics, like the Brazilian José de Alencar in the 1870s, and widely treated by writers of the River Plate area, such as the Uruguayans Eduardo Acevedo Díaz, Carlos Reyles, or Javier de Viana, and Argentines, from the telluric Hernández to the stylized Güiraldes; which tends to the allegorical in Gallegos in order to be given, back in Brazil again, at the height of the phase of preconsciousness of underdevelopment, an excellent portrayal in Graciliano Ramos's *Vidas secas* [Barren Lives], without vertigo at the distances, without tournaments or duels, without *caballadas* [herds of horses] or *vaquejadas* [herds of cows], without the centaurism which marks the others.

Regionalism was a necessary stage which led literature, especially the novel and the story, to local reality. Occasionally it was an opportunity for good literary expression, although the majority of its products have not aged well. Nevertheless, from a certain angle, perhaps it cannot be said that it is a thing of the past: many who attack it today, actually practice it. The economic facts of underdevelopment maintain the regional dimension as a living reality, although the urban dimension has become more and more important. We should bear in mind that some good writers, even some of the best ones, find material in it for books which are universally valid, such as José María Arguedas, Gabriel García Márquez, Augusto Roa Bastos, and João Guimarães Rosa. Only in the countries where the culture of the big cities absolutely predominates, like Argentina, Uruguay, and perhaps Chile, has regional literature become a real anachronism.

It is necessary to redefine the problem critically and verify that it is not exhausted by the fact that today no one considers regionalism a privileged form of national literary expression, and in fact, as we have said, it can be especially alienating. But we must think of its transformations, remembering that, under various names and concepts, the same basic reality continues. In effect, in the phase of exalted consciousness of a new country, characterized by the idea of backwardness, we had picturesque regionalism, which in several countries was held to be *the* true literature. That particular form became outmoded long ago, or reduced to the level of subliterature. Its finest and most tenacious manifestation in its golden era was perhaps the River Plate *gauchismo* [cult of the gaucho], while the most spurious form, without doubt, was the Brazilian *sertanejismo* [cult of the backlands]. And this is what irremediably mars certain more recent novels, like those of Rivera and Gallegos.

During the phase of preconsciousness of underdevelopment, in the thirties and forties, we had problematic regionalism, which was called *social novel*, *Indianism*, *novel of the Northeast*, depending on the country, and which is largely, although not exclusively, regionalistic. This regionalism interests us more as a precursor of the consciousness of underdevelopment, but it is only fair to recognize that, long before this, writers like Alcides Arguedas and Mariano Azuela had already demonstrated a more realistic sense of the living conditions and the human problems of the forsaken groups. Miguel Ángel Asturias, Jorge Icaza, Ciro Alegría, Jorge Amado, José Lins do Rego, and others are among the writers who next proposed the demythification of American reality with analytic vigor and sometimes with high artistic quality. All of these writers, in at least a portion of their work, write social novels which are quite related to regional aspects and frequently show traces of negative picturesqueness, which is combined with a certain humanitarian overview which permeates their writing.

However, they are characterized by having gone beyond patriotic optimism and by their adoption of a type of pessimism which is different from that found in naturalistic fiction. While naturalism focused on the poor man, considering him as an element in the way of progress, the later novelists dealt with the situation in its complexity, turning against the dominant classes and seeing man's degradation as a result of the situation. The paternalism of *Doña Bárbara* (which is a kind of apotheosis of the good *patrón* [boss]) suddenly seems archaic, when contrasted to the manner of George Grosz, in Icaza or Amado, in whose books traces of the picturesque and of melodrama are overshadowed by social unmasking which allows us to foresee the change from "consciousness of a new country" to "consciousness of an underdeveloped country," with the political consequences this includes.

Despite the fact that many of these writers are characterized by spontaneous and irregular language, the weight of social consciousness sometimes acts as a positive factor in their writing and occasions a search for interesting solutions adapted to the portrayal of inequality and injustice. The consummate craftsman Asturias who, like Icaza, writes clearly and obviously of social problems, owes his enduring popularity less to the indignant vehemence of his outcry against the exploiters than to some stylistic devices which he uses to express poverty. This is the case in *The Villagers*, too, in the way diminutives are employed, in the rhythm of grief in speech, in the reduction to animal level; all of this portrays the diminution of man, his reduction to elemental functions, which are associated with linguistic babble in order to symbolize privation. In *Barren Lives*, Graciliano Ramos carries his habitual verbal struggle to an extreme, reducing verbal expression to ellipsis, monosyllable, and minimal syntax in order to express the human suffocation of the cowboy, trapped in the minimal levels of subsistence.

It is appropriate to say that the case of Brazil may be different from others, since regionalism, which began there at the time of romanticism, has never produced works considered as first class, even by their contemporaries, and it has always been a literary movement of secondary importance. So it is only in the second phase of consciousness, which we are trying to characterize now, that regionalist tendencies, now sublimated and transfigured by social realism, achieve recognition as significant works, while in other places, especially in Argentina, Uruguay, and Chile, these traits were being phased out or had been rejected altogether.

The best products of Brazilian fiction were always *urban*, most of them stripped of all picturesqueness, following the dictates of the influential Machado de Assis, who, in 1880, showed the fragility of descriptivism and local color, which he proscribed from his books of prose and verse.

The overcoming of these modalities and the critical attack that they endure are demonstrations of maturity. For this reason, many writers would feel insulted if they were called *regionalists*. However, this does not mean that the regionalist dimension is not still present in many works of great importance, although it is not in any way imposed as a requisite of a mistaken national consciousness.

What we see now, from this point of view, is a novelistic flowering marked by technical refinement through which regions are transfigured and their contours subverted, causing the aspects which were previously picturesque to become disembodied and acquire universality.

Shedding sentimentalism and rhetoric, nourished by elements which are nonrealistic, like surrealism, the absurd, the magic of situations or by antinaturalistic techniques, like interior monologue, simultaneous points of view, foreshortening, and ellipsis, the contemporary novel takes advantage, however, of what used to be the very substance of nativism, of exoticism, and of social documentation. This would lead us to propose the distinction of a third phase, which could be called that of *superregionalism*. It corresponds to the lacerated consciousness of underdevelopment and entails going beyond the type of naturalism which was based on reference to an empirical view of the world, naturalism which was an aesthetic trait of a specific era in which bourgeois mentality triumphed and was the time when our literatures became consolidated.

A tributary of this superregionalism in Brazil is the revolutionary work of João Guimarães Rosa, solidly based on what could be called the "universality of the region." The fact that it has gone beyond the picturesque and the documental does not make the presence of the region less vivid in fiction like that of Juan Rulfo, neither in the fragmentary and obsessive reality of *The Burning Plain* nor in the phantasmal sobriety of *Pedro Páramo*. For this reason, it is necessary to reexamine drastic and in fact just judgments like those expressed by Alejo Carpentier in an essay where he writes that although our nativist novel has become assigned reading in schools, it no longer otherwise finds readers, even in its places of origins. This is undoubtedly true if we think of the first phase mentioned in our attempt at classification, true to a certain extent if we think of the second, not true at all for the last, bearing in mind that the third phase contains an important dose of regional ingredients, owing to the very fact of underdevelopment. As we have said, they constitute the stylized actuation of the peculiar dramatic conditions of regionalism, and they play a part in the selection of the themes and of the subject matter, sometimes in the way language is used.

It is no longer demanded, as perhaps it used to be, that Cortázar should sing the life of Juan Moreira or that Clarice Lispector should use the *sertanejo* [rural] vocabulary. But it is also necessary to recognize that, writing with refinement and surpassing academic naturalism, Guimarães Rosa, Juan Rulfo, and Vargas Llosa practice in all or part of their writing, as do Cortázar or Lispector within the universe of urban values, a new kind of literature which still deals in a transfiguring way with the very material of *nativismo* [nativism].

Notes

1.   The word *Modernism* in Brazil designates the movement of the literary vanguards of the twenties. To call attention to this, I use quotation marks every time I use it, in the two meanings which it has in the literary history of the Latin American countries of the Spanish and Portuguese language.

2.   I use *regionalism* here according to the tradition of Brazilian criticism, including all the fiction connected with regional description and rural customs since romanticism; and not in the manner of the majority of Hispanic-American critics, who in general restrict it to the movements which took place more or less between 1920 and 1950.

12 / Literature and Society

JOSÉ ANTONIO PORTUONDO

There is a constant in the Latin American cultural process, and it is the one determined by the predominantly instrumental—Alfonso Reyes would say "ancillary"—character of literature, placed at the service of society the greater part of the time. It should be emphasized that it is not a matter of the immediate dialectical relationship between the economic base and the various spheres of the superstructure—literature prominently included—nor of the reflective character of artistic manifestations, as Marxist aesthetics sustains. Although we reject the ingenuous concept of the reflection as a mirror-image reproduction of reality—expounded as a formula of critical realism by Stendhal— we fully accept its legitimate Leninist formulation—deepened and amplified by Pavlovian reflexology—as a *conditioned response* to a *signal*, integral to reality, which provokes and determines, not a servile copy of it, but rather a new reality in which that which is signaled reveals itself and extends its frontiers, bringing us ever closer to the essential rhythm of the universe. The relationships between Latin American reality and literature are characterized because to a great extent, or at least, in a more ostensible and constant way, life and literature of our America make mutual use of each other, they act in concert and continually blend together in unbreakable unity. Right from their beginnings, the verse and prose of the Hispanic countries of the New World reveal a certain attitude toward their environment and make an effort to have influence over it. There is no important writer or work which does not reveal deep concern for American social reality, and even the greatest escapists have apologetic or critical moments in regard to things and people. Parallel to educated expression, popular expression goes along filling us in with growing acuteness and wit, on the daily existence of the diverse human groups that are making an effort to become nations, against all the colonialists—old and *neos*—and in the face of all the imperialisms. And thus, from the earliest times, the Hispanic literatures of the new continent flow along through continuously confluent channels of the educated and the popular, reflecting and urging on the struggle of Latin American life, with occasional meanders into preciosity in which literature seems to forget the surrounding life and becomes escapist. But even in these cases, the escapism denounces a lack of adjustment between the writer and his social medium which sometimes is made explicit in a verse, in a paragraph, or in some other manifestation marginal to pure creative activity. In any form, literature is influenced by social existence and, in turn, has influence upon it, in an interminable dialectic play of reciprocal actions, of contrasted forces.

LITERATURE AND REVOLUTION

José Carlos Mariátegui (1895–1930) pointed out in his *Seven Interpretative Essays on Peruvian Reality* (1928), one of the major books of Latin American thought, that "elements of three different economies coexist in Peru today. Underneath the feudal economy inherited from the colonial period, vestiges of the indigenous communal economy can still be found in the sierra. On the coast, a bourgeois economy is growing in feudal soil; it gives every indication of being backward, at least in its mental outlook."[1] This situation, with slight variants, characterizes all of the Latin American nations, in which the invasion of imperialist financial capital left the feudal system of land management almost intact, and in some cases even reinforced it in the existence of enormous *latifundios* where the peasant—white, Indian, black, or mestizo—remained a true serf belonging to the land. Parallel to the Modernist poetry which was escapist, *preciosista*, and aristocratic, naturalist narratives denounced that reality. *Birds Without a Nest: A Story of Indian Life and Priestly Oppression in Peru* (1889), by the Peruvian Clorinda Matto de Turner (1854–1909), appeared barely a year after *Azul*, initiating a long series of Indianist novels in which authors from the whole continent denounce, with compassion or with anger, the exploitation of the Indian. Other stories will tell of the pain and even of the occasional rebellion of the urban worker and the sufferings of the petite bourgeoisie. The Zolaesque naturalism and its derivatives offer formulas for the denunciation of all social excrescences and deformations. Imperialism buys up real estate in the underdevelopment of our countries, maintains it, and submerges it with the complicity of dictators and of the new caste of bourgeois kings denounced by Darío. We refer back to Lenin:

> Imperialism is the epoch of finance capital and of monopolies, which introduce everywhere the striving for domination, not for freedom. The result of these tendencies is reaction all along the line, whatever the political system, and an extreme intensification of the existing antagonisms in this domain also. Particularly acute becomes the yoke of national oppression and the striving for annexations, *i.e.*, the violation of national independence (for annexation is nothing but the violation of the right of nations to self-determination). Hilferding justly draws attention to the connection between imperialism and the growth of national oppression.
>
> "In the newly opened countries themselves," he writes, "the capitalism imported into them intensifies contradictions and excites the constantly growing resistance against the intruders of the peoples who are awakening to national consciousness. This resistance can easily become transformed into dangerous

measures directed against foreign capital. The old social relations become completely revolutionised. The age-long agrarian incrustation of 'nations without a history' is blasted away, and they are drawn into the capitalist whirlpool. Capitalism itself gradually procures for the vanquished the means and resources for their emancipation and they set out to achieve the same goal which once seemed highest to the European nations: the creation of a united national state as a means to economic and cultural freedom. This movement for national independence threatens European capital [or North American, we add] just in its most valuable and most promising fields of exploitation, and European capital [or North American] can maintain its domination only by continually increasing its means of exerting violence."[2]

This long quotation from Lenin, based on Hilferding, eliminates the need for more detailed description of Hispanic-American reality illustrated by the literary output which followed the great generational experience of the Mexican agrarian revolution of 1910. Emiliano Zapata's cry of "land and liberty" echoed across the entire continent and engendered a rich literary expression of a libertarian and antiimperialist nature. It is not necessary to specify quantities of names or quotations in order to justify these affirmations. We are speaking of contemporary history, that which began with the first rebellions against imperialism and in defense of the free will of nations, of their right to liberty and culture; that history which we are making right now with the feverish rhythm which marks the main historical event of our time: the socialist Cuban Revolution. Faced with this event, the writers of the whole world have felt called to an urgent assessment of conscience and self-awareness which is agonizing for those of our own continent. And this assessment affects both the impassioned denouncers of injustice who maintained the position of Father Las Casas and the hyperbolical exalters of the deformed and the baroque, of the magic or the absurd quality which the daily expression of a persistent underdeveloped vision of reality tends to have among us, a vision enjoyed more as it becomes more distant, by the depraved European palates, and which possess an absolute and relevant aesthetic validity. A perceptive Spanish critic, José María Castellet, recently pointed out the transcendence of what he called "the Cuban meridian," and upon describing the characteristics of contemporary Latin American literature, seen from Europe, he emphasizes four suggestive and fruitful aspects which constitute, according to him, the great teaching of Latin American literature in the present era. The aspects are, first, "reflection and meditation, the effort to penetrate deeply each national reality." And he sees this—Castellet affirms—in novelists like Julio Cortázar just as much as in Mario Vargas Llosa, Juan Carlos Onetti, and Gabriel García Márquez. He adds:

Another characteristic which has been very impressive, and I think very fruitfully so to Spanish writers, is the great formal liberty of these novelists, that is, each writer tries to seek through precisely that reflection about each national reality in search of an entity; he tries to find the appropriate media for expression, and since in reality it is a matter of different societies, I think it is absolutely normal that formal models emerge—to put it that way—from these writers which are very different from each other and very diverse.... The third aspect which I would like to point out is that which I would call "fantasy as embellishment of reality...". On the other hand, I think that it is necessary to point out another very important thing for the Spanish writers: and that is the great linguistic freedom, the great freedom in creation, in the re-creation of the language.[3]

Castallet very perceptively indicates the dominant characteristics of today's Latin American literature, and although he is thinking particularly of narrative prose, his affirmations are valid for verse, as can be inferred from the discussions by other authors in the series of which the Spanish critic's lecture is a part. Critics as different in a geographical sense and in aesthetic perspective as the Argentinian Juan Carlos Portantiero[4] and the Cuban José Juan Arrom[5] agree with Castellet in indicating the characteristic nationalist and telluric qualities of Latin American literature. And this eagerness to penetrate into the essence of what is ours, of the national, and, by extension, of the American, is present even in works in which magic or the marvelous contribute to illuminate active aspects of the collective consciousness. The magic realism of Alejo Carpentier's *The Kingdom of This World*, for example, represents the normal vision of people who still interpret the phenomena of the surrounding world through a mythology which precedes the scientific explanation of reality and which is as legitimate and as valid for them as science is for us. When Gabriel García Márquez erases the boundaries between the real and the fantastic in *One Hundred Years of Solitude*, he is only continuing the tradition of a naturalistic antimetaphysical religiousness, beautifully illustrated in his own Colombia by the Antioquian Tomás Carrasquilla (1858–1940). And Columbus's amazement when he beheld the natural baroquism of our great tropical trees covered with and masked by parasitic plants, does this not perhaps anticipate the fascination which works like *Paradiso*, by the Cuban José Lezama Lima, hold for the European or Europeanized reader?

But this is not only a time for amazement, fascination, and magic, but also for action. Although Columbus's time of discovery is still with us, we are now in the midst of the impassioned and angry era of Father Las Casas. In 1928, to celebrate the second anniversary of the appearance of his journal *Amauta*, Mariátegui wrote these words of impressive immediacy:

> *New generation, new spirit, new sensibility*, all these terms are old-fashioned. the same would have to be said of these other labels: *vanguard, leftist*, and *renovation* were good and new terms in their time. We have made use of them to establish provisional boundaries, for contingent reasons of topography and orientation. Today they seem too generic and amphibolous. Under these labels, enormous amounts of contraband are being shipped. The new generation will not be effectively new except to the extent to which it finally knows how to be adult and creative.

The very word *revolution*, in this America of small revolutions, lends itself to misunderstanding. We must revindicate it rigorously and intransigently. We must restore to it its strict and exact meaning. The Latin American revolution will be nothing more and nothing less than a stage, a phase of the worldwide revolution. It will be simply and purely the socialist revolution. To this word add, depending on the case, all the adjectives you wish: *antiimperialist*, *agrarian*, *nationalist-revolutionary*. Socialism assumes them, anticipates them, includes them all.

Against capitalist, plutocratic, imperialist North America, it is only possible to oppose effectively a socialist Latin or Ibero America.The era of competition in the capitalist economy has ended in all fields and in all aspects. We are in the era of monopolies, that is, of empires. The Latin American countries are late arrivals to capitalist competition. The first places are already definitively assigned. The destiny of these countries, within the capitalist order, is that of simple colonies. The opposition of languages, of races, of spirits, has no decisive meaning. It is ridiculous to still speak of the contrast between a materialistic Saxon America and an idealistic Latin America, between a blond Rome and a pale Greece. All these are hopelessly discredited topics. Rodó's myth no longer operates—it has never operated—usefully and fruitfully upon souls. Let us inexorably discard all these caricatures and images of ideologies and come to terms, seriously and frankly, with reality.[6]

This coming to terms with reality has begun already, in our America, with the socialist Cuban Revolution, and, in its wake, life and literature both on the continent and away from it have begun to follow new ways. In the light of this, it seems evident now that there will be no appreciable novelty in literature if substantial novelty in life has not preceded it; that there is no valid formal renovation if it does not depend upon a renovated content; that no revolution will endure in words if it has not revolutionized action beforehand. And something else becomes evident from this Cuban experience: that it is no longer a matter, in literature and in art, of trying out poses as rebels or free shooters—which is another form of Bohemian entertainment or intellectual snobbism—but of the unified, disciplined, militant march of the creators who know themselves to be members of an army on the way to the decisive battle for the definitive liberation of America, that they have perceived that the revolution is not a rhetorical exercise, but a real fight against imperialism, in which it is not the men of letters who set the pace. It is not a matter, however, of allowing the clamor of arms to drown out the pure voices of the most delicate instrument, nor of allowing revolutionary discipline to impose specific themes or manners, destroying free expression. In his *Palabras a los intelectuales* [Words to the Intellectuals], Fidel Castro affirmed:

> The revolution should try to win over the greater part of the people to its ideas; the revolution should never give up counting on the majority of the people, counting not only on the revolutionaries but on all honest citizens who, although they may not be revolutionaries, that is, although they may not have a revolutionary attitude toward life, are with it. The revolution should only renounce those who

are incorrigibly counterrevolutionary. And the revolution must have a political plan for these people; the revolution has to have an attitude toward those intellectuals and writers. The revolution must comprehend that reality and, meanwhile, act in such a way that that sector of artists and intellectuals who are not genuinely revolutionary may find within the revolution a place where they can work and create and where their creative spirit, even when they are not revolutionary writers or artists, will have the opportunity and freedom to express itself within the revolution. This means that within the revolution, everything; against the revolution, nothing.[7]

But the interaction between literature and life, between Latin American literature and the medium in which it arises, is not only evident in our century. A quick look at our American past will provide an overview of some of the outstanding moments in this constant dialectic process.

THE COLONIAL PAST

When the newly found America still lacks its own voice—since the great pre-Columbian cultures were not understood and were brutally silenced—and it is only a theme of European curiosity, it already imposes new qualities on the accounts of travelers and chroniclers and inaugurates tones which will remain in the future literature of the New World. Its first discoverer and describer, Christopher Columbus (1451–1506) initiates the modern forms of commercial propaganda when he hyperbolically ponders the merchandise he tries to impose. Columbus, a great traveler who, according to his own admission, knew all the Atlantic coasts from England to Guinea[8] and was also familiar with the beautiful landscapes of the Mediterranean, says that he is in a state of constant amazement before the shoals, islets, and islands which his caravels pass, and before the naked and ingenuous Arawaks, when he determinedly seeks the fabulous lands of the Orient described by Marco Polo. He had to interest the Catholic monarchs in his poor and meager discoveries on this first voyage to the unknown, and he does not even take the precaution of varying or gradating his adjectives. The little island of San Salvador [*Guanahaní*], the first land his tired keels run into, "all of it is green, which is a pleasure to gaze at." Fernandina [*Inagua chica*] "is a very green and level and extremely fertile island"; the parastic plants which disguise the big tropical trees in such diverse and deformed ways seem to him "the greatest marvel of the world," and he goes on to add: "At this time I walked thus among those trees, which is the most astonishing thing I have ever seen." Isabela [*Inagua grande*] seems to be "the most beautiful island I saw; if others are very beautiful, this one is more so." Then he adds: "And when I arrived here, to this promontory, I smelled the good and gentle odor of flowers or trees of the earth, which is the sweetest thing in the world." It is already known that of Cuba he said: "that island is the most beautiful that eyes have seen"; and referring to the port which is today called

Nuevitas, Father Las Casas notes in his transcription of the *Diary of Columbus*: "He says more, that that *puerto de Mares* [seaport] is one of the best in the world." Of the Cuban lands of Maisí, on the eastern end of the island, he asserts with absolute rotundity: "And I certify to Your Highnesses that under the sun, it does not seem to me that there can be better [lands] in fertility, in temperateness of cold and heat, in abundance of good and healthy waters." But immediately he will say of La Española (today Haiti and Santo Domingo) "that it is the most beautiful thing in the world," reinforcing the affirmation in this form: "In all Castille there is no land which can compare to it in beauty and goodness"; and he goes on to ratify, farther along: "Your Highnesses may believe that these lands are so extremely good and fertile and especially those of this *island española* [Spanish island], that there is no one who would not say so, and no one can believe it without seeing it."

When he addresses himself to the capitalist partners of his enterprise, to whom he cannot offer gold or precious stones or spices, Columbus reverts, with a canny sense of capitalist commercial propaganda, to an exciting, although not varied, description of fertile lands in which to pour out the human surplus of the Reconquest, lands which even include slave labor, ready for their service.

Hyperbole arrived with Columbus. With Fray Bartolomé de las Casas (1474–1566) the polemic will begin, the ardent struggle for justice. Partisans of Las Casas and Sepúlveda still argue passionately today about the crimes and the "Black Legend" of the Conquest, but all the scholarly furors with which they claim to prove the paranoia of the friar are, nevertheless, unable to suppress, in the face of the genocide of yesterday and that of today, the impassioned justice and the generous militant humanism of Father Las Casas: "Humanity is one," he writes, "and all men are equal in their creation and all natural things, and no one is born a genius. From this it follows that all of us should be guided and helped at the beginning by those who were born before us. And the savage people of the earth may be compared to the uncultivated ground from which weeds and useless thorns grow, but they have within them such natural virtue that with work and cultivation they may be made to produce healthy and beneficial fruits."

Hyperbole and impassioned denunciation are at the root of our literature. The sensual pleasure in the apparent, the baroque delight in exuberant fruit and flower, with the parasitic and deformed, which already dazzled Columbus, live together with, are opposed to, and are sometimes combined with the cutting word, the sober presentation, or the fighting spirit, throughout the length of the Latin American literary process. And both contribute to illuminate and to stimulate the life of our people. When the conquerors began to settle on the new lands, cultivated verse and prose surged to describe what is found and to tell of what is lived, and beside them, the voice of the people is also raised to give its version of the events and to claim its part of the spoils. There is that formidable Mexican dialogue of the walls, in the first half of the sixteenth century in the anonymous verses which the discontented soldiers wrote on the white walls of Coyoacán, asking the conqueror for their part of the gold which, they suspected, he had hidden away. The first known poet is Hernán Cortés himself, who every day, with ingenuity and good humor, answered the malicious ones in verse until, tired of such impertinence, he put an end to the poetic joust with an epigraph which is almost Latin in its concision: "Pared blanca, papel de necios" ["White wall, paper of fools"]. But the bold ones did not give up, and the next day they answered in smooth prose: "Aun de sabios, y Su Majestad lo sabrá de presto" ["Of wise men too, and His Majesty will know it soon"].[9]

And His Majesty received memorials and poems like that composed by the Mexican Francisco de Terrazas (1525?–1600?), *Nuevo Mundo y Conquista* [New World and Conquest], in the stanzas of which he mourns the oblivion the conquerors and their descendants have suffered, placed behind the newcomers. One of these fortunate newcomers, Bernardo de Valbuena (c. 1562–1627), will undertake to exalt, in hyperbolic tercets, *La grandeza mexicana* [Mexican Greatness], printed in Mexico in 1604. But there will also be a voice that revindicates the conquerors and leaves us the memory of their greatness, so new and unfamiliar in Renaissance Europe that everyone will dismiss it as another example of the excessive American hyperbole, and some consider the *Royal Commentaries* (1609–1617) of the Inca Garcilaso de la Vega (1539–1616) as such today. But in that hour of the birth of capitalism, many perceptive thinkers have a presentiment of its excesses and dangers, and propose, as a remedy for the evil which is being born, a return to ideal times and places which stimulate the fabulous tales circulating about the New World, with its paradisical islands and its uncorrupted, unmalicious people, in order to situate, in one of them, a *Utopia*, or to construct wisely ordered kingdoms like the *City of the Sun*. Very soon Thomas More's (1478–1535) *Utopia* (1516) will return to America in the Franciscan saddlebags of Fray Juan Zumárraga (d. 1548), first archbishop of Mexico, and will inspire the colonizing experiment of Fray Vasco de Quiroga (c. 1470–1565) in Michoacán.

Literature and life, in an unstoppable dialectic process, breathe inspiration in the new American lands, are mixed with baroque splendor in the epic efforts of the Chilean Pedro de Oña, (1570–c. 1643), in the lyric discretions of the Mexican Sor Juana Inés de la Cruz (1651–1695), or in the biting Lima satire of Juan del Valle Caviedes (1652?–1697). From the humble captaincies general, simple little forts or transit stations—like Cuba—of the vast Spanish Empire, down to the proud viceroyalties which compete with the metropolis in material and cultural wealth, the new Latin American accent is raised, the voice of a new man, product of new geographic, economic, social, and cultural circumstances which compose the New World. As Afrânio Coutinho affirms, referring specifically to Brazil, but with validity for all Latin America:

Once arrived here, in contact with the new reality, the European "forgot" the old situation and, adjusting to the new one, became another man, who was joined by other new men born and raised here. That new man, American, Brazilian, engendered by the vast and profound process of miscegnation and acculturation which took place here, could not express himself in the same language as the European and so he transformed it, adapted it, conditioned it to the new expressive needs, in the same way that he adapted to the new geographic, culinary, and ecological conditions, to the new human and animal relationships, the same way he adapted his taste buds to the new fruits, creating, consequently, new feelings, attitudes, affections, hates, and fears, motives for behavior, for fighting, happiness and sadness. This whole new cultural complex had to lead to a new art, a new poetry, a new literature, a new dance, a new song, new legends and popular myths.[10]

In summary: on new economic bases, a new man and a new culture appeared in the New World.

During the eighteenth century, a Creole bourgeoisie begins to establish itself which already has full consciousness of itself and resents the incomprehension and the ignorance with which some on the distant peninsula view American affairs. And when someone, like the dean of Alicante, Manuel Martí, tries to dissuade his compatriots from seeking their fortunes in America because of the backwardness—principally intellectual— of the colonies, from all corners of the New World are heard Creole voices of protest, like those of the erudite Peruvian Pedro de Peralto Barneuvo (1663–1743), hyperbolical himself but hyperbolically praised by Feijóo, the Mexican Juan José de Eguiara y Eguren (1695–1763), father of Latin American literary historiography, and the Cuban historian José Martín Félix de Arrate (1701–1765) who, in answer to Dean Martí's nonsense, follows the example of Peralta Barnuevo, "obliged also by the desire and obligation," he says, "to manifest that these climates are not as lacking in good people or virtuous men as has been said, nor is it true that the offspring of the Castillians degenerate like good seed in barren earth."[11]

On the contrary, the fruitful land stimulates the desire for knowledge on the part of those who make it produce, and engenders a rich generation of learned men like José Celestino Mutis (1732–1808), a naturalist who, from Colombia, vies with Linnaeus and Alexander von Humboldt; like the Ecuadorian mestizo Francisco Eugenio de Santa Cruz Espejo (1747–1795), a medical doctor, philosopher, critic, and journalist, one of the most brilliant figures of the Latin American Enlightenment, who contributed to the struggle against Scholasticism and to the introduction of a concept of the world in accord with the new economic realities.[12] This enterprise is well served by the journalistic press which appears in this century, always in the hands of a Creole patriarchy of studious men, determined to spread the news in America of the new discoveries in science and technology indispensable to its economic and ideological progress. The Creoles make a great effort to improve the level of public information and to develop American agriculture and industry in accord with the newest procedures. And to this end they unite their efforts around the

"Economic Societies of Friends of the Country," in which poets and economists, educators and philosophers, join together in a fertile marriage of creative effort. The Creoles also begin to feel the need to know their past. Resentful because of the expulsion decreed against them by Charles III in 1767, the Latin American Jesuits react as Creoles wounded by the Bourbon despotism and proudly revindicate their pre-Hispanic past and their right to live on their own land. Thus, the study of pre-Cortesian history is begun and exalted by the Mexican Jesuits Francisco Xavier Alegre (1729–1788), Francisco Xavier Clavijero (1731–1793), Andrés Cavo (1739–1803), Juan Luís Maneiro (1744–1802), Pedro José Márquez (1741–1820), and others. The Guatemalan Jesuit Rafael Landívar (1731–1793) sang his *Rusticatio Mexicana* in magnificent Latin verse, exalting the American land. They all contribute to create the separatist consciousness of the Creole landholding bourgeoisie. In Brazil, the writings of Antonio Vieira (1608–1697) and Gregorio de Matos (1633–1969)—with whom the whole of mulatto life floods in, full of color and sensuality, of a population made of Indian and white and black components—prepare the way for the localism of the Arcadian narrative poetry of José Basilio da Gama (1740?–1795), whose poem "Uraguai" expresses sentiment against the conquerors, already revealed by the poet in a sonnet dedicated to the great Peruvian revel Tupac Amaru. The Creoles feel their hearts vibrate before the concepts of *liberty*, *independence*, and *revolution* which reach them from the thirteen colonies just liberated from England, and from France, which has just proclaimed a *Déclaration des droits de l'homme*. The Colombian Antonio Nariño (1765–1823) translated and printed the declaration secretly, in 1794, managing to send it to the most isolated corners of the southern tip of the continent. Thus when Napoleon invades Spain and the deputies from the colonies are sent to the courts of Cádiz, one of them, the most eloquent, the Ecuadorian José Mejía (1777–1812) dares to say: "There is talk of revolution and of how this should be renounced. Sir, I feel regret not that there must be revolution, but that there has not been one. The words *revolution, philosophy, liberty*, and *independence* are all of the same character: words which are seen by those who do not know them as bad omens, but those who have eyes may judge for themselves. Judging for myself, I say that it is a cause for sorrow that there is no revolution in Spain."

LITERATURE AND THE EMANCIPATION

In Spain there was not, nor could there be, a revolution,[13] but there certainly was one in the American colonies, where the Creole bourgeoisie of land-holders had come to be a class fully conscious of itself and aspired to endow the new relationships of production which had arisen in the New World with a political and administrative superstructure capable of maintaining them and making them prosper. It is not necessary to insist upon the close relationships between literature and life during the struggle for independence, if we remember that Simón Bolívar (1783–1830) has left pages of indisputable literary value, and that there is hardly one of the liberators who has not left traces in his own national literature. It will be, however, the Venezuelan Andrés Bello (1781–1856) who will take it upon himself to launch, in sonorous neoclassic verses, the proclamation of our intellectual independence. His "Alocución a la poesía [Allocution to Poetry] appeared in London in 1823, before the battle of Ayacucho, and in it he exhorts "Divine Poetry":

> tiempo es que dejes ya la culta Europa,
> que tu nativa rustiquez desama,
> y dirijas el vuelo donde te abre
> el mundo de Colón su grande escena.
> ....
> No te detenga, ¡ oh diosa!,
> esta región de luz y de miseria,
> en donde tu ambiciosa
> rival Filosofía,
> que la virtud a cálculo somete,
> de los mortales te ha usurpado el culto;
> donde la coronada hidra amenaza
> traer de nuevo al pensamiento esclavo
> la antigua noche de barbarie y crimen;
> donde la libertad vano delirio,
> fe la servilidad, grandeza el fasto,
> la corrupción, cultura se apellida.

> [it is time now for you to leave cultured Europe / which your native rusticity detests, / and direct your flight to where / Columbus's world opens its great stage to you / ..../ Do not be detained, oh goddess!, / by this region of light and misery / where your ambitious / rival Philosophy / who submits virtue to the calculation / of mortals has usurped your cult; / where the crowned hydra threatens / to again establish enslaved thought / the ancient night of barbarity and crime / where liberty is vain delirium / faith servility, greatness pomp, / corruption is called culture.]

The chorus of poets who sing to independence and to its heroes will come later; the Ecuadorian José Joaquín de Olmedo (1780–1847), who had been at the Courts of Cádiz and had spoken in favor of the Indians, the Mexican Andrés Quintana Roo (1787–1851), the Argentinian Juan Cruz Varela (1794–1839), all of them to some extent "official" poets who are soon involved and shaken by the *caudillista* [local leadership] struggles.

For this reason, perhaps, their tone finally becomes disenchanted and bitter, as though tinged by the intense melancholy of the unfulfilled yearning for liberty in the impassioned verse of the poet who is then the first romantic, beyond his neoclassic trappings, the Cuban José María de Heredia (1803–1839). Bello and Heredia are eminent examples of militant Americanism: both carry their creative passion beyond their native lands and become part of the Mexican or Chilean way of life, making consciences as Bolívar had raised nations. The independence movement had scattered writers and warriors all over the continent, contributing to the propagation of the essential Latin American ideological unity, founded on the basic similarity of economic, political, and social problems. It does not matter that independence touches off the fights between caudillos, disguised as Federalists and Centralists, nor that each nation makes an effort to flaunt its particular characteristics in competition against the others. There is an unreasonable eagerness to establish the precise national boundries of each country, while the common literature discovers the unity of American consciousness. Thus when José Joaquín Fernández de Lizardi (1776–1827) dissects Mexican society, each national group feels that it has been portrayed, and finally, the nativist enthusiasm that fires the verses of the Argentinian Bartolomé Hidalgo (1788–1823), of the Peruvian Mariano Melgar (1791–1815), and the West Indian Domingo del Monte (1804–1853) is the very same enthusiasm. In all of them it is the desire to express the new American consciousness, beginning with the common man who has burst into flower in the struggle. Del Monte follows an erroneous path when he attempts to use a traditional Spanish form, the ballad, already forgotten by the Cuban masses, to enclose the new message. But Melgar will return to the *yaraví*, and Hidalgo will know how to find in gaucho speech an appropriate vehicle for this poetry of pure popular roots. Del Monte in Cuba, like José Joaquín Pesado (1801–1861) in Mexico, represents the patrician decision to submit the new impulses of popular base, which surge up explosively with romanticism, to traditional and conservative reactionary molds.

The neoclassic poets who sang of the wars for independence and of their heroes, who later converted into rival caudillos, had expressed with extraordinary eloquence the world view of a social class, the landholding aristocracy, which aspired to replace Spanish domination by that of the great Creole rural property owners, without making substantial changes in the existing economic and social structure. But the mass of the armies was made up of men of the land—Indians, poor whites, blacks and mestizos of all kinds—and it was necessary to heed their demands somehow, especially when their own organic caudillos emerged from among their ranks, leaders who came to be comparable to the aristocrats in military power. What had cost centuries of sweat and blood in Europe—the transition from feudal fragmentation to national unity—had to be accomplished in less than three decades in our America. And in the light of much later European experiences, the Latin American thinkers realized that it was necessary to begin by changing life in order to change literature radically. The Argentinian Esteban Echeverría (1805–1851) typifies the type of Latin American romantic writer who wished to endow his country, torn apart by civil strife, with a new style, both in life and in literature. Attempts have been made to minimize Echeverría's merits as a founder and instigator, emphasizing his intellectual indebtedness, but his *Dogma socialista* [A Social Dogma] is no less valuable because of what it owes to Saint-Simon and Lammenais, Mazzini or Lerminier. Nor can the weaknesses of *La cautiva* [The Captive] obscure its fertile popularity nor make us forget the powerful breath which emanates from the realistic pages of *The Slaughterhouse*. But with all his limitations, Echeverría continues to endure above all because of the unity of his life and writing.

THE STRUGGLE FOR LIBERTY AND JUSTICE

After him—and after all of the romantics who lived and wrote more or less like him—came the generation of the founders, of the ideologues of that liberal bourgeoisie that tried to replace the superannuated system of landowners by modern capitalism. It is the hour of Alberdi (1810–1884), of Mitre (1821–1906) and of Sarmiento (1811–1888). Alberdi's *Las bases* [The Bases] are the foundation of Argentinian constitutional life, exiling anarchy; Sarmiento's *Life in the Argentine Republic* will always be one of the major books of our America, an early example of that peculiar interpenetration of genres—sociology, biography, novel and history—which some ingenuously believe to be the exclusive patrimony of our present time, and which is only the expression of the immediate need to unify life and poetry in the agonized investigation of the root of our great collective problems. Literature indicates possible paths or announces future action, constitutes the program which will be carried into effect later by Mitre and Sarmiento as presidents of the Argentine Republic, just as later Benito Juárez (1806–1872) will propagate and realize the ideals of the Mexican Reform. This is an era of writers who are passionately involved in political activity; they have achieved, for the first time, control over public matters. Then there appear the educated caudillos of a liberal bourgeoisie, of an incipient capitalism which, to apply again the words of Andrés Bello, open the fertile and almost unexploited countryside of America to the immigrants and to foreign investors. Civilization, which comes from Europe and North America with men and capital, invades the land where nomad barbarity flees or disappears. Literature will immediately reflect, above all in *Martín Fierro* by the Argentinian José Hernández (1834–1879), the protest of the man of the land, driven off it. Literature will also denounce the presence of the immigrant, and the novel and the theater will continue to show his slow penetration of and occasional fusion with the Creole population. Literature now participates in a conscious manner in social life; it is written deliberately in order to influence collective destinies. And when the reactionary educated caudillos appear, they will be met violently, uncontainably, by the denouncing words, insulting them when necessary, of the Ecuadorian Juan Montalvo (1832–1889) or the Peruvian Manuel González Prada (1848–1918). With the gradual penetration of foreign capital, cities prosper and industry develops, interest and concern for science and contemporary technology grow. The rural theme, above all in narrative literature, reveals the profound transformation which America undergoes in its landscapes and its people, in its customs and even in its language. Along with the recently sprouted factories a new humanity is born which is made up of human beings who have come from all over, without roots in the land and with only one characteristic in common: their exploitation, their poverty. The Latin American proletariat makes its entrance into life and into literature.

When a new historical phase begins in the world with the development of imperialism, our America has the passive role of territory-to-be-conquered and of battleground. America has already known the symptoms of imperialism and had to fight, in the north and in the south, against foreign invaders. Mexico had suffered the North American invasion (1846–1848) which would take away the northern half of its territory, and soon afterward, from 1862 to 1867, the French invasion and the imperial farce of Maximilian. But the new invaders of financial imperialism did not need, for the moment, either arms or armies. Along with thousands of immigrants from impoverished countries came branches of banks and representatives of monopolies and trusts of the great powers loaded with pounds sterling, francs, marks, and dollars. The cities and small towns contemplated the new spectacle in amazement. "In 1889," writes Adolfo Mitre in his prologue to the novel *La bolsa* [The Stock Market] (1891), by Julián Martel (José Miró, 1868–1896), "three hundred thousand immigrants arrive in the port of Buenos Aires; one hundred and thirty four corporations inscribe themselves on mercantile registers, with a capital of more than five hundred million pesos, and in the Commercial Stock Exchange—located on the Plaza de Mayo—the transactions reach fifteen hundred million pesos a month."[14] Fertilized by foreign capital, a new bourgeoisie grows and prospers, a golden race of bourgeois kings like the one described by Rubén Darío (1867–1916) in *Azul* (1888), inspired by a real person, Eduardo MacClure, director of the newspaper *La Época* of Santiago, Chile, for which the young Nicaraguan poet worked.[15]

We already know that Darío's Bourgeois King "had a splendid palace, where he had accumulated riches and marvelous art objects," that his refined taste mixed books by Jorge Ohnet "or beautiful books about grammatical questions, or splendiferous criticism. But definitely: he was a most vigorous proponent of academic taste in literature, of affected mannerisms in art; sublime soul, lover of polish and of orthography." One day they brought him a poet, hungry, naturally, but still with the energy to wield the quill of Echeverría and dream of revolutions. And the poet said: "I have wanted to be powerful! Because the time of the great revolutions is coming, with a Messiah who is all light, all agitation and strength, and it is necessary to receive his spirit with the poem which will be a triumphal arch, of steel stanzas, of golden stanzas, of stanzas of love." But the Bourgeois King, who was not, naturally, an advocate of revolutions, answered the poet: "You will turn a crank. You will close your mouth. You will make a music box play waltzes, quadrilles and galops, unless you prefer to die of hunger. A piece of music for a piece of bread. No jargon or ideals."

Darío reveals the attitude of the new plutocracy stimulated by imperialism, and he even will point out, later on, the significance and the danger of this plutocracy, but, opening the path for a great number of the writers of his time, he will prefer to turn the crank of the waltzes rather than face up to the Bourgeois King and his foreign masters. Imperialism is the generational experience which the men of the Modernist movement come up against, and for some, headed by Darío, it is an occasion for the cultivation of sensual, *preciosista* verse and prose, for hyperbolic escapism; for others, like José Martí (1853–1895), it awakes, instead, the combative passion and puts formal preciosity at the service of an incessant struggle for liberty and justice. The whole body of Martí's writing is dedicated to a lucid battle for the liberty of our America and to achieve—they are his own words—"the equilibrium of the world." His political vision surpasses the goals of the democratic-bourgeois ideologues who preceded him and opens the way to new horizons converting the fight for the national liberation of Cuba into a deeper and wider struggle against imperialism, sustained on the shoulders of the working masses. He was not a Marxist, but he prepared the way for socialist solutions. And since he understood—and said—that "each social state has its expression in literature, so that through the different phases of literature it would be possible to tell the history of the various peoples with greater truth than through their chronicles and their chapters," for this very reason he made a great effort to find the appropriate expression for his historical time, that of the struggle against imperialism, which is still our era today, and for this reason, too, his exhortation to the poet is still absolutely up to date:

> Junta en haz alto, y echa al fuego, pesares de contagio, tibiedades latinas, rimas reflejadas, dudas ajenas, males de libros, fe prescrita, y caliéntate a la llama saludable del frío de estos tiempos dolorosos en que despierta ya en la mente la criatura adormecida, están todos los hombres de pie sobre la tierra, apretados los labios, desnudo el pecho bravo y vuelto el puño al cielo, demandando a la vida su secreto.

> [Gather up into a great bundle and hurl into the fire all your infectious sorrows, Latin inertia, reflected rhymes, others' doubts, wrongs from books, prescribed faith, and warm yourself at the healthy flame of the cold of these sorrowful times in which the sleeping babe awakes in the mind; all men are on their feet on earth, their lips compressed, their brave chests bare and their fists raised to the sky, demanding of life its secret.]

Notes

1. José Carlos Mariátegui, *Seven Interpretative Essays on Peruvian Reality*, trans. Marjory Urguidi (Austin: University of Texas Press, 1971), p. 16.

2. V. I. Lenin, *Imperialism; The Highest Stage of Capitalism* (New York: International Publishers, 1939), pp. 120–121.

3. José María Castellet, "La actual literatura latinoamericana vista desde España" in *Panorama de la actual literatura latinoamericana*, series organized by the Centro de Investigaciones Literarias de la Casa de las Américas (Havana: Casa, 1969), pp. 35–38.

4. "If the present meaning of our literature can be characterized schematically in any way, it will be by its impassioned attempt to take on the reality which surrounds us, naked and essential." Juan Carlos Portantiero, *Realismo y realidad en la narrativa argentina* (Buenos Aires: Procyon, 1961).

5. Arrom characterizes the "Generation of 1954," still thriving, in accord with his periodological computation, up to 1984, with these words: "Installed in a world of reduced distances, as a group it is very universalist in vision and at the same time very nationalistic in origin. Threatened by the danger of a nuclear conflagration, it tends to replace metaphysical anguish by an angry pose. It identifies itself with the destiny of contemporary man, it wants its writing to be a testimony of its time and for its time. And convinced that a past in ruins is of no use in resolving the questions of the present, it does not accept living on inherited values nor does it wish to write according to antiquated aesthetics. Therefore, it disdains the literature of fastidiousness and diversions and seeks the essential word, direct language, connection to immediate things: bread is bread again, and wine is wine, but it is a bitter wine and a bread kneaded in anger. It writes, then, facing reality. And since the ire is everywhere—in the spirit and in the word—in general the hard phrase predominates, the acid verse, the neorealistic story and novel, the denunciatory and severe essay, and the theater of the absurd appears on the stage." José Juan Arrom, *Esquema generacional de las letras hispanoamericanas. Ensayo de un método* (Bogotá: Instituto Caro y Cuervo, 1963).

6. José Carlos Mariátegui, "Aniversario y balance," *Amauta*, year 3, no. 117 (Lima, September 1928).

7. Fidel Castro, *Palabras a los intelectuales* (Havana: Consejo Nacional de Cultura, 1961).

8. "I have spent twenty-three years at sea, without leaving it for any appreciable time, and I saw all the Levante and Poniente, on the way to Septentrión, which is England, and I have been to Guinea..." Christopher Columbus, *Diario de navegación* (Havana: Comisión Nacional Cubana de la Unesco, 1961), p. 143. All the quotations from Columbus are from this edition.

9. Antonio Castro Leal, prologue to Francisco de Terrazas, *Poesías* (Mexico: Porrua, 1941), p. 1x.

10. Afrânio Coutinho, *Conceito de literatura brasileira (ensaio)* (Río de Janeiro: Livraria Academica, 1960), pp. 18–19.

11. José Martín Félix de Arrate, *Llave del nuevo mundo antemural de las Indias Occidentales. La Habana descripta: noticias de su fundación, aumentos y estado* (Havana: Comisión Nacional Cubana de la Unesco, 1964), p. 238.

12.   Cf. Monelisa Lina Pérez-Marchand, *Dos etapas ideológicas del siglo xviii en México a través de los papeles de la Inquisición* (Mexico: El Colegio de Mexico, 1945), and Pablo González Casanova, *El misoneísmo y la modernidad en el siglo xviii* (Mexico: El Colegio de Mexico, 1948).

13.   See, in regard to this, Marx's acute analysis in his articles on "Revolutionary Spain" in the *New York Daily Tribune*, September–December, 1854, collected in K. Marx and F. Engels, *The Spanish Revolution* (Moscow: Editions in Foreign Languages, n.d.), pp. 5–72.

14.   *La bolsa* (Buenos Aires: Estrada, 1946), p. ix.

15.   Cf. Armando Donoso, "La juventud de Rubén Darío," in *Nosotros* (Buenos Aires, April 1919).

13 / A Permanent Discussion

JOSÉ MIGUEL OVIEDO

During a period of less than fifteen years, centered around the 1920s, the Latin American contemporary novel was founded: in 1916, Azuela's *The Underdogs* appeared; in 1918 Barrios' *Un perdido* [A Lost Man]; in 1919, Alcides Arguedas's *Raza de bronce* [The Bronze Race]; in 1924 Rivera's *The Vortex*; in 1926, Güiraldes's *Don Segundo Sombra*; in 1928, Mario de Andrade's *Macunaíma*; in 1929, Gallegos's *Doña Bárbara*. With these books, a new novel is born, together with the *isms* which best define it: Indianism, Creolism, regionalism, and urban naturalism. All of these variants concur, however, in a common tendency: the documentary, which tries to provide an inventory of the reality of each country, whether it be geographic or social, agricultural or political, always with the intent to demonstrate and portray. This attachment to nature and, in general, to the immediate models offered by reality, is the consequence of a missionary vocation: on one hand, the novels of that period function as records of accusation and denunciation of the violence and injustice which govern the life of the American man; on the other hand, they serve as substitutes for travel books: they describe the country to those who do not know it or who do not know it well, they go into the jungle, onto the plains, or into the mine tunnels to carry a message of national identity which surmounts the abysmal differences which official politics only camouflage. They postulate a morality and a faith, sometimes a militancy; at bottom, they are affirmative and hopeful, even when the scenes they depict are depressing and terrible: they are informed by compassion and vindicatory zeal.

These are exceptions, of course, like *Don Segundo Sombra*, which transcends River Plate Creolism when it proposes a mythological "poetic" image of the gaucho, and a hyperartistic treatment of reality: the author makes a land novel from the arm of Valery Larbaud and the ultraists, he "enobles" the material with aesthetic elaboration. "I have the feeling," says Güiraldes in a letter, "that certain works extricate themselves from their origins by achieving a formal realization that enables them to be self-sufficient."[1] But Güiraldes's novel, although it was a success, was swimming against too swift a current to be able to change its course. Around the same time, a solitary man, a misanthropist, a tormented man who wandered lost in the remote area of Misiones, wrote his best (his most terrible) stories—for example, those of *Los desterrados* [The Exiled Ones] (1926)—which used one of the favorite settings of regionalism—the vegetal infernos of the jungle—but only in order to submerge himself in the murky world of psychological abnormalities, of hallucination, and of the supernatural. His name was Horacio Quiroga, he was peripheral to Modernism, and the scars of his bedeviled art would destroy him. The historic moment pulled the novel away from those idyllic and paternalistic visions of the rural American world that Güiraldes proposed, and from the morbid studies of abnormal consciousness attempted by Quiroga. The genre passed through its hour of collective bitterness and social pathos which should have led to ideological faith. Around the thirties, with César Vallejo's *El tungsteno* [Tungsten] (1931) and Jorge Icaza's *The Villagers (Huasipungo)* (1934), this tendency would find its most vehement expression: the Indianist and antiimperialist novel conceived as a direct instrument for the political struggle of our people.

Thus, during the course of only a few years, our novel had moved from a telluric pantheism and a fascination with geography—"the novel of the land" as Arturo Torres-Rioseco called it in 1941—to ideological prophecy and partisan agitation. Aesthetically, the act was not innocent: the novel by Vallejo and the first books by the Brazilian Jorge Amado (like *Jubiabá*, 1935) are already Latin American adaptations of social realism. But even in less extreme cases than these, literature functioned as one of the ways of fulfilling political obligations, of identifying oneself with the militant groups that studied reality, of giving Marxist lessons to peoples who were illiterate, hungry, and oppressed by injustice. This is not a novelty in Latin America, where literary and artistic creation had always had to serve its turn in the role of school and tribune, of journalism and chronicle: during the era of emancipation, during the years of the organization of our republics, during the nineteenth century (when the first definitions and cultural institutions of modern mold are being launched), politics and art, government and creation were only interchangeable aspects of a common Americanist preoccupation. For this reason, ours has been a Janus-faced culture: in the men who made it, there often coexisted, significantly, a type of personality seduced by direct action—when the opposite was not the case. It is a Latin American custom for the race of Bolívar and Che Guevara to mix with that of Sarmiento and Javier Heraud. The man of letters also had to be a public man; sometimes the first duty of the country was the establishment of a prize to recognize literary success (the most illustrious example in the twentieth century is that of Rómulo Gallegos, but the more recent case of Juan Bosch in the Dominican Republic should not be forgotten), although the recompense could be more modest: ministerial, diplomatic, or bureaucratic. People thought, with automatic candor, that good writers must also be good citizens. In principle, there is nothing wrong with countries honoring their artists and adding them to their list of great men; in practice, this had a double and fatal consequence: first, it fostered the illusion that literature could fit comfortably into the odd moments allowed by demanding public activities and that it could be practiced as Sunday dilettantism rather than as a profession worthy of the name; second, it encouraged a certain passive and lazy attitude toward the problems of creativity by confusing the art of writing with the excellence or the immediacy of the themes, and even, piously, with the correct ideological stance of the work. Literature fell into the traps of over-simplification, pedagogy, and the message.

LITERATURE OF SALVATION

What was basically being affirmed by these writers and these works was the social function of literature, that famous and eternal question which has been so passionately discussed in Latin America amid rivers of ink. A novel or a poem sometimes took the place of the speech, the article, or the reforms which did not exist or turned out to be insufficient to rescue the forgotten men who populated these unknown countries; it was indubitably a noble intention, but it frequently operated as a hindrance: the public did not read the novels as novels; it sought an Aristotelian resemblance of art to the physical territories or the social circumstances which the novels described; they might not be realistic, but they had to seem *real*, bleeding slices of American life. The Indianist movement (José Carlos Mariátegui could write, in his *Seven Interpretative Essays on Peruvian Reality*, 1928)

> does not depend on simple literary factors but rather on complex social and economic factors. What gives the Indian the right to dominate the vision of the Peruvian of today is, above all, the conflict and the contrast between his demographic predominance and his social and economic servitude—not just inferiority. The presence of three to four million men of the indigenous race in the mental panorama of a population of five million should not surprise anyone in an era in which this population feels a need to find the equilibrium which until now it has lacked in its history.... If the Indian occupies the first plane in Peruvian literature and art, it is certainly not because of his literary or plastic interest, but rather because the new forces and the vital impulse of the nation tend to reclaim him.[2]

The literature of Latin America had been born under this impulse, and it could hardly renounce its vocation well into the twentieth century. It was a problem of conscience for the writers who knew themselves to belong to an elite of the privileged, with access to culture, amid a country of ignorant and dispossessed people. On one hand, the writers themselves assumed the role of public defenders and tried to identify with the masses. They touched the wounds with their own hands and put their feet on the physical territories where their books later were set, as part of an intellectual solidarity. On the other hand, those same masses saw them as their last redeemer and silently demanded of them a literature of salvation or of *agit-prop*: it was necessary to keep faith alive in the midst of sad reality. Love of the land was its most prestigious and most characteristic manifestation; from it surged that abundance of idyllic agricultural narratives, that folkloric and dialectical obsession, that (false) idea that Latin American novels had no better characters than their infinitely varied natural scenarios and their anonymous exploited masses. Our protagonists are the land and the people, said the explicators and literary critics of the thirties; the authors themselves believed it implicitly. Explaining the genesis of his *Doña Bárbara*, Gallegos tells of his visit to the highlands of the Apure in 1927, the upheaval produced in him by the majestic landscape, and he writes: "One could not react pessimistically to that spectacle, and my Venezuelan desire to have every part of my country one day achieve prosperity and guarantee happiness assumed literary form in this sentence: 'Widespread, ample land, opening all horizons to hope, all possibilities to desire...'. Thus I already had the major character for a novel destined to have good luck. And in effect, I had: the highland landscape, untamed nature, forger of strong men. All those of human nature who appear in this book, are they not creatures of that savage land?"[3] As can be seen, the stimulus is that of the landscape, but the intention is civic, of national affirmation.

In the field of poetry, the concept of literature as a direct instrument in the social reclamation of America also left profound traces. The "Americanist" concern, the pro-Indianism, and the tellurianism were really carry-overs from something much older: Modernism had propagated them in its heliographs of the beginning of the century, but romanticism, too, and all the academic poetry of the end of the nineteenth century, had demonstrated a similar proclivity. In general, it was a matter of the exoticism of faraway lands, very popular at a time when the ideal escapisms to the Orient, to the medieval age, or to rococo France had reached the level of saturation. The first really contemporary poetic movements are the black poetry of the West Indies and the nativism or *cholismo* of the Andean countries (Peru, Ecuador, Bolivia). They are hybrids of a conjunction of cultural influences: the European vanguard movements, Marxism, the immediacy of the Indian question, and the problem of the races in America. For example, black poetry—with its street language, electric rhythm, and exclamative involvement—was a result of the symbiosis between ultraism and the African substratum (with a dose of García Lorca); nativist poetry—telegraphic, paradoxically exotic and even racist—owed debts to Marinetti's futurism and to the ideological teachings of Mariátegui (with its touch of Mayakovski). Both were answers to and denials of pure poetry, which was sometimes nourished by the same cultural sources; both were preparing the way for the truly social poetry that would inundate America toward the end of the thirties: the poetry of Vallejo, Neruda, Nicolás Guillén, Raúl González Tuñón, and so forth. The Spanish civil war, the world menace of fascism, and the presence of the United States as a power along beside countries which were poor and weak, aroused the spirit of these and other poets, obliging them to effect a profound revision of their aesthetic values.

The choice was clear: you were for or against the threatened countries. During these hard and truceless years, the crises of conscience and the ideological and aesthetic repositionings are numerous. Without a doubt, those of Vallejo and Neruda turn out to be the most influential. From 1927 on, Vallejo's articles and critical commentaries reveal the distance which separates him from the poet who could write *Trilce* (1922): in 1930, he writes the early *Autopsia del surrealismo* [Autopsy of Surrealism] and defines himself ideologically:

> Breton is wrong. If in fact he has read and has agreed with Marxism, I do not understand how he could forget that, within this doctrine, the role of writers is not to provoke moral and intellectual crises which are more or less serious or general, that is, to effect the revolution "from above," but rather, on the contrary, to promote it "from beneath." Breton forgets that there is only a single revolution, the proletarian, and that this revolution will be effected by workers with action and not by intellectuals with their "crises of conscience."[4]

Vallejo and Neruda register the impact of the Spanish civil war with an immediate reaction in their poetry: *Spain, Take This Cup Away from Me*, and *Spain in My Heart* are their respective bitter fruits. In addition, the Spanish tragedy will lead Neruda to a poetic reencounter with a profound American reality: by 1938, the poet is already writing his epic *General Song* which would be published only much later, in 1950; that same year, in Chile, he gives a speech which clearly indicates his new poetic ideals, with explicit allusion to the struggle between his obligations and his profound uneasiness:

> During this year of strife, I have not even had time to look closely at what my poetry adores: the stars, the plants and the grains, the stones of the rivers and of the roads of Chile. I have not had time to continue my mysterious exploration, that which orders me to lovingly touch the stalactite and the snow so that the earth and the sea can yield up their mysterious essence to me. But I have advanced along another road, I have managed to touch the naked heart of my people and to realize with pride that in this heart lives a secret which is stronger than the springtime, more fertile and more sonorous than the oats and the water, the secret of the truth, which my humble, solitary, and forsaken people gather from the dregs of their hard land and raise high in their triumph, so that all the people of the world may consider it, respect it and imitate it.[5]

And more drastically still, he discusses his struggle a year later, in Montevideo: "I cannot, I cannot maintain my position of silent examination of life and of the world, I must come out to shout through the streets and I will be this way until the end of my life. We have solidarity and responsibility for peace in America, but that task also gives us the authority and shows us the obligation that humanity, with our intervention, should emerge from delirium and be reborn in the storm."[6]

In its turn the American solidarity of Neruda and Vallejo is part of their adhesion to worldwide revolution: poetry also passes on reports of the battles of Stalingrad, China, Prague, and so forth. Vallejo will say:

>   Mas sólo tú demuestras, descendiendo
>   o subiendo del pecho, bolchevique,
>   tus trazos confundibles,
>   tu gesto marital,
>   tu carta de padre,
>   tus piernas de amado,
>   tu cutis por teléfono,
>   tu alma perpendicular
>   a la mía...
>   ("Salutación angélica" [Angelic Salutation])

[But only you reveal, descending / or rising from your chest, Bolshevik, / your indistinguishable traits, / your marital face, / your identity as a father, / your legs of a loved one, / your skin by telephone, / your soul perpendicular / to mine...]

And Neruda:

>   Yo pongo el alma mía donde quiero.
>   Y no me nutro del papel cansado,
>   adobado de tinta y de tintero.
>   Nací para cantar a Stalingrado
>   ("Nuevo canto de amor a Stalingrado" [New Love Song to Stalingrad])

[I put my soul where I want. / And I do not nourish myself with tired paper, / decorated with ink and inkwell. / I was born to sing to Stalingrad]

Nicolás Guillén had also reached the same crossroads at around this time: his black poetry gave voice in 1934 to a shout of social indignation before the spectacle of some of the West Indies that were imprisoned in the nets of dependency: in *West Indies Ltd.* he wrote mocking and ferocious verses:

>   Aquí están los servidores de Mr. Babbitt.
>   Los que educan sus hijos en West Point.
>   Aquí están los que chillan: hello, baby,
>   y fuman "Chesterfield" y "Lucky Strike."
>   Aquí están los bailadores de fox trots,
>   los boys del jazz band
>   y los veraneantes de Miami y de Palm Beach.
>   Aquí están los que piden bread and butter
>   y coffee and milk.
>   Aquí están los absurdos jóvenes sifilíticos,
>   fumadores de opio y de mariguana,
>   exhibiendo en vitrinas sus espiroquetas
>   y cortándose un traje cada semana.
>   Aquí está los mejor de Port-au-Prince,
>   lo más puro de Kingston, la high life de La Habana...

[Here are the servants of Mr. Babbitt. / Those who educate their sons at West Point. / Here are those who shriek: hello, baby, / and smoke Chesterfields and Lucky Strikes. / Here are the dancers of fox-trots, / the boys of the jazz band / and those who summer in Miami and Palm Beach. / Here are those who order bread and butter / and coffee and milk. / Here are the absurd syphilitic youths, / smokers of opium and of marijuana, / exhibiting their spirochetes in store windows / and ordering a new suit every week. / Here are the best of Port-au-Prince, / the purest of Kingston, the high life of Havana...]

In 1937, his *España* [Spain], "poem in four anguishes and a hope," appeared, and his *Canción a Stalin* [Song to Stalin], in which the Soviet leader appears in a context of Afro-Cuban divinities:

> Stalin, Capitán,
> a quien Changó proteja y a quien resguarde
> Ochún...

> [Stalin, Captain / may he be protected by Changó and be guarded by / Ochún...]

From 1940 to 1950, this poetry of explicit social and political testimony will predominate in America; in some countries, in Peru for example, it will achieve its greatest height between 1950 and 1960, while in other places, at the same time, this kind of poetry has already entered into a period of poetic and intellectual crisis.

SYMPTOMS OF CRISIS

Various deficits began to exhaust that type of literature which Indianism and social poetry had made popular. Certainly, it was not reprehensible—on the contrary, it was desirable—that the writers of Latin America should, in their works, seek communion with their own land, with their people, with their collective hopes. But as it happened, certain methods for achieving this were aesthetically negligible if not merely demagogic. They were based upon simplifications and dealt with generalities; the desire to demonstrate encouraged a dissimulated idealization of the real objects and situations. In some way, writers believed that the revolution (which the politicians were not making) would be made with books. This was an illusion, for books only reached the more educated social levels, which were not always the most progressive, that is, a system of access to the masses was lacking; a literature intended to affect the political consciousness of a country was only being read by a select few. This in itself made prediction and ideological provincialism easier: converted into the oracle of his country, the Latin American writer announced to it, in its hour of catastrophe, that justice was right around the corner; however, this utopia was delayed and was less simple than had been imagined. Few writers knew how to write of it in all of its magnificent complexity. Vallejo's *El tungsteno*, conceived within the molds of socialist realism, supposes, for example, that intellectuals will fill a secondary and passive role in the revolution ("The only thing you can do for us [the workers] is to do what we tell you to do and listen to us and put yourselves at our orders and at the service of our interests," says Servando Huanca); he confuses the class struggle with racial hatred and personal vengeance ("We must be avenged! We must be avenged upon the injustices of the rich!"); he emphasizes the symbolic meaning of the storm—the imminent revolution announced by the wind on the last page of his book—with the key words (*exploitation, petite bourgeoisie, capital, Marx*, etc.) which dance in the imagination of a proletariat recently indoctrinated.

It is interesting to note that *Broad and Alien Is the World*, by Ciro Alegría (1940), culminates in a very similar scene: this time it is not the howling of the wind which carries the revolutionary message; now "the stampede of the Mausers [which] continue to sound" is in accord with the victory which awaits the peasants beyond the killings. Less allegorical, much less rigid in its ideological stance, Ciro Alegría's novel still bridles its undeniable emotion and its expressive sweetness within a framework of generic intellectual concepts of the social life of Indian Peru: the way of feeling its topic is richer than its way of thinking about it; a certain epic aspiration, a certain awareness that a thesis is being proved simultaneously, blunts the realistic force of the story. In reality, Alegría represents the culmination and the crisis of the novelistic art inaugurated by Azuela, Rivera, Gallegos, and others. A contradictory art, made of virtues and defects, of vigor and weakness, with focuses which belong to nineteenth century social romanticism and to the strategy of the anti-imperialist struggle. The Indianist novels, the novels of the land, and the works of American naturalism all possess an underlying sure and true vision of reality: words can define it conveniently, separate its lights and shadows, and solve its problems just as a theorem can be solved. Well then, the moment will arrive when this intellectual confidence can no longer function in the face of the evidence of new events.

Emir Rodríguez Monegal[7] has already observed that in the same year when Alegría published his third and last book, Juan Carlos Onetti's second novel, *Tierra de nadie* [No Man's Land] appeared, heralding the new manner of writing novels which would be developed from then on, "one which explores the complexities of human nature rather than those of spectacular external nature, one which extends the frontiers of realism." This new manner was indicated by a change of scenario, that is, from the country to the city, as well as by a substantial change in its intent: literature was not trying to prove anything or put itself at anyone's service; it wanted to be valued for itself alone. Without ignoring, as is logical, the presence of a few precursors (like Quiroga, like Arlt), Mario Vargas Llosa considers that Onetti is the first "creative" novelist to appear in Latin America (the last to be recognized, too); he is the author of a world both scrupulous and coherent, which is important in itself and not for the informative material it contains, and which is accessible in any language to readers anywhere because the subject matter has acquired, by virtue of a "functional" language and technique, a universal dimension. It is no longer an artificial world we are presented with, but a world that is human before it is American and one which, like all creations of a lasting nature, consists in the objectification of something subjective, where the primitive novel had constituted the subjectivization of a selected objective reality.... It no longer serves reality, but serves itself from reality.[8]

The exchange of barbarous lands for the city is explained easily: literature tries to keep up with the social process in Latin America, which witnesses the excessive growth of the capital cities and the depopulation of the countryside in a movement of internal migration which has still not ended. The cities are converted into a dramatic synthesis of the nation: for example, the insolent wealth and the most abject poverty, culture and illiteracy, skyscrapers and marginal hovels, modern comfort and the survival of primitive ways of life—all share contiguous and simultaneous spaces. there is no need to go out to the countryside to find new themes: the country has come to the city and has crudely revealed problems which seemed remote or fantastic. And readers begin to be less interested in exotic themes and geographic explorations: they prefer to read books which deal with a reality they can recognize as their own. The city is a nucleus of individual and social conflicts, demanding a psychological refinement of the descriptions which were previously perhaps not necessary: the jungle always devoured men. The old epic struggle against nature has become fragmented and liberated on many simultaneous fronts; it is called "solitude, alienation, anguish, noncommunication." This does not mean to say that the old themes of Indianism and regionalism disappear in the new panorama, but simply that they have become much less photographic and more expressive, less missionary and more literary.

This renovation is produced in many forms: in *Pedro Páramo* (1955), Juan Rulfo descends to the deepest roots of the Mexican peasant and discovers that they are interwoven with those of time and of death, that they multiply him in existences which are mythic and even beyond the tomb; in *Men of Maize* (1949), Miguel Ángel Asturias submerged himself in a sea of sounds, words, and astounding Mayan fantasies which configure a cosmogony where the true history of the Guatemalan people may be read; Guimarães Rosa writes at least one novel (*The Devil to Pay in the Backlands*, 1956) and various stories (*Primeiras estorias* [First Stories], 1962), whose territories are terribly real but whose atmosphere is miraculous, when it is not supernatural or frankly demoniacal; the *sertão* of Guimarães is adjacent to a "beyond" where souls transmigrate and where evidence is illusory; in *Son of Man* (1960), Augusto Roa Bastos recorded the best rhapsody of the violent and suffering life of Paraguay, which unfolds the resources of classic realism, of the chronicle, of poetry, of the war journal, of popular legend, and so forth; and in his two great novels (*Deep Rivers*, 1959; *Todas las sangres* [All the Bloods], 1964),

José María Arguedas rescued, from the depths of his memory and of his Andean nostalgia, the true psychologies of the Peruvian Indian and mestizo, with all of their conflictive complexities of a cultural, sexual, and religious order. The case of Arguedas is particularly important because it illustrates what has happened to the Indianist movement during these last years. Arguedas and Alegría both began to write around 1935 (the year they published *Agua* [Water] and *The Golden Serpent*, respectively), but Arguedas's writing would evolve into a more personal writing after 1941 (a year which marks nearly the ends of Alegría's writing career) and would represent a new level of evolution of the genre in Peru: the era in which the characters and their little internal activities replace the Manichean cardboard figures with fixed patterns of behavior. Arguedas—he himself a transplant who had to learn Spanish in the capital—proves that the country is not divided into Indians and whites, but into infinite strata, into plural societies, separated by irreconcilable but subtle interests which pit themselves against each other. Indianist unilaterality had piously hidden that image of reality from us.

REVOLUTION AND THE WORD

On the other hand, literature's change of intent—no longer a means but an end—was inevitable since it was increasingly difficult to sustain that it should fulfill the tasks of political and ideological agitation: these activities had moved over into other fields, not realistic but real, which assumed greater complexity, rigor as well as intellectual and practical responsibility. At the beginning of the 1960s, a new Latin America began to emerge: the armed struggle in several countries, and the reappearance (behind dissimulated masks) of the old fascism were evidence of this. But above all, the presence of the Cuban Revolution operated as a catalyzing phenomenon of political, cultural, and artistic life on the continent. The intellectuals, especially, understood the beautiful lesson of that first —and still only—socialist revolution in America: utopia had been converted into a difficult, conflictive, and, for this very reason, more admirable reality; it was not enough to defend it: it was necessary to reevaluate everything and act in consequence. Furthermore, the field for doing this was very wide and flexible because this was a revolution within which intellectual affairs had a specific meaning and place (some were to say, exaggerating, no doubt, that the intellectuals were the only privileged class of Cuba). A revolution, too, which did not come to impose any aesthetic canon, which did not believe in the pedagogic virtues of socialist realism, and which broadcast, with the same energy, Marx and Joyce, Martí and Kafka. For the socialist camp, where the relationships between the intellectual and the state have not been exactly comfortable, it meant both a promise and a challenge. The existence of the revolution clarified many things and liberated literature from many dogmas that weighed heavily on it. Above all, it revealed the secret immorality of the simplistic and familiar schemes; it refreshed our political thought, it connected it with reality.

The 1960s saw the frontiers of the zones of influence in the world substantially modified. To begin with, Cuba declared itself a socialist republic only a hundred miles away from the United States. For their part, Russia and China carried their dispute between giants to a level unimaginable to proletarian internationalism and provoked a schism in Communist parties everywhere. The strategy had to change, and it did change. Carlos Fuentes writes:

> In the twentieth century, the intellectual himself had to struggle within a society which was much more complex, internally and internationally, where the weapons of reason and morality would not suffice to dominate a situation which had stopped being the regional patrimony of an oligarchic minority opposed to an anonymous mass in a banana republic, to be converted into one of the central events of our time: the revolt and the ascent, contradictory, complex, and internationalized, of the subindustrial world. A transition from epic simplification to dialectical complexity has begun, from the security of answers to the battleground of questions.[9]

In this way, if the presence of the Cuban Revolution intensified political belligerence in other countries, intellectual and artistic language had to become more refined, lucid, and skeptical: the old sermonizing literature of moral "thesis" was outmoded. Writers begin to understand that their art has been invaded by concerns which films, journalism and, in general, the media of mass communication—despite being still in the hands of merchants—now potentially express better; no novel can stand up to comparison with the impact which a half-hour documentary or a television interview can produce. Literature reconquers its own terrain; however, with the imaginary invention of realities, which do resemble reality but are not obliged to be its faithful portrait, or its identity papers. Narrators understood that their objective was to narrate, simply, not to *demonstrate*; they were seduced by the possibility of creating autonomous worlds and giving them to the real world, not to repeat it, but to denounce the essential poverty and falsity of it; they explored, restructured, and invented. The raw materials of a writer are words; with a few exceptions, Latin Americans did not really know this, or did not use them fully. Then they discovered that one could reach out and touch things through possession of a language; that the great Latin American swindle, the true rape of our continent, was that of the language; that its lost authenticity must be recovered in order to make it possible to create true representations of reality. And here one must recognize the indisputable mastery of Borges, of his myths and theologies, of his paradoxes and his metaphors, which taught us the pleasure of the verbal—that is ideal—condition of art, a way of thinking which, being a typical fruit of Buenos Aires, is universal. Borges made us see that for a Latin American, the *Odyssey* was just as much a part of his heritage as *Martín Fierro*.

But among the novelists (Borges refused—energetically, he would say—to become one), Carpentier is the one who best exemplifies this fundamental communion between verbal creation and the representation of the world which it invents. For the Cuban novelist, to name is to create; the names of things are the things themselves. And that is an obsession which explains his point of view: America is a continent crammed with objects which are waiting to be specifically designated so that they can begin to exist in the world of art. The work of Carpentier takes on meaning in this ordering of the natural chaos, in the transition from genesis to history. In this passage from *Explosion in a Cathedral*, we have evidence of this process:

> Contemplating a snail—one alone—thought Esteban in the presence of the Spiral, through millennia and millennia, before the daily gaze of villages of fishermen, still incapable of understanding them or of perceiving, even, the reality of their presence. He meditated on the sea urchin's carapace, the mollusk's helix, the scallop's striations, astonishing himself before that Science of the Forms unfolded during such a long time before a humanity still without eyes to think about it. What might there be around me that is already defined, registered, and present, and which I may not be able to understand yet? What sign, what message, or what warning is in the frills of the chicory, the alphabet of the mosses, the geometry of the rose apple? Look at a snail shell. Just one. *Tedeum.*

In *Hopscotch*, Cortázar goes beyond this and dares to negate the novel he is writing (or rather, to propose others, just as valid as that one), to detonate his language, to take apart the whole Swiss-watchlike mechanism of the traditional novel, to plunge a familiar way of thinking and of understanding man into the most horrifying ridicule. His protagonist Morelli expounds the book's program:

> To provoke, to take on a text which is disarranged, at loose ends, incongruous, and minutely antinovelistic (although not antinovelesque). Without forbidding the grand effects of the genre when the situation demands it, but remembering the advice of Gide: "ne jamais profiter de l'élan acquis." Like all the chosen creatures of the West, the novel is contented with a closed order. Reluctantly in opposition, to seek here...to cut all systematic construction of characters and situations off at the root. The method: irony, incessant self-criticism, incongruence, and imagination at no one's service.

And another character clarifies more: "What he wants to do is to transgress the total literary deed, the book, if you like. Sometimes in the word, sometimes in what the word transmits. He proceeds like a warrior, he destroys what he can and the rest follows along. Don't think that he isn't a man of letters." Lezama Lima's *Paradiso* is a *novel-poem*, not in the sense this term ordinarily has (when it designates novels where the language is the showy decor of a content in itself poor), but in the sense that its topic—with the pretext of the childhood and adolescence of José Cemi—is the image, the possibility of knowing through the image. Thus, the novelist is precisely a poet, a seer who explores "the reality of the invisible world." He is guided by "the exercise of poetry, the verbal search for unknown finality.... When his vision gave him a word in whatever relationship it might have with reality, that word seemed to him to pass into his hands, and although the word might remain invisible to him, liberated from the vision it had left, it went along acquiring a wheel where the invisible modulation and the palpable shaping turned incessantly."

Two other novelists, very different from each other, García Márquez and Vargas Llosa, have made major contributions to the genre: the Colombian, with his unrestrained return to the world of the imagination, the logic of dreams, the time of the origins and popular mythology, upon which he founds his triumphant *One Hundred Years of Solitude*; and the Peruvian, with his implacable but impartial realism, his orchestrations of vast social worlds, his penetrating immersion in the infernos of liberty, violence, and human passions, his astonishing technical sureness in the handling of spatio-temporal planes, the melodramas of sex and the poetry of pure brutality. In general, the Latin American novel, which was previously closer to the essay or to reporting (sometimes it replaced it), now shares the domains of poetry. The sometimes juridical or pedagogic prose of our primitive Indianists and indigenists has been replaced by a more creative language: the language of fable, myth, and image, whose meanings cannot only be multiple but also contradictory.

MASTERS AND DISCIPLES OF DISSIDENCE

Poetry has undergone a series of changes which are no less revolutionary. A group of poets, somewhat younger than Neruda, infected by the spirit of the vanguard and principally by that of surrealism are the founders of that poetry which prevails today and which, in some way, is orienting the experiences of the new poets of the present: they are Octavio Paz, Enrique Molina, and Nicanor Parra (the most surrealist of them all, the Peruvian César Moro, wrote an important poetic work which still awaits continental distribution). Through this thirty years of writing poetry, Paz has amassed an important capital which few can challenge; in Mexico, at least, he has stimulated entire generations of poets. Complemented by his extremely rich and lucid critical writing, the poetry of Paz has sought (and found) key objectives: the dialectic of opposites, the erotic outburst, the mystic revelation, the essential ambiguity of the poetic cosmos, and so forth. In recent years, his experience has become even more radical and has contributed to the negation of poetic discourse itself by means of "visual disks" and different forms of aleatoric poetry (*Blanco* is the most extreme example) which conquer and combine space, word, and silence in an adventure of absolute liberty. Parra's "antipoetry" is the apotheosis of the prosaic and the commonplace which are turned around to reveal the absurd and the sinister humor of the contemporary world:

Yo no permito que nadie me diga
Que no comprende los antipoemas
Todos deben reír a carcajadas.
Para eso me rompo la cabeza
Para llegar al alma del lector.
Déjense de preguntas.
En el lecho de muerte
Cada uno se rasca con sus uñas.

[I don't allow anyone to tell me / That he doesn't understand anti-poems / Everyone should laugh out loud. / This is why I break my head / To reach the reader's soul. / Stop asking questions. / On his death bed / Everyone scratches himself with his own nails.]

With him, there is no doubt about it, the process of rhetorical decomposition begins which will pull Latin American poetry out of a stalemate; he represents a movement toward the reconciliatory irony and the heterodox truth which predominate among the young poets. Molina maintains his allegiance to surrealism, not because of loyalty to a literary movement, but because of its consequence to himself, as proven by his poetry that is populated with erotic images, marine visions, and incitations to adventure. The masters of Brazilian poetry are others, certainly: Manuel Bandeira, Carlos Drummond de Andrade, Vinicius de Moraes, and above all the great Jorge de Lima, the poet of the memorable *Invencão de Orfeu* [Invention of Orpheus] (1952).

Another great original voice of the poetry of our America is that of Ernesto Cardenal (disciple of the versatile Colonel Urtecho), the poet of the *Epigramas* [Epigrams] against the dictatorship, the mystic of the *Psalms of Struggle and Liberation*, the tortured witness of our apocalypse in *Oración para Marilyn Monroe* [Prayer for Marilyn Monroe], the interpreter of pre-Hispanic civilizations in *Mayapán* and *Economía del Tahuantinsuyo* [Economy of the Tahuantinsuyo]; the inventor, finally, of an unmistakable diction, which contains aspects of chronicle, of memorandum, and of public prayer. Other poets follow along this route of colloquial simplicity; Benedetti, Sabines, recently José Emilio Pacheco. Carlos Germán Belli constitutes a case—a value—apart, with his (almost) neoclassic language, with his allegories and puns, his cultisms and archaisms, which move along revealing an absolutely horrifying vision of inner and social life: the self is a cripple, society, a hierarchy of masters and slaves. The precise and profound verse of João Cabral de Melo Neto; the critical penetration of Enrique Lihn and of Heberto Padilla; the vehement assumption of the West Indian *négritude* of René Depestre; the eroticism of Homero Aridjis; the furors and calcifying vertigos of Rafael Cadenas and Juan Calzadilla (who come from the groups "Tabla Redonda" and "El Techo de la Ballena," important for their virulent poetic action in Caracas); the clean young voice of Javier Heraud (singer of the river of life, prophet of his death, living legend in Peru); and the antibourgeois sarcasm and zoological parables of Antonio Cisneros are some of the other paths of poetry.

TWO LINES

During these last years, the novel and the story have also undergone a rapid transformation in the hands of writers who are younger or less well known than the great consecrated figures. Although inevitably rigid, it is possible to place these writers in two major groups; one is the realist group which postulates a definite story as the basis of the narration and which tries to renovate the tradition of Latin American realism while operating within that same tradition. That wide spectrum includes the politically involved realism of David Viñas (*Los hombres de a caballo* [Men on Horseback]), the magic-psychological realism of Daniel Moyano (his stories in *El monstruo* [The Monster], and Reinaldo Arenas (*Celestino antes del alba* [Celestino Before Dawn]), the expressionist and sometimes baroque realism of Carlos Martínez Moreno (*Los aborígenes* [The Aborigines], *La otra mitad* [The Other Half]), the realism that is critical of the decomposed bourgeoisie of José Donoso (*This Sunday*) and Jorge Edwards (*Temas y variaciones* [Themes and Variations]). The other group, whose notorious inspirers are the recent Carlos Fuentes (*A Change of Skin*, *Holy Place*), to some extent Cortázar, and much more fully Guillermo Cabrera Infante (*Three Trapped Tigers*), nearly omits the story or subordinates it to an almost exasperated formalist search. Belonging to this group are Severo Sarduy (*From Cuba with a Song*), Manuel Puig (*Betrayed by Rita Hayworth*, *Heartbreak Tango*), Néstor Sánchez (*Siberia Blues*), Vicente Leñero (*El garabato* [The Scrawl]), Salvador Elizonda (*El hipogeo secreto* [The Secret Vault]) and Gustavo Sáinz (*Obsesivos días circulares* [Obsessive Circular Days]). While the first group is trying to redeem the realism of its illusionist devices by manipulating it with greater delicacy and effectiveness, less candidly, those of the second group can do without it or use it merely as a pretext for their verbal games and distortions: writing novels which intend to mock the very concept of the novel. It may be of interest to add two facts concerning literary geography: those of the first group tend to come from Chile and other Pacific coast countries, those of the second group, from Mexico and Argentina.

THEATRICAL RENOVATION

The true Cinderella of our continent's culture continues to be the theater (because even the cinema, which is incipient, can count on a handful of master works: those of Glauber Rocha, that of Getino-Solanas, those of the new Cuban film). A lack of continuous effort has affected the existence of a theatrical tradition; so has the extremely small audience drama addresses itself to (sometimes because it assesses its relationship to its public incorrectly) and the almost strictly national recognition of the authors. A realist and social vocation has always distinguished the Latin American theater; at least it became established as that in the models which may be considered as most influential until the beginning of the Second World War: Rodolfo Usigli and Celestino Gorostiza in Mexico and Samuel Eichelbaum in Argentina. The somewhat stiff and mimetic style (when it wanted to be popular) of this tradition is later filtered through to the work of such dramatists as the Cubans Virgilio Piñera and Abelardo Estorino, and the Colombian Enrique Buenaventura, who know how to register more intimate tones, use a really economical dialogue, and unfold authentic dramatic force. A wave of renovation invades our theater with the fresh air of the postwar period. The impact of the theater of the absurd and of the forms which tend to return ritual character to drama is generally felt, but the French existential theater, Brecht, and the European political theater are influential, too. What is the situation now? In the first place, one must point out the endurance of certain places— Argentina, Chile, and, to some extent, Mexico—as theatrical centers. The Argentines Agustín Cuzzani, Osvaldo Dragún, Roberto Cossa, and Ricardo Talesnik, the Chileans Egon Wolff and Jorge Díaz, the Mexicans Emilio Carballido and Jorge Ibargüengoitia, and the Guatemalan (but active in Mexico) Carlos Solórzano have made notable contributions to the new drama. But the most interesting phenomena are not in these places, but in Cuba and Brazil. The triumph of the Cuban Revolution gave an impetus and meaning to the national theater: the public enthusiasm, the access of a new public to the theatrical spectacle, and the state support of the authors, directors, and technicians were the principle stimuli. Together with the already mentioned Piñera and Estorino who, within the revolution, renew their creative vigor, appear José Triana (known worldwide for *The Criminals*), Antón Arrufat, Héctor Quintero, Jesús Díaz, and others. They are the new Cuban theater, where we find everything from grotesque vanguardist puppet shows to scenic chronicles of the revolutionary struggle. The best social theater is that which is written, produced, and seen today in Brazil. It is essentially realistic (perhaps it could not be otherwise), but what it seeks is immediacy between the spectacle and its public. To achieve this it uses many media: popular music and dance, informal systems of representation, admirable use of folklore, choral movements and re-creation of classical formulas (e.g., autos, allegories, parables). Testimony to this are the works of Jorge Andrade (*Vereda da Salvacão* [Pass of Salvation]), Joáo Cabral de Melo Neto (*Muerte y vida Severina* [Life and Death of Severina]), Alfredo Días Gomes (*Journey to Bahia* [also translated as *Payment as Pledged*]), Oduvaldo Viana (*Cuatro cuadras de tierra* [Four Square Blocks of Land]), and Plinio Marcos (*Navalha na carne* [Navalha in My Flesh]).

THE MOST RECENT PERIOD

Since the present situation is fluid, to describe a particular point in its process is to distort it subtly: it cannot be said to be, it *is being*. One of the factors which have made this last period so conflictive, rich, and vigorous is the powerful gravitation of the Cuban culture into the Latin American intellectual mainstream, and vice versa. During these years, many of the things which have happened to our literary and artistic life have revolved around the peculiar situation of Cuba as a center of creativity and diffusion of a revolutionary and socialist culture for the continent; inevitably, the Cuban example has had to constitute a challenge to Latin American intelligence. The Cuban focus has made itself felt in many ways.

Recent years have rapidly changed the terms of the debate and even the positions of the contenders: now it is not unusual for the most ardent polemicists to find themselves simultaneously on the same side and for the defenders to emerge from the opposite trenches. At the end of 1967, the discrepant attitudes became fully visible in an interview in the magazine *Casa de las Américas* [House of the Americas]; in the issue dedicated to examining the "situation of the Latin American intellectual," the positions have been defined, sometimes belligerently. Julio Cortázar reaffirms his faith in socialism; he justifies the prolongation of his exile in France "which is my home [and] continues to seem to me the ideal place for a temperament like mine"; and he declares the autonomy of his work as a writer in respect to his ideas: "At the risk of disillusioning the catechists and the advocates of art at the service of the masses, I continue to be that *cronopio* who... writes for his own personal suffering or pleasure without the least concession, without 'Latin American' or 'socialist' obligations understood as programmatic a prioris." The position of Vargas Llosa, as we know, coincides with that of the Argentine writer; he distinguishes between the obligations of the creator and those of the citizen; fidelity to the first may signify an involuntary subordination of the second ones; in any case, it is a matter of two separate fields of moral decisions, each with its own laws. Speaking of Sebastián Salazar Bondy, he writes: "He knew how to involve himself politically while safeguarding his independence, his creative spontaneity, because he knew that as a citizen, he could decide, calculate, or rationally premeditate his actions, but that as a writer, his mission consisted in serving and obeying the orders, often incomprehensible for the creator, the caprices and obsessions of unpredictable consequences, of the solitary one (literature), that free master, voluntarily admitted into his being." Benedetti, for his part, insists that the responsibility of the writer is *always* a joint one, "that of his art and that of his surroundings," denying "that improbable dividing line which many intellectuals, guarding against imaginary dangers, prefer to draw between the literary work and the human responsibility of the writer." And the Peruvian poet Alejandro Romualdo, more violently, condemns Latin American writers who accept "fellowships, translations into English, the numerous prizes, like the 'Rómulo Gallegos,' or the honors of the Order of the Sun of Peru." The sentence is full of concrete allusions, among them to Vargas Llosa himself and to Neruda, and it announces a series of internal tensions which are even sharper.

It is not a coincidence: the revolution was maturing in the midst of problems which demanded the vigilance of its vanguards—and the intellectual vanguard was a very important one. In all of Latin America, the struggles for national liberation and the guerrilla movements survived desperately, confronted failure and death, attacked and obtained only a renewed enforcement of repression. The sacrifice of Che, the division of the Communist parties into proinsurrection and antiinsurrection factions, and the statement of political solutions in military terms also had to affect the internal Cuban situation and displace the emphases of intellectual action onto certain matters which had not merited this kind of notice. The image of the successful writer—the novelists who make up what has quite stupidly been called the *boom*—with assured translations within a powerful publishing system, with access to prizes, professorships, and invitations all over the place, defender of a generally European exile and an absolute professionalism of literature, involved but not militant about a part, began to seem particularly uncomfortable to an intellectual sector which demanded a transparent revolutionary adherence not only in political acts, but in the creative task of each person. The curious thing is that the pressure manifested itself exclusively in regard to literature, but not in other fields of art (painting, film, theater, etc.) where experimental and vanguardist forms which originated in the repudiated consumer societies (like pop and op-art) continued to proliferate and dominate the Cuban aesthetic reality. Two kinds of groups had formed: Cortázar and Vargas Llosa, on one side, as representatives of the intellectuals who offered critical and not militant support to the revolution, and Benedetti, Depestre, and Dalton, principally, as paradigms of the intellectual with internal experience of the revolution, active within cultural or party organizations, totally integrated with and given over to the practice of socialism. As we see, those who appear eminently on this side of the line of fire are Latin American writers and not only Cubans.

This polemic—which is just one among many others that have agitated Latin American literature in recent years, like that of Cortázar and Arguedas about cosmopolitanism and regionalism—achieves greater transcendence precisely because its origin and stimulus is in Cuba, where an old intellectual hope continues to have come true: the lack of an aesthetic canon for a socialist culture. The proof is that the opinions in favor and against the point in question are listened to with equal attention there, making possible a dialogue which is surely impossible in almost all the rest of the American countries. What new theories and interpretations of the literary phenomenon will come out of this tense interchange of opinions? What marks will it leave on intellectual creation? It is still too early to know the results; for the time being, we can only present the positions which are influencing the process of our literature.

Notes

1. Quoted by Guillermo Ara, *Ricardo Güiraldes* (Buenos Aires: La Mandrágora, 1961), p. 79.

2. José Carlos Mariátegui, *Siete ensayos de interpretación de la realidad peruana* (Lima: Amauta, 1964), p. 290.

3. Quoted by Juan Liscano, *Rómulo Gallegos y su tiempo* (Caracas: Monte Avila, 1969), p. 102.

4. In *Variedades*, Lima, 26 March, 1930.

5. Quoted by Emir Rodríguez Monegal, *El viajero inmóvil* (Buenos Aires: Losada, 1966), pp. 99–100.

6. Ibid., p. 101.

7. Emir Rodríguez Monegal, *Narradores de esta América*, 2d ed. (Montevideo: Alfa, 1969), vol. 1.

8. *Times Literary Supplement*, London, 14 November 1968, p. 1287.

9. Carlos Fuentes, *La nueva novela hispanoamericana* (Mexico: Joaquin Mortiz, 1969), p. 13.

14 / Image of Latin America

JOSÉ LEZAMA LIMA

After the image had provided the momentum for the most frenetic or careful expeditions through the *terra incognita*, through *incunabula*, it had to slow down. Columbus, like Marco Polo, suffered imprisonment after his discoveries and adventures, as though an imposed respite were necessary after the fever of the *imago*. Probably thanks to their imprisonments they achieved an ambivalence between what they had really seen and what they were going to relate, as though to escape being the prisoners of the image of what they had divided up even before touching or recognizing it. Men of decision through the compulsion of blood and of the image which their blood obeyed, it is necessary to recognize these two impulses in their adventures, or if we see the two interwoven, we must discern the form in which the image determined in their adventurous blood their risks and their encounters with marvels.

In recent years, in the era of Spengler or Toynbee, the topic of cultures has been extemely seductive, but cultures can disappear without destroying the images which represent them. If we contemplate a Minoan jar decorated with marine motifs or some of their murals, we can, through the image, feel the present vitality, as though that culture were intact right now, without making us feel the year 1500 B.C. when it was extinguished. Cultures move toward their ruin, but after ruin they live again through the image. The image blows on the embers of the spirit of the ruins. The image is interwoven with the myth which is at the threshold of all cultures, which both precedes them and follows their funeral procession. It favors their initiation and their resurrection.

The conquest and colonization of America develop in ways which are opposed to the established riverbeds of Roman tradition. This tradition was a corpus, a force of historical diffusion which constantly expanded its historic contours, the expression of a world which had achieved plenitude and which was convinced of the barbarity which surrounded it, although upon occasion, as on their incursions into the Orient, it had to pay the price of the change of its gods, of its beliefs, losing through expansion its unified strength and having to adapt the mask of its imperial dualism in the West and in the East. But in its conquests of England, France, and Spain, the Roman Empire still acted from a center which managed to include these barbarians. It imposed laws, bridges, aqueducts, roads, superstitions, with the style, with the energy and the arrogance of a distinctive gesture. With great local effort, the Celts, the Normans, the Bretons, and the Druids achieved the survival of their *imago* in the face of the avalanche of legionnaires that paraded through continuously before finally corralling and destroying them. Latin grammar and legionary discipline refined verbs and reduced nature and instincts. Thus, it has been possible to affirm that at the root of Hispanic expression is the struggle between Latin grammar and the rebellious Celt. And in our greatest writers, from Sarmiento to Martí, that combat continues with an immediacy which suggests its permanence.

Perhaps that ordering, that final glazing, as ceramists say, almost forced those barbaric currents to liberate themselves, as by a new configuration, which canceled out the old, of that central deglutition. The infinity of the Eros in the Tristram, liberated from the extension of the eye, of the finity, of the *logos okulos*, the choral magic of King Arthur's companions, the recognizable trace of the flying cape of the Grail before the treasure guarded within it, flew up in a fury at the imposition of ancient Greek myths and their Latin versions. New swarms of images emerged, Provence replaces Athens, the Ponto Euxino and the Pillars of Hercules are replaced by Cathay or Cipango. The Mediterranean opened onto the Atlantic and the dying shipwreck victims who reached the Azores brought the tale of the new *colombas* that faded the memory of the ancient tale of the buzzard upon the older foundations. From the point of view of the kingdom of the image, the small peninsula of Armórica resists the Roman advance with its ghosts, witches, and fairies. And if the image, as we have affirmed, reorganizes and unifies cultures after their extinction, the dance of the Celtic witches upon a Roman bridge lends it the resistant mist of eternity.

But the relationship of the American situation to the image was antithetical to that of Europe before the Roman Conquest. Medieval Hispanic chaos was far from being unified. The Islamic world, the Jews, the tendency toward feudal atomization, theology in defense of a merely temporal problematicism, the incompatability between an innate roughness and a refinement imported by the house of Borgoña or by the Arabs, transferred all problematicism, engendered by an absorbing central power and by the resistance of the centrifugal forces, to a struggle between chaos, which was not in any case the primitive chaos, when the wind rippled the waters, but rather historical dispersion seeking an exit given it finally by chance, this was its true primitive state and what we have called *gnostic space*, the dimension which engenders the tree, the space which engenders and knows just as it was seen by the Taoists, strength germinating in the empty space. The Inca Empire, without the possibility of contact with the Roman Empire, acts only as space, in its appearance its resources are inertia and passivity, but I doubt that Roman civilization offers as germinative an image as that of Viracocha: it breaks chronology, it brings about a time of simultaneity, it creates a magic hilozoism, since he sees a possible or actual man in every stone, he makes warriors out of stones and after the victory the warriors become stones again. He has in him something of Hamlet and of Charlemagne, but he is always the one who arrives to reinforce and who disappears like a ghost without touching the ground. He is a Hamlet who does not refuse to appear at the opportune moment to help and a Charlemagne who does not weigh so heavily on the historical intrigue as the Carolingian cudgel which he gives to each of the twelve pairs.

Some medievalists affirm that it was a late Middle Ages which passed through America, and we can add that with the incorporation of a technique and with the fragmentary spirit of a civilization which we have only half incorporated, that medievalism has continued to be the root of Latin America. There existed among the first American settlers, from the Chichimecas to the Incas, a tendency toward empires, to great planetary dimensions ruled from a center. Sánchez Albornoz has emphasized that he is forced to recognize in the discovery and conquest of America, the last heroic age of the Western world, the last period of the epic Middle Ages.

The chronicler of the Indies carries the novel of chivalry to the landscape. Bernal Díaz del Castillo's way of writing reveals that he read and heard stories from books of chivalry. The forest teems with enchantments and the flora and the fauna are recognized insofar as they correspond to these described in old bestiaries, collections of fables and of magic plants. The solanaceae, which were also called *consolers*, and during the Middle Ages were applied to the bedeviled and the possessed, are replaced by quinine, and mezcal and coca construct the most sumptuous cathedrals in the air, but without support and without reality. Gonzalo Hernández de Oviedo calls the lizards *dragons*. Every little animal as it is discovered leads the conquerors to recall Pliny the Elder. First he carefully establishes the similarity and then the difference with other known animals, in a form of violent emphasis. The same chronicler compares spiders with sparrows, bees with flies. With each animal or plant, the chroniclers emphasize its similarities to those they carry in memory and in image, and afterward they rescue its individuality by noting the differences. Speaking of the mamey, the same chronicler emphasizes that its color is like that of the grafted pear, "but a little harder and heavier," the guanabana is compared with the melon, but "on its outer surface it has some subtle tracings that seem to indicate scales." Imagination establishes resemblances, but touch and sight achieve notice of individual particularities and new beauties. In America, during the first year of the Conquest, imagination was not "the family lunatic" but a principle of organization, of recognition, and of legitimate differentiation.

The decomposition into images of whatever we perceive has served the American ever since the Conquest as magical protection and security in choice. It is true that we received a result, a product, but we guided it toward the prism of the image. Hence the maturity of Cervantes's prose or the refinement of Gongorine sayings march accompanied by the appearance of the chroniclers of the Indies, in whom the primitivity of expression is united with the refinement of the image. The image becomes profound and refined because to the freight taken from Europe, from Pliny to the bestiaries, is added the abundance of new marvels. The gravitation of the image takes root among us right from the beginning, the image aimed toward the center of the earth and which is totally liberated from magical reason. The image produced by this space which knows, which creates a *gnosis*, covers us like a placenta which knows, which protects us from the ctonic world, from the mortal darkness which could destroy us before our time.

Thus as Europe, as Vico could note, moved from fables to myths, in America we have had to go from myths to the image. How the image has created culture, how that image has been most stimulating, how and when the image can no longer be fabulation or myth, are questions which only poetry and the novel can gradually answer. And above all, in what form the image will take part in history, will have effective powers, metaphorical strength so that the stones may again become images.

Góngora bases his two *Soledades* [Solitudes] on Ovid and his reference to Proserpina, to the gossip Ascálafo, and to the descents of the moon to the dark valley. His weddings of country girls are illuminated by the appearance of the god Pan in the Sicilian valleys. His poetic perspective is formed by the Greco-Latin tradition and the splendor of the baroque cornucopia of fishes and falcons. It is only a space illuminated by the lantern of a wedding, a lightning flash which allows us to glimpse the frenzy of the dances of the goatherds and the shepherds. The goat of Amaltea, of ancient tradition, animates those dances with its astral leaps. But neither the story nor the descriptions have anything to do with a novelizable form, nor is there the least possibility that those vistas, we could say, depart from the metallic glow of each of his metaphors. But in contrast let us see the *Poema heróico* [Heroic Poem] in honor of Saint Ignatius of Loyola, by the Colombian Domínguez Camargo. In this novel-length poem, Domínguez relates all the vicissitudes of the saint, from his birth and baptism until he takes the road to Rome to obtain the recognition of the order. Domínguez Camargo is one of Góngora's most important disciples, he is an epigone, but his work is radically different from that of his master. There where Góngora attempts a lightning flash, a light which allows us to glimpse the dances for an instant, Domínguez Camargo forges a story, the contour of a life. I would say that to the Gongorine metaphor, Domínguez opposes a very American image of space and development. Vossler observed that there is no landscape in Góngora's work, but in Domínguez's poems the decoration of the baroque cornucopia is replaced by the forest and the mountains which surround the lovely little church of Tunja, while at the same time Góngora's shepherds and goats leap about in the historic Sicilian valley, in accord with the pattern established by Homer and Vergil, Theocritus and Longo.

In his travels through Spain, Columbus came to the cathedral of Zamora where some exquisite tapestries are kept. Gallant scenes of ladies and warrior are depicted, surrounded by all the Provençal glories of color and of forms. The gallantry, the birds and the flowers, blend the splendor of the deeds with the most highly refined nature in their elegance. One of the tapestries depicts a coronation, that of Tarquin during Rome's early years; the other depicts the Trojan Wars, on this tapestry a medieval ship appears and a sailor is untying the cables. Everywhere there are Byzantine noblemen, Greek merchants, splendid colored figures. While the horseman advances toward the battle, the ladies watch from a balcony while what is for them like a tournament unfolds. There are flowers all around the battleground as in a Provençal review of arms. If after contemplating those tapestries of the cathedral of Zamora we read a few pages of Columbus's *Journal*, we are impressed by that eagerness to convert nature into a tapestry, emphasize the beauty of the fleet birds that blend with the many-hued leaves. Columbus's imagination is full of dolphins and Mediterranean sirens and poetic games and Provençal warriors' tournaments.

It cannot surprise us that an Italian, who goes to Spain during the era of Charles V, should write about things he never saw and subordinate himself more to the imagination we have called *Sicilian* than to the reality of a new landscape which he did not know. His description of Cuba is based only on his imaginative memories, on the derivations from his readings: "Everything is tempered by humidity, everything rich in gold products. Its caves, like so many open mouths, disgorge into the waters of the rivers. There are horrible caverns, there are dark valleys, there are calcareous rocks," that is, they are the same whirlpools, caverns, rivers, and rocks that his imagination has taken from his readings of Homer and Ovid and which serve him to match his Sicilian images with a truly new landscape, before which his imagination is helpless and must seek those points of support in the familiar. Thus, Pedro Mártir de Anglería relates that a Haitian chief had in his lakes a manatí which ate from his hands and carried men and children across to the other shore. The chronicler has replaced the seas around the island by the Mediterranean and by depending on the slightest of similarities, he equates a manatí with a siren. Unhappily we pass from ambivalence and similarity of images to an inconceivable destructive furor and today the manatí is almost an extinct species. It would have been better for this species' survival to have maintained the levity of an error of imagination.

The American image is liberated under pressure from the gnostic space which replaces dimension by the image, as in the ancient world exile, captivity and liberation begin to populate the stellar and to react on history. The colossal dimensions achieved by the Incas or by the Aztecs can only be compared with the Ninevite Empire, the Persians or the Egyptians in the most significant epochs of their history. That sense of space seduces the Incas from the beginning: in one of their most primitive fables, they emerge through the windows of some cliffs which are near Cuzco; four men and four women appeared in this way (remember the first Chinese dynasties, where the series of brothers appear). They came out through the middle window, the royal window. In the window they had to see a space where the stellar and the human conjoined. In the center of the window a navel appears, which is the city of Cuzco. Creative space already appears in this fable, with its navel or center, salt, pepper, dances, and joyfulness. Immediately, the conquerors want to equate the window in the rock with the window of Noah's Ark, but the fact that the Inca should consider himself the descendant of all nature, waterfalls, coyotes, or birds, which lead him to a total divinization of the entire external world, has to seem indecipherable to the conquerors, since their old image, nourished with infinite analogies, encounters a new space which disconcerts it and makes it tremble.

The Incaic space and the Aztec are similar in many ways, the umbilical window of the Incas coincides with the *quincunce* [radiating center] of the Aztecs, both are similar to what in Doctor Kungtse's (Confucius) era was called the *middle path*, between sky and earth. Yáhuar Huacac, seventh king of the Incas, or "Cries Blood," seems to have anticipated the terror of Moctezuma, he lives surrounded by omens, fears, insecurities. But Yáhuar manages to overcome his fears by the apparition of a ghost, of an image, but the most curious thing is that the ghostly prince is called *Viracocha* and the son of Yáhuar who saves him has the same name. There is a fusion of the historical character and the mythological one. But Moctezuma begins by decapitating the dreams. He sets up a kind of office for ill-omen dreams in his palace. And all those who dream of the disappearance of his empire are condemned to death.

What we have called "the American era of the image" has its most evident expressions in the new meanings of the chronicler of the Indies, the baroque dominion, the rebellion of romanticism. There the image acts as a *quantos* which is converted into a *quale* by the discovery of a center and the proportionate distribution of the energy. Exile and captivity are at the very root of these images. The chronicler of the Indies brings his already-formed images, and the new landscape bursts them open. The baroque seigneur begins his contortions and repolishings anchored in fable tradition and Greco-Latin myths, but very soon the incorporation of the phytomorphic and zoomorphic elements which waylay him, lizards, hummingbirds, coyotes, *ombú*, *ceiba*, *hylam-hylam*, create new collections of fables which grant a new center of gravity to his work. The romantic rebellion among us is something more than a rupture or the simple demoniac search for something else; on the contrary, it forms part of and expresses the historic circumstance. The verbal rebellion of the great American romantics, from Sarmiento to Martí, equates their inventions in language with their creations as builders of nations. Our romanticism fused Calimachus and Licophron with Licurgus and Solon. In the history of the West, Dante, for example, after his great symbolic verbal construction, never had any essential historico-political predominance over Florentine destinies. In American history the greatest builder and renovator of language we have had, without any doubt José Martí, creates a most innovative revolution. The image is finally incarnated by history; poetry becomes a choral canticle.

Simón Rodríguez communicates to Bolívar, from the time of his adolescence on, a sense of American historical grandeur through the Inca Empire. Bolívar, like Napoleon, was dazzled in his adolescence by General Miranda. From Russia to Spain, Miranda dominated European space. Bolívar, during the first years after his return to Caracas, believes, pressured by Miranda, that with the help of the liberal aristocracy it is possible to achieve independence. In that equivocal dimension Monteverde destroys Miranda and gets rid of Bolívar by exiling him. But successive encounters with Simón Rodríguez, the Rousseauian enamored of Incaic space, lead him to delve deeper and to seek new ethnic elements along the length of the Andean region which wish to express themselves. After the death of Bolívar, Simón Rodríguez continues to be immersed in the Incaic dimension, he knows that the intuition of that dimension by Bolívar was the root which made independence possible, he knows that the deeper exploration of that dimension will mean the enlightenment of the American space.

The search for that center of the American space was even more tragic in Simón Rodríguez. In his struggle to find that center of the immense Incaic space, the *quincunce* of the Aztecs, that is, the "radiating center" of the energies of the space, he arrived at the most immoderate grandeur. When he was nearly eighty years old we see Simón Rodríguez wandering about the shores of Lake Titicaca, surrounded by his children, with his Indian wife, living in the most desolate poverty. In the center of American history, in the *quincunce* of the Incaic space, he continues to win the most decisive battles for the image, the secret pulsations of the invisible toward the image, as eager to know as to be known.

GENERAL

Alegría, Fernando, *Historia de la novela hispanoamericana*, Mexico, De Andrea, 3d ed., 1966.

Anderson Imbert, Enrique, *Historia de la literatura hispanoamericana*, Mexico, Fondo de Cultura Económica, vol. I: *La Colonia, cien años de república*, 1954; vol. II: *Época contemporánea*, 1961.

————— y Eugenio Florit, *La literatura hispanoamericana*, New York, Holt, Rinehart and Winston, 1960.

Arrom, José Juan, *Esquema generacional de las letras hispanoamericanas. Ensayo de un método*, Bogotà, Instituto Caro y Cuervo, 1963.

Bazin, Robert, *Histoire de la littérature américaine de langue espagnole*, Paris, Hachette, 1953.

Benedetti, Mario, *Letras del continente mestizo*, Montevideo, Arca, 1967.

Campos, Augusto, Haroldo de Campos y Décio Pignatari, *Teoria da poesia concreta (textos críticos e manifestos), 1950/60*, São Paulo, Invenção, 1965.

Cândido, António, *Formação da literatura brasileira*, São Paulo, Livraria Martins, 1964, 2 vols.

—————, *Introducción a la literatura del Brasil*, Caracas, Monte Ávila, 1968.

Carilla, Emilio, *Hispanoamérica y su expresión literaria*, Buenos Aires, EUDEBA, 1969.

Carpentier, Alejo, *Tientos y diferencias*, Mexico, UNAM, 1964.

Coutinho, Afranio, ed., *A literatura no Brasil*, Rio de Janeiro, Sul Americana, 1955–1958, 5 vols.

Díez-Canedo, Enrique, *Letras de América*, Mexico, El Colegio de Mexico, 1944.

Dorfman, Ariel, *Imaginación y violencia en América*, Santiago, Universitaria, 1970.

Fernández Moreno, César, *La realidad y los papeles*, Madrid, Aguilar, 1967.

Fuentes, Carlos, *La nueva novela hispanoamericana*, Mexico, Joaquín Mortiz, 1969.

Harss, Luis, *Los nuestros*, Buenos Aires, Sudamericana, 1966.

————— and Barbara Dohmann, *Into the Mainstream*, New York, Harper & Row, 1967.

Henríquez Ureña, Max, *Breve historia del modernismo*, Mexico, Fondo de Cultura Económica, 1954.

—————, *Las corrientes literarias en la América hispánica*, Mexico, Fondo de Cultura Económica, 2d ed., 1954.

—————, *Obra Crítica*, Mexico, Fondo de Cultura Económica, 1954.

Lafforgue, Jorge, ed., *Nueva novela latinoamericana*, Buenos Aires, Paidós, 1969–1972, 2 vols.

Lazo, Raimundo, *Historia de la literatura hispanoamericana*, Mexico, Porrúa, 1963–1967, 2 vols.

Leal, Luis, *Historia del cuento hispanoamericano*, Mexico, De Andrea, 1966.

Lida, Raimundo, *Letras hispánicas*, Mexico, Fondo de Cultura Económica, 1958.

Loveluck, Juan, ed., *La novela hispanoamericana*, Santiago de Chile, Editorial Universitaria, 1969.

Mariátegui, José Carlos, *Siete ensayos de interpretación de la realidad peruana*, Lima, Biblioteca Amauta, 1928.

Ortega, Julio, *La contemplación y la fiesta. Notas sobre la novela latinoamericana actual*, Caracas, Monte Ávila, 1969.

—————, *Panorama de la actual literatura latinoamericana*, Havana, Casa de las Américas, 1969.

Paz, Octavio, *El arco y la lira*, Mexico, Fondo de Cultura Económica, 1956, 1967.

—————, *Los hijos del limo*, Barcelona, Seix-Barral, 1974.

—————, *Puertas al campo*, Mexico, UNAM, 1967.

—————, *Corriente alterna*, Mexico, Siglo XXI, 1967.

Portuondo, José Antonio, *El heroísmo intelectual*, Mexico, Fondo de Cultura Económica, 1955.
Pup-Walker, E., ed., *El cuento hispanoamericano ante la crítica*, Madrid, Castalia, 1973.
Rama, Ángel, *Diez problemas para el novelista latinoamericano*, in *Casa de las Américas*, Havana, No. 26, Oct.–Nov. 1964.
Reyes, Alfonso, *La experiencia literaria*, in *Obras completas*, vol. XIV, Mexico, Fondo de Cultura Económica, 1962.
Rodríguez Monegal, Emir, *El arte de narrar*, Caracas, Monte Ávila, 1968.
_____ , *Narradores de esta América*, Montevideo, Alfa, 1969, vol. I and II.
Solórzano, Carlos, *El teatro latinoamericano en el siglo xx*, Mexico, Pormaca, 1964.
Sucre, Guillermo, *La máscara, la transparencia*, Caracas, Monte Avila, 1975.
Torre, Guillermo de, *Claves de la literatura hispanoamericana*, Madrid, Cuadernos Taurus, 1959.
Yurkiévich, Saúl, *Celebración del modernismo*, Barcelona, Tusquets, 1976.
_____ , *Fundadores de la nueva poesía latinoamericana*, Barcelona, Barral, 1971.
Zum Felde, Alberto, *Indice crítico de la literatura hispanoamericana*, Mexico, Guarania, vol. I, 1954; vol. II, 1959.

Anthologies

Caillet-Bois, Julio, *Antología de la poesía hispanoamericana*, Madrid, Aguilar, 2d ed., 1965.
Jiménez, José Olivio, *Antología de la poesía hispanoamericana contemporánea, 1914–1970*, Madrid, Alianza, 1971.
Latchman, Ricardo, *Antología del cuento hispanoamericano contemporáneo*, Santiago, Chile, Zig-Zag, 2d ed., 1962.
Onis, Federico de, *Anthologie de la poésia Ibero-Américaine*, Paris, Nagel, 1956.
Pellegrini, Aldo, *Antología de la poesie viva latinoamericana*, Barcelona, Seix-Barral, 1966.
Rodríguez Monegal, Emir, *The Borzoi Anthology of Latin American Literature*, 2 vols., New York, Knopf, 1977.
Solórzano, Carlos, *El teatro hispanoamericano contemporáneo. Antología*, Mexico, Fondo de Cultura Económica, 1964, 2 vols.

CHAPTER ONE

Arrom, José Juan, *Certidumbre de América*, Havana, Anuario Bibliográfico Cubano, 1959.
_____ , *El teatro hispanoamericano en la época colonial*, Mexico, De Andrea, 1967.
Ballagas, Emilio, *Mapa de la poesía negra*, Buenos Aires, Pleamar, 1947.
Barrera Vásquez, Alfredo, *El libro de los libros de Chilam Balam*, Mexico, Fondo de Cultura Económica, 1948.
_____ , *Libro de los cantares de Dzitbalché*, Mexico, Instituto Nacional de Antropología e Historia, 1965.
Brathwaite, Edward, *Masks*, London, Oxford University Press, 1968.
Buarque de Holanda, A., *O romance brasileiro*, Rio de Janeiro, Edições O Cruzeiro, 1952.
Calcagno, Francisco, *Poetas de color*, Havana, Solar y Cía., 1878.
Césaire, Aimé, *Culture et colonisation*, Paris, Présence Africaine, 1956.
The Book of Chilam Balam of Chumayel, trans. by Ralph L. Roys, Norman, University of Oklahoma Press, 1967.
Coulthard, G. R., *Survey of British West Indian Literature in the Commonwealth*, Ithaca, Cornell University Press, 1961.
_____ , ed., *Caribbean Literature*, London, Oxford University Press, 1962.
_____ , *Race and Colour in Caribbean Literature*, London, Oxford University Press, 1962.
Damas, León, *Poetes d'expression française*, Paris, Editions du Seuil, 1947.

Dathorne, O. R., *Caribbean Verse*, London, Heineman, 1967.

——, *Caribbean Narrative*, London, Heineman, 1966.

Fanon, Frantz, *Peau noire,masques blancs*, Paris, Editions du Seuil, 1943.

Fernández de Castro, J. A., *Tema negro en la literatura cubana*, Havana, 1943.

Figueroa, John, *Caribbean Voices* (vol. I), 1966.

Firmin, Anténor, *De l'égalité des races humaines*, Paris, F. Pichon, 1885.

Garcilaso de la Vega, el Inca, *Royal Commentaries of the Incas, and General History of Peru*, trans. by Harold V. Livermore, Austin, University of Texas Press, 1966.

Guirao, Ramón, *Órbita de la poesía afrocubana, 1928–37*, Havana, Ucar, García y Cía., 1939.

Guzmán, Augusto, *Tupaj Katari*, Mexico, Fondo de Cultura Económica, 1944.

Kesteloot, Lilyan, *Anthologie négro-africaine*, Verviers, Marabout University, 1967.

León-Portilla, Miguel, *Visión de los vencidos*. Introd., selección y notas: Miguel León-Portilla; Versión de textos nahuas: Angel Ma. Garibay K., Havana, Casa de las Américas, 1972.

Madden, Richard R., *Poems by a Slave of the Island of Cuba, Recently Liberated*, London, Thomas Ward, 1840.

Mariátegui, José Carlos, *Seven Interpretive Essays on Peruvian Reality*, trans. by Marjory Urquidi, Austin, University of Texas Press, 1971.

Marinello, Juan, *Poética, ensayos en entusiasmo*, Madrid, 1933.

——, *Sobre una inquietud cubana*, in *Revista de Avance*, Havana, 1930.

Martínez Estrada, Ezequiel, *La poesía afrocubana de Nicolas Guillén*, Montevideo, Arca, 1967.

Masdeo Reyes, Jesús, *La raza triste*, Havana, 1924.

Molina, Cristóbal de, *Relación de fábulas y mitos de los incas en el tiempo de su infidélidad*, Lima, Sanmartí y Cía., 1916.

Pereda Valdés, Ildefonso, *Antología de la poesía negra americana*, Montevideo, BUDA, 1953.

Poma de Ayala, Felipe Huaman, *New Cronicle* (sic) *and Good Government*, translation notes and introd. by G. R. Coulthard, Jamaica, University of the West Indies, 1968.

Portuondo, José Antonio, *Bosquejo histórico de las letras cubanas*, Havana, Ministerio de Relaciones Exteriores, 1960.

Porras Barrenchea, Raúl, *Guamán Poma de Ayala*, Lima, Mercurio Peruano, 1946.

Price, Hannibal, *De la réhabilitation de la race noire*, Port-au-Prince, Imprimerie Vellerat, 1900.

Mars, Jean-Price, *Ainsi parla l'oncle*, Port-au-Prince, Imprimerie de Compiègne, 1928.

Ramchand, Kenneth, ed., *West Indian Narrative*, London, Nelson, 1966.

Sodi, Demetrio, *La literatura de los mayas*, Mexico, J. Mortiz, 1964.

St. Louis, Carlos, y Maurice Lubin, *Panorama de la poésie haitienne*, Port-au-Prince, H. Deschamps, 1950.

Varela, J. L., *Ensayos de poesía indígena en Cuba*, Madrid, Edición Cultura Hispánica, 1961.

Viatte, Agusto, *Histoire littéraire de l'Amérique française des origines à 1950*, Paris, Presses Universitaires de France, 1954.

Vila Selma, José, *Procedimientos técnicos en Rómulo Gallegos*, Seville, Escuela de Estudios Hispano-Americanos, 1954.

Vitier, Cintio, *Cincuenta años de poesía cubana 1902–1952*, Havana, Ministerio de Educación, 1952.

CHAPTER TWO

Studies

Carter, Boyd G., *Historia de la literatura hispanoamericana a través de sus revistas*, Mexico, De Andrea, 1968.

Carvalho, Ronald de, *Pequena história da literatura brasileira* (5th ed.), Río de Janeiro, Briguiet y Cía., 1938.
Jones, Willis Knapp, *Breve historia del teatro latinoamericano*, Mexico, De Andrea, 1956.

Anthologies

Alcina Franch, José, *Floresta literaria de la América indígena, antología de la literatura de los pueblos indígenas de América*, Madrid, Aguilar, 1957.
Gaos, José, *Antología del pensamiento de lengua española en la edad contemporánea*, Mexico, Séneca, 1945.
Nicolau d'Olwer, Luis, *Cronistas de las culturas precolombinas, antología*, Mexico, Fondo de Cultura Económica, 1963.

Translations

Arreola, Juan José, *Confabulario and Other Inventions*, trans. by George D. Schade, Austin, University of Texas Press, 1964.
Asturias, Miguel Ángel, *The President*, trans. by Frances Partridge, Harmondsworth, England, Penguin Books, 1972.
Bastos, Augusto Roa, *Son of Man*, trans. by Rachel Caffyn, London, Gollancz, 1965.
Borges, Jorge Luís, *Fictions*, edited and with an introduction by Anthony Kerrigan, London, John Calder, 1965.
Campo, Estanislao del, *Faust*, adapted from the Spanish by Walter Owen, Buenos Aires, Walter Owen, 1943.
Casares, Adolfo Bioy, *The Invention of Morel*, trans. by Ruth L. C. Simms, Austin, University of Texas Press, 1964.
Darío, Rubén, *Selected Poems*, trans. by Lysander Kemp, Austin, University of Texas Press, 1965.
Fuentes, Carlos, *A Change of Skin*, trans. by Sam Hikman, New York, Farrar, Straus, and Giroux, 1968.
Guzmán, Martín Luís, *The Eagle and the Serpent*, trans. by Harriet de Onís, New York, Knopf, 1930.
Hernández, José, *The Gaucho Martín Fierro*, trans. by Frank G. Carrino, Alberto J. Carlos, and Norman Mangouni, Albany, State University of New York Press, 1974.
Machado de Assis, *Joachim Maria, The Posthumous Memoirs of Braz Cubas*, trans. by William L. Grossman, Sao Paulo, Sao Paulo Editore, 1951. Reprinted as *Epitaph of a Small Winner* New York, Noonday Press, 1952.
———, *Philosopher or Dog?*, trans. by Clotilde Wilson, New York, Noonday Press, 1954. Also published as *the Heritage of Quincas Borba*, London, W. H. Allen, 1954.
———, *Dom Casmurro*, trans. by Helen Caldwell, New York, Noonday Press, 1954.
Neruda, Pablo, *Residence on Earth*, trans. by Donald D. Walsh, New York, New Directions, 1973.
———, *Selected Poems*, trans. by Ben Belitt, New York, Grove Press, 1963.
Onetti, Juan Carlos, *A Brief Life*, trans. by Hortense Carpentier, New York, Grossman Publishers, 1976.
Pietri, Arturo Uslar, *The Red Lances*, trans. by Harriet de Onis, New York, Knopf, 1963.
Ramos, Graciliano, *Anguish*, trans. by L. C. Kaplan, New York, Knopf, 1946.
Rojas, Manuel, *Born Guilty*, trans. by Frank Gaynor, London, Gollancz, and New York, Library Publishers, 1955.

Sarmiento, Domingo Faustino, *Life in the Argentine Republic in the Days of the Tyrants, or Civilization and Barbarism*, trans. by Mrs. Horace Mann, Hurd and Houghton, 1868. Reprinted by Collier, 1961.
Villaverde, Cirilo, *Cecilia Valdes*, trans. by Sydney G. Gest, New York, Vantage Press, 1962.
Yáñez, Agustín, *The Edge of the Storm*, trans. by Ethel Brinton, Austin, University of Texas Press, 1963.

CHAPTER THREE

Criticism

Torre, Guillermo de, *Literaturas europeas de vanguardia*, Madrid, Caro Raggio, 1925.
_____ , *Historia de las literaturas de vanguardia*, Madrid, Guadarrama, 1965.

Concrete Poetry

An Anthology of Concrete Poetry, prepared by Emmett Williams, New York, Something Else Press, 1967.
Anthology of Concretism, selected by Eugene Wildman for *The Chicago Review*, Chicago, The Swallow Press, 1968.
Antologia do verso e a poesia concreta, 1949/62, São Paulo, Noigandres, 5, 1962.
Poesía concreta, Lisbon, Embassy of Brazil, 1962.
Solt, Mary Ellen, *A World Looks at Concrete Poetry*, introduction to number 3–4 of *Artes Hispánicas/Hispanic Arts*, New York, Indiana University, Macmillan, 1968.

Translation

Asturias, Miguel Ángel, *Men of Maize*, trans. by Gerald Martin, New York, Delacorte Press/ Seymour Lawrence, 1975.

CHAPTER FOUR

Alonso, Dámaso, *Versión en prosa de "Las soledades" de Luis de Góngora*, Madrid, Sociedad de Estudios y Publicaciones, 1956.
Bakhtine, Mikhail, *La Poétique de Dostoïewski*, Paris, Seuil, 1970.
Barthes, Roland, *Système de la mode*, Paris, Seuil, 1967.
Charpentrat, Pierre, *Le mirage baroque*, Paris, Minuit, 1967.
Chomsky, Noam, *Structures syntaxiques*, Paris, Seuil, 1969.
d'Ors, Eugenio, *Lo barroco*, Madrid, Aguilar, 1964.
Jammes, Robert, *Etudes sur l'oeuvre poétique de Don Luis de Góngora y Argote*, Bordeaux, Institut d'Etudes Ibériques, 1967.

CHAPTER FIVE

Alegría, Fernando, *La poesía chilena*, Mexico, Fondo de Cultura Económica, 1954.
Alvarez Bravo, Armando, *Orbita de Lezama Lima*, Havana, Orbita, 1966.

Arrieta, Rafael, ed., *Historia de la literatura argentina*, Buenos Aires, Peuser, 1959.

Bachofen, J. J., *Myth, Religion and Mother Right*, Princeton, Bollingen Series, Princeton University Press, 1967.

Borges, Jorge Luis, y Adolfo Bioy Casares, *Poesía gauchesca*, v. I, Mexico, Fondo de Cultura Económica, 1955.

The Poem of the Cid, trans. by Lesley Byrd Simpson, Berkeley, University of California Press, 1959.

Diccionario de escritores mexicanos, Mexico, UNAM, 1968.

Fuentes, Carlos, *Casa con dos puertas*, Mexico, Mortiz, 1970.

Ghiano, Juan C., *Poesía argentina del siglo xx*, Mexico, Fondo de Cultura Económica, 1957.

Heidegger, Martin, *Being and Time*, trans. by John Macquarrie and Edward Robinson, New York, Harper, 1962.

Leger, Alexis Saint-Leger, *Anabasis*, trans. by T. S. Eliot, London, Faber and Faber, 1930.

Montezuma de Carvalho, Joaquim de, *Panorama das literaturas das Américas*, Angola, Nova Lisboa, 1958–1959.

Richardson, Jack, "Gabriel Garcia Marquez, Masterwork," *The New York Review of Books*, Volume XIV, Number 6, March 26, 1970.

Rosemberg, Harold, *La tradición de lo nuevo*, Caracas, Monte Ávila, 1969.

Torres Rioseco, Arturo, *Breve historia de la literatura chilena*, Mexico, De Andrea, 1950.

Xirau, Ramón, *Octavio Paz; el sentido de la palabra*, Mexico, Joaquín Mortiz, 1970.

CHAPTER SIX

Auerbach, Erich, "Germinie Lacerteux," *Mímesis*, Mexico, Fondo de Cultura Económica, 1950.

Barthes, Roland, *Le degré zéro de l'écriture*, Paris, Editions du Seuil, 1953.

Benedetti, Mario, *Juan Carlos Onetti y la aventura del hombre*, in *Literatura uruguaya del siglo xx*, Montevideo, Alfa, 1963.

Blanchot, Maurice, *René Char*, in *La part du feu*, Paris, Gallimard, 1948.

———, *Gide et la littérature d'experience*, in *La part du feu*, Paris, Gallimard, 1948.

Borges, Jorge Luis, *Ultraísmo*, in *Nosotros*, no. 151, xv, Buenos Aires, 1921.

Buenos Aires Literaria, no. 9, 1 (about Macedonio Fernández), Buenos Aires, 1953.

Communications, no. 11 (on "Le vraisemblable"), Paris, Editions du Seuil, 1968.

Cortázar, Julio, *La vuelta al día en ochenta mundos*, Mexico, Siglo XXI, 1968.

Change, No. 1 (on "Le montage"), Paris, Editions du Seuil, 1968.

Chomsky, Noam, "Contributions de la Linguistique à l'étude de la pensée," *Change*, Paris, Editions du Seuil, 1968.

———, *Language and Mind*, New York, Harcourt, Brace, 1968.

Duquesne Hispanic Review, No. 3, II (about Manuel Gálvez), Duquesne, Duquesne University, 1963.

Genette, Gerard, *Frontier du récit*, in *Communications*, no. 8, Paris, Editions du Seuil, 1966.

Gómez de la Serna, Ramón, *Prólogo*, in Macedonio Fernández, *Papeles de Recienvenido*, Buenos Aires, Losada, 1944.

Jean, Raymond, *Qu'est-ce que lire*, in *La Nouvelle Critique* ("Littérature et Linguistique"), Paris, 1968.

Jitrik, Noé, *Procedimiento y mensaje en la novela*, Cordoba, Universidad Nacional, 1962.

———, *El 80 y su mundo (presentación de una época)*, Buenos Aires, Jorge Alvarez, 1968.

Kristeva, Julia, *La productivité dite texte*, in *La Nouvelle Critique* ("Littérature et Linguistique"), Paris, 1968.

Lagmanovich, David, *"Rayuela," una novela que no es novela pero no importa*, in *La Gaceta*, Tucumán, 29 March 1964.

Macherey, Pierre, *Borges et le récit fictif,* in *Pour une théorie de la production littéraire,* Paris, Maspero, 1966.

Rozitchner, León, *Persona, cultura y subdesarrollo,* in *Revista de la Universidad de Buenos Aires,* 5 época, no. 1, VI.

Schmucler, Héctor N., *Rayuela: juicio a la literatura,* in *Pasado y Presente,* no. 9, III, Cordoba, 1965.

Todorov, Tzvetan, *Teoría de la literatura de los formalistas rusos,* Buenos Aires, Signos, 1970.

Viñas, David, *Literatura argentina y realidad política,* Buenos Aires, Jorge Alvarez, 1964.

Visca, Arturo S., *Prólogo,* in *Cartas inéditas de Horacio Quiroga,* v. 1, Montevideo, Instituto Nacional de Investigaciones y Archivos Literarios, 1959.

Yurkiévich, Saúl, *Valoración de Vallejo,* Resistencia (Argentina), Universidad Nacional del Nordeste, 1958.

CHAPTER SEVEN

Alegría, Fernando, *Literatura chilena del siglo xx,* Santiago de Chile, Zig-Zag, 2nd ed., 1967.

Dalton, Roque, *La ventana en el rostro,* Mexico, Ediciones de Andrea, 1961.

Fernández Moreno, César (with Horacio Jorge Becco), *Antología lineal de la poesía argentina,* Madrid, Gredos, 1968.

Rojas, Gonzalo, *Contra la muerte,* Santiago, Universitaria, 1964.

Sender, Ramon, *The King and the Queen,* trans. by Mary Low, New York, Vanguard Press, 1948.

———— , *The Sphere,* trans. by F. Giovanelli, London, The Gray Walls Press, 1950.

CHAPTER EIGHT

Abril, Xavier, *César Vallejo o la teoría poética,* Madrid, Taurus, 1962.

Alazraki, Jaime, *La prosa narrativa de Jorge Luis Borges,* Madrid, Gredos, 1968.

Alegría, Fernando, *Las fronteras del realismo: literatura chilena del siglo xx,* Santiago de Chile, Zig-Zag, 1962.

Alonso, Amado, *Poesía y estilo de Pablo Neruda. Interpretación de una poesía hermética,* Buenos Aires, Losada, 1940; Buenos Aires, Sudamericana, 1951.

Anderson Imbert, Enrique, *La crítica literaria contemporánea,* Buenos Aires, Gure, 1957.

———— , *Crítica interna,* Madrid, Taurus, 1961.

Andrade, Mário de, *Movimiento modernista,* Río de Janeiro, CEB, 1942.

Araujo, Orlando, *Lenguaje y creación en la obra de Rómulo Gallegos,* Buenos Aires, Nova, 1955.

Barrenechea, Ana María, *La expresión de la irrealidad en la obra de J. L. Borges,* Mexico, El Colegio de Mexico, 1957.

Borges, Jorge Luis, *Inquisiciones,* Buenos Aires, Proa, 1925.

———— , *Evaristo Carriego,* Buenos Aires, Gleizer, 1930, and Emecé, 1955.

———— , *Discusión,* Buenos Aires, Gleizer, 1932, and Emecé, 1957, 1961.

———— , *Historia de la eternidad,* Buenos Aires, Viau y Zona, 1936, and Emecé, 1953.

———— , *Otras inquisiciones,* Buenos Aires, Sur, 1952, and Emecé, 1960.

———— , *Leopoldo Lugones* (with Betina Edelberg), Buenos Aires, Troquel, 1955, Pleamar, 1965.

Carballo, Emmanuel, *Cuentistas mexicanos modernos,* Mexico, Biblioteca Minima Mexicana, 1956.

Carpeaux, Otto María, *Origins e fins*, Río de Janeiro, Casa do Estudante do Brasil, 1943.
_____ , *Presenças*, Río de Janeiro, Instituto Nacional do Livro, 1958.
Coutinho, Afrânio, *Correntes cruzadas*, Río de Janeiro, A. Noite, 1953.
_____ , *Da crítica e da nova crítica*, Río de Janeiro, Civilização Brasileira, 1957.
_____ , *Introdução a literatura no Brasil*, Río de Janeiro, São José, 1959.
Coyné, André, *César Vallejo su obra poética*, Lima, Letras Peruanas, 1958.
Escobar, Alberto, *Patio de letras*, Lima, Caballo de Troya, 1965.
Fernández Moreno, César, *Esquema de Borges*, Buenos Aires, Perrot, 1957.
_____ , *Introducción a la poesia*, Mexico, Fondo de Cultura Económica, 1962.
Freyre, Gilberto, *Vida, forma e cor*, Río de Janeiro, José Olympio, 1962.
García Canclini, Néstor, *Cortázar, una antropología poética*, Buenos Aires, Nova, 1968.
Goic, Cedomil, *La poesía de Vicente Huidobro*, Santiago de Chile, Ed. de los Anales de la Universidad, 1956.
_____ , *La novela chilena. Los mitos degradados*, Santiago de Chile, Editorial Universitaria, 1968.
Gutiérrez Girardot, Rafael, *Jorge Luis Borges. Ensayo de interpretación*, Madrid, Insula, 1959.
Jitrik, Noé, *Horacio Quiroga, una obra de experiencia y riesgo*, Buenos Aires, Ediciones Culturales Argentinas, 1959.
Lezama Lima, José, *Analecta del reloj*, Havana, Orígenes, 1953.
_____ , *La expresión americana*, Havana, Instituto Nacional de Cultura, 1957.
Liscano, Juan, *Rómulo Gallegos y su tiempo*, Caracas, Universidad Central de Venezuela, 1961.
Mallea, Eduardo, *El sayal y la púrpura*, Buenos Aires, Losada, 1947.
Martínez Estrada, Ezequiel, *Muerte y transfiguración de Martín Fierro*, Mexico, Fondo de Cultura Económica, 1948.
_____ , *El mundo maravilloso de Guillermo Enrique Hudson*, Mexico, Fondo de Cultura Económica, 1951.
Martins, Wilson, *Interpretações*, Río de Janeiro, José Olympio, 1946.
_____ , *A crítica literária no Brasil*, São Paulo, Departamento de Cultura, 1952.
Monguió, Luis, *César Vallejo. Vida y obra*, Lima, Perú Nuevo, 1960.
Paz, Octavio, *Las peras del olmo*, Mexico, Universidad Nacional Autónoma, 1957.
_____ , *Cuadrivio*, Mexico, Mortiz, 1965.
Picón Salas, Mariano, *Obras selectas*, Madrid, Edime, 1961.
_____ , *Estudios de literatura venezolana*, Madrid, Edime, 1962.
Pino Saavedra, Yolando, *La poesía de Julio Herrera y Reissig*, Santiago de Chile, Prensas de la Universidad de Chile, 1932.
Reyes, Alfonso, *Cuestiones estéticas*, in *Obras completas*, v. I, Mexico, Fondo de Cultura Económica, 1955.
_____ , *Simpatías y diferencias*, in *O.c.*, v. IV, Mexico, FCE, 1956.
_____ , *El deslinde*, in *O.c.*, v. XV, Mexico, FCE, 1963.
Rodríguez Monegal, Emir, *Literatura uruguaya del medio siglo*, Montevideo, Alfa, 1966.
_____ , *El viajero inmóvil. Introducción a Pablo Neruda*, Buenos Aires, Losada, 1966.
_____ , *El desterrado. Vida y obra de Horacio Quiroga*, Buenos Aires, Losada, 1968.
Rosenblat, Ángel, *La primera visión de América y otros ensayos*, Caracas, Ministerio de Educación, 1965.
Sábato, Ernesto, *El escritor y sus fantasmas*, Madrid, Aguilar, 1963.
Tamayo, Marcial, and Adolfo Ruiz-Díaz, *Borges, enigma y clave*, Buenos Aires, Nuestro Tiempo, 1955.
Vita, Luis Wáshington, *Tendencias do pensamento estético contemporâneo no Brasil*, Río de Janeiro, Civilização brasileira, 1967.
Xirau, Ramón, *Tres poetas de la soledad*, Mexico, Antigua Librería Robredo, 1955.
_____ , *Poesía hispanoamericana y española*, Mexico, Imprenta Universitaria, 1961.

CHAPTER NINE

Bachtin, Michail, *Dostoevskij. Poetica e stilistica* [Italian translation of the 1963 Russian text], Turin, Einaudi, 1968.

Bakhtin, Mikhail, *Rabelais and His World*, Cambridge, Mass., MIT, 1968.

Bann, Stephen, *Concrete Poetry. An International Anthology*, London, London Magazine Editions, 1967.

Bense, Max, *Der Begriff Text*, in *Augenblick*, no. 3/58, Darmstadt, J. G. Bläschke.

_____ , *Text und Kontext*, in *Augenblick*, no. 1/59, Darmstadt, J. G. Bläschke.

_____ , *Theorie der Texte*, Cologne, Kiepenheuer & Witsch, 1962.

_____ , *Konkrete Poesie* (anlässlich des Sonderheftes *Noigandres* zum zehnjährigen Bestehen dieser Gruppe für "Konkrete Poesie" in Brasilien), *Sprache im Technischen Zeitalter*, no. 15/65, Stuttgart, Kohlhammer.

_____ , *Brasilianische Intelligenz*, Wiesbaden, Limes, 1965.

Borges, Jorge Luis, *Prólogo* in *Nueva antología personal*, Buenos Aires, Emecé, 1968.

Brito, Mário da Silva, *Pensamento e ação de Oswald de Andrade*, in *Revista Brasiliense*, no. 16/58, São Paulo, Editôra Brasiliense.

Campos, Augusto de, *Pound (Made New) in Brazil*, in *Ezra Pound*, vol. 1, Paris, L'Herne, 1965.

Campos, Augusto de, *Balançó da Bossa*, São Paulo, Perspectiva, 1968.

_____ , *Musica popular de vanguarda no Brasil*, in *Revista de Letras*, no. 3/69, Mayagüez, Universidad de Puerto Rico.

_____ , y Haroldo de Campos, *Re/Visão de Sousândrade*, São Paulo, Invenção, 1964.

_____ , y Haroldo de Campos, *Sousândrade*, Río de Janeiro, Agir, 1966.

Campos, Haroldo de, *Miramar na Mira*, introduction to *Memórias Sentimentais de João Miramar*, by Oswald de Andrade, São Paulo, Difusão Européia do Livro, 1964 (2d ed.).

_____ , *Uma poética da radicalidade*, introduction to *Poesias Reunidas O. Andrade*, São Paulo, Difusão Européia do Livro, 1966 (2d ed.).

_____ , *Metalinguagem*, Petrópolis, Vozes, 1967.

_____ , *Oswald de Andrade*, Río de Janeiro, Agir, 1967.

_____ , *O jôgo de amarelinha* (on *Rayuela*), *Correio da Manhã*, Río de Janeiro, 30 July 1967.

_____ , *Romantismo e poética sincrônica*, in *Correio da Manhã*, Río de Janeiro, 26 November, 1967.

_____ , *Morfologia do Macunaíma*, in *Correio da Manhã*, Río de Janeiro, 23 April, 1967.

_____ , *A arte no horizonte do provável*, São Paulo, Perspectiva, 1969.

_____ , *Avanguardia e sincronia nella letteratura brasiliana odierna*, in *Aut-Aut*, no. 109–110/69, Milan, Lampugnani Nigri.

Cândido de Mello e Souza, António, *Brigada ligeira*, São Paulo, Livraria Martins Editôra, 1945.

_____ , *Literatura e sociedade*, São Paulo, Editôra Nacional, 1965.

Cortázar, Julio, *Notas sobre la novela contemporánea*, in *Realidad*, no. 8/48, Buenos Aires.

_____ , *Situación de la novela*, in *Cuadernos Americanos*, no. 4/50.

Curtius, Ernst Robert, *Literatura européia e idade méida latina*, [Portuguese trans. of the German text of, 1948], Río de Janeiro, Instituto Nacional do Livro, 1957.

Eliot, T. S., *Dante*, in *Los poetas metafísicos y otros ensayos* [Spanish trans. of Selected Essays (1917–1932)], Buenos Aires, Emecé, 1944.

Erlich, Victor, *Russian formalism*, 's-Gravenhage, Mouton, 1955.

Fernández Moreno, César, *Introducción a Macedonio Fernández*, Buenos Aires, Talía, 1960.

Gomringer, Eugen, *Die ersten Jahre der Konkreten Poesie*, in *Worte sind Schatten*, Reibek bei Hamburg, Rowohlt, 1969.

Grembecki, Maria Helena, *Mário de Andrade e "L'Esprit Nouveau"*, São Paulo, Instituto de Estudos Brasileiros, 1969.

Harss, Luis and Barbara Dohmann, *Into the Mainstream; Conversations with Latin American Writers*, New York, Harper and Row, 1967.

Hegel, G. W. Friedrich, *Esthétique*, [French trans. of the German text of 1835], Paris, Aubier, 1944.

Hocke, G. R. *Manierismus in der Literatur*, Hamburg, Rowohlt, 1959.

Hurtado, Efraín, *Entrevista con Severo Sarduy*, in *Actual*, no. 5/69, Mérida, Universidad de los Andes.

Jauss, H. R., *Littérature médiévale et théorie des Generes*, in *Poétique*, no. 1/70, Paris, Seuil.

Jakobson, Roman, *Linguistics and poetics*, in *Style in Language* (T. A. Sebeok editor), Cambridge, Mass., MIT, 1960.

———, *Essais de linguistique générale*, Paris, Minuit, 1963.

Kristeva, Julia, *Bakhtine, le mot, le dialogue et le roman*, in *Critique*, no. 239/67, Paris, Minuit.

Le tesi del '29 (Il Circolo Linguistico di Praga), Milan, Silva, 1966. *Les théses de 1929* [Reprint of French original], *Change*, no. 3/69, Paris, Seuil.

Langer, Susanne, *Feeling and Form*, London, Routledge and Kegan Paul, 1953.

Mallarmé, Stéphane, *Oeuvres complètes* (especially: *Crise de vers, Etalages, Le livre, instrument spirituel*), Paris, Gallimard, 1945.

Marx, Karl, and Friedrich Engels, *Sur la littérature et l'art (textes choisis)*, Paris, Editions Sociales, 1954.

McLuhan, Marshall, *Joyce, Mallarmé and the Press, Sewanee Review*, no. 1/54, Sewanee, Tennessee, The University of the South.

———, *The Gutenberg Galaxy*, Toronto, University of Toronto, 1962.

———, *Understanding Media: The Extensions of Man*, New York, McGraw Hill, 1965.

Mendilow, A. A., *Time and the Novel*, London, Peter Nevill, 1952.

Mukarovsky, Jan, *The Esthetics of Language*, in *A Prague School Reader on Esthetics, Literary Structure and Style* (Paul L. Garvin, editor), Washington, Georgetown University, 1964.

Obieta, Adolfo de, *Macedonio Fernández*, in *Papeles de Macedonio Fernández*, Buenos Aires, Editorial Universitaria de Buenos Aires, 1964.

Orfeo, revista de poesía y teoría poética, "Homenaje a Vicente Huidobro," no. 13–14, Santiago, Chile.

Paz, Octavio, *Poesía en movimiento* (anthology), Mexico, Siglo XXI, 1966.

———, *The Word as Foundation*, in *The Times Literary Supplement*, London, 14 November 1968.

Pignatari, Décio, *Informação Linguagem. Comunicação*, São Paulo, Perspectiva, 1968.

Pound, Ezra, *ABC of Reading*, London, G. Routledge and Sons, 1934.

Prado, Paulo, *Poesia pau-brasil, Poesias reunidas O. Andrade*, São Paulo, Difusão Européia do Livro, 1966 (2d ed.).

Proença, M. Cavalcanti,*Roteiro de Macunaíma*, São Paulo, Anhembi, 1955.

———, *Mário de Andrade*, Río de Janeiro, Agir, 1960.

Propp, Vladimir, *Morfologia della fiaba* [Italian trans. of the Russian text of 1928], Turin, Einaudi, 1966.

Romero, Sílvio, *História da literatura brasileira*, Río de Janeiro, Garnier, 1888.

Sarduy, Severo, *Escrito sobre un cuerpo*, Buenos Aires, Sudamericana, 1969.

Sklovskij, Viktor, *Theorie der Prosa* [German trans. of the 1925 Russian text], Frankfurt am Main, S. Fischer, 1966.

Sola, Graciela de, *Julio Cortázar y el hombre nuevo*, Buenos Aires, Sudamericana, 1968.

Sousândrade's Stock in *The Times Literary Supplement*, London, 24 June 1965.

Toppani, Gabriella, *Intervista con Borges*, in *Il Verri*, no. 18/65, Milan, Feltrinelli.

Valéry, Paul, *Variété II*, Paris, Gallimard, 1930.

Videla, Gloria, *El ultraísmo*, Madrid, Gredos, 1963.

Undurraga, Antonio de, *Teoría del creacionismo*, in Vicente Huidobro, *Poesía y prosa*, Antología, Madrid, Aguilar, 1957.

Wellek, René, and Austin Warren, *Literary Theory*, New York, 1955, 2d ed.
Wilson, Edmund, *Axel's Castle*, New York, Charles Scribner's, 1931.

CHAPTER TEN

See relevant issues of the journal *Casa de las Américas* (Havana) devoted to specific themes. For example: on the new Latin American novel, number 26, October–November 1964; on the influence of Rubén Darío, number 42, May–June 1967; on the situation of the intellectual in Latin America, number 45, October–November 1967.

Translations

Cortázar, Julio, *All Fires the Fire and Other Stories*, trans. by Suzanne Jill Levine, New York, Pantheon, 1973.
Garcilaso de la Vega, el Inca, *Royal Commentaries of the Incas, and General History of Peru*, trans. by Harold V. Livermore, Austin, University of Texas Press, 1966.
Hugo, Victor Marie, *The Man Who Laughs*, New York, NBI Press, 1967.
Mariátegui, José Carlos, *Seven Interpretative Essays on Peruvian Reality*, trans. by Marjory Urquidi, Austin, University of Texas Press, 1971.

CHAPTER ELEVEN

Beyhaut, Gustavo, *Sociedad y cultura latinoamericanas en la realidad internacional*, Montevideo, CIR, 1959.
Bomfim, Manoel, *A América Latina—males de origem*, Río de Janeiro, H. Garnier, 1905.
Cortázar, Julio, interview, *Life*, vol. 33, no. 7, 7 April 1969, pp. 45–55.
Franco, Pablo, *La influencia de los Estados Unidos en la América Latina*, Montevideo, Ediciones Tauro, 1967.
Furtado, Celso, *Desenvolvimento e subdesenvolvimento*, Río de Janeiro, Editôra Fôndo de Cultura, 1961.
———, *Subdesenvolvimento e estagnação na América Latina*, Río de Janeiro, Civilização Brasileira, 1966.
Lacoste, Yves, *Geografia do subdesenvolvimento* (trans. from French), São Paulo, Difusão Européia do Livro, 1966.
Stavenhagen, Rodolfo, *Siete tesis equivocadas sobre América Latina*, in *Política Exterior Independiente*, I, 1, Río de Janeiro, 1965, pp. 67–80.
Vieira de Mello, Mário, *Desenvolvimento e cultura—O problema do estetismo no Brasil*, São Paulo, Companhia Editora Nacional, 1963.

CHAPTER TWELVE

Agosti, Héctor P., *Por una política de la cultura*, Buenos Aires, Procyon, 1956.
Lenin, V. I., *Imperialism: The Highest Stage of Capitalism*, New York, International Publishers, 1939.
Mariátegui, José Carlos, *Seven Interpretive Essays on Peruvian Reality*, trans. by Marjory Urquidi, Austin, University of Texas Press, 1971.
Marinello, Juan, *Literatura hispanoamericana*, Mexico, Universidad Nacional de Mexico, 1937.

Schulman, González, Loveluck, Alegría, *Coloquio sobre la novela hispanoamericana*, Mexico, Fondo de Cultura Económica, 1967.

Torres Rioseco, Arturo (ed.), *La novela iberoamericana. Memoria del Quinto Congreso del Instituto de Literatura Iberoamericana*, Albuquerque, N. M., The University of New Mexico Press, 1952.

Yáñez, Agustín, *El contenido social de la literatura iberoamericana*, Mexico, El Colegio de Mexico, 1944.

CHAPTER THIRTEEN

Essays

Collazos, Oscar, Julio Cortázar y Mario Vargas Llosa, *Literatura en la revolución y revolución en la literatura*, Mexico, Siglo XXI, 1970.

Mariátegui, José Carlos, *Seven Interpretive Essays on Peruvian Reality*, trans. by Marjory Urquidi, Austin, University of Texas Press, 1971.

La naturaleza y el hombre en la novela hispanoamericana, first International Seminar on Hispanic American Literature, Antofagasta, Universidad del Norte, 1969.

Anthologies

Arbeláez, Fernando, *Nuevos narradores colombianos*, Caracas, Monte Ávila, 1968.

Caballero Bonald, José Manuel, *Narrativa cubana de la Revolución*, Madrid, Alianza, 1968.

Carballo, Emmanuel, *Narrativa mexicana de hoy*, Madrid, Alianza, 1969.

Cotelo, Rubén, *Narradores uruguayos*, Caracas, Monte Ávila, 1969.

Escobar, Alberto, *Antología de la poesía peruana*, Lima, Paraíso, 1968.

Oviedo, José Migues, *Antologia de la poesía cubana*, Lima, Paraíso, 1968.

———— , *Narradores peruanos*, Caracas, Monte Ávila, 1968.

Translations

Asturias, Miguel Ángel, *Men of Maize*, trans. by Gerald Martin, New York, Delacorte Press/ Seymour Lawrence, 1975.

Gallegos, Rómulo, *Doña Bárbara*, trans. by Robert J. Malloy, New York, P. Smith, 1948.

Notes on Contributors

ALEGRÍA, FERNANDO

Chilean writer and critic (born Santiago, 1918). Principal works: *La poesía chilena* [Chilean Poetry], Mexico, 1954; *Walt Whitman en Hispanoamerica* [Walt Whitman in Hispanic America], Mexico, 1954; *Caballo de copas* [Horse of Hearts] (n), Santiago, 1957; *Las fronteras del realismo* [The Frontiers of Realism], Santiago, 1962; *Historia de la novela hispanoamericana* [History of the Hispanic American Novel], Mexico, 1963; *Literatura chilena del siglo xx* [Twentieth-Century Chilean Literature] (e), Santiago, 1967; *Los dias contados* [The Numbered Days] (n), Mexico, 1970; *Amerika, Amerikka, Amerikkka,* Santiago, 1971; *Literatura ya revolución* [Literature and Revolution], Mexico, 1971; *El paso de los gansos* [The Goose-Step] (n), New York, 1975; *Homenaje a Neruda—Homage to Neruda* (p), Palo Alto, California, 1978. Has taught at the University of Chile and at the University of California (Berkeley), and served as Cultural Attache of the Embassy of Chile in Washington, D.C., during 1971–73. Currently professor of Hispanic-American literature at Stanford University.

BERG, MARY G.

North American essayist and teacher of Latin American studies (New York, 1940). Has written about, and translated, works of nineteenth- and twentieth-century Latin American fiction. Has taught at Harvard University, the University of Colorado (Boulder), and is currently at the California Institute of Technology (Pasadena).

CAMPOS, HAROLDO DE

Brazilian poet and essayist (Sao Paulo, 1929). Principal works: *Auto de possesso* [Document of the Possessed], (p), Sao Paulo, 1950; *Servidão de passagem* [Servitude of Passage] (p), Sao Paulo, 1962; *Teoria da poesia*

Abbreviations: (a) anthology, (e) essays, (n) novel, (s) short stories, (sw) selected or collected works, (p) poetry.

concreta: textos criticos e manifestos [The Theory of Concrete Poetry: Critical Texts and Manifestos] (with Augusto de Campos and Decio Pignatari), Sao Paulo, 1965; *Metalinguagem: ensáios de teoria e crítica literária* [Metalanguage: Essays in Literary Theory and Criticism], Petrópolis, 1967; *A arte no horizonte do provável* [Art on the Horizon of the Probable] Sao Paulo, 1969, *Guimarães Rosa em três dimensões* [Guimarães Rosa in Three Dimensions] (e), Sao Paulo, 1970; *A operação do texto* [Operation of the Text] (e), Sao Paulo, 1976; *Ideograma: lógica, poesia, linguagem* [Ideogram: Logic, Poetry, Language], Sao Paulo, 1977; *Macunaíma: el héroe sin ningún carácter* [Macunaíma: a Hero Without Character] (e), Barcelona, 1977; *Ruptura dos gêneros na literatura americana* [The Rupture of Genres in American Literature] (e), Sao Paulo, 1977. Member of the concrete-poetry group *Noigandres*.

CÂNDIDO, ANTÓNIO

Brazilian critic (Rio de Janeiro, 1918). Principal works: *Formaçao da literatura brasileira (1750–1880)* [The Formation of Brazilian Literature, 1750–1880], 2 volumes, Sao Paulo, 1964; *Introducción a la literatura de Brasil* [Introduction to Brazilian Literature], Caracas, 1968; *Literatura e sociedade: Estudos de teoria e história literária* [Literature and Society: Studies in Literary Theory and History], Sao Paulo, 1976; *Tese e antítese* [Thesis and Antithesis] (e), Sao Paulo, 1978. Currently professor of literary theory and comparative literature at the University of Sao Paulo.

COULTHARD, GEORGE ROBERT

English critic, resident of Jamaica (Bradford, 1921–1974). Principal works: *Visitor of Mist* (translations of the poetry of Jorge Carrera Andrade), London, 1950; *Race and Color in West Indian Literature*, Oxford, 1962; *Anthology of Caribbean Literature*, London, 1966. Was professor of New World literature at the University of the West Indies (Mona).

FERNÁNDEZ MORENO, CÉSAR

Argentine poet and essayist (Buenos Aires, 1919). Principal works: *Introducción a Macedonio Fernández* [Introduction to Macedonio Fernández] (e), Buenos Aires, 1960; *Introduction a la poesía* [Introduction to Poetry] (e), Mexico, 1962; *Argentino hasta la muerte* [Argentine to the Bitter End], (p), Buenos Aires, 1963; *Los aeropuertos* [Airports] (p), Buenos Aires, 1967; *La realidad y los papeles* [Reality and Papers] (e), Madrid, 1967; *Ambages* [Circumlocutions] (p), Caracas, 1972; *Argentina* (e), Barcelona, 1972; *Buenos Aires, me vas a matar* [B.A., You're Going to Kill Me] (p), Mexico, 1977. Has been director of Unesco's Regional Culture Office for Latin America and the Caribbean.

FERNÁNDEZ RETAMAR, ROBERTO

Cuban poet and essayist (Havana, 1930). Principal works: *La poesía contemporánea en Cuba, 1927–1953* [Contemporary Cuban Poetry, 1927–1953], Havana, 1954; *Idea de la estilística* [Notion of the Study of Style], Havana, 1958; *Ensayo de otro mundo* [Essay of Another World], Havana, 1967, and Santiago, 1969; *Poesía reunida (1948–1965)* [Collected Poems (1948–1965)], Havana, 1966; *A quien pueda interesar. Poesía, 1958–1970* [To Whom It May Concern. Poetry, 1958–1970], Mexico, 1970; *Calibán. Apuntes sobre la cultura en nuestra América* [Caliban. Notes on Culture in Our America], Mexico, 1971; *Cuba, nuestra América, los Estados Unidos* [Cuba, Our America, the United States] (sw), Mexico, 1973; *Cuaderno paralelo* [Parallel Notebook] (p), Havana, 1973; *Circunstancia de la poesía* [The Circumstance of Poetry] (e), Buenos Aires, 1974; *Nuestra América y el Occidente* [Our America and the West], Mexico, 1978. Has taught at Yale University and currently teaches at the University of Havana; is director of the Cuban journal *Casa de las Américas* [House of the Americas].

JITRIK, NOÉ

Argentine writer (Rivera, 1928). Principal works: *Feriados* [Holidays] (p), Buenos Aires, 1956; *Horacio Quiroga, una obra de experiencia y riesgo* [Horacio Quiroga, Experience and Risk in His Work] (e), Buenos Aires, 1959; *Procedimientos y mensaje en la novela* [Method and Message in the Novel] (e), Córdoba, 1962; *El escritor argentino: dependencia o libertad* [The Argentine Writer: Dependence or Freedom] (e), Buenos Aires, 1967; *Ensayos y estudios de literatura argentina* [Essays and Studies of Argentine Literature], Buenos Aires, 1970; *El 80 y su mundo* [The Generation of 1880 and Its World], Buenos Aires, 1968; *El fuego de la especie* [The Fire of the Species] (e), Buenos Aires, 1971; *La novela futura de Macedonio Fernández* [The Novel of Macedonio Fernández as Forerunner], Caracas, 1973; *Comer y comer: poemas 1965–1970* [To Eat and Eat: Poems, 1965–1970], Buenos Aires, 1974; *El no existente caballero: la idea de personaje y su evolución en la narrativa latinoamericana* [The Nonexistent Gentleman: The Idea of the Character in Latin American Fiction and Its Evolution] (e), Buenos Aires, 1975; *Producción literaria y producción social* [Literary Production and Social Production] (e), Buenos Aires, 1975; *Las contradicciones del modernismo: productividad poética y situación sociológica* [The Contradictions of Modernism: Poetic Productivity and Sociological Situation] (e), Mexico, 1978. Has taught at the universities of Córdoba, Buenos Aires, and Besançon; currently teaches at El Colegio de México (Mexico City).

LEZAMA LIMA, JOSÉ

Cuban writer (Havana, 1910–1976). Principal works: *Tratados en la Habana* [Treatises in Havana], Havana, 1958; *Paradiso* (n), Havana, 1966;

Órbita de Lezama Lima [The Orbit of Lezama Lima] (sw), Havana, 1966; *La expresión americana* [American Expression] (e), Santiago, Chile, 1969; *La cantidad hechizada* [The Charmed Duration] (e), Havana, 1970; *Poesía completa* [Whole Poetry] (sw), Havana, 1970; *Las eras imaginarias* [the Imaginary Eras], Madrid, 1971; *Introducción a los vasos órficos* [Introduction to Orphic Vessels], Barcelona, 1971; *Oppiano Licario* (n), Mexico, 1977. Founder and director of the journal *Orígenes* [Origins] (Havana, since 1944).

MARTÍNEZ, JOSÉ LUIS

Mexican critic (Jalisco, 1918). Principal works: *Situación de la literatura mexicana contemporánea* [The State of Contemporary Mexican Literature], Mexico, 1948; *Literatura mexicana siglo xx* [Twentieth-Century Mexican Literature], Mexico, 1949; *Los problemas de nuestra cultura literaria* [The Problems of Our Literary Culture], Guadalajara, 1953; *La expresión nacional* [Our National Expressiveness], Mexico, 1955; *Unidad y diversidad de la literatura latinoamericana* [The Unity and Diversity of Latin American Literature], Mexico, 1972; *Obras: poesías, teatro, artículos y cartas* [Works: Poetry, Theater, Articles and Letters], Mexico, 1975. Professor at the National University of Mexico.

ORTEGA, JULIO

Peruvian writer (Casma, 1942). Principal works: *De este reino* [Of This Kingdom] (p), Lima, 1964; *Teatro* [Theater], Lima, 1965; *Las Islas Blancas* [The White Islands] (s), Lima, 1966; *La contemplación y la fiesta: Notas sobre la novela latinoamericana actual* [Contemplation and Feast: Notes on the Contemporary Latin American Novel], Caracas, 1969; *Mediodía* [Noon] (n), Buenos Aires, 1970; *Figuración de la persona* [Imagining the Personage] (e), Barcelona, 1970; *Imagen de la literatura peruana actual* [Image of Current Peruvian Literature] (e), Lima, 1971; *Antología* [An Anthology of José Martí], Barcelona, 1973; *Relato de la utopía; notas sobre narrativa cubana de la revolución* [A Narrative of Utopia: Notes On Cuban Fiction of the Revolutionary Period], Barcelona, 1973; *La imaginación crítica; ensayos sobre la modernidad en el Perú* [The Critical Imagination: Essays on Modernity in Peru], Lima, 1974; *César Vallejo*, Madrid, 1974; *Guillermo Cabrera Infante* (e), Madrid, 1974; *Rituales* [Rituals] (p), Lima, 1976; *La cultura peruana: Experiencia y conciencia* [Peruvian Culture: Experience and Consciousness] (e), Mexico, 1978. Has taught at the universities of Pittsburgh, Yale, and Florida, and is currently at the University of Texas at Austin.

OVIEDO, JOSÉ MIGUEL

Peruvian critic (Lima, 1934). Principal works: *César Vallejo, estudio crítico-biográfico* [César Vallejo, A Critical Biography], Lima, 1964; *Genio y figura*

de Ricardo Palma [The Genius and Stature of Ricardo Palma], Buenos Aires,
1965; *Piezas dramáticas* [Dramatic Pieces], Lima, 1967; *Narradores
peruanos* [Peruvian Storytellers] (a), Caracas, 1968; *Antología de la poesía
cubana* [Anthology of Cuban Poetry], Lima, 1968; *Antología del cuento
cubano* [Anthology of the Cuban Short Story], Lima, 1968; *Mario Vargas
Llosa: la invención de una realidad* [Mario Vargas Llosa: The Invention of
His Reality], Barcelona, 1970; *Conversaciones* [Conversations], Lima, 1972;
Estos 13 [These Thirteen] (sw), Lima, 1973. Has taught at the University of
Essex (England), the University of San Marcos, and the Catholic University
of Lima, and is currently at the University of Indiana.

PORTUONDO, JOSÉ ANTONIO

Cuban critic (Santiago, 1911). Principal works: *Proceso de la cultura cubana*
[The Process of Cuban Culture], Havana, 1939; *El contenido social de la
literatura cubana* [The Social Content of Cuban Literature], Mexico, 1944;
José Martí, crítico literario [José Martí, Literary Critic]. Washington, 1953;
El heroísmo intelectual [Intellectual Heroism], Mexico, 1955; *Bosquejo
histórico de las letras cubanas* [Historical Sketch of Cuban Literature],
Havana, 1960; *Estética y revolución* [Esthetics and Revolution], Havana,
1963; *Crítica de la época y otros ensayos* [Critique of the Age and Other
Essays], Havana, 1965; *El pensamiento vivo de Maceo* [The Living Thought
of Maceo], Havana, 1971; *Concepto de la poesía y otros ensayos* [The
Concept of Poetry and Other Essays], Havana, 1971, and Mexico, 1974;
Sobre el concepto marxista del héroe, a propósito de Camilo y el Che [On the
Marxist Concept of the Hero, with Reference to Camilo and Che], Havana,
1975. Has taught at the University of Havana and directed its Institute of
Literature and Linguistics. Currently ambassador of Cuba before the Holy
See.

RODRÍGUEZ MONEGAL, EMIR

Uruguayan critic (Melo, 1921). Principal works: *El juicio de los parricidas:
la nueva generación argentina y sus maestros* [The Judgment of the
Parricides: The New Argentine Generation and Its Teachers], Buenos Aires,
1956; *Narradores de esta América* [Storytellers of Our America], Monte-
video, 1961; *El cuento uruguayo, de los orígenes al modernismo* [The
Uruguayan Short Story, From Its Origins Until Modernism], Buenos Aires,
1965; *El viajero inmóvil (Introducción a Pablo Neruda)* [The Stationary
Traveler (An Introduction to Pablo Neruda)], Buenos Aires, 1966, and
Caracas, 1977; *El desterrado (Vida y obra de Horacio Quiroga)* [The Exile
(The Life and Work of Horacio Quiroga)], Buenos Aires, 1967; *El otro
Andrés Bello* [The Other Andrés Bello], Caracas, 1968; *El arte de narrar
(Diálogos)* [The Art of Storytelling (Dialogues)], Caracas, 1968; *Borges par
lui-même*, Paris, 1970; *Notas sobre (hacia) el boom* [Notes On (Toward) the
Boom in Latin American Literature], Caracas, 1972; *Rodó en el novecientos*

[Rodó At the Turn of the Century] (e), Montevideo, 1976. Teaches Latin American and comparative literature at Yale University.

SARDUY, SEVERO

Cuban writer and essayist (Camagüey, 1937). Principal works: *Gestos* [Gestures], Barcelona, 1963; *De dónde son los cantantes* [Where Are the Singers From] (n), Mexico, 1967; *Escrito sobre un cuerpo* [Writings on a Body] (e), Buenos Aires, 1969; *Cobra* (n), Buenos Aires, 1972; *Overdose*, Las Palmas, 1972; *Barroco* [Baroque] (e), Buenos Aires, 1974; *Big Bang*, Barcelona, 1974; *Maitreya*, Barcelona, 1978. Resides in Paris, and is literary consultant to Éditions du Seuil.

SCHULMAN, IVAN A.

North American critic and professor (New York, 1931). Principal works: *Symbol and Color in the Works of José Martí* (e), Madrid, 1960, 1970; *Genesis of Modernism: Martí, Nájera, Silva, Casal* (e), Mexico, 1966, 1968; *El modernismo hispanoamericano* [Hispanic American Modernism] (e), Buenos Aires, 1969; *Coloquio sobre la novela hispanoamericana* [Colloquium on the Hispanic American Novel] (e, sw), Mexico, 1967; *Martí, Darío, y el modernismo* [Martí, Darío, and Modernism] (with Manuel Pedro González) (e), Madrid, 1969, 1974; *Juan Francisco Manzano, Autobiografía de un esclavo* [Juan Francisco Manzano, Autobiography of a Slave], Madrid, 1975. Has taught at the universities of California, Michigan, Rio de Janeiro, and Washington University (St. Louis), and is presently Graduate Research Professor and Director of the Center for Latin American Studies of the University of Florida.

SUCRE, GUILLERMO

Venezuelan poet and essayist (Ciudad Bolívar, 1933). Principal works: *Mientras suceden los días* [As the Days Flow By] (p), Caracas, 1961; *Borges, el poeta* [Borges, the Poet] (e), Mexico, 1967; *La mirada* [The Glance] (p), Caracas, 1970; *Jorge Luis Borges* (e), Paris, 1971; *Acerca de Octavio Paz* [About Octavio Paz], Montevideo, 1974; *La máscara, la transparencia: ensayos sobre poesía hispanoamericana* [The Mask, the Transparency: Essays on Hispanic American Poetry], Caracas, 1975. Has directed the journal *Imagen* [Image] (Caracas) and has taught at the Central University of Venezuela and the University of Pittsburgh.

XIRAU, RAMÓN

Mexican essayist and philospher (Barcelona, 1924). Principal works: *Sentido de la presencia* [The Meaning of Presence], Mexico, 1953; *Tres poetas de la soledad* [Three Poets of Solitude], Mexico, 1955; *Introducción a la historia de la filosofía* [Introduction to the History of Philosophy], Mexico, 1964; *Genio y figura de Sor Juana Inés de la Cruz* [The Genius and Stature of Sister Juana Inés de la Cruz], Buenos Aires, 1967; *Palabra y silencio* [The Word and the Silence], Mexico, 1968; *The Nature of Man* (with Erich Fromm), New York, 1968; *Ciudades* [Cities], Mexico, 1970; *Octavio Paz: el sentido de la palabra* [Octavio Pax: The Meaning of the Word], Mexico, 1970; *Pintura moderna de México y cultura mexicana* [Modern Mexican Painting and Mexican Culture], Mexico, 1970; *Poesía iberoamericana: doce ensayos* [Ibero-American Poetry: Twelve Essays], Mexico, 1972; *Mito y poesía; ensayos sobre literatura contemporánea de lengua española* [Myth and Poetry: Essays on Contemporary Spanish-Language Literature], Mexico, 1973; *Poesía y conocimiento: Borges, Lezama Lima, O. Paz* [Poetry and Understanding: Borges, Lezama Lima, O. Paz], Mexico, 1978. Teaches at the Autonomous National University of Mexico and directs the journal *Diálogos* [Dialogues] published by El Colegio de México.

Nélida Negri and Fernando Burgos

Index